BIOGRAPHICAL ENCYCLOPEDIA OF
20th-Century
World Leaders

BIOGRAPHICAL ENCYCLOPEDIA OF
20th-Century
World Leaders

Volume 1
Abdul – Clemenceau

Editor
John Powell
Pennsylvania State University, Erie

Marshall Cavendish
New York • London • Toronto • Sydney

Marshall Cavendish Corporation
99 White Plains Road
Tarrytown, New York 10591-9001

© 2000 Marshall Cavendish Corporation
Printed in the United States of America
09 08 07 06 05 04 03 02 01 00   5 4 3 2 1

Library of Congress Cataloging-in-Publication Data

Biographical encyclopedia of 20th-century world leaders / John Powell
p. cm.
    v. cm.
    Includes bibliographical references and index.
    1. Heads of state Biography Encyclopedias.   2. Statesmen Biography Encyclope-
dias.   3. Biography 20th century Encyclopedias.   I. Powell, John, 1954-   . II. Title:
Biographical encyclopedia of twentieth-century world leaders
    ISBN 0-7614-7129-4 (set)
    ISBN 0-7614-7130-8 (vol. 1)
    D412.B56   1999
    920'.009'04—dc21
                                                                        99-34462
                                                                        CIP

∞ This paper meets the requirements of ANSI/NISO Z39.48-1992 (R1997)
Permanence of Paper for Publications and Documents in Libraries and Archives

CONTENTS

VOLUME 1

Publisher's Note xi
Contributors xiii
Key to Pronunciation xvii

Abdul Rahman 1
Ralph David Abernathy 4
Dean Acheson 7
Gerry Adams 11
Konrad Adenauer 14
Emilio Aguinaldo 18
Akihito 21
Madeleine Albright 24
Edmund Henry Hynman Allenby 27
Salvador Allende 30
Idi Amin 34
Kofi Annan 38
Corazon Aquino 41
Yasir Arafat 44
Oscar Arias Sánchez 49
Jean-Bertrand Aristide 52
H. H. Asquith 55
Hafez al-Assad 59
Tobias Michael Carel Asser 63
Nancy Astor 65
Kemal Atatürk 68
Clement Attlee 72
Lloyd Axworthy 76
Muhammad Farah Aydid 79
Nnamdi Azikiwe 82
Ibrahim Babangida 86
Fredrik Bajer 89
Stanley Baldwin 91
Arthur Balfour 95
Surendranath Banerjea 99
Edmund Barton 102
Fulgencio Batista y Zaldívar 105
José Batlle y Ordóñez 109
Auguste-Marie-François Beernaert 111
Menachem Begin 114
Edvard Beneš 118

David Ben-Gurion 122
Richard Bedford Bennett 126
W. A. C. Bennett 129
Theobald von Bethmann Hollweg 132
Bhumibol Adulyadej 135
Benazir Bhutto 138
Zulfikar Ali Bhutto 142
Hugo L. Black 146
Tony Blair 149
Léon Blum 153
William E. Borah 157
Robert Laird Borden 160
Louis Botha 163
Lucien Bouchard 166
Houari Boumedienne 169
Léon Bourgeois 172
Boutros Boutros-Ghali 174
Omar N. Bradley 178
Louis D. Brandeis 181
Willy Brandt 184
Karl Hjalmar Branting 188
Wernher von Braun 190
William J. Brennan, Jr. 193
Leonid Ilich Brezhnev 196
Aristide Briand 200
Alan Francis Brooke 204
Stanley Bruce 207
Gro Harlem Brundtland 210
William Jennings Bryan 213
Zbigniew Brzezinski 217
Nikolai Ivanovich Bukharin 220
Bernhard von Bülow 224
Ralph Bunche 227
Warren E. Burger 230
George Bush 233
Mangosuthu Gatsha Buthelezi 237
Richard E. Byrd 240
James Callaghan 244
Plutarco Elías Calles 247
Kim Campbell 250

Henry Campbell-Bannerman 253
Lázaro Cárdenas 256
Pat Carney 259
Jimmy Carter 261
René Cassin 265
Fidel Castro 268
Nicolae Ceausescu 272
Austen Chamberlain 276
Neville Chamberlain 279

Chen Duxiu 283
Chiang Kai-shek 286
Joseph Benedict Chifley 290
Shirley Chisholm 293
Jean Chrétien 296
Winston Churchill 300
Joe Clark 304
Georges Clemenceau 307
Index 313

VOLUME 2

Bill Clinton 333
Hillary Rodham Clinton 337
Michael Collins 340
Joseph Cook 343
Calvin Coolidge 345
Sheila Copps 349
William T. Cosgrave 352
Pierre de Coubertin 355
William Randal Cremer 358
John Curtin 360
George Nathaniel Curzon 364
The Dalai Lama 367
Charles G. Dawes 371
Moshe Dayan 374
Alfred Deakin 378
Alcide De Gasperi 380
F. W. de Klerk 383
Jacques Delors 386
Deng Xiaoping 389
Eamon de Valera 393
Diana, Princess of Wales 397
Porfirio Díaz 400
John G. Diefenbaker 404
Milovan Djilas 408
Samuel K. Doe 410
Robert Dole 414
Karl Dönitz 417
Tommy Douglas 420
William O. Douglas 423
Alexander Douglas-Home 425
Alexander Downer 428
José Napoleon Duarte 431
Alexander Dubček 434

W. E. B. Du Bois 438
John Foster Dulles 442
Maurice Duplessis 446
François Duvalier 449
Jean-Claude Duvalier 453
Abba Eban 456
Félix Éboué 460
Anthony Eden 463
Edward VII 467
Edward VIII 471
Dwight D. Eisenhower 473
Elizabeth II 477
Enver Pasha 481
Matthias Erzberger 484
Herbert Vere Evatt 487
Arthur William Fadden 489
Fahd 491
Faisal 494
Faisal I 498
Geraldine Ferraro 501
Andrew Fisher 504
Gerald R. Ford 506
Francis Michael Forde 509
Francis Ferdinand 511
Francis Joseph I 514
Francisco Franco 518
Felix Frankfurter 522
Malcolm Fraser 524
Hedy Fry 527
Alberto Fujimori 529
J. William Fulbright 533
Indira Gandhi 536
Mahatma Gandhi 540

Contents

Rajiv Gandhi 544
Alfonso García Robles 547
Marcus Garvey 550
Charles de Gaulle 553
George V 557
George VI 561
John H. Glenn, Jr. 564
Charles Albert Gobat 566
Robert H. Goddard 568
Joseph Goebbels 571
Mikhail Gorbachev 574
Al Gore 578
Hermann Göring 581
John Grey Gorton 584
Antonio Gramsci 586
Herbert Gray 589
Alan Greenspan 591
Andrei Andreyevich Gromyko 594

Heinz Guderian 598
Che Guevara 601
Guo Moruo 605
Juvénal Habyarimana 608
Alexander M. Haig 612
Haile Selassie I 615
William F. Halsey 619
Dag Hammarskjöld 621
Warren G. Harding 625
William Averell Harriman 629
Hassan II 632
Charles James Haughey 635
Václav Havel 638
Robert Hawke 642
Víctor Raúl Haya de la Torre 644
Edward Heath 646
Arthur Henderson 650
Index 655

VOLUME 3

Édouard Herriot 675
Chaim Herzog 678
Rudolf Hess 682
Heinrich Himmler 685
Paul von Hindenburg 688
Hirohito 692
Adolf Hitler 695
Oveta Culp Hobby 699
Ho Chi Minh 702
Oliver Wendell Holmes, Jr. 706
Harold Holt 709
Erich Honecker 712
Herbert Hoover 715
J. Edgar Hoover 719
Félix Houphouët-Boigny 722
John Howard 725
Victoriano Huerta 728
Charles Evans Hughes 730
William Morris Hughes 733
Cordell Hull 737
Hubert H. Humphrey 741
Hussein I 744
Saddam Hussein 748
Hayato Ikeda 752

İsmet İnönü 755
Itō Hirobumi 758
Jesse Jackson 762
Cheddi Jagan 765
Jiang Qing 767
Jiang Zemin 770
Mohammed Ali Jinnah 774
Joseph-Jacques-Césaire Joffre 777
John XXIII 779
John Paul II 782
Lyndon B. Johnson 785
Barbara Jordan 789
Juan Carlos I 792
János Kádár 795
Constantine Karamanlis 798
Rashid Karami 800
Kenneth Kaunda 803
Karl Kautsky 807
Paul Keating 810
Frank B. Kellogg 813
George F. Kennan 816
John F. Kennedy 819
Robert F. Kennedy 823
Jomo Kenyatta 827

Aleksandr Fyodorovich Kerensky 831
Albert Kesselring 835
John Maynard Keynes 837
Ruhollah Khomeini 841
Nikita S. Khrushchev 845
Kim Il Sung 849
Ernest Joseph King 853
Martin Luther King, Jr. 856
William Lyon Mackenzie King 860
Jeane Kirkpatrick 863
Henry A. Kissinger 866
Horatio Herbert Kitchener 870
Ralph Klein 873
Helmut Kohl 875
Juscelino Kubitschek 879
Robert M. La Follette, Jr. 881
Henri-Marie La Fontaine 885
Fiorello Henry La Guardia 887
Christian Lous Lange 890
Julia C. Lathrop 892
Wilfrid Laurier 894
Pierre Laval 897
Bonar Law 901
T. E. Lawrence 903
Le Duc Tho 906
Lee Kuan Yew 909
Vladimir Ilich Lenin 912

Jean-Marie Le Pen 916
René Lévesque 919
Lin Biao 921
Li Peng 923
Maksim Maksimovich Litvinov 926
Liu Shaoqi 929
David Lloyd George 932
Henry Cabot Lodge 936
Huey Long 939
Erich Ludendorff 942
Patrice Lumumba 945
Albert Lutuli 947
Douglas MacArthur 950
Ramsay MacDonald 954
Samora Moisès Machel 958
Harold Macmillan 960
Francisco Madero 964
Ramón Magsaysay 966
Datuk Seri Mahathir bin Mohamad 968
John Major 971
Makarios III 975
Malcolm X 978
Georgi M. Malenkov 982
Nelson Mandela 985
Winnie Mandela 989
Wilma P. Mankiller 992
Index 997

VOLUME 4

Michael Manley 1017
Carl Gustaf Mannerheim 1020
Preston Manning 1023
Mao Zedong 1025
Ferdinand E. Marcos 1029
George C. Marshall 1032
Thurgood Marshall 1036
Paul Martin 1039
Tomáš Masaryk 1041
Marcel Massé 1044
Vincent Massey 1046
William Ferguson Massey 1048
Joseph R. McCarthy 1050
William McMahon 1054
Arthur Meighen 1056

Golda Meir 1058
Carlos Saúl Menem 1062
Robert Gordon Menzies 1065
Slobodan Milošević 1068
William Mitchell 1072
François Mitterrand 1074
Mobutu Sese Seko 1077
Mohammad Reza Pahlavi 1081
Vyacheslav Mikhailovich Molotov 1085
Bernard Law Montgomery 1088
Henry Morgenthau, Jr. 1091
Mohammad Mossadegh 1093
Louis Mountbatten 1096
Hosni Mubarak 1099
Robert Mugabe 1103

Contents

Muhammad V	1107	John J. Pershing	1228
Robert Muldoon	1109	Philippe Pétain	1231
Brian Mulroney	1111	Henry Petty-Fitzmaurice	1234
Yoweri Kaguta Museveni	1115	Augusto Pinochet Ugarte	1236
Benito Mussolini	1118	Pius XI	1240
Alva Myrdal	1122	Pius XII	1243
Imre Nagy	1124	Raymond Poincaré	1246
Gamal Abdel Nasser	1128	Pol Pot	1250
Jawaharlal Nehru	1132	Georges Pompidou	1253
Benjamin Netanyahu	1136	Adam Clayton Powell, Jr.	1256
Nicholas II	1140	Colin Powell	1259
Chester W. Nimitz	1144	Pu-yi	1263
Richard M. Nixon	1146	Muammar al-Qaddafi	1266
Kwame Nkrumah	1150	Manuel Quezon	1269
Philip John Noel-Baker	1153	Yitzhak Rabin	1272
Manuel Noriega	1155	Hashemi Rafsanjani	1275
Julius Nyerere	1158	Fidel Ramos	1279
Milton Obote	1162	Jeannette Rankin	1281
Álvaro Obregón	1165	Jerry John Rawlings	1283
Sandra Day O'Connor	1168	Ronald Reagan	1287
Seán T. O'Kelly	1171	William H. Rehnquist	1291
Thomas P. O'Neill, Jr.	1174	George Houston Reid	1294
Daniel Ortega	1177	Louis Renault	1296
Turgut Özal	1180	Janet Reno	1298
Ian Paisley	1184	Syngman Rhee	1301
Andreas Papandreou	1186	Joachim von Ribbentrop	1305
Franz von Papen	1190	Hyman G. Rickover	1308
Park Chung Hee	1194	Matthew B. Ridgway	1310
Vallabhbhai Jhaverbhai Patel	1197	Mary Robinson	1313
George S. Patton	1199	Erwin Rommel	1315
Paul VI	1202	Eleanor Roosevelt	1317
Lester B. Pearson	1205	Franklin D. Roosevelt	1321
Peng Dehuai	1208	Theodore Roosevelt	1325
Shimon Peres	1211	Elihu Root	1329
Javier Pérez de Cuéllar	1215	Nellie Tayloe Ross	1332
Eva Perón	1218	Gerd von Rundstedt	1334
Juan Perón	1221	Index	1339
H. Ross Perot	1225		

VOLUME 5

Dean Rusk	1359	António de Oliveira Salazar	1371
Carlos Saavedra Lamas	1361	Augusto César Sandino	1375
Anwar el-Sadat	1363	Eisaku Satō	1377
Andrei Sakharov	1367	Jeanne Mathilde Sauvé	1380

Gerhard Schröder 1382
James Henry Scullin 1385
Hans von Seeckt 1387
Léopold Senghor 1389
Eduard Shevardnadze 1392
Muhammad Siad Barre 1396
Norodom Sihanouk 1400
William Joseph Slim 1403
Joseph Roberts Smallwood 1406
Alfred E. Smith 1408
Ian Smith 1412
Margaret Chase Smith 1416
Jan Christian Smuts 1419
Anastasio Somoza García 1422
Paul-Henri Spaak 1426
Joseph Stalin 1428
Adlai E. Stevenson 1432
Henry L. Stimson 1435
Louis St. Laurent 1439
Gustav Stresemann 1442
Alfredo Stroessner 1445
Suharto 1448
Sukarno 1452
Sun Yat-sen 1456
Robert A. Taft 1460
William Howard Taft 1463
Mother Teresa 1467
U Thant 1471
Margaret Thatcher 1474
Clarence Thomas 1478
Bal Gangadhar Tilak 1481
Alfred von Tirpitz 1484
Josip Broz Tito 1487
Hideki Tojo 1491
Leon Trotsky 1495
Pierre Elliott Trudeau 1499
Rafael Trujillo 1503
Harry S Truman 1505
Moïse Tshombe 1509
William V. S. Tubman 1512
John Napier Turner 1516

Desmond Tutu 1518
Tz'u-hsi 1522
Walter Ulbricht 1524
Georges Vanier 1527
Getúlio Vargas 1529
José María Velasco Ibarra 1532
Eleuthérios Venizélos 1534
Pancho Villa 1537
Vo Nguyen Giap 1540
Kurt Waldheim 1544
Lech Wałęsa 1547
George C. Wallace 1551
Wang Jingwei 1554
Earl Warren 1556
Chaim Weizmann 1559
Ida B. Wells-Barnett 1563
Walter Francis White 1565
Gough Whitlam 1568
Elie Wiesel 1570
Simon Wiesenthal 1573
William II 1577
Harold Wilson 1581
Woodrow Wilson 1585
Isoroku Yamamoto 1589
Ahmed Zaki Yamani 1592
Boris Yeltsin 1595
Yuan Shikai 1599
Saʿd Zaghlūl 1603
Emiliano Zapata 1606
Ernesto Zedillo 1609
Zhao Ziyang 1612
Zhou Enlai 1615
Zhu De 1619
Georgy Konstantinovich Zhukov 1623
Mohammad Zia-ul-Haq 1626

Appendix: Governments and Leaders . . . 1629

Leaders by Area of Achievement 1655
Leaders by Country 1663
Index 1671

Publisher's Note

In the twentieth century, the people of the world saw unprecedented changes and great political upheavals. The world's leaders faced challenges on many fronts. Established nations experienced revolutions, economic depression, and world wars. New nations were born and struggled with basic issues of freedom and survival. Some leaders fit into long-established traditions; others created their own governments and states according to their personal ideologies. Types of government ranged from monarchies to parliamentary and presidential democracies to military and fascist dictatorships.

The five volumes of the *Biographical Encyclopedia of 20th-Century World Leaders* profile 483 leaders from ninety-eight countries who left their mark on a country, a region, or, in some cases, the political landscape of the world. Although many wrote significant works, individuals are included here primarily for the influence of their actions rather than their writings. Beyond heads of state and other high-level government figures, this encyclopedia includes people who achieved breakthroughs in civil rights, law, diplomacy, and military endeavors. It focuses on personages who are significant in the social sciences and humanities curricula of grades 6 through 12, curricula intended to educate young citizens of a culturally diverse democratic society in an interdependent world.

Among the major countries with leaders profiled here are the United States (with 105 individuals covered), Great Britain (41), Canada (32), Germany (28), Australia (24), China (19), France (17), the Soviet Union (15), and Mexico (11). Among the dozens of other countries with leaders in the encyclopedia are Japan, Malaysia, Chile, Pakistan, Haiti, Sweden, Cuba, Congo, Rwanda, South Africa, the Ivory Coast, Iran, the Philippines, Vietnam, and Turkey. Government figures include presidents, prime ministers, kings and queens, dictators, secretaries of state,

and other significant officials. Diplomats include Nobel Peace Prize winners, U.N. secretaries-general, and disarmament and arms-reduction advocates. Military leaders include generals and admirals as well as advocates of specific military technologies. Influential figures in law include jurists and central personages in international law. Civil rights leaders include individuals involved in struggles for racial, religious, and political rights around the world.

The *Biographical Encyclopedia of 20th-Century World Leaders* is arranged alphabetically, beginning with Abdul Rahman of Malaysia and ending with Mohammad Zia-ul-Haq of Pakistan. Articles are approximately 750 or 1250 words long. Each begins with a capsule description of the leader's importance, with dates in office or service given as appropriate. Lines providing birth and death information (dates and places) follow. The main text of the essay is a discussion of the development of the individual's career that includes his or her philosophy and actions. Subheads highlight important aspects of the leader's contributions. Articles also include sidebars that present key events, organizations, concepts, and pieces of legislation with which the leader is identified. Sidebars may cover events in which the individual was involved or concepts that provide salient background information that aids in understanding the essay. Shorter articles contain one sidebar, and longer articles contain two. Articles conclude with brief bibliographies, many of which include works by the article's subject. All articles are signed by academicians.

The set includes a number of features especially designed for young students. More than a thousand photographs provide portraits of the leaders and illustrate the historical events discussed in the text. A phonetic pronunciation guide for each individual profiled follows the first mention of the person's name in the article. In recognition of the fact that the readership of this work will be multicultural, pronunciations are given for English-language as well as foreign names. A key to the pronunciation guide is found at the front of each volume; it gives the combinations of letters used to represent various sounds and provides examples of words in which the sounds appear. In addition, the set's comprehensive index may be found at the end of each volume.

The transliteration of foreign names adheres to widely used systems. For Chinese names, the Pinyin system of transliteration was used except in a few cases (Chiang Kai-shek, for example) in which the individual is almost universally known by a non-Pinyin name. In the index, cross-references are provided from the older Wade-Giles transliterations to the Pinyin system and, conversely, from Pinyin to the name used in non-Pinyin transliterations. Place-names are also treated in Pinyin. Russian names are rendered according to the system used by the U.S. Board on Geographic Names. Arabic names are rendered in the most widely familiar forms; these generally align with the *American Library Association-Library of Congress Romanization Tables.*

Following the last article in volume 5 is an appendix by editor John Powell entitled "Governments and Leaders," broken into two parts. Part 1, "Types of Government," is in essay form. It first introduces three general approaches to government—authoritarianism, anarchism, and pluralism—along with the forms of government, from dictatorship to democracy, associated with these approaches. Next the essay discusses major political ideologies, including liberalism, conservatism, socialism, fascism, and Marxist-Leninism. Also covered are such central concepts as nationalism, capitalism, and imperialism. Part 2, "Political Leaders and Types of Government," after an introduction, lists the governmental leaders covered in the *Biographical Encyclopedia of 20th-Century World Leaders,* categorized by the types of government in which they participated. "Multiparty Liberal Governments," for example, is subdivided into four categories of leaders, including "Constitutional or Liberal Monarchists" and "Liberals, Democrats, Liberal Democrats, Centrists." Following the appendix are two categorized lists of all the leaders in the set: one organized by country, the other by area of achievement (government, diplomacy, the military, law, or civil rights). These lists are followed by a comprehensive index.

Particular thanks are due John Powell, who served as the set's editor, and pronunciation editor Eric v. d. Luft. We also thank all the scholars and academicians who contributed their expertise. A list of their names and affiliations appears on the following pages.

Contributors

Patrick Adcock
Henderson State University

Richard Adler
University of Michigan, Dearborn

William Allison
University of Saint Francis

Earl R. Andresen
University of Texas at Arlington

Stanley Archer
Texas A&M University

Mary Welek Atwell
Radford University

Bryan Aubrey
Fairfield, Iowa

James A. Baer
Northern Virginia Community College

Barbara Bair
Duke University

Carl L. Bankston III
University of Southwestern Louisiana

David Barratt
Chester, England

Maryanne Barsotti
Warren, Michigan

Alvin K. Benson
Brigham Young University

Milton Berman
University of Rochester

Cynthia Bily
Adrian College

Nicholas Birns
The New School for Social Research

Russell Blackford
Phillips Fox Lawyers

Steve D. Boilard
Sacramento, California

Helen Bragg
University of Guelph

Peter Brigg
University of Guelph

William S. Brockington, Jr.
University of South Carolina, Aiken

Keith H. Brower
Salisbury State University

Anthony R. Brunello
Eckerd College

Fred Buchstein
John Carroll University

Joseph P. Byrne
Belmont University

Susanna Calkins
Purdue University

Nancy M. Campbell
Portland, Oregon

Edmund J. Campion
University of Tennessee

John W. Cavanaugh
University of South Carolina

Ranès C. Chakravorty
Salem, Virginia

Maria Hsia Chang
University of Nevada, Reno

Paul J. Chara, Jr.
Loras College

Paul Christensen
Texas A&M University

Lawrence Clark
Delaware, Ohio

Thomas Clarkin
Lake Hills, Texas

William H. Coogan
University of Southern Maine

Lisa-Anne Culp
University of Arizona

Frank Day
Clemson University

Peng Deng
High Point University

Andy DeRoche
Front Range Community College

M. Casey Diana
University of Illinois at Urbana-Champaign

David J. Dranchak
Portland, Oregon

Steven L. Driever
University of Missouri, Kansas City

David G. Egler
Western Illinois University

H. J. Eisenman
University of Missouri, Rolla

Robert P. Ellis
Northboro, Massachusetts

Randall Fegley
Pennsylvania State University

Gregory C. Ference
Salisbury State University

Dale L. Flesher
University of Mississippi

Carol G. Fox
East Tennessee State University

Tom Frazier
Cumberland College

Richard A. Fredland
Indiana University, Indianapolis

John C. Fredriksen
Salem, Massachusetts

Barbara B. Frisbie
Kalamazoo, Michigan

Gloria Fulton
Humboldt State University

Robert L. Gale
University of Pittsburgh

Keith Garebian
Mississauga, Ontario

K. Fred Gillum
Colby College

Melanie Beals Goan
University of Kentucky

Nancy M. Gordon
Amherst, Massachuseetts

Robert F. Gorman
Southwest Texas State University

Lewis L. Gould
University of Texas at Austin

Daniel G. Graetzer
Seattle, Washington

Johnpeter Horst Grill
Mississippi State University

Michael Haas
Loyola Marymount University

Irwin Halfond
McKendree College

Michael S. Hamilton
University of Southern Maine

C. James Haug
Mississippi State University

Louis D. Hayes
University of Montana

Peter B. Heller
Manhattan College

Diane Andrews Henningfeld
Adrian College

Steven R. Hewitt
University of Saskatchewan

Ronald K. Huch
University of Papua New Guinea

Caralee Hutchinson
Canby, Oregon

Raymond Pierre Hylton
Virginia Union University

Robert Jacobs
Central Washington University

Willoughby Jarrell
Kennesaw State University

Maude M. Jennings
Ball State University

Sheila Golburgh Johnson
Santa Barbara, California

Leigh Husband Kimmel
Herrin, Illinois

Grove Koger
Boise Public Library

Eugene Larson
Pierce College

Steven Lehman
John Abbott College

Thomas T. Lewis
Mount Senario College

Guoqing Li
The Ohio State University Library

Roger D. Long
Eastern Michigan University

Herbert Luft
Pepperdine University

Susan MacFarland
Canton, Georgia

Paul Madden
Hardin-Simmons University

Patrick N. Malcolmson
St. Thomas University

Barry Stewart Mann
Atlanta, Georgia

Carl Henry Marcoux
University of California, Riverside

Jeffrey J. Matthews
University of Kentucky

Steve J. Mazurana
University of Northern Colorado

Erin K. McClain
Washington, D.C.

Michelle C. K. McKowen
New York, New York

Michael E. Meagher
University of Missouri, Rolla

William V. Moore
College of Charleston

Christina J. Moose
Pasadena, California

B. Keith Murphy
Fort Valley State University

Norma C. Noonan
Augsburg College

Charles H. O'Brien
Western Illinois University

Elvy Setterqvist O'Brien
Williamstown, Massachusetts

Lisa Paddock
Cape May Court House, New Jersey

Ranee K. L. Panjabi
*Memorial University of
Newfoundland*

William A. Paquette
Tidewater Community College

Wayne Patterson
St. Norbert College

W. David Patton
Boise State University

Brian A. Pavlac
King's College

William A. Pelz
Institute of Working Class History

Nis Petersen
New Jersey City University

Lela Phillips
Andrew College

Julio Cesar Pino
Kent State University

J. P. Piskulich
Oakland University

Karan B. Pittman
Andrew College

Michael Polley
Columbia College

Clifton W. Potter, Jr.
Lynchburg College

Dorothy Potter
Lynchburg College

John Powell
Pennsylvania State University, Erie

Verbie Lovorn Prevost
University of Tennessee at Chattanooga

R. Kent Rasmussen
Thousand Oaks, California

Paul L. Redditt
Georgetown College

Matthew A. Redinger
Montana State University, Billings

Rosemary M. Canfield Reisman
Charleston Southern University

Douglas W. Richmond
University of Texas at Arlington

James W. Riddlesperger, Jr.
Texas Christian University

Edward A. Riedinger
Columbus, Ohio

Henry O. Robertson
Louisiana State University at Alexandria

Carl Rollyson
Baruch College, CUNY

John Alan Ross
Eastern Washington University

Irving N. Rothman
University of Houston

Thomas E. Rotnem
Brenau University

Irene Struthers Rush
Los Osos, California

Jerry P. Sanson
Louisiana State University at Alexandria

Richard Sax
Madonna University

Robert O. Schneider
University of North Carolina at Pembroke

Rose Secrest
Signal Mountain, Tennessee

Robert M. Seiler
The University of Calgary

Ollie Shuman
Healdsburg, California

R. Baird Shuman
University of Illinois at Urbana-Champaign, emeritus

Narasingha P. Sil
Western Oregon University

Charles L. P. Silet
Iowa State University

Donald C. Simmons, Jr.
Mississippi Humanities Council

Andrew C. Skinner
Brigham Young University

Christopher E. Smith
Michigan State University

Dale Edwyna Smith
St. Louis, Missouri

Jean M. Snook
Memorial University of Newfoundland

David J. Snyder
Southern Illinois University

George Soule
Carleton College

William H. Stewart
The University of Alabama

Gerald J. Stortz
St. Jerome's University

Taylor Stults
Muskingum College

Timothy E. Sullivan
Towson University

Glenn L. Swygart
Tennessee Temple University

William A. Taggart
New Mexico State University

Robert D. Talbott
University of Northern Iowa, emeritus

Donald G. Tannenbaum
Gettysburg College

Terry Theodore
University of North Carolina at Wilmington

Nicholas C. Thomas
Auburn University at Montgomery

Andrew Trescott
Dallas, Texas

Paul B. Trescott
Southern Illinois University

Michael W. Tripp
University of Victoria

Catherine Udall Turley
Mesa Community College

Robert D. Ubriaco, Jr.
St. Louis, Missouri

Jiu-Hwa Lo Upshur
Eastern Michigan University

William T. Walker
Chestnut Hill College

George C. Y. Wang
The George Washington University

Robert P. Watson
University of Hawaii at Hilo

Donald A. Watt
Southern Arkansas University

Henry G. Weisser
Colorado State University

Judith Barton Williamson
Sauk Valley Community College

Michael Witkoski
Columbia, South Carolina

Lisa A. Wroble
Redford Township District Library

Laura M. Zaidman
University of South Carolina at Sumter

Key to Pronunciation

As an aid to users of the *Biographical Encyclopedia of 20th-Century World Leaders*, guides to pronunciation for all profiled leaders have been provided with the first mention of the name in each entry. These guides are rendered in an easy-to-use phonetic manner. Stressed syllables are indicated by capital letters.

Letters of the English language, particularly vowels, are pronounced in different ways depending on the context. Below are letters and combinations of letters used in the phonetic guides to represent various sounds, along with examples of words in which those sounds appear and corresponding guides for their pronunciation.

Symbols	Pronounced As In	Spelled Phonetically
a	answer, laugh	AN-sihr, laf
ah	father, hospital	FAH-thur, HAHS-pih-tul
aw	awful, caught	AW-ful, kawt
ay	blaze, fade, waiter	blayz, fayd, WAYT-ur
ch	beach, chimp	beech, chihmp
eh	bed, head, said	behd, hehd, sehd
ee	believe, leader	bee-LEEV, LEED-ur
ew	boot, loose	bewt, lews
g	beg, disguise, get	behg, dihs-GIZ, geht
i	buy, height, surprise	bi, hit, sur-PRIZ
ih	bitter, pill	bih-TUR, pihl
j	digit, edge, jet	DIH-jiht, ehj, jeht
k	cat, kitten, hex	kat, KIH-tehn, hehks
o	cotton, hot	CO-tuhn, hot
oh	below, coat, note	bee-LOH, coht, noht
oo	good, look	good, look
ow	couch, how	kowch, how
oy	boy, coin	boy, koyn
s	cellar, save, scent	SEL-ur, sayv, sehnt
sh	issue, shop	IH-shew, shop
uh	about, enough	uh-BOWT, ee-NUHF
ur	earth, letter	urth, LEH-tur
y	useful, young	YEWS-ful, yuhng
z	business, zest	BIHZ-ness, zest
zh	vision	VIH-zhuhn

BIOGRAPHICAL ENCYCLOPEDIA OF
20th-Century
World Leaders

Abdul Rahman

Born: February 8, 1903; Alor Setar, Kedah, Malaya (now Malaysia)
Died: December 6, 1990; Kuala Lumpur, Selangor, Malaysia

First prime minister of independent Malaya (1957-1963) and of Federation of Malaysia (1963-1979)

Tunku (Prince) Abdul Rahman Putra Alhaj (TUHNG-kew AHB-duhl RAH-muhn POOT-rah al-HAJ) was the seventh son of Prince Abdul Rahman Albni Hamid Halim Shah, sultan of Kedah, and Nerang, the daughter of Luang Nara Borirak, a descendant of the chieftain of Mataban, Thailand. A graduate of St. Catherine's College, Cambridge University, in England, Rahman returned to Malaya after graduation to hold a series of administrative posts. He married three times, the last to Roziah Barakbah of Kedah. Rahman had one son and one daughter from his first marriage, and he and his wife adopted two Chinese children, a daughter and a son. Early in life, Rahman had a reputation as a fun-loving sportsman, but after World War II he entered politics and helped to lead his country to independence in 1957. Prior to that time, Malaya was a part of the British Empire.

Early Years

After several years in the Kedah civil service, Rahman returned to England in 1947, where he was called to the bar in 1949. At this time, he was appointed a deputy public prosecutor in the Malayan Federal Legal Department. He resigned this post in 1951 to begin his political career. He was elected president of the United Malay National Organization (UMNO) in 1951.

As president of UMNO, Rahman created an alliance between UMNO and the Malayan-Chinese Association (MCA) in 1952. This coalition, known as the Alliance Party, also included the Malayan Indian Congress (MIC) by 1955. The Alliance Party captured fifty-one of fifty-two seats in the 1955 election, and Great Britain relinquished its power in Malaya. Rahman traveled to London in 1956 to negotiate for independence, which was declared by Malaya on August 31, 1957. Rahman became the first prime minister of the independent country.

Prime Minister

As Malaya's first prime minister, as well as foreign minister, Rahman proceeded to negotiate an end to the communist guerrilla warfare that had plagued northern Malaya since World War II. By 1960 the Malayans had succeeded in ending the communist terrorism. In 1963

Abdul Rahman *(Corbis/Bettmann-UPI)*

Rahman played the most significant role in negotiating the union of Malaya with Singapore, North Borneo (Sabah), and Sarawak. The Federation of Malaysia was formed on September 16, 1963, with Rahman as its first prime minister. On August 7, 1965, Rahman reluctantly requested Singapore to withdraw from the federation because of political problems.

The political drive of the Malays, primarily expressed through UMNO, characterized postwar Malaysia. Tensions between the Malays and Chinese erupted in rioting in Kuala Lumpur on May 13, 1969. Abdul Rahman suspended the constitution and declared a state of emergency. Facing a deteriorating racial situation and under attack for supposedly placating the Chinese to the detriment of the Malays, Rahman resigned as prime minister in 1970 and was succeeded by Abdul Razak.

Later Life

In 1987 Rahman stepped forward to condemn the actions of the Malaysian government, which had arrested seventy-nine political and civil leaders in an attempt to stop racial unrest. Rahman campaigned against the policies of the new prime minister, Datuk Seri Mahathir bin Mohamad, from his wheelchair. Throughout his retirement, Rahman continued to serve his homeland through newspaper columns, books, and speeches that emphasized national unity and religious tolerance.

University of Malaysia students in Kuala Lumpur protesting against Abdul Rahman during a wave of unrest in 1969. *(AP/Wide World Photos)*

The Alliance Party

The Alliance Party of Malaysia was formed in 1952 by the combining of the United Malay National Organization (UMNO) and the Malayan Chinese Association (MCA). Under the leadership of party president Abdul Rahman, the Alliance Party had gained the support of the Malayan Indian Congress (MIC) by 1955. This powerful coalition became the nation's dominant party, and in the 1955 election it won fifty-one of fifty-two seats. The alliance favored national independence within the British Commonwealth within four years. Great Britain granted independence in 1957.

The party suffered a setback in 1969. Rioting after the election, primarily between the Malays and the Chinese, resulted in a state of emergency. By 1971, however, the alliance had achieved a two-thirds majority. In 1973 the Alliance Party formed a broader coalition, consisting of the UMNO, MCA, MIC, and eight other minority parties. Known as the National Front, this ruling coalition exerted a powerful influence on Malaysian politics for many years.

Bibliography

Andaya, Barbara Watson, and Leonard Y. Andaya. *A History of Malaysia*. New York: St. Martin's Press, 1982.

Healy, Allen. *Tunku Abdul Rahman*. New York: University of Queensland Press, 1982.

Ongkill, James. *Nation Building in Malaysia, 1946-1974*. New York: Oxford University Press, 1985.

Roff, William R. *Origins of Malay Nationalism*. New York: Oxford University Press, 1995.

Ryan, N. J. *The Making of Modern Malaysia and Singapore*. London: Oxford University Press, 1969.

Karan A. Berryman

Ralph David Abernathy

Born: March 11, 1926; Linden, Alabama
Died: April 17, 1990; Atlanta, Georgia

American civil rights leader, a founder of the Southern Christian Leadership Conference (1957)

Ralph David Abernathy (RALF DAY-vihd A-bur-na-thee) was born in Linden, Alabama, the son of William L. and Louivery (Bell) Abernathy. His early years were spent on the family farm, where he learned hard work and dedication from his father. Abernathy served in the army during World War II. He then earned a degree in mathematics from Alabama State College in 1950, after having been ordained a Baptist minister a year earlier. By 1951, Abernathy had completed a master's degree in sociology from Atlanta University.

Ralph David Abernathy *(Library of Congress)*

In that same year, Abernathy became the pastor of the First Baptist Church in Montgomery, Alabama. While he was a graduate student in Atlanta, Abernathy met Martin Luther King, Jr. They remained friends for the remainder of King's life.

The Montgomery Bus Boycott

Abernathy first rose to prominence during the 1955-1956 Montgomery, Alabama, bus boycott. At the time, all buses in Montgomery had segregated seating. On December 1, 1955, Rosa Parks refused to give her seat up to a white man. She was immediately arrested. Joining forces with other African American leaders, Abernathy began planning a bus boycott to protest the arrest. Abernathy suggested that his friend Martin Luther King, Jr., be included in the planning. The protest began on Monday, December 5, 1955, the day of Rosa Parks's trial. The buses of Montgomery ran 90 percent empty on that day. On November 13, 1956, the Supreme Court decided that Alabama bus segregation laws were unconstitutional. On December 21, 1956, more than a year after Rosa Parks's arrest, Ralph Abernathy and King rode on the first integrated bus in Montgomery, Alabama.

Southern Christian Leadership Conference

In January, 1957, Abernathy, King, and African American leaders from other southern states met in Atlanta to form a group that would coordinate existing protest groups. This group took the name Southern Christian Leadership Conference (SCLC). It became one of the most important civil rights organizations in the country. The Supreme Court's decision and the formation of the SCLC led to violence in Montgomery. Abernathy's

The Southern Christian Leadership Conference

The Southern Christian Leadership Conference (SCLC) was founded by Ralph David Abernathy, Martin Luther King, Jr., and other African American leaders from across the South in 1957. The group was first organized to coordinate civil rights protests. The SCLC leaders preached passive resistance and assertive non-violence as a means of social change. The SCLC was perhaps most famous for organizing the 1963 March on Washington, a march that drew some 250,000 people to the nation's capital. After the death of SCLC president Martin Luther King, Ralph Abernathy became president, a position he held until 1977.

home and church, along with King's home and four additional homes, were bombed. The violence did not deter Abernathy and King. They organized sit-ins, marches, and voter registration drives in their quest to desegregate the South.

In 1967, Abernathy and King began to organize a march to Washington, D.C. King, however, was assassinated in March, 1968. After King's death, Abernathy assumed the reins of the SCLC. He finished the plans for the Poor People's Cam-

An empty bus drives through Montgomery, Alabama, in 1956. Ralph David Abernathy and Martin Luther King, Jr., were the main strategists behind a boycott that led to the integration of the city's bus system. *(AP/Wide World Photos)*

Ralph David Abernathy (right) became head of the Southern Christian Leadership Conference after the death of his friend Martin Luther King, Jr. (left). *(Library of Congress)*

paign and led a large-scale protest in Washington, D.C., in May and June, 1968.

Later Years

Abernathy continued to lead the SCLC until 1977, when he resigned under pressure from other leaders. He decided to run for Congress but was unsuccessful in his bid. During the following years, he worked on his autobiography, *And the Walls Came Tumbling Down*, published in 1989. After a long career as a minister and fighter for civil rights, Ralph David Abernathy died in Atlanta on April 17, 1990.

Ralph David Abernathy was at the heart of the great American Civil Rights movement and was an important figure in the Montgomery bus boycott. Perhaps Abernathy's greatest contribution to the movement was the counsel, advice, and friendship he gave King during the years they led the SCLC together.

Bibliography

Abernathy, Ralph David. *And the Walls Came Tumbling Down*. New York: Harper and Row, 1989.

Garrow, David J. *Bearing the Cross: Martin Luther King, Jr., and the Southern Christian Leadership Conference*. New York: William Morrow, 1986.

Kasher, Steven. *The Civil Rights Movement: A Photographic History, 1954-1968*. Foreword by Myrlie Evers-Williams. New York: Abbeville Press, 1996.

Murray, Paul T. *The Civil Rights Movement: References and Resources*. New York: G. K. Hall, 1993.

Diane Andrews Henningfeld

Dean Acheson

Born: April 11, 1893; Middletown, Connecticut
Died: October 12, 1971; Sandy Spring, Maryland

U.S. secretary of state (1949-1953)

Dean Gooderham Acheson (DEEN GOO-dur-uhm A-cheh-suhn) was the son of Canadian immigrants to the United States. His father was a minister and was later Episcopal bishop of Connecticut. The Achesons, including Dean's mother, loved the outdoors and shared a vivid and lively sense of humor that occasionally discomfited Acheson as secretary of state in later years.

Acheson attended the Groton School, one of the most famous boys' preparatory schools in the United States. During the summer after graduation he obtained a job with the work crew of the Grand Trunk (now Canadian National) Railway then being pushed westward through Canada. His work in the North Woods helped form Acheson's sturdy and self-confident character. After a summer's work in the wilderness, he attended Yale University, graduating in 1915. He was admitted to the Harvard Law School that year, where his brilliance brought him to the attention of Professor Felix Frankfurter (later an associate justice of the U.S. Supreme Court). Frankfurter was later to recommend Acheson for a year's Supreme Court clerkship with Justice Louis D. Brandeis. In 1917, while still at the law school, Acheson married Alice Stanley; they had three children.

Early Professional Years

After wartime duty as an ensign in the naval auxiliary reserve, Acheson began his duties with Justice Brandeis in 1919. The excellence of his work prompted Brandeis to ask him to stay for an additional year. Acheson happily accepted, and after two years with Justice Brandeis he joined the law firm of Covington and Burling. Acheson spent the next ten years solidifying his reputation as a skilled lawyer, specializing in international law and labor law. The Achesons became the center of a group of politically involved liberals who supported Franklin D. Roosevelt's candidacy for the presidency in 1932. In May, 1933, he was asked to become undersecretary of the Treasury. In this post he received his introduction to the world of diplomacy, because of the importance of international monetary issues during the Depression. Acheson resigned from the Treasury Department in 1934 following a policy disagreement with Roosevelt.

Dean Acheson in 1945, shortly after being named U.S. undersecretary of state. *(Library of Congress)*

Point Four

Among the most important accomplishments of the Truman administration was its successful promotion of aid to underdeveloped countries. Point Four was the fourth foreign policy plank in President Harry S Truman's 1949 inaugural address. It called for the provision of agricultural and industrial technical assistance to the Third World. This equivalent of the Marshall Plan (which aided European recovery after World War II) fell to Secretary of State Dean Acheson to promote and administer. With the help of Senator Arthur S. Vandenberg of Michigan, Acheson persuaded Congress to pass the program. One of the domestic attractions of the Point Four program was that it required a much smaller investment than the massive aid programs that the United States was undertaking on behalf of its European allies.

Acheson believed that it was more important to assist impoverished nations to become productive than to provide them with large capital loans before they had acquired the technical and managerial skills needed to use them successfully. Thus Point Four, whose formal name was the Technical Aid Program, was never lavishly funded by Congress. Yet it may have been more effective than the United States' other foreign-aid programs in enhancing prosperity in underdeveloped nations and in reducing the vulnerability of Third World countries to Soviet penetration. Point Four was considered one of the cornerstones of the containment policy.

At the State Department

After his resignation, Acheson returned to the practice of law, but in 1939 and 1940 the looming world war persuaded him to support President Roosevelt's rearmament policies. He was particularly influential in helping to promote the lend-lease program, a plan which allowed the United States to provide weapons and other material assistance to Britain before the United States officially entered World War II. In February of 1941 he accepted the post of assistant secretary of state for economic affairs. He was to spend all but a few months of the remainder of his working life in the State Department as assistant secretary, as undersecretary to Secretaries of State James Byrnes and George C. Marshall, and ultimately as President Harry S Truman's secretary of state from 1949 to 1953.

World War II ended in 1945. Acheson was one

U.S. secretary of state Dean Acheson signing the North Atlantic Treaty Organization (NATO) agreement in 1949 as U.S. president Harry S Truman and vice president Alben Barkley observe. *(Archive Photos)*

Dean Acheson (center) with President Harry S Truman and Chief Justice Fred M. Vinson after taking the oath of office as U.S. secretary of state in 1949. *(AP/Wide World Photos)*

of the principal architects of American foreign policy during the crucial years just after World War II when the Soviet threat was first being recognized. Acheson supported the containment policy, a plan to resist the spread of communism. He was heavily engaged in the negotiations which established the North Atlantic Treaty Organization (NATO), a military alliance devised to counter the Soviet military threat in Europe. He persuaded Congress to abandon the older isolationist tenets of American foreign policy. This early Cold War period was a time of domestic anticommunism and fears of communist infiltration. Acheson had nothing but contempt for those he saw as witch hunters, and he did everything he could to shield the State Department from what he was later to call "the attack of the primitives."

Both in his congressional relations and within the State Department hierarchy, Acheson was known as both witty and intolerant of foolishness. His impatience with error and his occasionally wicked tongue sometimes antagonized political opponents, especially right-wing isolationists in Congress. As an administrator he was excellent: the Department of State and the Foreign Service had strong, centralized leadership and coordination under his guidance. American foreign policy was as competently coordinated and executed as at any time in the nation's history.

On June 24, 1950, the military forces of North Korea attacked South Korea across the partition line at the thirty-eighth parallel. Acheson, called to the telephone in the middle of the night, notified President Truman as soon as reports of the

Containment

The policy of containment of the Soviet Union was devised in 1949 and 1950. It was based on the assumption that the Soviet Union was attempting to dominate the world by means of political, economic, ideological, and military pressure. The Soviet Union was viewed by most of the world's democracies as the greatest post-World War II threat. This view of Soviet policy had been most cogently expressed by George Kennan, a gifted Foreign Service officer and colleague of Dean Acheson, in his famous "long telegram" to the State Department in 1946. The containment policy, which was incorporated into a National Security Council paper, NSC-68, called for resistance to Soviet expansion by a combination of military and economic measures. European recovery from World War II was to be assisted, political and economic resistance to communism was to be promoted, and a military security perimeter was to be established by the United States and its allies. Although the precise tactics varied over the years, the policy of containment was followed for the forty years of the Cold War, coming to an end only with the collapse of the Soviet Union in the early 1990's.

attack could be verified. During the following week Truman, Acheson, and the State and Defense Departments forged the policy that led to the United Nations' first exercise of collective military security in history. Although the United States bore the heaviest weight of the fighting in the Korean War, many other nations provided forces to help fend off the North Korean attack. Acheson's Korean policy succeeded, but not until after China had been drawn into the war and after the American commander of the U.N. effort, General Douglas MacArthur, had been dismissed by President Truman.

Acheson left the State Department when Truman's second term ended in January, 1953. In retirement, Acheson continued to advise presidents on foreign policy and wrote a number of books and memoirs. He died of a stroke at his farm in Maryland in 1971.

Bibliography

Acheson, Dean. *Morning and Noon*. New York: Houghton Mifflin, 1965.

_____. *Present at the Creation: My Years in the State Department*. New York: W. W. Norton, 1969.

Chace, James. *Acheson*. New York: Simon & Schuster, 1998.

McCullough, David. *Truman*. New York: Simon & Schuster, 1992.

McLellan, David S. *Dean Acheson: The State Department Years*. New York: Dodd, Mead, 1976.

Truman, Harry S. *Memoirs: Years of Decision*. Garden City, N.Y.: Doubleday, 1955.

_____. *Memoirs: Years of Trial and Hope*. Garden City, N.Y.: Doubleday, 1955.

Robert Jacobs

Gerry Adams

Born: October 6, 1948; Belfast, Northern Ireland

Northern Irish political figure, leader of the Sinn Féin party

Gerard "Gerry" Adams (JEH-rahrd "JEH-ree" A-duhmz) was the first of thirteen children born to a strongly nationalist family in the Catholic working-class neighborhood of West Belfast. He socialized with Protestants as a child, and his first job as a teenager was in a pub mainly frequented by Protestants. However, his political sympathies were with the Catholics who sought to reunite Ireland, and he rose to leadership of the Republican political party Sinn Féin. Adams married Colette McArdle in 1971; they and their three children made their home in Belfast.

Early Activism

Adams's political activism was sparked in 1964 during street riots resulting from the display of the Irish flag, which was forbidden in Northern Ireland. Adams joined Sinn Féin, the political party associated with the Irish Republican Army (IRA). The party's goal was the reunification of British-ruled Northern Ireland with the predominantly Catholic Irish Republic. Subsequently, Adams helped to organize a number of action committees and civil rights groups to protest discrimination in housing, jobs, and political representation against Irish Catholics in the North. Between 1969 and 1972, the civil unrest escalated to urban warfare, culminating in the British suspension of the constitution of Northern Ireland (also known as Ulster) and imposition of direct British rule. Adams was arrested and imprisoned without trial in 1972, but later that year he was secretly sent to London to participate in cease-fire negotiations. In 1973, he was again arrested and was held without trial until 1977 in Long Kesh, a British prison camp near Belfast. There Adams taught other prisoners Irish history, discussed strategies to end British rule in Northern Ireland, read extensively, and became fluent in the Irish language.

Political Leadership

After his release from Long Kesh, Adams was part of a group of young northerners who wrested control of the Provisional Sinn Féin from an older group of leaders from the Republic. Adams was elected vice president of Provisional Sinn Féin in 1978, and he became president in 1983. In 1982, when Great Britain restored home rule to Northern Ireland, Adams was elected to the Northern Irish Assembly. In 1983, Adams was elected as a minister of Parliament from West Belfast. He refused to take his seat in Parliament, however, because that would require his taking

Gerry Adams *(Popperfoto/Archive Photos)*

11

Gerry Adams (fourth from left) marching with other Sinn Féin leaders and supporters in 1989. *(Reuters/Rob Taggart/ Archive Photos)*

The 1997 Belfast Peace Negotiations

In the 1920's Ireland was partitioned into the Irish Republic and smaller Northern Ireland, the latter a part of the British Empire. In Northern Ireland, the partition has caused decades of conflict between Protestants loyal to the British crown and Irish Catholics determined to reunite the six counties of the North with the Republic. In 1988, Adams began secret meetings with John Hume, leader of the Social Democratic and Labour Party (the SDLP, a Catholic nationalist party at odds with Sinn Féin). The talks eventu-

ally led to peace negotiations involving the leaders of the Irish Republic and Great Britain, with the intervention and support of U.S. president Bill Clinton. In April, 1998, a peace agreement was signed; it was endorsed a month later by 71 percent of voters in the North. Hume and David Trimble (leader of the Protestant Ulster Unionist Party) shared the 1998 Nobel Peace Prize. Although Adams was not formally recognized, he was acknowledged by Hume as a major factor in the peace process.

Gerry Adams addressing supporters in West Belfast in 1997. *(AP/Wide World Photos)*

an oath of allegiance to the British queen.

In 1984, a daylight assassination attempt severely and permanently wounded Adams. Reelected to Parliament in 1987, he was defeated in 1992 by Catholic Joseph Hendron when Protestants from the district threw their support to Hendron rather than to the Protestant candidate so as to unseat Adams. Adams, however, was again elected to Parliament in 1997.

Many restrictions have been placed on Adams by the British government. For example, from 1988 to 1994, it was illegal to broadcast the voices not only of members of outlawed Irish paramilitary groups such as the IRA but also of leaders of the legal Sinn Féin party. Therefore, when Adams was interviewed on radio or television, his answers had to be repeated by an anonymous reader. British pressure also prevented the U.S. government from issuing Adams a visa to travel in the United States. In 1994, however, a two-day visa was granted. Adams's visit raised U.S. consciousness about "the troubles" in Northern Ireland.

Bibliography

Adams, Gerry. *Before the Dawn: An Autobiography*. New York: William Morrow, 1997.

_____. *Free Ireland: Towards a Lasting Peace*. Niwot, Colo.: Roberts Rinehart, 1994.

O'Day, Alan, ed. *Political Violence in Northern Ireland: Conflict and Conflict Resolution*. London: Praeger, 1997.

Stevenson, Jonathan. *We Wrecked the Place: Contemplating the End to the Northern Irish Troubles*. New York: The Free Press, 1997.

Irene Struthers Rush

Konrad Adenauer

Born: January 5, 1876; Cologne, Germany
Died: April 19, 1967; Rhöndorf, West Germany

First chancellor of post-World War II West Germany (1948-1963)

Konrad Adenauer (KON-raht AH-deh-now-er) was the son of a Prussian civil servant and was the third of five children. He grew up in modest circumstances in Cologne, where his father served as an official of the highest provincial court. After completing college preparatory work, he studied law and economics. After taking his degree, Adenauer worked briefly for a private attorney, then as an associate judge in the provincial court. In 1904 he married Emma Weyer, a member of a prominent Cologne family. They had three children. His first wife having died in 1916, Adenauer married Auguste Zinsser in 1919; together they had four children. Adenauer remained throughout his life a devout Roman Catholic.

Mayor of Cologne

In 1917, although he had been severely injured in an automobile accident that disfigured him, Adenauer was elected mayor of Cologne. That same year Emperor William II named him principal mayor of Cologne and appointed him to the upper house of the Prussian legislature. The end of World War I in 1918 led to the occupation of part of the German Rhineland by British troops. Adenauer successfully forged a good relationship with the occupation authorities. Throughout his tenure as chief mayor of Cologne, Adenauer worked tirelessly to make Cologne the economic and cultural center of western Germany.

As a steadfast member of the Center Party, which had arisen in 1870 to represent the Catholic elements in the new German Empire, Adenauer quickly rose to a leadership position. He represented the party in the upper house of the Prussian legislature from 1921 onward and was annually elected chairman of the party's representatives there until 1933.

Hounded by the Nazis

In 1933, the National Socialist Party, or Nazis, rose to power in Germany. This fascist government engineered the exclusion of Adenauer from the office of chief mayor of Cologne on March 12, 1933; he was formally dismissed on July 17. He never held office during the Nazi period, was forced to take refuge for a while in a monastery, and was imprisoned by the Nazis on several

Konrad Adenauer *(Library of Congress)*

The Christian Democratic Union

The Christian Democratic Union (CDU), founded in 1945, was intended to appeal to those elements in Germany that believed in free enterprise and opposed socialism. It comprised some individuals who had belonged to the old Center Party of the empire and the Weimar Republic, but it rejected the close ties with the Catholic Church that had characterized the Center Party. Drawing its greatest strength from the predominantly Catholic Rhineland, Konrad Adenauer's home ground, it was an ideal vehicle for his political advancement. The party's appeal cut across class lines, though following the reorganization of the Social Democratic Party (SPD) in the late 1950's as a broad liberal party, it became more conservative. Throughout Adenauer's tenure as chancellor he worked actively to build the party organization and to strengthen its electoral appeal, and during the 1950's he was successful on both counts. He strongly supported the party's official commitment to social reconciliation, known as the social market philosophy.

On a 1955 state visit, West German chancellor Konrad Adenauer attends services at the only Roman Catholic church in Moscow. *(Library of Congress)*

occasions. Following a failed coup against German chancellor and Nazi leader Adolf Hitler in July, 1944, both Adenauer and his wife were imprisoned. She contracted an illness in prison from which she died in 1948.

Resuming Political Activity

On May 4, 1945, after Nazi Germany's defeat in World War II, the American occupation authorities restored Adenauer to the mayoral office. Adenauer soon resumed his activities with the newly founded Christian Democratic Union (CDU). The CDU was intended to be the heir to the old Center Party but to comprise all faiths. Adenauer became the party chairman in the North Rhineland, as well as a member of the CDU in the state legislature of North Rhineland. He was soon elevated to chairman of the party's caucus.

The decision by the Western Allies to re-create a central government for the part of Germany under their control (West Germany) opened a new opportunity for Adenauer, thanks to his unblemished record as an opponent of the Nazis. He became a member of the Parliamentary Council, created to draft a new constitution or basic law for the three Western occupation zones. He was

Konrad Adenauer (left) with French president Charles de Gaulle in the late 1960's. *(AP/Wide World Photos)*

ture) on August 14, 1948, Adenauer won a seat as a member of the CDU, and on September 15 he was elected chancellor of a coalition government comprising the CDU, its affiliate the Christian Social Union (CSU), the Free Democratic Party (FDP), and the small German Party. Adenauer won by one vote.

Accomplishments as Chancellor

As chancellor, Adenauer had two main goals for West Germany. First, he wanted to rehabilitate Germany politically so that it might once more play a role in European politics. Second, he sought to heal the social divisions among the German people that had existed before the war but were exacerbated by the widespread destruction of World War II. Half of Germany's housing stock had been damaged or destroyed, and its industries mostly lay in ruins.

By cooperating closely with the Western occupation authorities, he won their trust and confidence so that they supported giving ever more

elected chairman of the council on September 1, 1948, and played a leading role in drafting a new constitution based on federal principles. His was the dominant influence leading to the selection of Bonn as the capital of the new West German state. In the first elections for the Bundestag (legisla-

The European Coal and Steel Community Treaty

Konrad Adenauer took an active part in pushing the Schuman Plan, proposed by Robert Schuman, foreign minister of France, in the early 1950's. The Schuman Plan proposed to create an international authority to manage the coal and steel industries of Western Europe—the European Coal and Steel Authority. The nations involved were collectively termed the European Coal and Steel Community (ECSC). Directed by a council first chaired by Adenauer, the European Coal and Steel Community was soon dominated by Jean Monnet of France. Adenauer

signed the treaty creating the authority in Paris in April, 1951; it was ratified by the Bundestag in early 1952. The authority supervised the reconstruction of the coal and steel industries following their extensive damage during World War II. The ECSC provided a model for other multinational bodies, notably the European Defense Community (EDC) and Euratom. It also led to the creation of the European Common Market, which evolved into the European Economic Community.

authority to the new German government. He made special efforts to establish reconciliation with France. These efforts coincided with the movement among the French for multinational authorities that would make the outbreak of another war between France and Germany impossible. Adenauer's cooperation in integrating Germany into European entities and into the North Atlantic Treaty Organization (NATO) led to the end of the Allied occupation in 1955. Adenauer supported codetermination, the process by which German unions gained representation on the boards of large industrial enterprises. He also advocated the sale of stock at favorable prices to people of modest means, notably when the Volkswagen company was privatized.

The reconstruction of the Social Democratic Party in the late 1950's into a genuine liberal party led to the loss of CDU votes in the 1961 election. The coalition that Adenauer had created ten years earlier began to fall apart. On October 15, 1963, Adenauer resigned as chancellor, though he remained a member of the legislature until his death. Nicknamed *der Alte*, the Old Man, Adenauer was a towering figure in the re-creation of Germany after World War II.

Bibliography

Adenauer, Konrad. *Memoirs*. Translated by Beate Ruhm von Oppen. Chicago: H. Regnery, 1966.

Hiscocks, Richard. *The Adenauer Era*. Philadelphia: J. B. Lippincott, 1966.

Pommerin, Reiner, ed. *The American Impact on Postwar Germany*. Providence, R.I.: Berghahn Books, 1997.

Wighton, Charles. *Adenauer, a Critical Biography*. New York: Coward-McCann, 1964.

Nancy M. Gordon

Emilio Aguinaldo

Born: March 23, 1869; near Cavite, Luzon, Philippines
Died: February 6, 1964; Manila, Philippines

Filipino revolutionary and guerrilla leader

Emilio Aguinaldo y Famy (ay-MEE-lyoh a-gee-NAHL-doh ee FAH-mee) was born to a well-to-do family in a rural area of the Philippines. He completed his education at the Spanish-founded University of Santo Tomás in Manila. While still in his twenties, he became mayor of Cavite Viejo, and in 1896 he became the local leader of the Katipunan, a secret society dedicated to overthrowing Spanish colonial control of the Philippines.

The Struggle Against Spain

The Katipunan was founded by the revolutionary leader Andres Bonifacio. Its goal was to free the Philippines from Spain, which had ruled the islands since the sixteenth century. Aguinaldo soon proved himself a much more capable guerrilla leader than the Katipunan's founder. Following a dispute over leadership of the movement, Aguinaldo put Bonifacio on trial; Bonifacio was executed.

The war for independence quickly began to turn against the Philippine independence movement, and Aguinaldo entered into negotiations with Spain. In December of 1897 he agreed to leave the Philippines in return for a payment and a promise of political reforms for the Philippines. Once abroad, he continued maneuvering for Philippine independence. In Hong Kong and Singapore, he made contact with representatives of the United States, then on the verge of war against Spain over the Spanish colony of Cuba. With American backing, he returned to the Philippines on May 19, 1898, and resumed the war.

War with the United States

American forces quickly defeated the Spanish. Spain agreed to grant Cuban independence and to cede the Philippines, Guam, and Puerto Rico to the United States for twenty million dollars. Many Filipinos saw this as a betrayal by their American allies. On January 23, 1899, an assembly in the town of Malolos declared the Philippines an independent republic with Aguinaldo as its president. The following February, fighting broke out between American and Philippine forces in Manila. Aguinaldo declared war against the United States. After three years of fighting, the Americans captured Aguinaldo. The Filipino leader took an oath of allegiance to the American government, received a pension, and retired from public life.

Emilio Aguinaldo *(Library of Congress)*

18

The Philippine Insurrection

After the American victory over Spain in 1898, Spain handed over the Philippines to the United States. Tension quickly grew between American troops and Filipino soldiers, who had been fighting against Spain and had at first welcomed the Americans.

In February, 1899, fighting broke out between American and Filipino soldiers in Manila. The well-equipped Americans quickly established control over Manila and other major cities, and Philippine president and military commander Emilio Aguinaldo retreated to the northern part of the island of Luzon to conduct guerrilla warfare. The outgunned guerrillas fought a bitter war that most American historians call the Filipino Insurrection and most Filipino historians call the Philippine-American War. More than four thousand American soldiers and about twenty thousand Filipino soldiers died in the fighting. American efforts to push the guerrillas from the countryside devastated farmland. Many historians estimate that at least 200,000 Filipino civilians died from starvation or American guns. In 1901 the struggle came to an end when American forces captured Aguinaldo.

Later Life and Legacy

Aguinaldo entered politics again in 1935, when the United States allowed the Philippines to form a commonwealth government in preparation for independence. He ran for president of the new commonwealth but was defeated by Manuel Quezon.

In late 1941, the Japanese invaded the Philippines; they occupied the country in 1942. Aguinaldo made speeches on behalf of the Japanese. It is not entirely certain why he worked with the Japanese; perhaps he thought it was in the best interest of his country, or perhaps he was forced to do so. After the war, he was imprisoned for collaborating with the enemy. He was granted amnesty, however, and in 1950 President Elpidio Quirino appointed him to the Council of State. For the rest of his life, he devoted himself to promoting

Emilio Aguinaldo arriving in Malolas, the Philippines, for his inauguration as president of the First Philippine Republic. *(Library of Congress)*

19

Philippine insurgents proclaimed independence from the United States under Emilio Aguinaldo's leadership in 1899; the fighting lasted three years. *(Library of Congress)*

democracy and nationalism in the Philippines.

Many Filipino historians criticize Aguinaldo for his execution of Bonifacio and for the help he later gave to the Japanese. Nevertheless, he is widely regarded as a national hero by Filipinos and is honored as the nation's first president.

Bibliography

Bain, David Haward. *Sitting in Darkness: Americans in the Philippines*. Boston: Houghton Mifflin, 1984.

Tebbel, John William. *America's Great Patriotic War with Spain: Mixed Motives, Lies, and Racism in Cuba and the Philippines, 1898-1915*. Boston: Marshall Jones, 1996.

Vinnanueva, Alejo L. *Bonifacio's Unfinished Revolution*. Detroit, Mich.: Cellar Book Shop, 1990.

Carl L. Bankston III

Akihito

Born: December 23, 1933; Tokyo, Japan

Emperor of Japan (from 1989)

Akihito Tsugunomiya (ah-kee-hee-toh tsew-gew-noh-mee-yah) was the fifth child and eldest son of Japan's Emperor Hirohito and Empress Nagako. Although he spent much of the World War II years in Karuizawa, west of Tokyo, he received his education through the Gakushuin School and Gakushuin University, graduating in 1952 with a degree in politics. In addition, he was tutored by philosopher R. H. Blyth and Philadelphia Quaker Elizabeth Grey Vining in the English language and Western culture. He would thus be the first in the imperial household to have an international outlook and fluency in English. In 1952 he was formally invested as crown prince, the heir to the Japanese throne.

Break with Tradition

As crown prince, Akihito attended the coronation of Britain's Queen Elizabeth II as the official representative of Emperor Hirohito in the spring of 1953. The event marked the first overseas visit by the Japanese royal family since World War II. He then went to visit thirteen countries in Europe and North America. In the subsequent two decades he was to visit thirty-seven countries in twenty-two separate trips. In addition, as honorary president, he hosted the Eleventh Pacific Science Congress in 1966, the Sports Universiade 1967 in Tokyo, the Expo 1970 world's fair in Osaka, and the International Ocean Exposition in Okinawa in 1975. He was the first imperial family member to visit Okinawa since its return to Japan in 1972.

In April of 1959, Akihito married Michiko Shoda, the daughter of a company president and a commoner. Extensive press coverage of the "romance on the tennis court" was a symbol of what was seen as the democratization of the imperial court. The couple had two sons and a daughter.

The eldest son, Naruhito, would be crown prince but, in a break with tradition, the second son, Akishino, was allowed to marry before his brother. Both sons studied at Oxford University.

A New Emperor

Emperor Hirohito died of cancer on January 7, 1989. During the previous year, during Hirohito's illness, Akihito had taken charge of imperial state duties. Now he was to become the 125th emperor in the world's longest unbroken imperial line. Shinto religious ceremonies that date from before

Akihito *(Archive Photos)*

Akihito on a state visit to Great Britain in 1998. At right is the Duke of Edinburgh. *(AP/Wide World Photos)*

Akihito's China Visit

Akihito visited China in October, 1990, in the midst of a tense diplomatic situation. During World War II Japan's attacks on China had caused twenty million casualties. Japanese war reparations (thirty-four warships from the Imperial Navy) never compensated the Chinese who were the victims. Japan had argued that its postwar aid donations, loans, investment, and trade all represented sufficient compensation. Akihito's words were weighed carefully in this tense situation. He said he "deplored" the "unfortunate period" in which Japan "inflicted great suffering on the people of China." With "a sense of deep reproach" the Japanese people "believe such a war must never be repeated" and "resolve to tread the path of a peaceful nation." Since the words "deplore" and "reproach" have less severe meanings in Japanese than they do in English, it seemed to many that the emperor had not made a full apology. However, the Chinese government gained recognition from the imperial visit and benefited because the visit helped deflect criticism of the Tiananmen Square massacre in 1989.

recorded history brought him officially to the throne almost two years later in November, 1990. There were forty separate rituals, costing $95 million, that were widely covered in the Japanese press and attended by 170 foreign dignitaries. The reign title chosen was Heisei (achieving peace). The year 1990 became the first year of Heisei in the Japanese alternative calendar.

The Japanese constitution of 1947 forbids that the emperor be considered a god or a descendant of the sun goddess. However, the most important ritual in the Shinto accession ceremony involves the emperor becoming *arahitogami* (the man representing the imperial ancestral deities in this world). It could be argued that this ritual crosses the line between the human world and that of the deities. Akihito is the first emperor to have been confronted with this confusing constitutional problem. In all other ways, Akihito strove to change the imperial image into a worldly one. He and his wife published poetry, wore stylish Western suits, and acquired the habit of speaking colloquial Japanese to ordinary citizens. He inherited his father's interest in marine biology, studied cello, and learned to ski, play tennis, and ride horses. By throwing the first ball at the beginning of baseball season, Akihito solidified his image as a leader engaged in the life of the Japanese citizenry.

Japanese emperor Akihito speaking at the opening ceremonies of the 1998 Winter Olympic Games at Nagano, Japan. *(AP/Wide World Photos)*

Bibliography

Chapman, William. *Inventing Japan: The Making of a Postwar Civilization*. New York: Prentice Hall, 1991.

Crump, Thomas. *The Death of an Emperor: Japan at the Crossroads*. Oxford, England: Oxford University Press, 1989.

Field, Norma. *In the Realm of a Dying Emperor: A Portrait of Japan at Century's End*. New York: Pantheon Books, 1991.

Smith, Patrick. *Japan: A Reinterpretation*. New York: Pantheon Books, 1997.

Vining, Elizabeth Grey. *Windows for the Crown Prince*. Rutland, Vt.: Charles E. Tuttle, 1952.

David G. Egler

Madeleine Albright

Born: May 15, 1937; Prague, Czechoslovakia

First woman to occupy the position of U.S. secretary of state (named 1996)

The father of Madeleine Jana Korbel Albright (MA-deh-lehn YAH-nah KOHR-behl AHL-brit) served as a Czechoslovakian diplomat before immigrating to the United States, where he taught international relations at the University of Denver. During World War II, her family moved to London in 1939 to escape from the Nazis. They returned after the war but had to flee again ten years later when communists seized power in Czechoslovakia. This time they went to the United States. Madeleine graduated with a degree in political science from Wellesley College in 1959, and three days later she married journalist

Madeleine Albright *(Reuters/Rick Wilking/Archive Photos)*

Joseph Albright. They had three daughters and were married for twenty-three years. While raising her children, Albright also earned a doctorate from Columbia University.

Educational and Political Background

After her children were grown, Albright went to work as chief legislative assistant to Senator Edmund S. Muskie from 1976 to 1978. She then served as a staff member for the National Security Council and adviser on foreign policy for the White House from 1978 to 1981. Her work on the influence of the press on political changes in Poland won her a fellowship at the Woodrow Wilson International Center for Scholars at the Smithsonian Institution from 1981 to 1982.

The next ten years were spent in scholarly pursuits, including work as research professor of international affairs and director of women in foreign service programs at Georgetown University's School of Foreign Service, where she taught graduate and undergraduate courses. From 1989 until 1993 she was also president of the Center for National Policy, a nonprofit research organization that promotes study and discussion of domestic and international issues.

Global Responsibilities

In 1993 Albright's foreign policy expertise earned her President Bill Clinton's appointment as U.S. ambassador to the United Nations. As chief U.S. representative to the United Nations, Albright not only promoted U.S. interests in that global organization but also focused on educating the public about U.S. policy toward Bosnia, Haiti, Iraq, and sub-Saharan Africa. She also worked to gain congressional acceptance of U.S. support for a more streamlined and efficient United Nations. In 1995 she led the U.S. delegation to the 1995 Women's Conference in Beijing sponsored by the United Nations.

Albright continued to concentrate on educating the American public about U.S. foreign policy when she became the first woman to be appointed secretary of state in 1996. She also continued her efforts to persuade Congress to pay the United Nations the millions of dollars it owed the organization in unpaid dues. In addition to her role as chief foreign policy adviser to the president, Albright worked to improve relationships between the United States and the United Nations, and specifically between Congress and the United Nations.

Albright was a major influence on the March, 1999, decision by the United States and other countries in the North Atlantic Treaty Organization (NATO) to launch air strikes against Yugoslavia. The attacks were intended to prevent further deaths in Yugoslavia's Kosovo province as a result of Yugoslavian Serbs' policies of persecuting and mur-

Madeleine Albright speaking in the White House in January, 1997, after being sworn in as secretary of state. At left is President Bill Clinton, at right Vice President Al Gore. *(AP/Wide World Photos)*

dering members of Kosovo's ethnic Albanian population, policies sometimes referred to as "ethnic cleansing."

In a world characterized by interdependence, Albright considered it important to make U.S.

The U.N. Debt Controversy

Throughout the 1980's, some members of Congress argued that the United Nations had grown too big, powerful, and expensive. They held that it was no longer in the United States' national interest to continue its financial support. These views continued to be enunciated in the 1990's by Senator Jesse Helms, the powerful Republican leader of the U.S. Senate Committee on Foreign Relations. As U.S. ambassador to the United Nations and then secretary of state, Madeleine Albright advocated U.S. support for the United Nations. One of her goals was to convince Congress to pay its overdue U.N. bills. She developed a plan to pay off the debt, reduce the U.S. share of the U.N. budget, and streamline the U.N. bureaucracy. Although the plan had strong congressional and executive branch support, a small group of House members blocked final passage of the measure in 1997. The defeat saddened Albright, who responded that "one can either curse the darkness or light a candle to find the way out."

U.S. secretary of state Madeleine Albright with Israeli prime minister Benjamin Netanyahu (left) and Palestine Liberation Organization leader Yasir Arafat at the Wye River peace conference in 1998. *(AP/Wide World Photos)*

foreign policy more understandable and accessible to American citizens. Her efforts to attain that goal earned her a reputation as an unusually forthright secretary of state, a reputation that extended to her dealings with both congressional and world leaders.

Bibliography

Blood, Thomas. *Madam Secretary: A Biography of Madeleine Albright*. New York: St. Martin's Press, 1997.

Byman, Jeremy. *Madam Secretary: The Story of Madeleine Albright*. Greensboro, N.C.: Morgan Reynolds, 1997.

Freedman, Suzanne. *Madeleine Albright: She Speaks for America*. New York: Franklin Watts, 1998.

Maas, Robert. *U.N. Ambassador: A Behind the Scenes Look at Madeleine Albright's World*. New York: Walker, 1995.

Susan MacFarland

Edmund Henry Hynman Allenby

Born: April 23, 1861; Brackenhurst, near Southwell, Nottinghamshire, England
Died: May 14, 1936; London, England

British military leader during World War I

Edmund Henry Hynman Allenby (EHD-muhnd HEHN-ree HIHN-muhn A-lehn-bee) spent a comfortable but vigorous childhood in the English countryside. His family spent half the year in the county of Suffolk and the other half in the county of Norfolk. Allenby prepared for a life in the army by attending the Royal Military College at Sandhurst. He married Adelaide Mabel Chapman in 1896, and the couple had one child, a son who was to die in World War I.

A Soldier's Life

Allenby was an energetic and dynamic leader who routinely earned the enthusiastic loyalty of those he commanded. His bold style was sometimes unpopular with his superiors, although he remained scrupulously attentive to their orders. These qualities, coupled with his solid physique and frequent outbreaks of temper, earned him the nickname Bull. Allenby's first active service was in British forays into native regions of southern Africa, in Bechuanaland (1884-1885) and Zululand (1888). More important, he served in the Second Anglo-Boer War (1899-1902), in which Great Britain fought Dutch settlers for control of what would become South Africa.

During World War I (1914-1918) Allenby served at first on the western (European) front, eventually receiving command of the Third Army in 1915. His most notable involvement in this theater of the war was a typical one, and it came in 1917 in the Battle of Arras. Allenby planned to intensify, then cut short, a British bombardment and to surprise the Germans with an unexpectedly early attack of infantry. His plans, however, were so compromised by his superiors and by Britain's French allies that British gains were minimal.

The Middle East

In 1917 Allenby was given an opportunity to command in which his dynamic approach was less likely to be undercut: He was put in charge of allied forces based in the recently declared British protectorate of Egypt. In the Middle East, fighting the troops of Turkey (or the Ottoman Empire, as it was then called), Allenby distinguished himself as one of Great Britain's most important generals. After a brief period of reorganization, Allenby successfully concentrated

Edmund Henry Hynman Allenby *(Library of Congress)*

The Egyptian Expeditionary Force

Edmund Allenby's success against Turkey was as much psychological as tactical. Taking command of the Egyptian Expeditionary Force (EEF) in June, 1917, Allenby visited as many units as possible. He was immediately able to inspire the mixture of troops— British, Australian, Indian, and New Zealander—and to meld them into disciplined fighting units. Under Allenby's command, the EEF swept northward parallel to the eastern coast of the Mediterranean Sea, taking Beersheba, Gaza, and finally Jerusalem in the latter weeks of 1917. The following year Allenby staged the last historically important use of cavalry at Megiddo (the ancient Armageddon). As a result of Allenby's success, Turkey withdrew from the war on October 30, 1918. Allenby recognized the need of some under his command to operate independently, and gave them considerable latitude. Among these individuals was T. E. Lawrence, afterward known as Lawrence of Arabia, who organized the tribes of the Arabian Peninsula into guerrilla units that staged disabling attacks on the Turks.

Edmund Henry Hynman Allenby speaking at London's Chelsea Hospital in 1926; in the post-World War I era he was famous as the hero of Jerusalem. *(AP/Wide World Photos)*

his troops against Turkish forces in Palestine at the eastern end of the Mediterranean Sea. He seized control of the holy city of Jerusalem in November, 1917. By the end of October, 1918, he had forced Turkey to withdraw from the war. In recognition of this achievement, Allenby was named a viscount by the British government and was awarded fifty thousand pounds.

Allenby was subsequently appointed high commissioner for Egypt. In this position he encountered many of the same frustrations that he had encountered in the military. One of his first and most controversial acts was to free nationalist leader Sa'd Zaghlūl from arrest and exile on the island of Malta. Against much opposition, he oversaw the recognition of Egypt as an independent country by Great Britain in 1922, but he resigned because of frustration with his superiors in 1925. During his life of service to his country he had helped add to the British Empire in southern Africa, fought the empire's enemies in World War I, and finally overseen an initial step in the empire's dissolution in Egypt.

A rendition of Field Marshal Edmund Henry Hynman Allenby with Jerusalem in the background. Allenby's troops took control of Jerusalem in November, 1917, during World War I. *(Library of Congress)*

Bibliography

Bullock, David L. *Allenby's War: The Palestine-Arabian Campaigns, 1916-1918*. London: Blandford Press, 1988.

Gardner, Brian. *Allenby of Arabia, Lawrence's General*. New York: Coward-McCann, 1966.

James, Lawrence. *Imperial Warrior: The Life and Times of Field-Marshal Viscount Allenby, 1861-1936*. London: Weidenfeld and Nicolson, 1993.

Wavell, Archibald Percival. *Allenby, a Study in Greatness: The Biography of Field-Marshal Viscount Allenby of Megiddo and Felixstowe, G.D.B., G.C.M.G.* 2 vols. New York: Oxford University Press, 1941, 1943.

Grove Koger

Salvador Allende

Born: June 26, 1908; Valparaíso, Chile
Died: September 11, 1973; Santiago, Chile

President of Chile (1970-1973)

Salvador Allende Gossens (sahl-vah-THOHR ah-YEHN-day GO-sehnz) was the fourth child of Salvador Allende Castro, a lawyer and mason, and Laura Gossens Uribe, daughter of Catholic French professionals who had immigrated to Chile. Allende attended the National Institute in Santiago until age fourteen, when he rejoined his family in Valparaíso. After finishing secondary school in 1925, Allende served a year's compulsory military service. He then enrolled in the School of Medicine of the University of Chile

Salvador Allende *(Express Newspapers/Archive Photos)*

(Santiago) and worked to help his ailing father support the family.

In 1931, Allende led a students' strike and participated in street protests against the presidency of General Carlos Ibáñez (1927-1931). He was arrested and imprisoned, was released under an amnesty for political prisoners, and was jailed again for protesting the overthrow of a twelve-day-old socialist government. Before being freed in late 1932 under another amnesty, Allende was allowed to attend his father's funeral, where he swore that he would dedicate his life to social struggle. In 1939, he met and married Hortensia Bussi Allende, a socialist also from Valparaíso. They had three daughters: Carmen, Beatriz, and María Isabel.

A Socialist Leader

Although Allende was a licensed physician, politics took priority over medicine in his life. In 1933, Allende helped found the Chilean Socialist Party and became its leader in Valparaíso. In 1935, he was sent into internal exile in Caldera, a northern fishing town. The resulting publicity made him a folk hero. Two years later, Allende was elected to represent Valparaíso in the Chamber of Deputies. When Pedro Aguirre Cerda won the presidency, Allende joined his administration (1938-1941). As minister of public health, Allende lobbied for worker-safety laws, established maternity care, instituted a free lunch program in the schools, and founded Chile's National Health Service.

Because in 1946 his party refused to defend the right of the Communist Party to exist legally, Allende founded the Popular Socialist Party. When, in 1952, the Popular Socialist Party united with the communists in the Front of the People,

Salvador Allende with his wife and daughter at a 1964 political rally. *(Express Newspapers/Archive Photos)*

Allende agreed to run as its presidential candidate. He won only a small number of votes in the election. Remaining active in Chile's senate, Allende again ran for the presidency in 1958 as head of the Popular Action Front (FRAP), an alliance of all leftist parties, and he barely lost the election. Again as FRAP's candidate, Allende ran a third time for the presidency in 1964, losing decisively

The Election of 1970

The presidential election of September 4, 1970, was a three-way race with Allende, candidate of the Unidad Popular (UP), receiving 1,075,616 votes (36.3 percent), Jorge Alessandri, an independent rightist candidate, 1,036,278 (34.9 percent), and Radomiro Tomic, candidate of the ruling Christian Democrats, 824,849 (27.8 percent). Under Chilean law, a joint session of the bicameral congress had to choose between the top two contenders. On October 24, it endorsed Allende by a vote of 153 to 35. Allende won in the election because the UP represented the largest leftist coalition in Chile's history. He prevailed in the congressional selection because the Christian Democrats were satisfied that Allende supported democracy and political pluralism.

Chile's Nationalization of U.S. Copper Companies

Chile's Frei administration of the 1960's had negotiated Chilean majority ownership of foreign copper firms in Chile and had signed an agreement with the Anaconda company for the progressive nationalization of its mines. However, Salvador Allende, believing that foreign mining companies had caused Chile's underdevelopment, wanted immediate control of the country's copper, which yielded about 80 percent of Chile's export income. On July 11, 1971, dubbed National Dignity Day for the occasion, the Chilean Congress unanimously approved a constitutional amendment authorizing President Allende to nationalize the properties of U.S.-owned Kennecott, Anaconda, and Cerro corporations. Allende alleged that Anaconda and Kennecott had made excess profits of $774 million and that their Chilean interests were worth $550 million. He therefore refused to pay for the expropriated properties. These two companies contested Allende's decision in the courts. They conducted an international campaign that depleted Chile's foreign-exchange reserves and dried up credit lines from international lending organizations.

to a centrist coalition headed by Eduardo Frei, a Christian Democrat. Despite the defeat, Allende was elected president of the senate in 1966.

The Presidency

After gaining the presidency in 1970, Allende talked of Chile becoming a "second model" of the transition to a socialist society. He wanted to move Chile to socialism, but only with democracy and political pluralism. Many in his large leftist coalition, although not the communists, wanted a Marxist-Leninist dictatorship of the proletariat as soon as possible. Allende refused to break off relations with the radical factions in his coalition, and he even invited Fidel Castro to visit Chile for one month in 1971 to shore up their support.

While the radicals created problems for Allende, so did his bold economic measures. Although they increased wages and stimulated consumer demand, they also discouraged investments in the private sector through excessive land expropriations, the nationalization of banks and mines, and state takeovers of many factories. His policies created rampant inflation (more than 300 percent in the last year of his presidency) and critical shortages of goods, including food.

Allende's Fall

The U.S. Central Intelligence Agency (CIA) went to great lengths to discredit Allende and to destabilize his government. Nevertheless, the CIA's role was secondary to growing Chilean opposition to Allende. A truckers' strike in the fall of 1972 so worried Allende that he suffered a serious heart attack, which was kept secret for fear the news would encourage a *coup d'état*. On June 29, 1973, a military coup was stopped by the army chief of staff, General Carlos Prats. In response, Allende urged workers to seize industries and the streets.

In August, General Prats resigned and was replaced by General Augusto Pinochet Ugarte. On the morning of September 11, the military under Pinochet carried out a coup. It began when the Chilean navy, engaged in war games with U.S. forces off Chile, steamed into port and seized Valparaíso. Learning of the situation, Allende hurried to La Moneda, the presidential palace, with his guards. Pinochet gave him a choice:

surrender and go into exile or be bombarded. In a last radio address from La Moneda, Allende vowed that he would defend with his life the authority vested in him by the Chilean people. He and the few who stayed by his side defended La Moneda, which was bombed by planes and then assaulted. When the smoke cleared, Allende was found dead. There are conflicting accounts of whether he was murdered or committed suicide; a public autopsy never was conducted.

Chile After Allende

The brutal suppression of Chilean leftists after Allende's death extinguished democracy in Chile for many years. Pinochet's regime abducted its opponents, who simply disappeared and were never seen again. By 1975 socialism in Chile had been erased and replaced with free-market capitalism, which made Chile one of the most prosperous Latin American countries. Buoyed by the economy, the Pinochet dictatorship (1974-1990) allowed non-Marxist political parties to organize in 1987. The following year, Pinochet permitted a referendum on his rule. If a majority voted yes, Pinochet would serve an eight-year presidential term; if the vote was no, presidential elections would be held in 1989. The referendum failed, and a center-left coalition won the election. The new government promised to improve conditions for poorer Chileans while maintaining Chile's economic growth. As Allende had predicted in his last radio address, Chile was again moving toward a better society.

In August, 1973, Chilean president Salvador Allende (right) named Augusto Pinochet commander in chief of the army. Less than a month later, Pinochet had taken power and Allende was dead. *(AP/Wide World Photos)*

Bibliography

Alexander, Robert J. *The Tragedy of Chile*. Westport, Conn.: Greenwood Press, 1978.

Falcoff, Mark. *Modern Chile, 1970-1989: A Critical History*. New Brunswick, N.J.: Transaction, 1989.

Garza, Hedda. *Salvador Allende*. New York: Chelsea House, 1989.

Kaufman, Edy. *Crisis in Allende's Chile*. New York: Praeger, 1988.

Salvador Allende. Moscow: Novosti Press Agency, 1973.

Steven L. Driever

Idi Amin

Born: c. 1925; Koboko, West Nile Province, Uganda

Ugandan political leader, head of Uganda (1971-1979)

Idi Amin Dada Oumee (EE-dee ah-MEEN dah-dah ew-MAY) was born, apparently in 1925 (some sources say as late as 1927), to Kakawa tribespeo-

Idi Amin *(AP/Wide World Photos)*

ple, in Koboko, a small village in the northwestern part of Uganda near Sudan. Amin's mother raised him in Lugazi, to which she relocated after abandoning his father. Amin received a fourth-grade education and remained functionally illiterate into his adult life. A large and physically powerful man, he was an exceptional athlete and the only black African to play on the prestigious Nile rugby team. He also held the Ugandan national boxing title from 1951 to 1960.

Military Advancement

In Uganda in the 1940's, the only opportunity for advancement lay in joining the British Colonial Army. Amin enlisted as a private in 1946, joining the Fourth (Ugandan) Battalion of the King's African Rifles. He quickly impressed his superiors with his physical prowess and his subservience. In World War II Amin served with the Allies during the Burma campaign. In the 1950's he fought against the Mau-Maus during their revolt against British colonialism in Kenya. He continued to advance through the British ranks until 1959, when he was named "effendi," a rank created for outstanding noncommissioned African officers.

As Uganda began preparing for independence in 1962, the colonial army rushed to become Africanized. In this rush, Amin became one of the first two Ugandans to become commissioned officers. As a result, he rose quickly through the ranks. His advancement was hastened by his relationship with Uganda's prime minister, Milton Obote. The Amin-Obote relationship began in 1962 after Amin committed atrocities while policing cattle rustling among Kenyan and Ugandan ethnic groups. British officials sent Amin to Obote to be punished. Instead, Obote chose the politically safe route and merely reprimanded him.

Amin became commander of the armed forces in 1966. Obote relied on him to crush any political opposition, and Obote turned deaf ears to reports of human-rights abuses and corruption. As Amin's power grew, however, Obote began to fear his protector. In 1969 Obote survived an attempted assassination and became wary of Amin. By 1970 Obote had decided to replace Amin, but, surprisingly, he first promoted him to chief of general staff, a position that gave Amin control of the military.

Seizing Power in Kampala

In January of 1971, Obote ordered Amin to prepare written reports to explain the disappearance of weapons and military funds. Obote then left Uganda for the Commonwealth Heads of State Conference. Amin, warned that he was about to be arrested by Obote's troops, raised his own loyal troops, mainly other Kakawas. On January 25, he seized control of Uganda.

Ugandans welcomed Amin as a leader. He was a charismatic figure who was still enough of a "common man" to participate in their traditional dances and rituals. Amin also chose wives from different tribal and ethnic groups within Uganda in order to portray himself as a nationalist. He continued to increase his

Idi Amin addressing a crowd in 1975. *(Express Newspapers/ Archive Photos)*

popularity by disbanding Obote's secret police, freeing and granting amnesty to fifty-five political prisoners (many of whom he himself had rounded up for Obote), and promising free elections by 1974.

The Burmese Campaign in World War II

During his time in the British Colonial Army, Idi Amin fought with the Allies during the Burma campaign. Japanese forces had occupied Burma, and they were able to keep Allied forces in India from providing supplies and support to the Chinese. In March of 1944, Allied troop-carrier units and air commandoes used gliders and C-47 transport planes to land some nine thousand raiders, pack animals, air-field construc-tion equipment, and more than 250 tons of supplies behind Japanese lines in Burma. These forces kept Japanese forces in Burma off-balance until Chinese troops and American guerrilla fighters seized the Myitkyina airfield in northern Burma in the spring of 1944. The Chinese troops were able to reopen the Burma Road to China in March of 1945.

Despite promises and hopes, Amin ruled Uganda with an iron fist. He used executions and forced exile to eliminate potential dissidents. He executed officers who remained loyal to Obote. Amin capitalized on the tribal and ethnic divisions in Uganda to keep the nation too fragmented to challenge his rule, and he maintained a campaign of institutionalized violence to maintain power. In June of 1975, he was named president for life by the Ugandan Defense Council.

In international affairs, Amin was sometimes a shrewd leader, sometimes an arrogant buffoon. In 1972 he expelled more than seventy thousand Asians from Uganda, claiming that God had told him in a dream to chase away the Asian exploiters and hand over the economy to Ugandans. In 1975, at the U.N. General Assembly, he called for the extinction of Israel. Despite incidents such as these and widely reported human-rights abuses, Amin was elected chairman of the Organization of African Unity in 1975.

By the late 1970's, Uganda's economy was in ruins. The Arab nations that had been providing financial aid to Uganda began balking because of reports that Amin was killing Ugandan Muslims in his purges. In addition, the business infrastructure that Amin had taken from the exiled Asians had been squandered.

By October, 1978, Amin had survived twenty-two assassination attempts. His luck finally ran out when he chose to mount an invasion of Tanzania in an attempt to divert his people's attention from Uganda's economic crisis. The invasion failed, and Tanzanian soldiers and Ugandan exiles mounted a campaign that pursued Amin

Ugandan president Idi Amin (left) lunching with Zairian president Mobutu Sese Seko in Kinshasa, Zaire (now Congo), in 1977. (AP/Wide World Photos)

Human Rights in Uganda

Uganda is composed of some twenty-eight ethnic groups, with the main skirmish lines being drawn between Nilotic tribes (Acholi and Langi) and the Bantu tribes. During the reign of Idi Amin, who was a Kakawa tribesman, the persecution of members of the Acholi and Langi tribes grew to genocidal proportions. In 1978 the International Commission of Jurists estimated that as many as ten thousand Ugandans had been slaughtered by Amin and his forces. Some experts argue that there may have been as many as 100,000 to 300,000 Ugandans tortured and murdered as Amin attempted to purge the Langi and Acholi from Uganda. In 1977, two years before his fall, African nations blocked a U.N. resolution that would have condemned Amin for these violations of human rights.

until his government fell on April 11, 1979. Amin fled to Libya, then to Saudi Arabia as an exile.

Amin left Uganda in political and economic shambles. The Ugandan economy became merely an appendage of the economy of neighboring Kenya. The impact of the human-rights abuses under the Amin regime continues to unfold. Perhaps the only positive aspect of Amin's reign is that his actions helped to bring both African ethnic violence and governmental human-rights abuses into the limelight.

Bibliography

Apter, David E. *The Political Kingdom in Uganda: A Study of Bureaucratic Nationalism*. Essex, England: Frank Cass, 1997.

Olok-Apire, P.A. *Idi Amin's Rise to Power: The Inside Story*. Westport, Conn.: Lawrence Hill, 1985.

Omara-Otunnu, Amii, and Amli Omara Otunnu. *Politics and the Military in Uganda, 1890-1985*. New York: St. Martin's Press, 1987.

B. Keith Murphy

Kofi Annan

Born: April 8, 1938; Kumasi, Gold Coast (now Ghana)

Ghanaian diplomat, secretary-general of the United Nations (named 1996)

Kofi Atta Annan (KOH-fee ah-TAH ah-NAHN) was born into a prominent family, the son of the governor of Ashanti Province in Ghana, which at the time was still a British colony called the Gold Coast. After attending a university in Ghana, Annan completed his bachelor's degree in economics at Macalester College in St. Paul, Minnesota. He pursued graduate studies in Geneva, Switzerland, at the Institut Universitaire de Hautes Etudes Internationales, and earned an M.S. in management at the Massachusetts Institute of Technology in the United States. He married Nane Lagergren, and they had one son and two daughters. By 1971, Annan had joined the United Nations and begun his lifelong career as a diplomat.

Kofi Annan *(Reuters/Peter Morgan/Archive Photos)*

U.N. Diplomat

Annan quickly gained experience in a wide variety of administrative positions at the United Nations. These included assistant secretary-general for program planning, budget, and finance; chief of personnel for the High Commission for Refugees; and administrative officer for the Economic Commission for Africa. In 1993, Annan became undersecretary-general for peacekeeping operations and took a role at the center of world events. He showed that he was willing to speak out when necessary. For example, he expressed his dissatisfaction that the international community had not taken action to stop the killing in Somalia, where a U.S.-led U.N. peacekeeping operation had been sent in 1992. Annan also regretted that the world had not acted forcefully to prevent the genocide in Rwanda in 1994, in which hundreds of thousands of people died.

Annan also played a role in events surrounding two other crises of the 1990's. He traveled to Iraq to negotiate the release of hostages and the safe transport of about 500,000 Asian workers who had become stranded there. Concerning Bosnia, where a civil war raged from 1992 to 1995, Annan took part in delicate negotiations among the United States, Britain, France, and Russia as they tried to broker an end to the war.

Becoming Secretary-General

In December, 1996, Annan reached the pinnacle of his career when he was named secretary-

Kofi Annan at a memorial site in Mwulire, Rwanda, in 1998, looking at the skulls of victims massacred during the genocide that occurred in Rwanda in 1994. Annan's stop at Mwulire was part of the U.N. leader's 1998 tour of Africa. *(AP/Wide World Photos)*

Sanctions Against Iraq

The United Nations imposed sanctions on Iraq following the Persian Gulf War in 1991. In that war, a U.S.-led international coalition forced Iraq to withdraw from neighboring Kuwait, which it had invaded in August, 1990. The sanctions included a trade embargo, part of which involved restricting the amount of oil (Iraq's chief export) that Iraq was permitted to sell in the world markets. Iraq claimed that the sanctions led to the deaths of thousands of Iraqi children because of malnourishment and a lack of medical supplies. The U.S. government, however, contended that the major cause of hardship in Iraq was Saddam Hussein's continued diversion of resources into military rather than civilian uses. Iraq repeatedly requested the lifting of sanctions. In his trip to Baghdad in 1998, Annan informed the Iraqi leadership that the U.N. Security Council would discuss the lifting of sanctions only if Iraq agreed to cooperate with U.N. inspectors.

U.N. secretary-general Kofi Annan speaking in Rome before the 1998 ceremony establishing an international criminal court. *(Reuters/Paolo Cocco/Archive Photos)*

general of the United Nations. He was the first black African to hold the job, and many observers believed that he had the experience, diplomatic skill, and leadership qualities to succeed in this tough assignment.

In his first speech, Annan announced that his top priority would be reform of the United Nations. The world body had been widely criticized during the 1990's as being ineffectual and irrelevant to the solving of the world's problems. The secretary-general also called upon the United States, which had been critical of the slow pace of U.N. reform, to pay its $1.3 billion in unpaid U.N. dues, saying that reform would be difficult without the U.S. contribution. The United States contributes 25 percent of the U.N. budget.

Annan won international respect in February, 1998, when he flew to Baghdad, Iraq, and negotiated a last-minute agreement that averted U.S. air strikes against Iraq. The dispute concerned Iraqi president Saddam Hussein's decision to expel U.N. weapons inspectors from his country. The inspectors were seeking to ensure that Iraq did not develop weapons of mass destruction. Under the deal engineered by Annan, Iraq agreed to cooperate fully with the weapons inspectors. Within months, Hussein changed his mind, and the threat of air strikes again loomed; by the end of 1998, a new agreement had been reached.

Bibliography

Basic Facts About the United Nations. New York: United Nations Publications, 1996.

Carpenter, Ted Galen. *Delusions of Grandeur: The United Nations and Global Intervention.* Washington, D.C.: Cato Institute, 1997.

Glassner, Martin Ira, ed. *The United Nations at Work.* Westport, Conn.: Praeger, 1998.

Bryan Aubrey

Corazon Aquino

Born: January 25, 1933; Tarlac Province, Philippines

President of the Philippines (1986-1992)

Maria Corazon Cojuangco (mah-REE-ah ko-rah-ZOHN koh-WAHNG-koh) was the sixth of eight children of Demetria and José Cojuangco, descendants of rich and politically powerful families. She met her future husband, Benigno S. "Ninoy" Aquino (ah-KEE-noh), at the age of nine at a birthday party for his father, a congressman who represented Tarlac. Her childhood in Manila was interrupted by World War II. When it was over Corazon was sent to Raven Hill Academy in Philadelphia, a convent school. Later, she attended the College of Mount Saint Vincent in Brooklyn, New York. In 1953 Corazon returned to Manila and enrolled at Far Eastern University for one semester. She married Aquino on October 11, 1954, uniting two of the country's most influential families. They would have four children.

The Widow as Candidate

In 1972 Philippine president Ferdinand E. Marcos was at the end of his second term and by law could not run again. However, he declared martial law and gave himself emergency powers, thereby managing to stay in power until 1986 (martial law lasted until 1981). Benigno Aquino, then a senator, was Marcos's most outspoken critic and would have been his most likely successor. Marcos had him imprisoned under martial law in 1972. After seven years, Marcos offered to free him if he would leave the Philippines. The Aquino family spent three happy years near Boston, but Aquino decided to return to the Philippines to organize the opposition again. He was assassinated in Manila a few moments after exiting a plane on August 20, 1983. The assassination made Aquino a martyr and inspired increased opposition to Marcos.

When a sick President Marcos was forced to call an election in 1985, the opposition tried to unite around a single candidate. Salvador Laurel, head of Unido, the largest opposition party, had been preparing for the presidency for three years. In 1984 a group met to decide on the process for selecting a candidate. Laurel established a National Unification Conference to select a candidate, splitting the opposition. In May, Laurel offered Corazon Aquino the Unido Party's vice-presidential nomination, but she declined. A group of businessmen started a drive to draft Aquino for president. After prayer and contem-

Corazon Aquino *(Ricardo Watson/Archive Photos)*

41

In Manila in 1987, Philippine president Corazon Aquino greets a huge rally for the country's new constitution.

She abolished the parliament and the constitution, which gave the president blanket authority. A constitutional commission was appointed. The commission drafted a constitution providing a presidential system, a bicameral legislature, and a requirement for a two-thirds Senate vote to approve treaties. It limited the president's power to declare martial law, and it established rights for prisoners that prohibited intimidation, violence, and torture.

Guerrilla warfare was a serious problem in the Philippines. About a fifth of the population supported a guerrilla group called the National People's Army. There was also a communist faction as well as a separatist Muslim movement. National elections for the new legislature were held in May, 1987. Before her own legislative powers ended on July 27, Aquino wrote more than three hundred

plation, she accepted the nomination and offered Laurel the vice presidency.

The Presidency

A month after she was inaugurated, President Aquino began major reforms of the government.

The People Power Movement

On election day, February 7, 1986, Corazon Aquino was elected president by popular vote, but President Ferdinand Marcos refused to concede. On February 22 a group of officers and soldiers took over the national defense building in Camp Aguinaldo, and rebel soldiers rushed to their aid. By evening, the media broadcast Defense Minister Juan Enrile's statement: "I cannot . . . recognize Marcos as the commander in chief of the armed forces."

The rebel forces were at first greatly outnumbered, but influential Catholic leader Cardinal Jaime Sin broadcast an appeal for help. By mid-

night, ten thousand Filipinos had surrounded Camp Aguinaldo, and by 1:30 A.M. there were fifty thousand. On the second day, a human shield massed to protect the rebel camp. Marcos's heavily armed troops arrived, but they were surrounded by more than a million Filipinos. On the third day, Marcos ordered helicopters to the camp, but when they landed on the parade ground, sixteen pilots jumped out waving white handkerchiefs. After further desperate but unsuccessful attempts to deal with the rebellion, Marcos capitulated on February 25, 1986. Aquino was inaugurated the same day.

Corazon Aquino reviews the honor guard after arriving in Singapore for a summit meeting in 1992. *(Reuters/Enny Nuraheni/Archive Photos)*

executive orders as well as the new constitution, and she established the Comprehensive Agrarian Reform Program to advance land reform. An unsuccessful coup was attempted by a military faction in 1987. Further trouble erupted: There was rivalry between the national military and local police, a communist insurgence began, and there was a rise in local vigilante groups.

Aquino's term was over in June of 1992, and although she refused to run again, her favored candidate, Fidel Ramos, was elected. He was a lieutenant general who had helped instigate the revolution against Marcos and had stood beside her through all attempts to oust her from power.

Bibliography

Komisar, Lucy. *Corazon Aquino: The Story of a Revolution*. New York: George Braziller, 1987.

Reid, Robert H., and Eileen Guerrero. *Corazon Aquino and the Brushfire Revolution*. Baton Rouge: Louisiana State University Press, 1995.

White, Mel. *Aquino*. Dallas, Tex.: Word Publishing, 1989.

Sheila Golburgh Johnson

Yasir Arafat

Born: August 4 or 24, 1929; Cairo, Egypt, or Jerusalem, Palestine

Chairman of the Palestine Liberation Organization (from 1969), winner of 1994 Nobel Peace Prize

Mohammed Abd al-Rauf Arafat al Qudwa al-Husseini (moo-HAH-muhd AB-dal rah-EWF AH-rah-faht al KUHD-wah al-huh-SAY-nee), known as Yasir Arafat (YAH-sir AH-rah-faht)), was born in either Gaza, Palestine, or Cairo, Egypt. (Arafat says that he was born in Palestine, but his only known birth record states that he was born in Cairo.) His father, Abder Rauf Arafat, had relocated his family to Egypt in 1927 seeking better business prospects.

Yasir Arafat *(Archive Photos/Imapress)*

The details of Yasir's childhood are somewhat murky, especially after the death of his mother, Hamida Abu Saud, in 1933. As a boy he was reputed to be hyperactive, with a penchant for adventures; despite his short stature, he stood tall among his cohorts because of his personality and leadership qualities. From 1933 to 1937, he lived with his maternal uncle in Jerusalem and thereafter returned to Cairo to live with his father.

In his teen years, Yasir became interested in politics. He learned about the Arab nationalist struggle from his relative Haj Amin al-Husseini, grand mufti of Jerusalem, Sheik Hassan Abu Saud, and the military leader Abdel Kader al-Husseini, founder of the Arab Higher Committee in Cairo.

Making of an Arab Nationalist

England's Balfour Declaration of November, 1917, called for a Jewish national homeland to be established in Palestine. The declaration left Palestine's Arab population in despair. After two abortive revolts between 1936 and 1939, the Palestinian nationalist movement was at its lowest point. Yet tensions between Palestinians and the Jews who were moving to Palestine mounted. Arafat became interested in an independent Arab Palestine from the 1940's, and he began to smuggle weapons to the Palestinians, who were barred by the British from arming themselves. (Palestine was under British control at that time.)

During his freshman year as an engineering student at the King Fuad University, Arafat joined the war between five Arab states and the newly created state of Israel in 1948. He was shocked to note that Arab soldiers did not welcome Palestinian irregulars as their cohorts and even confiscated their arms. To make matters worse, the defeated Arab states concluded a

The Palestine Liberation Organization (PLO)

The Palestine Liberation Organization (PLO) was founded in Jerusalem in 1964 at the urging of President Gamal Abdel Nasser of Egypt, then the dominant member of the Arab League (a group of independent Arab states organized in 1945 for the purpose of Arab unity). The purpose of the PLO was to shore up languishing Arab unity in the face of Israeli actions in Palestine. Its charter included provisions for armed struggle against Israel. Yet true to his political vision and style, Nasser eschewed militance and opted for a moderate nationalist stance. The PLO's first president, Ahmad al-Shukairy, was a Nasserite. Under him the PLO was essentially a political structure founded on the conviction that Palestine's liberation would come by conventional warfare under the direction of Arab armies. Israel's victory in the Arab-Israeli War of 1967 (the Six-Day War) led to the radicalization of the PLO and a sharper articulation of its goals and strategies.

With the induction of Yasir Arafat as its new head in 1969, the PLO became an organization of, by, and for Palestinians. In the early 1970's the PLO was responsible for a number of terrorist actions. However, it became increasingly moderate after 1974. Through the next two decades it was able to win recognition from the Arab states and many nations in the world.

peace with Israel that displaced more than 750,000 Palestinians. This experience prompted Arafat, upon his return to campus, to found a guerrilla movement, the Movement for the Liberation of Palestine (Harakat al-Tahrir al-Watani al Filastini, or al-Fatah—an acronym in reverse that stood for the Arab word for conquest). The organization adopted the strategy of armed resistance to recover Palestine.

Leader of Palestinian Nationalism

There were several efforts in the United Nations to come to terms with the Palestinian issue, but discussions were plagued by intra-Arab rivalries. This disarray encouraged Israel to divert the waters of the Jordan River for its own use. To counteract this Israeli move, President Gamal Abdel Nasser of Egypt proposed the formation of a "Palestinian entity." This proposal led to the founding of the Palestine Liberation Organization (PLO) in 1964. A moderate Palestinian nationalist, Ahmad al-Shukairy, was its president. Al-Shukairy was replaced by Yasir Arafat in 1969. At this time Arafat was not only the head of al-Fatah but also the hero of the Battle of Karameh against the Israeli army in Jordan on March 21, 1968.

The Palestinian State

Palestinian militants were expelled from Jordan by its moderate King Hussein in September of 1970. They relocated to Lebanon, from where they continued attacks on Israel. The PLO was implicated in the violence that had erupted in Lebanon between the country's Christian and Muslim populations and was consequently expelled from Beirut. Arafat relocated the PLO headquarters to Tunis in North Africa. Yet Arafat succeeded in uniting most of the Arabs under the aegis of the PLO. By the early 1970's the PLO contained a variety of factions, and Arafat did not always have control over them all. Terrorism increased during this period, some of it at the hands of a group within al-Fatah called Black September, which was responsible for the massacre of Israeli athletes at the 1972 Munich Olympics. The

Arab Summit Conference at Rabat in 1974 recognized the PLO as the legitimate representative of Arab nationalists. The U.N. General Assembly meeting of the same year conferred similar recognition on the PLO. Arafat, on his part, recognized Israel's need to be an independent state.

Arafat's increasingly moderate stance toward Israel caused a rift within al-Fatah. He faced increasing resistance from the younger radical members, who were receiving Syria's support. Arafat retrieved his position by aligning himself with the Palestinian uprising of December 9, 1987, in Gaza known as the *Intifada*. In November, 1988, at Algiers, the Palestinian National Congress (established in 1917 in response to the Balfour Declaration) proclaimed an independent Palestinian state on the West Bank and the Gaza Strip and implicitly recognized Israel's right to exist. On December 13, 1988, Arafat declared in a U.N. session in Geneva that the PLO abjured terrorism and supported the rights of all parties concerned in the Middle East. The state of Palestine received diplomatic recognition from seventy countries, and even the United States declared its intention to begin a diplomatic dialogue with the PLO. The ground thus gained was to some extent lost in the early 1990's, when Arafat supported Iraq's invasion of Kuwait. However, in August, 1993, Israel recognized PLO participation in the peace process (begun in late 1991). Arafat thereby recovered his stature.

Peace Agreements

A significant breakthrough in the Israeli-Palestinian relationship occurred on September 10 of 1993, when—following numerous negotia-

Palestine Liberation Organization leader Yasir Arafat meeting with U.S. president Bill Clinton at the White House in 1997. *(Reuters/Rick Wilking/Archive Photos)*

Yasir Arafat (right) with Israeli prime minister Benjamin Netanyahu at Erez Crossing, Gaza Strip, in December, 1998. They, and U.S. president Bill Clinton, were meeting to discuss Israel's decision to halt troop withdrawals from the West Bank. *(AP/Wide World Photos)*

tions between the representatives of the PLO and Israel in Oslo, Norway—Arafat and Prime Minister Yitzhak Rabin of Israel exchanged letters of mutual recognition. The Oslo Peace Accords were signed and sealed by both men in the United States three days later. They provided for Palestinian self-rule in Israeli-occupied Gaza and in the West Bank town of Jericho (later to extend to the entire West Bank territory). On May 4, 1994, Rabin and Arafat signed the Jericho-Gaza withdrawal agreement in Cairo. Arafat, Rabin, and Israel's Shimon Peres were awarded the Nobel Peace Prize in 1994 for their efforts.

In September and October of 1998, Arafat and Israeli prime minister Benjamin Netanyahu met in the United States for new peace talks. Relations between Israel and the Palestinians had been particularly troubled in the previous few years. In the Wye River Agreement (October 23, 1998), Israel pledged to return a significant amount of West Bank land to the PLO, and the PLO pledged to suppress terrorist attacks against Israel. The agreement immediately faced difficulties from both sides.

Bibliography

Hart, Alan. *Arafat: A Political Biography*. Rev. ed. London: Sidgwick & Jackson, 1994.

The *Intifada*

The *Intifada* (meaning "shake up") was a spontaneous revolt of Palestinian youth that began in Gaza on December 9, 1987, following an accident in which four Palestinians were killed and several others injured by an Israeli military vehicle. When a gathering of Palestinian mourners was fired upon by the Israeli army, Gaza and the West Bank burst into open insurrection. The movement was led by an underground local organization called the Unified National Leadership, comprising several members of the Palestine Liberation Organization. The strategy of the *Intifada* was civil disobedience, including strikes, the closure of business establishments, and a refusal to pay taxes until the Israelis stopped building settlements, confiscating Arab lands, and imposing special taxes on Palestinians. Arafat came to identify with the *Intifada*; through diplomacy and dialogue, he brought the Palestinians into the world arena.

Mishal, Shaul. *The PLO Under Arafat: Between Gun and Olive Branch*. New Haven, Conn.: Yale University Press, 1986.

Nassar, Jamal R. *The Palestine Liberation Organization: From Armed Struggle to the Declaration of Independence*. New York: Praeger, 1991.

Rubinstein, Danny. *The Mystery of Arafat*. Translated by Dan Leon. South Royalton, Vt.: Steerforth Press, 1995.

Wallach, Janet, and John Wallach. *Arafat: In the Eyes of the Beholder*. New York: Carol, 1990.

Narasingha P. Sil

Oscar Arias Sánchez

Born: September 13, 1941; Heredia, Costa Rica

President of Costa Rica (1986-1990), winner of 1987 Nobel Peace Prize

Oscar Arias Sánchez (OHS-kahr AH-ree-ahs SAHN-chays) was born into a wealthy coffee-growing family residing in Heredia, on the outskirts of San José, Costa Rica's capital city. His father played an active role in politics, running unsuccessfully for vice president on the National Liberation Party ticket with presidential aspirant Luis Monge in the 1970's.

The young Arias attended the local Catholic Colegio Saint Francis in San José and then went abroad to study medicine at Boston University in the United States. He found out quickly that he enjoyed social science courses more than medicine, so he gave up the idea of becoming a physician. During Arias's Boston sojourn, John F. Kennedy was running for U.S. president, and Arias identified with the rich American's liberal political philosophy. He returned to San José and the national university to study law and economics. After graduating in 1967, he continued his studies in England, earning a master's degree and subsequently a Ph.D. from the University of Essex, in political science. He also attended the London School of Economics and Political Science.

A Political Career

Returning to Costa Rica, Arias began teaching political science at the national university in San José. He soon turned to politics, accepting a position as economic adviser to President José Figueres, head of the National Liberation Party and Costa Rica's most prominent political leader. Figueres became young Arias's mentor and advanced him to the office of minister of planning. At the same time, Arias began his climb within the ranks of the National Liberation Party itself. He became its secretary-general in 1979.

The Arias Presidency

Arias ran for president in 1986, sixteen years after first entering politics. A liberal, he campaigned on a platform of providing new housing and more job opportunities. He won the presi-

Oscar Arias Sánchez addressing the U.N. General Assembly in 1989. *(Reuters/Ray Stubblebine/Archive Photos)*

49

The 1987 Central American Peace Accord

In the 1970's and 1980's, numerous attempts by outside parties failed to produce a program to bring peace to Central America's warring factions. Oscar Arias Sánchez of Costa Rica therefore began work on a peace plan of his own. The plan was termed Esquipulas II, after the Guatemalan city where negotiations began. Arias was able to persuade the other presidents of Central America—from Guatemala, El Salvador, Honduras, and Nicaragua—to discuss proposals for ending the fighting that had plagued the area for more than two decades. Arias's negotiations were complicated by the civil wars that existed at the time in Nicaragua, El Salvador, and Guatemala. Nevertheless he secured the cooperation of Central America's other leaders in adopting an agreement that led to peace throughout the area. The signing of the Arias peace plan by the assembled Central American presidents took place in Guatemala City on August 7, 1987.

dency in a hard-fought campaign with 52 percent of the popular vote. Arias felt that Costa Rica's economic future lay with the restoration of peace to the area. Once in office, he began laying plans for ensuring his country's neutrality in the ongoing civil war under way in neighboring Nicaragua. Moreover, he began to work on a plan to develop an overall peace program for Central America.

Arias prevailed on the other four Central American presidents—from Guatemala, Honduras, El Salvador, and Nicaragua—to meet with him to discuss his ideas. His commitment to strict neutrality flew in the face of U.S. foreign policy, which at that time supported the efforts of a rebel faction (the Contras) fighting to oust the Nicaraguan Sandinista government. Nevertheless, he succeeded in persuading the other Central American leaders to follow his suggestions for the adoption of an independent Central American peace plan.

Arias's domestic program proved equally dramatic. Persuading Costa Rica's congress to pass laws to increase taxes, he met 80 percent of his goal of constructing 21,700 new homes in the first year of his administration. The housing

Oscar Arias Sánchez in a 1993 interview in Mexico City at which he voiced support for the North American Free Trade Agreement. *(AP/Wide World Photos)*

construction drive also fulfilled his plans to alleviate unemployment, since the building program was heavily labor intensive.

After the conclusion of his presidency in 1990, Arias continued to campaign for peaceful solutions to global problems. In a speech at Wake Forest University on September 17, 1998, he reiterated his call for disarmament: "Restricted arms sales are necessary. The poor of the world are crying for schools and doctors, not guns and generals." For his efforts in search of peace, Oscar Arias Sánchez was awarded the 1987 Nobel Peace Prize. Because of Arias's philosophy, Costa Rica became the only country in Central America without a standing army.

Bibliography

Edelman, Marc, and Joanne Kenen, eds. *The Costa Rica Reader*. New York: Grove Weidenfeld, 1989.

Kenworthy, Eldon. *America/Americas*. University Park: Pennsylvania State University Press, 1995.

Rolbein, Seth. *Nobel Costa Rica*. New York: St. Martin's Press, 1989.

Carl Henry Marcoux

Jean-Bertrand Aristide

Born: July 15, 1953; Port Salut, Haiti

President of Haiti (1991, 1994-1996)

Jean-Bertrand Aristide (ZHAH bayr-TRAH ah-ree-STEED) grew up in Haiti's capital, Port-au-Prince, where he attended Catholic schools. He graduated from College Notre Dame at Cap-Haitian in 1974 and entered a seminary in the Dominican Republic the next year. He returned to Haiti for postgraduate training in philosophy and psychology, and in 1979 he left to study in Rome and Israel, concentrating on biblical theology. He was ordained a priest in Haiti in 1983, but he left the priesthood in 1988 because of his involvement in Haitian politics. He married attorney Mildred Trouillot in 1996, and together they had one child.

A Voice for the Poor

Aristide's first assignments as a priest were to parishes in the slums of Port-au-Prince. There he saw the abject poverty that afflicted almost 85 percent of Haiti's population under the dictatorship of Jean-Claude ("Baby Doc") Duvalier. Aristide became a vocal critic of the ruling regime and a spokesman for his poor parishioners. In sermons and in the radio addresses that brought him to national prominence, Aristide emphasized the human dignity of each person and criticized the system that permitted such tremendous social and economic inequity. His hopeful, pro-democracy message attracted thousands of followers, and Aristide's movement played an important part in the fall of the Duvalier regime in 1986. He was just as critical of the repressive military governments that followed Duvalier's. He was therefore a target of numerous assassination attempts by the Haitian military.

In September, 1988, his parish church was attacked by armed thugs during a service. Dozens of congregants were massacred, and the church was burned to the ground. This attack was so outrageous that it was partly responsible for the fall of the ruling military junta one week later. Aristide was expelled from his religious order in 1988 as a result of his political activities, but he continued to devote himself to social work and pro-democracy politics. In 1990 he announced his candidacy for the Haitian presidency.

President Aristide

Although many people feared that the elections would end in political violence, as had happened in 1987, international observers deemed

Jean-Bertrand Aristide *(Reuters/Arnd Wiegmann/ Archive Photos)*

Jean-Bertrand Aristide arriving in Port-au-Prince, Haiti, in 1994 after more than three years in exile. *(Reuters/Rick Wilking/Archive Photos)*

the 1990 elections free and fair. Aristide won 67 percent of the vote in a field of thirteen candidates. He attempted to institute governmental reforms but had been in office for only seven months when his government was overthrown by the military in September of 1991. Forced into exile in the United States, he fought for international support to restore democracy in Haiti.

Aristide was successful in garnering that support. Faced with the prospect of an invasion by twenty-three thousand U.S. troops, the military government of General Raul Cedras agreed to leave peacefully. Aristide returned to Haiti in October, 1994, and completed his presidential term, continuing his reform initiatives and completely dissolving the Haitian military. Free elections were held in 1995, and Aristide stepped down from office in 1996.

Blazing a Trail for Democracy

Jean-Bertrand Aristide is a remarkable figure in Haitian history. A leader of the common people, he gave voice to the hopes and frustrations of the poorest of Haitians. Instrumental in overthrowing the decades-long Duvalier dictatorship, he became the first freely elected president

Aristide's Dismantling of the Military

When President Jean-Bertrand Aristide was returned to office in 1994, the Haitian military, long riddled with corruption and prone to brutality, posed a serious problem. Military leaders had deposed Aristide in 1991, and during the period of his exile the military carried out a campaign of repression that targeted Aristide supporters, journalists, students, and others who were opposed to military rule. Beatings, torture, and murder of Haitian citizens increased dramatically under military rule. Rather than attempt to reform the military establishment that had terrorized Haitians during his exile, Aristide dismantled it entirely. In what was perhaps his most significant achievement as president, he suspended all Haitian armed forces—the army, navy and air force—reducing the size of the military from about seven thousand to fewer than one hundred. The military was replaced by a much smaller police agency under civilian control.

of Haiti. He began reforms to root out long-standing government and military corruption. Moreover, he took part in his country's first peaceful, democratic transition of power when, in 1996, he relinquished his presidency to his duly elected successor, René Préval.

Bibliography

Aristide, Jean-Bertrand, with Christophe Wargny. *Aristide: An Autobiography*. Translated by Linda M. Maloney. Maryknoll, N.Y.: Orbis Books, 1993.

Heinl, Robert, Nancy Heinl, and Michael Heinl. *Written in Blood: The Story of the Haitian People, 1492-1995*. Ann Arbor, Mich.: University Press of America, 1996.

Perusse, Roland. *Haitian Democracy Restored, 1991-1995*. Ann Arbor, Mich.: University Press of America, 1995.

Catherine Udall Turley

H. H. Asquith

Born: September 12, 1852; Morley, Yorkshire, England
Died: February 15, 1928; Sutton Courtney, Berkshire, England

Prime minister of Great Britain (1908-1916)

Herbert Henry Asquith (HUR-burt HEHN-ree AS-kwihth) was born into a family of small-scale mill owners and devout Puritans. After attending middle-class boarding schools, he won a scholarship to Balliol College, Oxford. He began legal studies in 1874, was called to the bar in 1876, and in 1877 married Helen Melland, raising a family of four sons and a daughter in a quietly well-ordered household before his wife's death from typhoid fever in 1891.

In 1886, Asquith was elected Liberal Party member of Parliament for East Fife. His 1888 service as a junior counsel for the Irish leader Charles Stewart Parnell brought him widespread public and legal attention. He became a queen's counsel in 1890, developing a lucrative High Court practice. From 1892 to 1895, Asquith served as home secretary, first under William Ewart Gladstone and then during the brief administration of Archibald Primrose, earl of Rosebery. Asquith's 1894 marriage to Margaret ("Margo") Tennant reshaped his personal life. The witty, uninhibited, unpredictable, and frequently tactless society lady seemed an odd partner for the conventional and restrained home secretary. Two children were born to this marriage. Because the Liberals were out of office from 1895 to 1905, Asquith resumed his legal practice to support his family and their more active social life.

When Arthur James Balfour and the Conservative Unionists resigned in December of 1905, new prime minister Sir Henry Campbell-Bannerman assembled a gifted Liberal cabinet with Asquith as chancellor of the Exchequer, Sir Edward Grey at the Foreign Office, and David Lloyd George as president of the Board of Trade. In the 1906 election the Liberal Party decided to cooperate with the Labour Party and adopted its promise of benefits for workers. Winners by a landslide, the Liberals embarked on an agenda of working-class legislation sometimes called "the New Deal in England."

H. H. Asquith *(Library of Congress)*

Prime Minister

When ill health forced Campbell-Bannerman to retire, Asquith was appointed prime minister on April 3, 1908. He named David Lloyd George as chancellor of the Exchequer and Winston Churchill as president of the Board of Trade. The new prime minister's first major achievement was the landmark Old Age Pension Act of 1908. The budget of 1909 was blocked by the House of Lords in an unprecedented invasion of House of Commons' traditional control of finance. Asquith proposed trimming the veto powers of the House of Lords, and this attack, by putting their lordships on the defensive, intimidated the peers into passing most of the Liberal reform bills. These included the Labour Exchanges Act to help people find jobs, the Trade Boards Act on wages and working conditions, and the House and Town Planning Act, all enacted in 1909. In 1911 came the National Insurance Act, covering sickness and unemployment, as well as the Parliament Act and an act providing salaries for members of the House of Commons. No previous administration had done as much for the working class. However, rising prices at the time caused many workers to strike for higher wages, agitation for women's right to vote increased, and in 1914 the passage of Irish home rule raised the threat of civil war and army mutiny. Therefore, much of the implementation of these measures was postponed to the end of World War I.

Wartime

During the European crisis of July-August, 1914 (the beginning of World War I), Asquith succeeded in delaying a decision on Britain's role until Germany invaded Belgium, alienating British public opinion. Then he brought Britain into the war with the support of both major political parties. British troops were deployed in France rapidly enough to take part in the crucial battles of August and September, 1914. Asquith's management of this changing political and military crisis was masterful, and his leadership role seemed assured. However, like most European political leaders of 1914, Asquith soon became a victim of the war. The press and public unrealistically expected quick and decisive victories, not stalemate and a strategy of attrition. Asquith did not originate any strategic plans, and his deliberate composure was not a substitute for leadership. There was also gossip and criticism about his conspicuous social life of motor trips and country weekends with golf, bridge, and brandy.

The Parliament Act of 1911

By rejecting the 1909 budget, the House of Lords not only forced a special election in January, 1910, on the budget issue but also renewed the controversy over their own veto power. H. H. Asquith proposed a bill limiting this by legislation, but the new king, George V, agreed to create enough new peers to pass the measure only after another mandate from the voters. The December, 1910, election gave the two major parties 272 seats apiece. However, Irish, Labour, and Liberal votes plus the king's support persuaded the Conservatives to let the bill through the House of Lords. The act provided that finance bills should go directly from the House of Commons to the king's approval and that all other bills could become law without the House of Lords' approval when passed by the House of Commons in three sessions over a two-year period. The Lords could delay, but could no longer veto, legislation.

British soldiers in their trench in World War I. Asquith's prime ministership fell victim to the ravages of the war as it dragged on. *(AP/Wide World Photos)*

His 1915 coalition government only postponed to December, 1916, Asquith's replacement as prime minister by Lloyd George, who formed a coalition with the Conservatives and promised to deliver "a knockout blow."

Out of Power

Asquith declined to serve under Lloyd George. Still in control of party machinery, he headed a Liberal opposition of more than a hundred in Parliament, but he led only one ineffective attack on the Lloyd George coalition in May of 1918.

Asquith Liberals soon became a minor party with only twenty-six seats, and Asquith himself was defeated at East Fife. His political fortunes rebounded slightly when the Conservatives abandoned Lloyd George, and the 1922 elections gave Asquith Liberals sixty seats to only fifty-seven for the Lloyd Georgeites.

After again losing his seat in the election of 1924, Asquith in 1925 accepted a peerage as earl of Oxford and Asquith. He was still nominally the head of the party, with Lloyd George as Liberal leader in the House of Commons, but in

Coalition War Governments

The political truce on wartime management ended in the spring of 1915. Allied failures at the Dardanelles and Gallipoli coincided with newspaper reports of a "shell shortage scandal," and critics sought a scapegoat. The Conservative Party leader, Bonar Law, on May 16 demanded that Winston Churchill be replaced at the Admiralty as the price of continued cooperation. H. H. Asquith promptly abandoned Churchill and formed an "all parties" coalition government. However, the Labour Party had only one member in the coalition, the Southern Irish did not join, and—except for Arthur James Balfour at the Admiralty—Conservatives filled only minor posts. Asquith relegated Law to the Colonial Office and never treated him as a political partner.

Asquith's problems continued in 1916 with the Irish Easter Rebellion, the death at sea of War Secretary Field Marshall Herbert Horatio Kitchener, the difficulties over introducing conscription, Field Marshall Douglas Haig's costly battle of attrition on the Somme, and the death at the front of Asquith's gifted son, Raymond. David Lloyd George demanded a larger role in war policy. Upon Asquith's refusal, he and the Conservatives formed a new coalition, without Asquith, in December of 1916. This government finished the war and held office until 1922.

actuality their personal split handicapped a party that was losing votes to both the Labour and Conservative Parties. Asquith spent his last years writing memoirs which were readable but of marginal historical importance.

H. H. Asquith's chief legacy was an impressive list of working-class reforms that laid the basis for the modern welfare state in Britain. Ironically, his own upper-class views, personality, and lifestyle made it difficult for the workers to enshrine him as a political idol. Asquith's wartime performance was more debatable.

Bibliography

Asquith, Herbert H. *Letters to Venetia Stanley*. New York: Oxford University Press, 1982.

Cassar, George. *Asquith as War Leader*. London: Hambledon Press, 1994.

Dangerfield, George. *The Strange Death of Liberal England*. Reprint. New York: G. P. Putnam's Sons, 1980.

Jenkins, Roy. *Asquith*. London: Collins, 1964.

Koss, Stephen. *Asquith*. London: Allen Lane, 1976.

K. Fred Gillum

Hafez al-Assad

Born: October 6, 1930; Qardāha, Latakia Province, Syria

President of Syria (took office 1971)

A member of the minority Alawite sect, which is viewed as heretical by mainstream Islam, Hafez al-Assad (hah-FEHZ ahl-ah-SAHD) was the ninth of the eleven children of Ali Sulayman al-Assad—a small landowner—and the fourth of his second marriage. Hafez attended secondary school in the city of Latakia, graduating in 1951. Thereupon he entered the flying school (later academy) in Aleppo, emerging as a lieutenant in 1955. He was then sent for further pilot training to Egypt, where he caught the Arab nationalist fever. In 1958, he married Aniseh Makhlaf, a union that was to produce four sons and one daughter (another daughter having died in infancy). That same year he went to the Soviet Union for jet-fighter training. Thereafter, Assad ascended the military hierarchy rapidly. By 1964, he was commander of the new Syrian air force. He was promoted to the rank of lieutenant general in 1968. Long before then, in 1946, the adolescent Assad had joined the Ba'th Party. As an organizer and activist, he participated in discussions about Syria's future.

Political Career

In May, 1963, Assad took a leading part in the coup that brought the Ba'th Party to power in Syria. After a further coup by the party's radical wing in February, 1966, Assad was made defense minister. In another coup, in February, 1969, Assad gained control of the party. He agreed to compromise in a coalition until October, 1970, when, in a final coup instigated by him, Assad seized complete power, retaining the position of minister of defense but additionally assuming the premiership. In March, 1971, a plebiscite endorsed his single candidacy by the Ba'th Party as president of Syria. He was reelected unopposed by overwhelming majorities in 1978, 1985, and 1992 to successive seven-year terms.

This long tenure enabled Assad to endow his country with an unaccustomed political stability following its turbulent post-independence years in the 1940's. In domestic policy, Assad followed the dictates of the Ba'th Party. He nationalized industries and achieved pragmatic state socialism; he championed the Arab cause. He endeavored to boost economic development through such projects as the Euphrates River Dam, intended to increase agricultural production. As-

Hafez al-Assad *(Archive Photos)*

The Baʿth Party

The Baʿth (Arab Socialist Renaissance) Party emerged in Syria in 1953 as a result of the fusion between the Syrian Socialist Party headed by Akram Hourani, a Sunni Arab, and the Resurrection Party led by Michel Aflaq, a French-educated Greek Orthodox Marxist. Baʿthism stands for Arab unity and freedom from foreign exploitation, the rebirth of Arab culture, and socialism. However, it does not demand the elimination of free enterprise or private ownership of property but rather the nationalization of key industries, extensive social services, and greater social justice. This program appealed to students—especially those belonging to such minorities as the Alawite sect, to which Hafez al-Assad belongs— and to disaffected intellectuals, workers, peasants, and others.

In the late 1950's, the Baʿth became a pan-Arab party with branches in Lebanon, Iraq, and Jordan. At first highly supportive of the Syrian-Egyptian merger as the United Arab Republic (UAR) in 1958, by 1959-1960, with the party now banned and contemplating its loss of program and power, the Baʿth helped to terminate the UAR in 1961. Still, it continued to support the idea of a looser pan-Arab union such as the Federation of Arab Republics that was proposed in 1971.

A series of coups beginning in 1963 was eventually, by 1970, to lead to Hafez al-Assad's emergence as the uncontested Baʿth leader. He purged or imprisoned his adversaries. Under his guidance, the new party high command nominated a 173-member People's Assembly, which drafted a plebiscite-approved constitution that went into effect in 1973. Accordingly, Assad's position as head of the ruling party, closely allied with the National Progressive Front, and its renewal of his presidency enabled him to lead Syria as a populist regime, an authoritarian one with an undisputed chief.

sad also expanded Syria's oil industry by liberalizing the economy and attracting foreign investments. However, domestic political concerns such as the repression of outlawed Islamic fundamentalists—especially the Muslim Brotherhood—and foreign policy problems within and outside the Arab world were challenging.

Policy Problems

Syria's relationship with Lebanon posed a major problem. Beginning in 1975, Assad in effect established a Syrian protectorate over the neighboring country to ensure that no unfriendly government could take over, but this undertaking involved a heavy Syrian financial and military commitment. Syria also generally opposed concessions to Israel. Israel therefore opposed the peace initiative begun by Egypt in the 1970's

despite Syria's inability to impose its own military solution. Assad's problems within the Arab world largely grew out of ideological differences within the pan-Arab Baʿth Party, specifically between its Syrian and Iraqi regions.

During the Iran-Iraq War of 1980-1988, Syria supported non-Arab Iran against Iraq, while in the Gulf War of 1991 Syria assisted the U.S.-led U.N. coalition against Baghdad. After the 1991 breakup of the Soviet Union, until then Syria's major military and political backer, Assad was in a weaker international position. Yet, except for a brief period prior to the return of Israel's hardline Likud coalition to office in 1996, Assad rejected strenuous American efforts to have him sign a permanent peace treaty with Israel, primarily because of Israel's continued occupation of the Golan Heights.

Hafez al-Assad waving to crowds in 1992; he is on his way to take the oath of office for his fourth term as president of Syria. *(Reuters/Ali Jarekji/Archive Photos)*

Assad's Importance

With Assad suffering a near-fatal heart attack in 1983 and the subsequent death of his eldest and most popular son and heir apparent, Basil, the question of succession assumed some urgency. Even though Assad's younger brother, Colonel Rifaat al-Assad, was considered a major contender for the presidency, Rifaat's accept-

The Golan Heights

The Golan (or Jawlan) Heights is a barren, hilly plateau of some 450 square miles (1,200 square kilometers) in southwestern Syria that was occupied by Israel during the Six-Day War of 1967. Its elevated strategic location—which is no longer as crucial because of improved long-range missiles—had been used by Syria to shell northern Israeli settlements.

In the October War (Yom Kippur War) of 1973, Syria failed to recapture the Heights. However, a disengagement agreement in 1974 positioned a U.N. force between the two antagonists after Israel withdrew from the Golan's major town, Quneitra, and some land that it had just captured. About fifteen thousand Syrians of the Druze religious sect and nearly as many Israeli settlers live in their respective zones of the Golan Heights. In 1981 Israel officially annexed its portion of the territory despite international opposition. Syria continues to demand its total return. The status of the Golan Heights has hampered the chances of a final negotiated Syrian-Israeli settlement agreement.

Hafez al-Assad (right), on a visit to Iran, is greeted by Iranian president-elect Seyyed Mohammad Khatami in 1997. *(AP/Wide World Photos)*

ability after his exile and temporary tenure as Syria's vice president was in doubt. At the close of the twentieth century, Syria faced serious economic and foreign policy difficulties; internally, reflecting its ethnic and religious mosaic, it tended to be politically unstable.

Assad's authoritarian rule has a checkered record regarding fundamental rights at home (the government massacred members of the Muslim Brotherhood in Hama in 1982, for example), and he allegedly aided and abetted terrorism abroad. Nevertheless, as a strong leader, al-Assad (literally, "the lion") can be credited with having given Syria three decades of respite from its customary internal political turmoil. His reputation as an astute Middle Eastern statesman is unequaled.

Bibliography

Gordon, Matthew S. *Hafez al-Assad*. New York: Chelsea House, 1990.

Maʿoz, Moshe. *Asad: The Sphinx of Damascus*. New York: Weidenfeld and Nicolson, 1988.

Patterson, Charles. *Hafiz al-Asad of Syria*. New York: Simon and Schuster, 1991.

Seale, Patrick. *Asad of Syria: The Struggle for the Middle East*. Berkeley: University of California Press, 1988.

Viorst, Milton. "A Reporter at Large: The Shadow of Saladin." *The New Yorker*, January 8, 1990, pp. 40-65.

Peter B. Heller

Tobias Michael Carel Asser

Born: April 28, 1838; Amsterdam, the Netherlands
Died: July 29, 1913; The Hague, the Netherlands

Dutch international-law scholar and peace activist

Tobias Michael Carel Asser (toh-BEE-ahs MEE-kah-ehl KAH-rehl AH-sur) was a brilliant student who came from a family with a tradition in the field of law. He earned his doctor's degree in law from the University of Amsterdam in 1860, and he practiced law for a short period of time prior to devoting his life to teaching, politics, and international law. In 1862, he accepted a teaching position at the University of Amsterdam, and he taught courses in private, international, and commercial law until 1893.

International Law Expert

Devoting himself to the problems of international law, Asser soon built a prominent reputation. He persuaded the Dutch government to call several conferences of European powers to codify international public law. Presiding over the first two conferences, held at The Hague in 1893 and 1894, Asser was influential in negotiating a treaty that established a uniform international procedure for conducting civil trials. He also presided over the conferences of 1900 and 1904, which resulted in several important treaties governing international family law, including matters relating to marriage, divorce, legal separation, and guardianship of minors.

International Affairs

Asser's scholarly prowess led him to write many important contributions to the literature of law and to help found an international law journal. He also participated in an international conference in Ghent that led to the founding of the Institute of International Law in 1873, an organization that he later headed. The organization received the Nobel Peace Prize in 1904.

Asser was an active participant in the practical politics of international affairs as well. He served as a member of the prestigious Dutch Council of State, as president of the State Commission for International Law in 1898, as a Dutch representative at the Hague Peace Conferences of 1899 and 1907, and as a member of the Permanent Court of Arbitration in 1900. Because of his skill as a negotiator, Asser was involved in virtually every treaty that was finalized by the Dutch government between 1875 and 1913.

Tobias Michael Asser *(The Nobel Foundation)*

63

The 1907 Hague Peace Conference

The objectives of the 1907 Hague Peace Conference were to codify international law, promote disarmament, and provide procedures for peacefully solving international disputes. These procedures were to include mediation, inquiry, and arbitration. Representatives from forty-four countries attended the conference, including all the Latin American countries that did not attend the first conference held at The Hague in 1899. The conference adopted eleven additional conventions to discuss the problems of armaments, the rules of modern warfare, and aspects of the law of naval war and neutrality. Although the 1907 conference made little progress toward disarmament or averting World War I—which began in 1914—it established an example for peace negotiations that later influenced the formation of both the League of Nations and the United Nations. In addition, a draft written by members of the conference for establishing a "Judicial Arbitration Court" laid the groundwork for the founding of the Permanent Court of International Justice in 1922.

Nobel Peace Prize

For his devoted work in establishing the Permanent Court of Arbitration in 1899 and his initiation and guidance of the peace conferences held at The Hague, Asser shared the Nobel Peace Prize with Austrian journalist Alfred H. Fried in 1911. Asser was also commended for his work as an arbitrator in the dispute between Russia and the United States over the Bering Strait (1902) and in the Pious Fund dispute between the United States and Mexico (1902). Because of his contributions to international law, an international library of law housed at the Peace Palace in The Hague is known as the Asser Collection.

International Significance

The efforts of Tobias Asser in the codification of public international law and the harmonization of private international law established him as an eminent international lawyer and a distinguished leader of modern jurisprudence. As a member of the Permanent Court of Arbitration, Asser was recognized worldwide as an arbiter of international disputes. The peace conferences held at The Hague that Asser initiated, and over which he presided, laid the foundation for other conventions that established uniformity in international law and led to greater public security and justice in international relations.

Bibliography

Bos, Maarten. *A Methodology of International Law.* New York: Elsevier, 1984.

Van Panhuys, H. F., ed. *International Law in the Netherlands.* Dobbs Ferry, N.Y.: Oceania, 1978.

Van Themaat, Peter Verloren. *The Changing Structure of International Economic Law.* Boston: Martinus Njhoff, 1981.

Alvin K. Benson

Nancy Astor

Born: May 19, 1879; Danville, Virginia
Died: May 2, 1964; Grimsthorpe Castle, Lincolnshire, England

British politician, first woman to hold a seat in House of Commons (1919-1945)

Nancy Witcher Langhorne Astor (NAN-see WIHT-chur LANG-hohrn AS-tur) was the eighth of eleven children of Civil War veteran Chiswell Dabney Langhorne and his wife Nancy. Because of her father's accumulated wealth in tobacco and railroads, Nancy lived affluently, but even when young was religious and concerned for the poor. She attended various schools but was largely self-educated. In 1897 she married Robert Gould Shaw II of Boston, but because of his alcoholism they separated and were divorced in 1903. On a trip to England in 1905 she met Waldorf Astor; they married in 1906. In 1910, Waldorf was elected a Conservative member of Parliament for Plymouth.

Astor Runs for Parliament

Though Nancy Astor became a successful political hostess, she sought new challenges. In 1914, after a serious illness, she became a Christian Scientist and, with characteristic enthusiasm, attempted to convert her family and friends. During World War I she engaged in hospital work in Plymouth and turned Cliveden, the family's country house, into a military hospital.

After Waldorf's father, Viscount Astor, died in October of 1919, Waldorf was obliged to enter the House of Lords. The Plymouth Conservatives asked Nancy to run for his seat in the House of Commons, which she won with a substantial majority over two male candidates. In 1918 women had been given the right to vote and be elected to Parliament. Since a female Irish nationalist had earlier refused to take the oath of allegiance, Nancy Astor became the first woman to sit in the House of Commons. She would represent Plymouth for twenty-five years.

Although the sole woman member for two years, Astor enjoyed the give and take of British politics. She was witty and could hold her own in debates, even against individuals such as Winston Churchill, who disapproved of female politicians. She worked for legislation on alcoholic beverage control, widows' pensions, nursery schools, and improving slum and dockyard conditions. She also entertained a varied circle of international politicians, Christian Scientists, American visitors, and literary figures such

Nancy Astor *(Library of Congress)*

Nancy Astor campaigning in the British general election of 1931. *(AP/Wide World Photos)*

as Henry James and George Bernard Shaw at Cliveden.

The 1930's and 1940's

Nancy created controversy in 1931 when she, Waldorf, and Bernard Shaw visited the Soviet Union and met Joseph Stalin. The charge of being sympathetic to dictators was raised again in the late 1930's when, as a supporter of Neville Chamberlain, she defended his policy of appeasement in response to Adolf Hitler and Nazi Germany. The Astors and their friends, the so-called Cliveden set, were accused of supporting the Nazis. When World War II began, Nancy threw herself into war work, but her political reputation suffered, while that of Churchill rose.

Despite numerous air raids and Nancy Astor's parliamentary duties, the Astors remained in Plymouth as much as possible. After the war, however, Nancy was reluctantly persuaded by Waldorf and their children not to seek reelection. Having no comparable vocation in retirement, her last decades were spent traveling, writing, and enjoying her family. In declining health the last four years of her life, she died following a stroke in 1964.

Inspiring both affection and dislike, even hatred, but never indifference, Nancy Astor's life was a mass of contradictions. She was an American who became the first woman member of Britain's Parliament, a wealthy socialite who crusaded for temperance, Christian Science, and the

The Cliveden Set

The term "Cliveden set" was coined in 1936 by an imaginative communist journalist, Claud Cockburn, in his small newspaper, *The Week*. Various articles supposedly exposed a pro-Nazi cell situated at Cliveden, the Astors' country house. Led by Nancy and Waldorf Astor and including Geoffrey Dawson, editor of the *Times*, this group was credited with manipulating British foreign policy in favor of Adolf Hitler. The wealthy Conservative Astors and their friends were convenient scapegoats for the various economic and social problems Britain was experiencing in the 1930's. Though the stories were in fact journalistic mythmaking, and the Astors denounced them as such, they were picked up by the press in both Britain and America. Despite its lack of reality, the phrase "Cliveden set," with its pro-Nazi implications, was periodically resurrected as late as 1942, much to the annoyance of the Astors.

poor, and a combative person who supported pacifism. While not a great politician, her concern for the rights of women and children and for world peace was her primary legacy.

Bibliography

Astor, Michael. *Tribal Feeling*. London: John Murray, 1963.

Grigg, John. *Nancy Astor: A Lady Unashamed*. Boston: Little, Brown, 1980.

Halperin, John. *Eminent Georgians: The Lives of King George V, Elizabeth Bowen, St. John Philby, and Nancy Astor*. New York: St. Martin's Press, 1995.

Langhorne, Elizabeth. *Nancy Astor and Her Friends*. New York: Praeger, 1974.

Sykes, Christopher. *Nancy: The Life of Nancy Astor*. New York: Harper and Row, 1972.

Dorothy Potter

Member of Parliament Nancy Astor addresses a crowd in London's Trafalgar Square in September, 1940. *(AP/Wide World Photos)*

Kemal Atatürk

Born: May 19, 1881; Salonika, Ottoman Empire (now Thessaloniki, Greece)
Died: November 10, 1938; Istanbul, Turkey

Founder of the Turkish republic and its first president (1923-1938)

Mustafa Kemal Atatürk (moos-tah-FAH keh-MAHL ah-TAH-tewrk), founder of Turkey and its first president, was the son of a middle-class customs official turned timber merchant and a mother who came from a farming family. His birth name was simply Mustafa. He was educated in military schools rather than the traditional religious schools. A high school mathematics teacher gave him the nickname of Kemal, which means "the perfect one." In 1905, he graduated from the military academy in Istanbul with the rank of staff captain.

Posted to Damascus, he and several other officers founded a short-lived clandestine society

Kemal Atatürk *(Library of Congress)*

to oppose the despotism and abuses of the Ottoman Empire's sultan. In 1907, he joined an anti-government group, the Committee of Union and Progress (CUP), in Salonika. The CUP was part of the nationalist and reformist Young Turks movement. The organization opposed the autocratic government of the Ottoman Empire, of which Turkey was a part. In 1909, the CUP forced the Ottoman Sultan Abdul Hamid II to abdicate.

Military Career

In 1911 and 1912, Atatürk fought against the Italian army in Libya. He organized the defense of the Dardanelles during the Balkan Wars of 1912 and 1913. During World War I (1914-1918), in which Turkey sided with Germany, Atatürk became a national hero. He played a crucial role in repelling the Allied invasion (which included Australian and British forces) at Gallipoli in 1915. His victory at Gallipoli won him the title of Saviour of Istanbul. In 1916, he was transferred to the Russian front and quickly promoted to general. He was the only Turkish general to win any victories over the Russians on the eastern front. His military reputation grew during Turkey's four-year War of Independence. He led the forces that expelled an invading Greek army.

On May 19, 1919, Mustafa Kemal Atatürk landed in the Black Sea port of Samsun to launch the War of Independence against the Ottoman regime in Istanbul. On April 23, 1920, he was elected president of the provisional government. Fighting on many fronts, he defeated several invading armies and rebel forces. The sultanate was abolished on November 1, 1922. Turkey was declared a republic on October 29, 1923, with Atatürk as president.

Turkish soldiers at a military review in Damascus during World War I. Kemal Atatürk became a national hero, the Saviour of Istanbul, during the war. *(AP/Wide World Photos)*

The Young Turks

Kemal Atatürk built his reputation as a military leader during the revolutionary period in Turkish history dominated by a group known as the Young Turks (also known as the Committee of Union and Progress). Group members were opposed to the repressive policies of Abdul Hamid II, the Ottoman Empire's sultan. In July of 1908, they forced the sultan to reinstate the constitution of 1876, which limited his powers and reestablished a representative government. Approximately a year later, the Young Turks forced him to abdicate. Later Atatürk disagreed with the direction the Young Turks movement was heading, including its military alliance with Germany during World War I. Atatürk spent the years between 1911 and the establishment of the Turkish republic in 1923 fighting the enemies of the shrinking Ottoman Empire. His defense of the strategically important Gallipoli Peninsula in 1915 earned him the title Saviour of Istanbul. In November of 1922, Turkish nationalists abolished the sultanate and forced the sultan into exile. Atatürk's victories over the Allied Powers in World War I led to the Treaty of Lausanne on July 24, 1923, which fixed Turkey's European border. He thus played a major role in helping Turkey win control of its own sovereignty.

President of Turkey

Turkey faced major problems. It lacked capital, industry, and technological expertise. Successive wars had decimated its manpower, agricultural production was at a low level, and the foreign debts of the defunct Ottoman Empire were significant. Atatürk's goal was to create a new and modern Turkey patterned directly on the societies of Western Europe. His Six Arrows reform program focused on the principles of republicanism, nationalism, populism, reformism, statism, and secularism. Throughout his presidency, he governed essentially by personal rule in a one-party state. He regarded his personal rule as a necessary transition to the democratic process.

Atatürk immediately undertook an ambitious and revolutionary program to turn Turkey into a self-sufficient, industrialized, twentieth-century state. Turkey was the first Muslim nation to become a republic. He excluded Islam from the official life of the nation: Religious laws were abolished and a secular system of law introduced. He eliminated the special rights and privileges the Ottomans had granted to some European powers. Turkey signed peace agreements with a number of countries and joined the League of Nations. Under Atatürk's leadership, the Arabic script, which had been used by the Turks for a thousand years, was replaced rapidly with the simpler Latin alphabet, with its twenty-nine letters (eight vowels and twenty-one consonants). The alphabet reform enabled children and adults to learn to read and write within a few months and to study Western languages with greater effectiveness. Atatürk banned the fez—the hat that had become a symbol of Ottoman and Islamic orthodoxy—outlawed polygamy, and championed rights for women. Women stopped wearing the veil. The Islamic calendar was replaced by the Western calendar. In 1935, he introduced his last reform—the surname. Until then, a Turk had only one name—the one given at birth. Now, to reduce confusion over names, Turks would follow Europe's example and adopt family names. This was when Mustafa was given the last name Atatürk, which means "father of the Turks." Collectively, these reforms dramatically overhauled Turkish culture, education, and society. Atatürk turned the mostly Muslim country into a largely secular state modeled on the nations of Western Europe.

Turkey's War of Independence

On May 19, 1919, Kemal Atatürk landed at Samsun on the Black Sea coast of Anatolia to start the war to liberate Turkey. The Turks were outraged that the European powers that had defeated Germany and its ally, the Ottoman Empire, were preparing to carve up their country as a prize for victory. Atatürk and his associates developed a plan for a national liberation movement. Fighting raged on many fronts and against many enemies, including British, French, Greek, and Italian troops. The Ottoman sultan tried unsuccessfully to stop Atatürk. The turning point came when a powerful Ottoman general decided to support Atatürk, placing eighteen thousand troops under his command. Atatürk gained official status as head of a nationalist provisional government in mid-1919. Atatürk and his armies defeated most of the Allied powers in a series of campaigns. On October 29, 1923, Turkey became an independent republic.

Importance

Mustafa Kemal Atatürk was a national hero, the liberator of the Turks from the Ottoman Empire and the founder of modern-day Turkey. He stopped the Western powers that were carving up Turkey for their own benefit and enrichment. He was a great general, pragmatic political leader, economic and social reformer, and peacemaker. He modernized, secularized, and westernized Turkey within a fifteen-year period. He ruled as a charismatic leader and teacher who trained, cajoled, and forced the government and the people of Turkey to act as he thought they should. Atatürk accomplished what he set out to achieve—the establishing of a democratic republic. This fact was demonstrated the day after his death, when the Grand National Assembly elected his successor. The second president of Turkey—İsmet İnönü—would eventually permit the creation of a multiparty political system and the holding of democratic elections.

Turkish leader Kemal Atatürk after his forces repelled the Greek army. *(Library of Congress)*

Bibliography

Armstrong, Harold Courtenay. *Gray Wolf: The Life of Kemal Atatürk.* New York: Capricorn Books, 1961.

Brock, Ray. *Ghost on Horseback: The Incredible Atatürk.* New York: Duell, Sloan and Pearce, 1951.

Kinross, Patrick Balfour. *Atatürk: A Biography of Mustafa Kemal, Father of Modern Turkey.* New York: Quill/Morrow, 1992.

Metz, Helen Chapin, ed. *Turkey: A Country Study.* Washington, D.C.: Federal Research Division, Library of Congress, 1996.

Pope, Nicole. *Turkey Unveiled: Atatürk and After.* London: John Murray, 1997.

Fred Buchstein

Clement Attlee

Born: January 3, 1883; London, United Kingdom
Died: October 8, 1967; London, United Kingdom

Prime minister of Great Britain (1945-1951)

Clement Richard Attlee (KLEH-mehnt RIH-churd AT-lee) came from a solid, upper-middle-class family. His father was a prosperous British solicitor, or lawyer. Clement attended a private school and Oxford University. He was called to the bar, or qualified as a lawyer, in 1905. Because he was strongly influenced by what he saw at a boys' club in the poor East End of London, he chose social work in London's worst neighborhoods instead of law. His concerns over social conditions later made him a keen activist in the Labour Party. He also lectured at the London School of Economics.

Clement Attlee *(Library of Congress)*

Attlee's life was altered by the outbreak of World War I in 1914. He served with distinction as an officer and was severely wounded. When he returned to civilian life, he continued in social work, was elected mayor of one East End district, and then a member of Parliament. He married and enjoyed an ordinary and unpretentious upper-middle-class family life thereafter.

In Parliament he became a cabinet minister, holding various posts under Labour's first prime minister, Ramsay MacDonald, in the 1920's. Yet when MacDonald decided to form a national government with the Conservative Party in 1931, Attlee opposed his chief, feeling that MacDonald had betrayed the cause of socialism because he was won over by the rich and stylish Conservatives. Attlee became deputy and then leader of the much smaller anti-MacDonald Parliamentary Labour Party, the group that refused to join the coalition.

World War II

As war threatened in the 1930's, Attlee used his considerable leadership skills to keep his party together. Most Labourites wanted disarmament and security through the League of Nations, but the growing menace of fascist aggression alerted him. He came to denounce Prime Minister Neville Chamberlain's appeasement of Nazi Germany. While Attlee saw the need for rearmament, his party remained divided on the issue.

After the war broke out it became clear to the Conservatives that they needed to form a coalition government with Labour. Attlee refused to support Prime Minister Chamberlain, and when Winston Churchill became prime minister in the spring of 1940, Attlee became a cabinet minister. He had risen to deputy prime minister by 1942.

British prime minister Clement Attlee (right) with King George VI in 1945; Attlee's Labour Party had just won a majority in Parliament. *(National Archives)*

When Churchill traveled widely to lead the war effort, Attlee found himself doing more and more of the day-to-day business of government, activities that eminently qualified him for the job of prime minister.

Throughout the war Attlee supported Churchill with great loyalty and kept the Labour members of Parliament in line. After Germany was defeated, Attlee was willing to continue the wartime coalition until Japan was defeated, but this

British Socialism

Clement Attlee campaigned for British socialism throughout his career. Nevertheless, he was anticommunist and anti-Marxist. The nature of British socialism explains his position: From its origins, British socialism operated within traditional British practices and institutions. It was democratic, accepting vote by ballot, majority rule, and the gradual achievement of socialism through ordinary legislation. Unlike communism, British socialism did not accept class war

and violent revolution. Above all, its goals were humanistic, seeking a better, fairer life for British subjects through economic justice. In Attlee's day, the establishment of the welfare state and nationalization of vital services and industries were the means to this end. British socialism did not seek to abolish capitalism but to operate a mixed economy containing an important public sector as well as a private sector.

The National Health Service

One major accomplishment of Clement Attlee's government of 1945-1951 was establishing the National Health Service. The service is free for all citizens from birth to death; no one has to prove that he or she receives less than a certain income to benefit from it. It is tax supported, and medical doctors are in charge of running it. Preventative medicine, such as screening children for early signs of illness, is an important part of the system.

Some of the National Health Service facilities and procedures are among the best in the world—for example, the centralized process that effectively tests for breast cancer. On the other hand, there have been numerous complaints, such as the long waits for certain types of elective surgery. If they wish, people with the financial resources can go to doctors who maintain private practices outside the system. Regardless of its shortcomings, Britain's National Health Service is an immense improvement over the spotty medical service that had existed previously, and it remains popular with the electorate. Even the most determined opponents of big government, such as former prime minister Margaret Thatcher, have been able to make only minor adjustments to a system so highly esteemed by British voters.

was not the wish of his party. In a 1945 election, the Labour Party won by an unexpected landslide, which made Attlee prime minister with a very comfortable majority.

The Attlee Government

The election campaign had been fought over what kind of postwar Britain the electorate wanted. It was not a contest between the charismatic personality of Churchill, now revered as the great war leader, and the rather quiet and plain personality of Clement Attlee. It was instead about planning for the future, and the Labour Party called for specific programs that would lead to full employment and cradle-to-grave welfare services for everyone. Churchill and the Conservatives offered only vague promises plus warnings about the dangers of socialism.

Attlee appointed able but often difficult men to run the government, and he kept them working together as an effective team. The Labour government of 1945-1951 nationalized key industries, established the National Health Service, and built up the welfare state, a prodigious accomplishment in light of the strained postwar economy. In foreign affairs, Attlee supported the United States in reconstructing and stabilizing Europe and resisting communist aggression. He also presided over the granting of independence to many parts of the British empire peacefully. When his highly effective government ran out of steam in 1951, the Conservatives won. Attlee retired in 1955 to become an earl, widely praised in the Labour Party as "the only man who could have kept us together."

Attlee's Achievement

Clement Attlee was the leader of the Labour Party for twenty years, the longest tenure in history, and was prime minister for six years. He effectively led the strong, active Labour government after World War II, establishing the welfare state and the mixed economy. Many of the changes he brought about are still in existence. Nonetheless, he had critics on the Labour left who found him insufficiently socialist and too willing to cooperate with U.S. foreign policy.

As a party leader he had extraordinary talents for healing divisions and reconciling factions. An excellent team player, he has been praised as the best leader that the Labour Party ever had. He was a man of principle who advanced clear concepts of social justice. He was modest in lifestyle, and people trusted in his absolute integrity. Although not a dramatic speaker, he was clear, calm, and articulate.

While his government was highly innovative, Attlee did not seek drastic restructuring of British laws or institutions. He was a patriot, a monarchist, and a gradualist who always believed in the British system of government. What he criticized was its economic injustice and imperialism. Attlee's government gained bipartisan support and public acceptance for its important legislation, which resulted in improved social conditions in a stable postwar Britain.

Clement Attlee (left) applauds remarks by U.S. secretary of state Dean Acheson in May, 1950. Acheson was in London to attend British-American-French meetings on the Cold War. *(AP/Wide World Photos)*

Bibliography

Brookshire, Jerry H. *Clement Attlee*. New York: Manchester University Press, 1995.

Burridge, Trevor. *Clement Attlee: A Political Biography*. London: J. Cape, 1987.

Harris, Kenneth. *Attlee*. London: Weidenfeld and Nicholson, 1982.

Henry G. Weisser

Lloyd Axworthy

Born: December 21, 1939; North Battleford, Saskatchewan, Canada

Canadian political leader, force behind the Ottawa Treaty (1997)

Lloyd Axworthy (LOYD AKZ-wur-thee) served first as a parliamentarian and then, in the 1980's and 1990's, as a Canadian cabinet minister. After attaining a bachelor's degree at United College in Winnipeg, Manitoba, Axworthy attended Princeton University. There he obtained both an M.A. and a Ph.D. in political science. He returned to Manitoba, where from 1965 to 1979 he was a professor of political science at the University of Winnipeg.

Entry into Politics

Axworthy made his first foray into politics at the provincial level. In 1973, he was elected as a provincial member for a Winnipeg-area riding (district). He would spend the next six years in provincial politics. In 1979, Axworthy made the decision to advance to the federal level. In May of that year he captured a Winnipeg riding for the federal Liberal Party under the leadership of Pierre Trudeau. Axworthy's victory was one of the few bright spots for the Liberals, who after eleven years in power found themselves defeated by the Progressive Conservative Party. The time in opposition was to be short for both the Liberals and Axworthy. In February, 1980, another election was held, and the Liberals returned to power. Axworthy was the party's only representative in all of western Canada. More than anything, he symbolized the regional split in Canadian party support, as the Conservatives dominated in the West while the Liberals held sway in the remainder of Canada.

In the Cabinet

Being the only Liberal member of Parliament from western Canada made it inevitable that Axworthy would have a role in the federal cabinet. His first position was as minister of employment and immigration, in which position he served from 1980 to 1983. Viewed as being on the political left of the Liberal Party, the new cabinet minister was given responsibilities that included dealing with the status of Canadian women. In 1983, he became the new minister of transportation. In 1984, the Liberals suffered a major political defeat and were forced out of office. Axworthy was one of the few Liberals to be reelected.

Now in opposition, Axworthy was appointed critic for several different areas that reflected his interests. These included industrial expansion, farming, international trade, and external affairs. He won his seat in 1988 and again in 1993, when the Liberals returned to power—this time with Jean Chrétien at the helm.

Lloyd Axworthy *(AP/Wide World Photos)*

Canadian foreign affairs minister Lloyd Axworthy signing the 1997 Ottawa Treaty banning antipersonnel land mines. Behind him are U.N. secretary-general Kofi Annan (center) and Canadian prime minister Jean Chrétien (right). *(Reuters/Peter Jones/Archive Photos)*

Back in the Cabinet

The return of the Liberals to office marked the reappearance of Axworthy in the federal cabinet. He was appointed as minister of human re- sources development, and the government made it known that the new minister would be at- tempting to reform Canada's welfare and post- secondary educational systems. Axworthy's in-

The Ottawa Treaty

In December, 1997, the Ottawa Treaty, an agreement to ban the use of antipersonnel land mines, was signed in the capital of Canada. That country, under the leadership of its minister of external affairs, Lloyd Axworthy, was the driv- ing force behind the treaty. The destructive force of land mines, especially upon noncombatants, had long been evident in countries such as Cam- bodia, Bosnia, and North and South Korea. The issue was given impetus and widespread pub-

licity by Diana, Princess of Wales, only a few months before her death as a result of a fatal automobile accident. Beginning at a conference in Oslo, Norway, lengthy bargaining culminated in the agreement. Even though 120 countries signed, and despite intense lobbying, the United States, Russia, and China refused to sign the treaty, primarily because it would have required them to destroy their supplies of land mines.

Lloyd Axworthy in 1997, alleging in the Canadian House of Commons that Israeli agents had used altered or forged Canadian passports in an attempt to assassinate a Hamas leader. *(Reuters/Pool/Archive Photos)*

itiatives, however, fell victim to a change in the Liberal government's priorities. Two years into its mandate, the government decided to place its emphasis on the reduction of Canada's federal budgetary deficit. With such an approach, the minister of finance became the leading figure in the cabinet, and Axworthy's plans were scrapped.

A New Job

Once it was clear that Axworthy's ideas of progressive domestic welfare reform would not be implemented, his focus shifted. In 1996 he became Canada's minister of external affairs. Axworthy played particularly important roles in two areas. He was centrally involved in the development of a treaty to ban land mines, which was signed in Ottawa in December, 1997. He also worked tirelessly for an agreement to begin the development of a world court. Frustrated in internal politics, Axworthy's work in external affairs gained him new influence.

Bibliography

Graham, Ron. *All the King's Horses: Politics Among the Ruins*. Toronto: McFarlane, Walter, and Ross, 1995.

Greenspon, Edward, and Anthony Wilson-Smith. *Double Vision: The Inside Story of the Liberals in Power*. Toronto: Doubleday Canada, 1996.

Newman, Peter C. *The Canadian Revolution: From Deference to Defiance*. Toronto: Penguin Books, 1995.

Steve Hewitt

Muhammad Farah Aydid

Born: c. 1930; Beledweyne, Italian Somaliland
Died: August 1, 1996; Mogadishu, Somalia

Somali political leader

The son of Somali nomads of the Habar Gedir subclan of Somalia's largest clan, the Hawiye, Muhammad Farah Aydid (moo-HAH-muhd FAH-rah ay-DEED) was the fifth child in a family of thirteen. Aydid (sometimes spelled Aydeed or Aideed) served in the Somali army and as a diplomat before leading opposition forces against Muhammad Siad Barre's regime in 1989. He overthrew Siad Barre in 1991 and contributed to the famine and anarchy that soon engulfed Somalia. He gained notoriety when his forces killed American and other foreign troops serving under the command of the United Nations in 1993.

The Making of a Military Man

As a teenager, Aydid worked with crews building airfields and highways, but his interest gradually turned toward soldiering. His official military career began in 1950, when he joined the Italian *Gendarmaria*. He received military and language training in Italy and went to the North Atlantic Treaty Organization (NATO) infantry school. He returned to Somalia in the late 1950's. His unit raised the Somali flag at Somalian independence ceremonies on July 1, 1960. During the 1960's Aydid advanced to the rank of captain and earned an overseas assignment to the Soviet Union as a military attaché.

Aydid's career received a setback when he warned the government about Siad Barre's plans for a coup in 1969. Siad Barre thus distrusted Aydid and, once in power, imprisoned him for six years. Two years after his release, Aydid was promoted to brigadier general because Somalia was preparing for war with Ethiopia (1977-1978). During the 1980's, Aydid embarked on a brief diplomatic career, serving as Somalia's ambassador to India, Sri Lanka, and Singapore.

Rebel and War Criminal

In the late 1980's members of the Hawiye clan who opposed the regime of Siad Barre met to organize and choose leaders. They called upon Aydid to join a new opposition group, the United Somali Congress (USC), as the commander of its military forces. Aydid agreed, and the USC was officially established in 1989. The military wing elected him as the head of the USC. Other USC

Muhammad Farah Aydid *(AP/Wide World Photos)*

79

Civil war and drought in Somalia caused a disastrous famine; here hungry children are held back after the food being distributed ran out. International intervention and relief efforts in 1992 and 1993 managed to save many lives. *(AP/Wide World Photos)*

figures opposed this move, however, and infighting between USC factions plagued the organization throughout the 1990's. Aydid made significant gains against Siad Barre's army during 1990, and in January, 1991, Siad Barre fled the capital of Mogadishu. Aydid pursued him and largely eliminated the government forces as a major contender in subsequent months. Infighting among the Hawiye continued. Ali Mahdi Muhammad, a member of the Agbal subclan, was declared interim president of Somalia, a position to which Aydid himself aspired.

During 1992, fighting in the countryside and among Hawiye factions in Mogadishu precipitated a disastrous famine that prompted international intervention. Although the famine was brought under control within months, U.N. forces eventually attempted to disarm Somali military groups, including Aydid's USC forces. The latter resisted all such attempts and eventually killed scores of Americans and other U.N. troops in a climate of urban guerrilla warfare. Branded a war criminal by the United Nations, Aydid eluded capture, and he thereby attained hero status among many Somalis. The eventual withdrawal of U.N. and American forces was a hollow victory for Aydid, who inspired as much fear among his Somali opponents as he did admiration among his followers. Months and years of infighting continued without any side gaining the upper hand. Aydid was eventually shot and killed in this climate of civil discord on August 1, 1996. Aydid's much less experienced son, Hussein Aydid, became chairman of the USC after Aydid's death. This change signaled the decline of USC fortunes and new opportunities for negotiation of a national reconciliation conference.

As long as Aydid vied for national ascendancy, his much-feared temper and imperial manner inspired determined opposition. Aydid had lived and died by the sword. It is ironic that his death created opportunities for a more determined path toward peace in Somalia.

Muhammad Farah Aydid (left) shakes hands with Ali Mahdi Muhammad after the two warring somali leaders signed a peace agreement in Mogadishu in 1992. *(Reuters/Hos Maina/Archive Photos)*

Famine in Somalia

The famine that wracked Somalia between 1991 and 1993 was a by-product not only of drought but also of the civil war that raged in the southern part of the country. Fighting occurred in and around the capital city of Mogadishu and in the agricultural regions between the Webi Shebelli and Juba Rivers. Much heavy fighting between Muhammad Farah Aydid's United Somali Congress (USC) and government forces took place in these agricultural areas, inhibiting the planting and harvesting of crops. The famine in turn provoked international intervention in December, 1992, to ensure the security of food aid and its delivery to starving people. Although famine-related starvation was brought quickly under control, the U.N. operation unwisely attempted to disarm Aydid's USC forces. These attempts prompted armed opposition and the eventual withdrawal of all U.N. forces, leaving Somalis to resolve their own internal conflicts.

Bibliography

Ghalib, Jama Mohamed. *The Cost of Dictatorship: The Somali Experience.* New York: Lilian Barber, 1995.

Samatar, Ahmed I. *The Somali Challenge: From Catastrophe to Renewal.* Boulder, Colo.: Lynne Rienner, 1995.

Robert F. Gorman

Nnamdi Azikiwe

Born: November 16, 1904; Zungeru, Nigeria
Died: May 11, 1996; Enugu, Nigeria

First president of independent Nigeria (1963-1966)

Born the son of Ibo parents stationed in northern Nigeria, Benjamin Azikiwe (BEN-jah-mihn ah-zih-KEE-way) later took the name Nnamdi (uhn-NAHM-dee). He attended primary schools in Nigeria, attaining fluency in the languages of the Hausa, Yoruba, and Ibo (also written Igbo), which are Nigeria's dominant ethnic groups. He worked briefly as a clerk in Lagos before commencing studies in the United States. He gained a reputation as a writer and teacher while earning advanced academic degrees in political science and journalism at American universities.

Nnamdi Azikiwe *(Archive Photos)*

Upon returning to West Africa he pursued careers in journalism and in politics. He earned a reputation as one of the continent's most prominent and well-liked nationalists. He served as Nigeria's first president until ousted by a military coup in 1966, and afterward he was prominent in efforts to unify Nigeria and heal its wounds after the Biafran War. Azikiwe was an active figure in Nigerian politics until his retirement in 1986. He remained a popular and revered elder statesman of Nigerian politics until his death in 1996.

African Nationalist

The life of Nnamdi Azikiwe closely follows the history of his native land. Nigeria was a British colony until 1960, when full independence was achieved. Thus, Azikiwe lived nearly two-thirds of his life as a subject of the British crown. His interest in politics and African independence was kindled during his studies in the United States, where he encountered the best and worst of American society. He acquired a fine undergraduate and graduate education at American universities but also frequently encountered racial bigotry. At Lincoln University he taught courses on pan-African ideology and wrote his first book, *Liberia in World Politics*, published in 1934. Upon his return to Africa in 1934, Azikiwe embarked on a career in journalism, first in the neighboring country of Ghana, and then in Nigeria. In Nigeria he founded a nationalist newspaper, the *West African Pilot*, in 1937.

During the next ten years Azikiwe built a journalistic empire of six Nigerian newspapers and began to participate in a range of political and economic activities designed to promote Nigerian nationalist sentiment and political independence. As a member of the Nigerian National

Democratic Party, he worked hard for the integration of the Nigerian and Cameroonian people. He held offices in the National Council of Nigeria and the Cameroons which he helped to establish toward that end. As a passionate nationalist, Azikiwe attracted much support among younger Nigerians, who formed the Zikist movement in 1946 to press more vigorously for independence. "Zik" (pronounced "zeek") was the affectionate nickname Azikiwe had acquired as a student in the United States and which was adopted by his Nigerian supporters.

Azikiwe published several works promoting Nigerian freedoms, including *Political Blueprint of Nigeria* (1943). During the 1950's he was the most active and prominent Nigerian nationalist. He held a number of public positions, including serving in the Nigerian Legislative Assembly and the Nigerian Senate, which were established under British rule in anticipation of Nigeria's eventual independence. Azikiwe had emerged as Nigeria's chief voice for independence, as an activist of great energy, and as an unusually keen political strategist.

Leading an Independent Nigeria

Azikiwe was appointed governor-general upon Nigeria's independence, and in 1963 he became the president of Nigeria after the country

Nnamdi Azikiwe (left) in London in 1959. Azikiwe was the leading voice for Nigerian independence in the 1950's. *(Express Newspapers/Archive Photos)*

The *West African Pilot*

The *West African Pilot* was established by Nnamdi Azikiwe in 1937 after his return to Nigeria from a short-lived journalistic career in Ghana, where he had edited the *African Morning Post*. In both papers, Azikiwe gained the reputation of being an ardent, deeply impassioned African nationalist. The motto of the *West African Pilot* was "Show the light and the people will find the way." The paper was published in Lagos but had a nationwide distribution and focus. Azikiwe used it to disseminate all kinds of news demonstrating the progress of Nigerians toward education, development, and distinction. He championed pan-African and West African causes but eventually focused on promoting Nigerian nationalism. Azikiwe's success in journalism, including an expanding chain of newspapers, was a major stepping-stone in launching his political career, which began in the mid-1940's.

Nnamdi Azikiwe in 1968, speaking as an adviser to Biafran leader Odumegwu Ojukwu. *(AP/Wide World Photos)*

became a republic. His tenure was short-lived, however, and marked by growing dissension among Nigeria's conflicting regions. The army overthrew the government in a 1966 coup. Not long after, Nigeria descended into a bloody civil war in which the Ibo-dominated eastern region sought independence from Nigeria as Biafra. With reluctance, Azikiwe supported the Biafran independence effort; it soon became clear, however, that Biafra could not succeed as an independent country. As the bloodshed mounted, Azikiwe realized that a unified Nigeria was the only realistic answer to the region's difficulties.

After the civil war, Nigerian politicians, including Azikiwe, worked to heal the wounds left by the war. Under military rule, the country gradually prepared for a return to a civilian government. As head of the Nigerian People's Party (NPP) from 1978 to 1983, Azikiwe stood for election to the presidency of the new republic in both 1979 and 1983. The new government was designed along the lines of the American federal constitution. Only parties that could claim national membership (rather than purely regional or ethnic membership) could take seats in the newly established legislature. With Azikiwe as its

The Secession of Biafra

Before Nigeria's independence in 1960, many people in the Ibo-dominated southeast region of Nigeria favored independence as a separate, distinct country. However, Nnamdi Azikiwe argued that Ibos should join the larger and more viable Nigeria rather than face independence as a small and separate nation. (Azikiwe, a committed pan-Africanist, had even hoped for the formation of a single West African state.) Nigerian politics proved to be highly combative; regional rivalries, political jealousies, and disputes dogged the new nation almost from the start. Azikiwe could not prevent them, and when Ibos eventually started their war of secession in 1967,

he reluctantly agreed that Biafran independence might be a necessary step in acknowledging irreconcilable regional differences. After two years of unsuccessful and very bloody conflict, however, Azikiwe realized that the secession attempt had been a mistake. About a million people died as a result of the war, some in the fighting and many more from starvation. He began to urge an end to the civil war. He was among the leaders who helped to fashion a humane reconciliation when the war ended in 1970. Biafra was surely and steadily reintegrated into Nigerian political life.

head, the NPP garnered considerable support beyond the Ibo regions. Although he lost the presidential elections on both occasions, Azikiwe remained an active voice in the political life of Nigeria until his eventual retirement from politics in 1986—after the military had once again overthrown the civilian government.

Nigerians from all ethnic backgrounds and regions came to admire and respect Nnamdi Azikiwe. He was the most influential founding father of the Nigerian nation, and although an Ibo, a statesman who desired what was best for his entire nation, not merely his ethnic homeland in the east. He was a leader who inspired affection and trust, in a country where deep-seated ethnic divisions and political disputes have too often marred national political life. His death in 1996

marked the passing of Nigeria's greatest and most truly national political figure.

Bibliography

Azikiwe, Nnamdi. *My Odyssey: An Autobiography*. New York: Praeger, 1970.

Jones-Quartey, K. A. B. *A Life of Azikiwe*. Baltimore: Penguin Books, 1965.

Oyewole, A. *Historical Dictionary of Nigeria*. Metuchen, N.J.: Scarecrow Press, 1987.

Schwarz, Frederick. *Nigeria*. Westport, Conn.: Greenwood Press, 1965.

Uwazurike, P. Chudi. *The Man Called Zik of Africa: Portrait of Nigeria's Pan-African Statesman*. New York: Triatlantic Books, 1996.

Robert F. Gorman

Ibrahim Babangida

Born: August 17, 1941; Minna, Nigeria

President of Nigeria (1985-1993)

Ibrahim Badamasi Babangida (ih-brah-HIHM bah-dah-MAH-see bah-BAHN-gih-dah) was born in Minna, in northern Nigeria. His father was a Muslim religious teacher, and Babangida received a complete elementary and secondary education. He joined the military immediately after he finished school, and he furthered his education at military academies in Nigeria, India, Great Britain, and the United States.

Military Career

While Nigeria experienced tensions between the Christians in the south and the Muslims in the north, Babangida stayed out of politics. He fought on the side of the government in Nigeria's civil war in the late 1960's and ascended in military rank through the 1970's. After Nigeria's third bloody *coup d'état* in 1976, he was appointed to the powerful Supreme Military Council. A year later, when another coup was attempted, Babangida went unarmed to talk with the rebel leaders and convinced them to give up without violence. He became a national hero, known for his intelligence and charm.

Babangida still had no apparent desire for public attention, and for several years he went quietly about his duties. Nigeria experienced a time of great wealth, fueled by the value of its huge oil reserves, but a corrupt government squandered most of the money. Little of it was used to improve the life of Nigeria's poor. As the nation grew through the 1980's, the gap between rich and poor widened. In 1983 Babangida played a prominent role in another coup which replaced a democratically elected government with a military ruler, Alhaji Shagari. Many people had expected Babangida to become the new leader, but he did not seek that position. However, twenty months later, Babangida announced that he had overthrown Shagari and assumed leadership.

President Babangida

Babangida promised to stop government corruption, end human rights abuses, and

Nigerian president Ibrahim Babangida with French president François Mitterrand during Babangida's 1990 visit to France. *(Reuters/Charles Platiau/Archive Photos)*

Ibrahim Babangida in Lagos, Nigeria, flanked by army officers a few days after Babangida took power in 1985. *(Reuters/Stringer/Archive Photos)*

Abuja, a New Capital

For the first three decades of Nigeria's independence, its capital city was Lagos, a coastal city that is still Nigeria's cultural and industrial center. Lagos is built on a number of small islands connected by bridges, and as its population increased there was no land on which to expand. Bridges, roads, and utilities could not be maintained or expanded rapidly enough to keep up with population growth. In addition, Lagos's location in the southwest corner of the country made it difficult for most Nigerians, with limited access to transportation, to visit their capital. In 1976, the government approved plans for a new capital, Abuja, a city that would be designed from the ground up in the center of Nigeria. Unlike muggy Lagos, Abuja would enjoy a mild climate and would not be in the center of any ethnic group's traditional land. Plans called for an airport, superhighways, dam-generated electrical power, and modern government buildings. Throughout the 1980's, construction was sporadic, intersrupted several times by changes in leadership and the mishandling of funds. Finally, in 1991, the new city was dedicated by President Ibrahim Babangida, who used its completion to demonstrate his commitment to serving his people.

eliminate censorship of journalists who criticized the government. He appointed members of different ethnic groups to important positions in an attempt to unify the country. Soon he became so trusted and so popular that he was able to convince the population to accept harsh financial measures that caused hardship to many in the short term in the hope of long-term stability. He promised to allow free and democratic elections in 1992, and he seemed willing to give up power if he could not win the election.

However, it gradually became clear that Babangida's government had its share of corruption and human rights abuses. Billions of dollars in oil profits had disappeared from the nation's treasury, and Babangida jailed his opponents without filing charges. When elections were held in 1993, it appeared that Babangida was losing by a large margin. Before the ballots could be counted, he declared that the election was fraudulent and its results would not stand; he would retain leadership. In the ensuing turmoil, Babangida was overthrown and replaced by another military ruler. In 1998, as Nigeria continued to struggle for a stable government, Babangida made a public speech calling for the end of military rule and urging democratic elections.

As independent Nigeria's longest-serving leader, Babangida brought a measure of stability to a poor and ethnically divided nation. His economic reforms led to a higher standard of living for most citizens and created a foundation for continued improvements.

Bibliography

Amuta, Chidi. *Prince of the Niger: The Babangida Years*. Lagos, Nigeria: Tanus Communications, 1992.

Duyile, Dayo. *Babangida: His Vision, His Mission, His Courage*. Ibadan, Nigeria: Ororo, 1991.

Levy, Patricia. *Nigeria*. New York: Marshall Cavendish, 1996.

Cynthia A. Bily

Fredrik Bajer

Born: April 21, 1837; Vester Egede, Denmark
Died: January 22, 1922; Copenhagen, Denmark

Danish diplomat and peace activist, winner of 1908 Nobel Peace Prize

Fredrik Bajer (FRIHT-rihk BI-ur) was the son of a Danish clergyman. As a youth, he loved military studies and idolized Napoleon Bonaparte. He attended the National Cadet Academy and was commissioned in the Danish Army. In 1864 war broke out between Denmark and Prussia over disputed territories. Bajer served well, but the experience of combat destroyed many of his illusions about war.

Becoming a Pacifist

After the war, Bajer worked as a translator and publicist, wrote articles on education, and became active in the Danish Pedagogical Society. In 1867 he learned about the French peace leader Frédéric Passy and immediately wrote offering to distribute information for Passy's new organization. In 1870 Bajer played a major role in the first conference of Danish, Norwegian, and Swedish educators in Göteborg, Sweden. The Association of Scandinavian Free States was established, and Bajer became editor of the federation's weekly journal. Bajer and his wife Mathilde were both devoted to political equality for women. In 1871 they founded the Dansk Kvindesamfund (Danish Women's Association) to promote women's rights.

National Politics

The following year, Bajer was elected to the Folketing (the Danish parliament). He was an outspoken proponent of liberal causes and vehemently opposed expenditures on fortifications and armaments. He wrote about the strategic positioning of the Scandinavian nations and advocated declarations of neutrality that would be internationally recognized. In 1882 Bajer gathered parliamentary colleagues to establish the

Foreningen til Danmarks Neutralisering (Association for Neutralization of Denmark).

He attended the International Conference of Peace Societies in 1884, at which he suggested the formation of an international peace society. A year later he organized the first Scandinavian peace conference. Hoping to set an international example, Bajer guided a proposal through Parliament in 1886 calling for arbitration agreements with Sweden and Norway. Through his lobbying, the Danish Interparliamentary Group was

Fredrik Bajer *(The Nobel Foundation)*

The International Peace Bureau

At the 1890 World Peace Congress in London, Fredrik Bajer proposed an international bureau to promote peace. At the 1891 Congress in Rome, the International Peace Bureau was established, to be headquartered in Bern, Switzerland. Bajer was its first chairman, and Elie Ducommun of France was secretary-general. Originally financed by pacifists Hodgson Pratt of Great Britain and German novelist Baroness Bertha von Suttner, the bureau later received grants from various governments.

The International Peace Bureau served as a clearinghouse for information and personnel in the peace movement. It helped to prepare for and implement resolutions of peace congresses, and it maintained a library of relevant publications. The bureau itself was awarded the Nobel Peace Prize in 1910. The organization moved to Geneva in 1924 to be closer to the League of Nations. Its work declined in the 1930's, and operations were suspended during World War II. The bureau was officially closed in 1959.

founded in 1891. Bajer was its first president and served in that post until 1917. Eventually the group included a majority of the Parliament's members.

International Leader

Bajer was the only Danish delegate at the founding session of the Interparliamentary Union in 1889. At the 1991 Peace Congress in Rome, the International Peace Bureau was formed, with Bajer as its first chairman. As a member of both the union and the bureau (both headquartered in Bern, Switzerland), Bajer served as a liaison between them. In 1893, he was elected to the union's council representing Denmark, Sweden, and Norway. In 1904 and 1905 Bajer was a primary force in the Danish adoption of peacetime treaties with Portugal, Italy, and the Netherlands.

In 1908 Bajer received the Nobel Peace Prize for his life's work. Because of his waning health, he was unable to attend the Nobel ceremony on December 10, 1908. He also stepped down as chairman of the International Peace Bureau and was named an honorary president. As World War I loomed, Bajer focused on arranging an international pact guaranteeing Danish neutrality. Despite decades of pacifist efforts, Bajer lived to see the eruption of global conflict in 1914.

A major figure in early peace movements, Fredrik Bajer was admired for his earnest idealism and indefatigable labors. He was both a passionate politician and a prolific writer on historical and diplomatic topics. The international peace movement he helped to build transformed diplomacy in the twentieth century.

Bibliography

Abrams, Irwin. *The Nobel Peace Prize and the Laureates: An Illustrated Biographical History, 1901-1987*. Boston: G. K. Hall, 1978.

Simon, Werner. "The International Peace Bureau: Clerk, Mediator, or Guide?" In *Peace Movements and Political Cultures*, edited by Charles Chatfield and Peter Van Dungen. Knoxville: University of Tennessee Press, 1988.

Wintterle, John, and Richard S. Cramer. *Portraits of Nobel Laureates in Peace*. London: Abelard-Schuman, 1971.

Barry Stewart Mann

Stanley Baldwin

Born: August 3, 1867; Bewdley, Worcestershire, England
Died: December 14, 1947; Astley Hall, Worcestershire, England

Three-time prime minister of Great Britian (1923-1924, 1924-1929, 1935-1937)

Stanley Baldwin (STAN-lee BAWL-dwihn) was the son of Alfred Baldwin, a member of Parliament, and Louisa Macdonald Baldwin, a daughter of the Reverend George Macdonald. He was also related to the prominent writer Rudyard Kipling. Baldwin was educated at Harrow and Trinity College, Cambridge. After Cambridge, Baldwin managed his father's extensive industrial holdings. In 1892 he married Lucy Ridsdale of Rottingdcan; they had a family of two sons and two daughters. In 1906 Baldwin made an unsuccessful bid for Parliament when he ran for the seat in Kidderminster. In 1908 he won the seat in Bewdley in Worcestershire. Baldwin held that seat until 1937, when he retired from politics and received a peerage.

Early Political Life

Stanley Baldwin's political life began during the Edwardian era; it was an age that predated the horrors of modern war and the revolutions that would characterize most of the twentieth century. Yet this first decade of the twentieth century reflected a new uncertainty in British politics; the external environment was forcing change on British society and its leaders. Great Britain was caught in a naval arms race with Germany and was experiencing domestic unrest caused by underemployment and a growing gap between the rich and the poor. Baldwin and other British politicians were confronted by challenges that had not existed previously.

Baldwin's political fortunes were linked to World War I, when his abilities in finance were recognized. After the collapse of Prime Minister H. H. Asquith's government in 1916 and the formation of a coalition government led by David Lloyd George, Baldwin was named parliamen-

tary private secretary to Bonar Law. Law was chancellor of the Exchequer and a prominent Conservative leader. In the next year Baldwin was appointed financial secretary to the treasury and served until 1921. In this capacity, Baldwin became an intimate member of the Conservative inner circle in the government. He played a significant role in the financial issues relating to the war, war debt, and reparations. In 1921 Baldwin was elevated to president of the Board of Trade, and in 1922 he aligned himself with Law to bring about the collapse of the Lloyd George coalition.

Stanley Baldwin *(Library of Congress)*

91

The General Strike of 1926

During the economic recovery from World War I, the gap between the British upper and working classes became more evident. In May of 1926 a crisis developed in the coal industry when government subsidies ceased and the mine owners demanded that the miners work for lower wages and work more hours each week. The Miners' Federation refused to accept these conditions, and it gained the support of the British union movement. A general or national strike was called by the Trade Union Council on May 3, 1926. It paralyzed the nation until May 12, 1926: railroads, shipping, roads, building, chemical, electrical, and natural gas industries were affected. Stanley Baldwin's government, which included Chancellor of the Exchequer Winston Churchill, responded effectively to the union efforts and kept the support of the middle class. The Trade Union Council was defeated, and its members suffered when they had to accept the demands of industrialists.

Prime Minister Law named Baldwin chancellor of the Exchequer in 1922; Baldwin's performance regarding war debt and reparations was criticized widely. Nonetheless, he sustained his position within the Conservative Party so that when Law resigned because of a terminal disease, Baldwin was asked to form a government in May, 1923.

Prime Minister Baldwin

Stanley Baldwin served three times as prime minister of Great Britain (twice between 1923 and 1929 and again from 1935 to 1937). He led Britain during a period in which the nation experienced a decline in its status, was plagued by mounting economic and social problems, and found itself in a weakened position as a defender of democratic institutions from the totalitarian forces of fascism and communism.

Baldwin's first ministry was brief, lasting less than a year. The Conservatives were defeated in the general elections of January, 1924, when the Labour Party came to power for the first time. Led by Ramsay MacDonald and focused on attacking Baldwin's protectionist trade policies, the Labour

British prime minister Stanley Baldwin returning to his residence shortly after the beginning of the 1926 general strike. *(Library of Congress)*

government proved inept. After ten months, the MacDonald ministry collapsed.

Baldwin's second term as prime minister began in November, 1924, and lasted until June, 1929. During these years Baldwin's Britain, in spite of difficulties associated with the General Strike of 1926, appeared to enjoy a limited economic revival. However, there were underlying problems that did not disappear. In addition to domestic economic issues, Britain's share of world trade diminished with the success of the United States and the rapid recovery of Germany.

Further, Britain was experiencing mounting problems with its empire, principally in India but also among the dominions (nations in the British Commonwealth), which were clamoring for enhanced controls. The veneer of British society attempted to restore itself, but the loss of almost an entire generation to World War I became increasingly evident. Perhaps Baldwin's greatest achievement during his second ministry was to appoint Winston Churchill as chancellor of the Exchequer. This post rehabilitated Churchill within the Conservative Party and enabled him

to establish a network of loyalists who would serve the nation well immediately prior to and during World War II. In June, 1929, Baldwin's government fell because of increasing unemployment.

Baldwin returned to government in 1931 as a member of a coalition national government led by Prime Minister Ramsay MacDonald; he held the post of lord president of the council until 1935. While Baldwin held a prominent position, the politics of the coalition did not permit him to express his mounting concerns regarding the emergence of Nazi Germany. He advanced his protectionist policies in the Ottawa Agreement (1932) and through his domestic tariff proposals.

In June, 1935, Baldwin began his third and final ministry as leader of the national government. In addition to finding himself unable to improve the dismal performance of the British economy, Baldwin found that he had little power or influence to confront the fascist advances in Ethiopia, the Rhineland, and Spain. The policy of appeasement had its origins during these years. Baldwin, while expending more funds for military equip-

The National Government

As the effects of the Great Depression widened in England in 1930 and 1931, with high unemployment, the collapse of businesses, and a lack of confidence in British institutions, the major political parties came to recognize their own vulnerability. In August, 1931, the Labour ministry of Ramsay MacDonald was paralyzed over a proposed reduction in unemployment benefits. Acting on the recommendation of Herbert Samuel, leader the Liberal Party, MacDonald formed a national government on August 24, 1931. In Britain's parliamentary system, a national government is a coalition in which various parties share power. MacDonald's national gov-

ernment consisted of a coalition of Labour, Conservative, and Liberal ministers. As leader of the Conservatives, Stanley Baldwin was a key participant in this process. In October, 1932, a general election endorsed the concept of national government, and MacDonald formed a second national ministry. MacDonald resigned in 1935 and was replaced by Baldwin as prime minister. The continuing economic depression, the rise of Nazi Germany, and the abdication of King Edward VII were the major issues confronting Baldwin through 1937, when he was replaced by Neville Chamberlain.

ment, contributed to appeasement by his lack of leadership. Domestically the most significant development of this ministry was the crisis of the abdication of King Edward VIII. Baldwin denounced the king's plans to marry the divorced American Wallis Simpson.

Stanley Baldwin led Britain during difficult and trying times. While his record is not noted for many remarkable achievements, Baldwin did keep the British nation together during the critical interwar years.

Bibliography

Ball, Stuart. *Baldwin and the Conservative Party: The Crisis of 1929-1931.* New Haven, Conn.: Yale University Press, 1988.

Middlemass, Keith, and John Barnes. *Baldwin: A Biography.* London: Weidenfeld and Nicolson, 1969.

Roberts, Bechhofer. *Stanley Baldwin: Man or Miracle?* New York: Greenberg, 1937.

Young, G. M. *Stanley Baldwin.* London: Rupert Hart-Davis, 1952.

William T. Walker

Arthur Balfour

Born: July 25, 1848; Whittinghame, East Lothian, Scotland
Died: March 19, 1930; Woking, Surrey, England

Prime minister of Great Britian (1902-1905)

Arthur James Balfour (AHR-thur JAYMZ BAL-fohr) was the son of James Maitland Balfour and Lady Blanche Gascoigne Cecil; his mother was the second daughter of the second marquis of Salisbury and a member of the great Cecil family, which had been prominent since the Elizabethan era in the early sixteenth century. Balfour was educated at Eton and at Trinity College, Cambridge, where he received his M.A. Balfour never married, and outside politics he pursued the life of an intellectual. He was the author of many books, including *A Defense of Philosophic Doubt* (1879), *Essays and Addresses* (1893), *The Foundations of Belief, Being Notes Introductory to the Study of Theology* (1895), *Economic Notes on Insular Free Trade* (1903), *Criticism and Beauty* (1909), *Theism and Humanism* (1914), and *Theism and Thought* (1923). Balfour was enmeshed throughout his life in the Victorian debate pitting religion against science; he consistently supported the cause and role of religion.

Early Political Life

Balfour entered politics by winning the seat for Hertford in 1874. As a nephew of Lord Salisbury, Balfour had access to the inner workings of Prime Minister Benjamin Disraeli's government, in which Salisbury served as foreign secretary. During the Russo-Turkish crisis of 1877-1878, Balfour accompanied Disraeli and Salisbury to the Congress of Berlin in June, 1878, where he served as a secretary; it was at Berlin that Balfour began his practical education in diplomacy. Balfour demonstrated keen skills as a parliamentary debater and was appointed to a series of posts in his uncle's ministries—president of the Local Government Board (1885-1856), secretary for Scotland (1886-1887), chief secretary for Ireland (1887-1891), first lord of the Treasury, and leader in the House of Commons (1891-1892 and 1895-1906). Balfour was opposed to Irish home rule (allowing Ireland to establish an independent government) but advocated reforms to eliminate abuses in Ireland.

Arthur Balfour *(National Archives)*

The Anglo-French Entente

At the beginning of the twentieth century, Anglo-French relations were precarious. The French effort to expand its holdings in east Africa resulted in the Fashoda Crisis of 1898-1899, in which British and French troops confronted each other in the Sudan. War was avoided through the skillful diplomacy of the French foreign minister. In 1902 Arthur Balfour succeeded his uncle, Lord Salisbury, as prime minister, and he served through early December, 1905. The most significant foreign-policy achievement of Balfour's ministry was the Anglo-French Entente (also known as the Entente Cordiale) of 1904. This colonial settlement improved ("normalized") relations between Britain and France.

The Anglo-French Entente also brought Britain into the Franco-Russian camp and subsequently resulted in British participation in the war against Germany in 1914. Specifically, the Anglo-French Entente concluded that northwestern Africa (Morocco) was a French sphere of influence and that northeastern Africa (Egypt, the Sudan, and, by implication, the headwaters of the Nile) was a British sphere of influence. The new, cooperative Anglo-French relationship was demonstrated in the First and Second Moroccan Crises with Germany. Furthermore, it paved the way for negotiations that resulted in the Anglo-Russian Entente of 1907.

Balfour found himself in a quandary over the Boer War (1899-1902): He opposed the rationale for the struggle but politically had no choice but to argue for a complete British victory.

Balfour as Prime Minister

Lord Salisbury's health had declined during the 1890's and took a decided turn for the worse during the spring of 1902. Salisbury resigned, and Balfour became prime minister in July, 1902. Balfour's achievements were substantive but not recognized by his contemporaries. The great parliamentary debater did not develop policies or positions based upon consensus. As a result, public enthusiasm for his programs was limited.

Domestically, Balfour's most important measures were the Education Act of 1902 and the Irish Land Purchase Act of 1903. The former law reorganized the administration of public and private schools, including those with religious affiliations; it eliminated abuses and introduced a series of progressive practices in the local management and funding of elementary and secondary schools. The latter created mechanisms

through which tenant farmers could purchase the land they worked.

In foreign affairs Balfour's achievements were somewhat controversial. There was general support for the establishment of a Committee of Imperial Defense in 1904. The committee coordinated strategic planning between Britain and the dominions and was very useful during World War I. The Anglo-French Entente, also in 1904, normalized relations with France. However, Balfour's importation of thousands of Chinese laborers to South Africa to work in the diamond and gold mines was denounced by a vehement coalition of anti-imperialists and humanitarians. Balfour was not a popular prime minister; in December, 1905, he resigned without dissolving Parliament. In the next month the Liberal government of Sir Henry Campbell-Bannerman acquired an overwhelming majority in the general election.

Later Years

After his own rather dissatisfying experience as prime minister, Balfour continued to lead the

Conservative Party until 1911, when younger leaders such as Bonar Law and Stanley Baldwin emerged as new forces within the party. Balfour was interested in returning to intellectual pursuits, but he continued to respond to the needs of the nation. In 1915, during World War I, he joined the government as first lord of the Admiralty. He replaced Winston Churchill, who had been discredited by the disastrous Gallipoli campaign against Turkey.

In 1916 Balfour joined Prime Minister David Lloyd George's government as foreign secretary; however, Balfour had little or nothing to do with the war, the articulation of war aims, or the Versailles settlement. His most significant achievement during this period was the issuance of the Balfour Declaration in 1917, which committed Britain to the establishment of a Jewish homeland in Palestine. After the war Balfour served as lord president of the council in governments led by David Lloyd George and Stanley Baldwin; his most significant postwar achievement was the Balfour Report of 1926, which defined the status of the dominions (nations in the British Commonwealth) and which was enacted in the Statute of Westminster a year after Balfour's death.

Arthur Balfour in Washington, D.C., for arms talks in 1922; on the left is Indian delegate Srinvasa Sastri. *(Library of Congress)*

The Balfour Declaration

The Zionist aspiration for the establishment of a Jewish state acquired support from Great Britain when Foreign Secretary Arthur Balfour clarified British policy in a letter to the leader of the British Zionist Federation on November 2, 1917. Balfour declared British support for a Jewish "national home" in Palestine as long as such action did not adversely affect the Arab Palestinians. In this, Balfour was responding to Zionist and Christian influences in Britain and was considering British war aims for the Middle East after World War I. The Balfour Declaration became the basis for the League of Nations' position on Palestine. The Israeli state came into existence in 1948.

Arthur Balfour was a nineteenth-century statesman and intellectual who survived into the turbulence of a new century that was not based on the same values, processes, or goals. While Balfour may not always have been effective, he was committed to a life of service to his nation and, in that context, his life was characterized by integrity, high intellectual attainments, and consistent devotion to his country.

Bibliography

Dugdale, Blanche. *Arthur James Balfour, First Earl of Balfour*. 2 vols. London: Hutchinson, 1936.

Egremont, Max. *Balfour: A Life of Arthur James Balfour*. London: Collins, 1980.

Mackay, Ruddock F. *Balfour: Intellectual States-man*. Oxford, England: Oxford University Press, 1985.

O'Callaghan, Margaret. *British High Politics and a Nationalistic Ireland: Criminality, Land, and the Law Under Forster and Balfour*. Cork, Ireland: Cork University Press, 1994.

Tomes, Jason. *Balfour and Foreign Policy: The International Thought of a Conservative Statesman*. New York: Cambridge University Press, 1997.

Young, Kenneth. *Arthur James Balfour: The Happy Life of the Politician, Prime Minister, Statesman, and Philosopher, 1848-1930*. London: Bell, 1963.

Zebel, Sydney H. *Balfour: A Political Biography*. Cambridge, England: Cambridge University Press, 1973.

William T. Walker

Surendranath Banerjea

Born: November 10, 1848; Calcutta, India
Died: August 6, 1925; Barrackpore, near Calcutta, India

Indian nationalist leader, founder of Indian National Congress

Surendranath Banerjea (soo-RAYN-dro-naht BA-nohr-jee) was the son of a well-known Calcutta physician. His father, though an orthodox (Kulin) Brahman, was a modernist and a liberal. Therefore, after a short period in a local-vernacular school, Surendranath was sent to an English-language school. He was an excellent student and graduated from Calcutta University in 1868.

Experiences with the British

In March, 1868, Banerjea went to England to take the Indian Civil Service Examinations. He passed the examination in 1869 but was removed from the list of successful candidates for being over age. He was indeed of the correct age and was reinstated after legal action. He returned to India in 1871 after completing the two years' probationary training in a year's time.

He was posted as an assistant magistrate under an Anglo-Indian magistrate who disliked him. He was dismissed from the civil service for a technical irregularity. Banerjea appealed for redress and even went to England, where he was turned down. He then fulfilled the requirements for practicing as a barrister-at-law. However, he was not granted the right to practice, because he had been dismissed from government service.

Educator and Politician

Banerjea was convinced of British discrimination against Indians and returned to Calcutta in June, 1875. Even though he greatly admired British liberalism and culture and the parliamentary system, he believed that Indians needed to have self-government under British supervision. His tribulations had caught public attention, and he was offered a post as professor of English at a noted school, the Metropolitan Institution, in Calcutta. He was an excellent teacher and infused his students with ideas of fairness and nationalism. In 1882 he took over a small school. Under his leadership the school prospered and became a college for students seeking the bachelor of arts, science, and law degrees at the Calcutta University. Banerjea named it Ripon College (after Lord Ripon, a viceroy of India). The college became an important educational insti-

Surendranath Banerjea *(Kim Kurnizky)*

tution in Calcutta and was later renamed for Banerjea.

In spite of his busy political life, Banerjea remained an active educator from 1875 to 1912, when he had to stop, as he became a member of the Indian Legislative Council. He was a member of the Calcutta University Senate for five years.

An extraordinary orator, Banerjea was one of the pioneers of Indian nationalism. He came in contact with the Brahmo Samaj—a modernist, universalist, liberal Hindu group. With two young members of this group, Banerjea founded the Indian Association on July 26, 1876. The association engaged Indian youth in political regeneration as well as social progress. Though himself a high-caste Brahman, Banerjea was active in social work such as women's liberation and widow remarriage. On behalf of the Indian Association he traveled extensively in northern, western, and southern India in 1877 and 1878, keeping large audiences spellbound with his oratory.

Journalist

In 1879 Banerjea bought a weekly newspaper, *The Bengalee*, which exposed British and Anglo-Indian inequities. Through its pages and his public speeches, Banerjea was active in all the political controversies of the day. He criticized an English judge of the High Court for his indifference to and contempt for Hindu religious traditions in an editorial and was sent to jail for two months. The event caused a great national protest.

Nationalist

The Indian Association was the forerunner of the Indian National Congress, with which it merged. Banerjea was one of the leading spirits of the Indian National Congress during its first twenty years. He presided over two of the annual sessions, in 1895 and in 1902 as a moderate who sought Indian self-government under British guidance. Extremists demanding total autonomy gradually took over the congress. Banerjea's influence had decreased by 1906, and he finally left the congress in 1918.

Banerjea had been a member of the Calcutta Municipal Corporation and the Imperial Legislative Council for many years. In 1919 he was elected to the Bengal Legislative Council and took office as a minister in 1921. This and his acceptance of a knighthood from the British government caused his fall from public favor. He was badly defeated in the election of 1923 by a relative newcomer. Thereafter he retired from the politi-

The Bengalee

The Bengalee was a weekly English-language newspaper published in Calcutta, India. It was launched in 1871 by Bacharam Chatterjee, who sold it to Surendranath Banerjea in 1879. Banerjea had returned from triumphal speaking tours of India in 1877 and 1878 and needed a vehicle to broadcast his ideas. Under Banerjea's editorship it quickly became an important vehicle for the dissemination of Indian nationalist sentiments. By 1900 it had become a daily. In 1909 Banerjea, its editor, was invited to the Imperial Press Conference in England; he was the only representative of the Indian Press to be invited.

The paper functioned smoothly under Banerjea's guidance until 1921, when he became a member of the Bengal Legislative Council and stepped down from the editorship. During these years *The Bengalee* was an influential organ in expressing the nationalist viewpoint. Its editorials and articles promoted Indian nationalism and protested British inequalities fearlessly. It was thus pivotal in bringing together Indians from all parts of the country.

The body of Surendranath Banerjea lying in state in Calcutta in September, 1925. Banerjea founded the Indian National Congress and published *The Bengalee*, a nationalist English-language newspaper. *(Gamma Liaison/Hulton Getty)*

cal arena. Surendranath Banerjea is rightly called *Rashtraguru*, or preceptor (teacher) of the nation.

Bibliography

Argov, D. *Moderates and Extremists in the Indian Nationalist Movement, 1883-1920: With Special Reference to Surendranath Banerjea and Lajpat Rai*. Bombay: Asia Publishing House, 1967.

Banerjea, S. N. *A Nation in Making*. New York: Oxford University Press, 1925.

Banerjee, Bani. *Surendranath Banerjea and History of Modern India*. New Delhi, India: Metropolitan, 1979.

Ranès C. Chakravorty

Edmund Barton

Born: January 18, 1849; Sydney, New South Wales (now Australia)
Died: January 7, 1920; Medlow Bath, New South Wales, Australia

First prime minister of Australia (1901-1903)

Edmund Barton (EHD-muhnd BAHR-tuhn) was the son of a financial agent and stockbroker. His mother ran a girls' school for a time. Barton was educated at Fort Street Model School, Sydney Grammar School, and the University of Sydney. He became a barrister in 1871 and a queen's counsel in 1889. After a long engagement, he married Jane Mason Ross in 1877.

Early Political Career

In 1876 and 1877, Barton stood unsuccessfully for the University of Sydney seat in the Legislative Assembly of the British colony of New South Wales. He finally won the seat in 1879. He was a member of the Legislative Assembly from 1879 to 1887, 1891 to 1894, and 1899 to 1900, holding various seats. In the years 1887-1891 and 1897-1898 he was in the upper house, the Legislative Council. Throughout this time, he held a number of ministerial portfolios, including attorney general from 1891 to 1893 and acting premier for several months in 1892.

Barton and Federation

Barton became a major presence in the movement to unite the Australian colonies in a single

Australian prime minister and minister for external affairs Edmund Barton, third from right in the front row, attending the Colonial Conference in London in 1902. *(Gamma Liaison/Hulton Getty)*

The Australian Commonwealth

From the 1840's there had been proposals for a national union of the Australian colonies, but the successful federation movement began in the 1880's. It was initially led by Henry Parkes. In 1890 the delegates to a federal conference in Melbourne agreed to hold a constitutional convention, which met in Sydney in 1891. Two further conventions took place in 1897, and another in 1898. Much of the debate concerned the power of the upper house of federal parliament, the Senate. Edmund Barton proposed a successful compromise. A referendum for the new constitution failed in New South Wales, the most populous Australian colony, but a modified constitution was accepted in a second referendum on June 20, 1899. It was then adopted by Western Australia in 1900.

The constitution had to be passed by the English Parliament, so Barton and other leading politicians traveled to London to reach an agreement with the British government. The Constitution Bill was introduced into the House of Commons in May, 1900, and the Commonwealth of Australia commenced on January 1, 1901.

federation. In 1891, he joined the committee established to draft a federal constitution. By 1897, he was the acknowledged leader of the federation movement, and in that year he served as chairman of a drafting committee. In 1900 he led a political delegation to London to secure British support for the proposed Commonwealth of Australia. An agreement was reached with the British government, and the new nation was formed in 1901.

Barton as Prime Minister

Australia's governor-general, the earl of Hopetoun, originally requested that William Lyne form a ministry and assume the office of prime minister. A power struggle ensued, and Barton emerged as Australia's first prime minister, leading a Protectionist government. During his period as prime minister, from 1901 to 1903, Barton was also minister for external affairs.

The Barton government made laws on customs tariffs and defense arrangements with Britain. Barton strongly supported the establishment of an Australian navy. His government restricted immigration and prohibited the importation of kanakas as laborers in the cotton and sugar industries. Kanakas were people from the Solomon Islands, New Hebrides, and New Guinea who were used as cheap labor. They were often treated almost as slaves, living and working in extremely harsh conditions.

High Court Judge

In September, 1903, Barton resigned from politics and was appointed as a judge of the High Court. His judgments favored states' rights within the Australian federation, especially in regard to commerce and labor relations. However, he supported the commonwealth's power to control the economy for defense purposes during World War I. Barton served on the Court until his death in 1920.

Barton's Achievement

Barton has sometimes been criticized for an element of laziness and an unwillingness to discipline his ministers. Yet he made an energetic contribution to the creation of the Commonwealth of Australia. He worked intensely toward his goal during the vital years at the end of the nineteenth century, when a consensus for federation had to be forged among the people of the colonies. As Australia's first prime minister, he gave the new nation a sound start, establishing its financial arrangements and machinery of government. With his vast political experience, he became a distinguished judge on his nation's highest court.

Bibliography

Clark, C. H. M. *The People Make Laws, 1888-1915*. Vol. 5 of *A History of Australia*. Melbourne, Australia: Melbourne University Press, 1981.

La Nauze, J. A. *The Making of the Australian Constitution*. Melbourne, Australia: Melbourne University Press, 1972.

Reynolds, John. *Edmund Barton*. Sydney: Angus & Robertson, 1948.

Rutledge, Martha. *Edmund Barton*. Melbourne, Australia: Oxford University Press, 1974.

Russell Blackford

Fulgencio Batista y Zaldívar

Born: January 16, 1901; Banes, Cuba
Died: August 6, 1973; Guadalmina, Spain

President of Cuba (1940-1944, 1952-1959)

Fulgencio Batista y Zaldívar (fewl-HAYN-thee-oh bah-TEES-tah ee sahl-DEE-vahr) came from a poor, rural family in eastern Cuba and had Chinese, European, and African ancestors. After working as a barber and cane cutter, he joined the army at age twenty because it offered steady employment. In the army he learned to read and write. Batista became a stenographer and confidential secretary to generals. He thus learned the inner workings of the military, and he later used that knowledge to seize power.

Seizure of Power

Batista joined the ABC Party, which was working secretly to overthrow Cuban dictator Gerardo Machado. After a revolt ousted Machado in August of 1933, Batista led a group of sergeants who staged a coup in September; the coup deposed the provisional president. Sergeant Batista walked into the office of the army chief of staff with a revolver in hand and took over his position. He had himself promoted to colonel. Batista installed as Cuban president Ramón Grau San Martín, a socialist, rabble-rouser, and Yankee hater who was a favorite among university students. Grau San Martín had been in office only four months when Batista removed him. Batista then ruled Cuba for seven years through a series of puppet presidents while remaining in the background.

Batista's Rule

Rather than the classic authoritarian dictator, Batista was an army commander and an astute political operator. He was popular with the common people, who could identify with his success. Critics of Batista could speak out in Congress or in political campaigns. Individuals and newspapers were free to attack him, and the courts had some degree of independence. Batista gave women the right to vote and encouraged workers to unionize on a major scale. He sponsored a law establishing a state-supported educational system. Laws to improve working conditions and provide safeguards against accidents, unemployment, and poverty in old age were instituted. Batista enacted all these measures for the people without popular pressure.

In his relations with the United States, Batista cooperated with the U.S. Good Neighbor Policy.

Fulgencio Batista y Zaldívar *(Library of Congress)*

Buildup to the Coup of 1959

In the 1950's Batista enjoyed the fruits of office but did nothing to extend social or economic reforms. Various groups—including intellectuals, students, and communists—became dissatisfied and organized opposition. The most effective organization was the secret ABC Party. Batista ruthlessly suppressed opposition. On July 26, 1953, brothers Fidel and Raúl Castro led a small band of men in an attack on an army post near Santiago and were captured. Batista was so unimpressed with them that he commuted their prison sentences to exile.

In 1954 Batista was elected to a four-year term. Although on the surface conditions in Cuba seemed good, there were basic problems that Batista ignored. Land was owned by a few wealthy Cubans and foreigners, rural and factory workers were underpaid, the government was inefficient and dishonest, politicians were corrupt, and schools were poor and few. Under Batista there seemed to be little hope of improvement. In exile in Mexico, Fidel Castro organized the invasion of eastern Cuba in December, 1956. The invasion was a failure, and many of the invaders were killed. The Castro brothers and the few remaining men escaped into the Sierra Maestra mountains. For two years Castro waged a political campaign as well as guerrilla warfare against Batista. Castro's propaganda campaign earned him recognition at home and abroad as the foremost leader of the opposition in Cuba.

Fulgencio Batista y Zaldívar at his desk in the presidential palace. *(AP/Wide World Photos)*

He did not protest the U.S. naval base at Guantánamo and accepted loans from the U.S. government. He identified himself with popular movements abroad and accepted the need for a common American democratic front. Batista was a cooperative ally of the United States during World War II.

The Presidency

In 1939 Batista could point to seven years of stability and growing prosperity. He decided to occupy the presidency himself. A new constitution that made him eligible was adopted in 1940, and Batista was elected that same year. During World War II, Cuban businessmen and rural workers enjoyed higher incomes. The United States purchased all the sugar that Cuba could produce. Increased mining of nickel and manganese and a revived tobacco industry provided greater employment. The United States improved roads, docks, and airports. Fewer tourists came to Cuba, but American servicemen made up for the loss of tourist revenue.

In 1944, Batista followed the advice of U.S. president Franklin D. Roosevelt. He did not run for office, nor did he dictate his successor. The candidate he favored lost the election to Grau San Martín, who was now estranged from Batista. Batista permitted the winner to take office and made a tour of South America. When evidence of malfeasance during his administration was uncovered, Batista established his residence in Florida, where he lived in luxury.

The Return of Batista

Batista returned to Cuba after he was elected senator in 1948. He remained a charismatic leader. He was popular with the masses as a self-made man and a benefactor who had done more for the people than any other ruler. Many expected him to be elected president in 1952. Batista and his supporters in the army, however, feared that the government would control the elections to prevent the election of Batista. Before the elections took place, they launched a barracks revolt that brought Batista to power without any difficulty or violence. The people seemed generally pleased, and reaction abroad was favorable. Batista spoke as if a significant revolution had happened, and he aroused hopes of reform. These hopes were not fulfilled.

Corruption became widespread in the Batista government of the 1950's. He allowed gangsterism and other abuses of power to permeate the army, and he alienated the people. As opposition developed, Batista used harsh repression to silence it—and thereby created more opposition.

The Cuban Constitutional Army

During his second term, Batista made political appointments to the Cuban Constitutional Army and used favoritism in the commissioning and promotion of officers. Many among the army's personnel were unscrupulous and used illegal methods to make money, often at the expense of the common people. In some cases they extorted money from businesses. Professional soldiers were passed over for promotions; morale in the army declined. When the July 26 movement began guerrilla warfare in 1956, the army responded with indiscriminate bombings, destruction of the property of peasants suspected of helping the guerrillas, and depopulation of villages. In contrast, the Twenty-sixth of July movement soldiers, under Fidel Castro's orders, treated the peasants fairly. They paid for all supplies taken and did no damage to peasant property. The peasants in turn provided the guerrillas with supplies, information, and recruits. Castro won the allegiance of the countryside.

At the beginning, the guerrilla forces avoided facing the Constitutional Army directly. Not until the army had become hated in the countryside did the guerrillas become bolder. The army soon suffered a complete demoralization. Soldiers deserted to the guerrillas on a large scale, taking their weapons with them. Before the end of Batista's regime, the army refused to fight, and the guerrillas operated without effective opposition. Batista fled on January 1, 1959, to Santo Domingo and then to Spain. Castro marched triumphantly across Cuba to Havana on foot and assumed control unopposed. Unsure of the loyalties of the remains of the Constitutional Army, Castro created the People's Militia as a counterforce. He recruited ordinary men and women and armed them. The People's Militia served other purposes as well. It was a method of spreading the revolution, pressuring the half-hearted, and keeping track of those whose loyalty was suspect. After the Constitutional Army was reformed, the two groups were merged.

Armored vehicles taking positions in front of the presidential palace in Havana after Fulgencio Batista y Zaldívar seized power in 1952. *(Library of Congress)*

One of the most effective opposition groups was led by Fidel Castro, who overthrew Batista in 1958. Batista fled into exile on January 1, 1959, finally settling in Spain. He lived there quietly, avoiding notice, until his death in August of 1973.

Bibliography

Farber, Samuel. *Revolution and Reaction in Cuba, 1933-1960: A Political Sociology from Machado to Castro.* Middletown, Conn.: Wesleyan University Press, 1976.

Gellman, Irwin F. *Roosevelt and Batista: Good Neighbor Diplomacy in Cuba, 1933-1945.* Albuquerque: University of New Mexico Press, 1973.

Quirk, Robert E. *Fidel Castro.* New York: W. W. Norton, 1993.

Robert D. Talbott

José Batlle y Ordóñez

Born: May 21, 1856; Montevideo, Uruguay
Died: October 20, 1929; Montevideo, Uruguay

President of Uruguay (1903-1907, 1911-1915)

José Batlle y Ordóñez (hoh-ZAY BAT-yay ee ohr-THOH-nyays), reform-minded president of Uruguay, twice elected to the presidency, was the son of a former president of Uruguay and leader of the Colorado Party. This party and its rival, the Blanco Party, originated from the frontier struggles of rival bands of ranchers for pastureland. From this struggle arose the tradition of the *caudillo*: the authoritarian individual who dominates and constantly fights over political and government power, frequently causing instability and violence.

Early Career

Initially intending to be a lawyer, the young Batlle abandoned law school and became a journalist. After a period in Paris, he became a follower of positivism, a spiritualist philosophy emphasizing technical progress, and repudiated his Catholic religion.

An increasingly noted writer and journalist, in 1886 he founded the newspaper *El Día*. This became the mouthpiece of the Colorado Party and among the most widely read newspapers in the country. His writing advocated stabilizing, modernizing reforms for the Uruguayan economy, society, and politics. His writings and political practices became the foundation of Batlle Doctrine. With his stature growing in the party, he was elected to the Chamber of Deputies and then to the Senate.

President of Uruguay

In 1903 Batlle was elected to his first four-year term as president of Uruguay. This event immediately led to an armed uprising by the head of the Blanco Party. Civil war ensued, ending only with the death of the Blanco leader the following

year. Batlle then effected several parts of his reform program. Secondary education was established in all cities, divorce was legalized, and some income taxes were abolished. Leaving the presidency in 1907, he went to live in Europe.

By the beginning of the twentieth century, profound changes were occurring in Uruguay, fundamentally altering the nature of the country. Refrigerated shipping appeared, allowing Uru-

José Batlle y Ordóñez *(Kim Kurnizki)*

109

The Batlle Doctrine

José Batlle y Ordóñez sought to modernize almost every aspect of Uruguay. At the heart of his program was the stabilizing of its political life, reducing its violent and authoritarian character. Although a leader of the Colorado Party, he sought to have the opposition Blanco Party share in power so that it would also have a stake in the stability of government.

Stabilization also meant a dynamic economy and a just society. To achieve economic growth he fostered the expansion of the economy through state development of business and manufacturing. The Batlle Doctrine modernized and brought under Uruguayan control the means of producing, transporting, storing, and shipping the meat exports that were the heart of the country's revenue.

The doctrine sought to achieve a more just society by supporting labor unions, an eight-hour workday, reform of suffrage, the right to education and divorce, and old-age pensions. The Batlle Doctrine made Uruguay one of the most stable and prosperous countries in Latin America during the first half of the twentieth century.

guayan ranchers to transport increased amounts of chilled meat to markets in Europe, particularly Britain. Income from exports significantly expanded, as did capital for investment, especially in manufacturing enterprises. Immigrants from Europe, generally from the southern part, flooded into the country, increasing the population. Settling in cities, primarily Montevideo, immigrants brought about the capital's rapid expansion. The urban population of the country began to increase in relation to the rural population.

While in Europe, Batlle came to be particularly impressed by the presidency of Switzerland, in which a committee replaced a single person, forming a plural or collegial type of executive. He thought that such a presidency would be appropriate for Uruguay as a means of replacing the strongman dominance of its politics and government. Elected again to a four-year presidential term in 1907, Batlle presided over the passage of an even greater part of his reform program. The eight-hour workday and old-age pensions were established, rural credit increased, electricity and telephone service expanded, foreign economic influence was curtailed, national industries were developed and fostered by the state, and labor unions were respected for their role in the national economy and society.

A modified version of collegial presidency was established in Uruguay by the constitution of 1919. This document also brought about the separation of church and state. Batlle, popularly known as Don Pepe, died in 1929, leaving an unprecedented legacy in Latin America for the modernization of his country.

Bibliography

Vanger, Milton I. *José Batlle y Ordóñez of Uruguay: The Creator of His Times, 1902-1907.* Cambridge, Mass.: Harvard University Press, 1963.

———. *The Model Country: José Batlle y Ordóñez of Uruguay, 1907-1915.* Hanover, N.H.: University Press of New England, 1980.

Weinstein, Martin. *Uruguay: The Politics of Failure.* Westport, Conn.: Greenwood Press, 1975.

Edward A. Riedinger

Auguste-Marie-François Beernaert

Born: July 26, 1829; Ostend, Belgium
Died: October 6, 1912; Lucerne, Switzerland

Belgian prime minister and peace activist, winner of 1909 Nobel Peace Prize

Auguste-Marie-François Beernaert (oh-GEWST mah-REE frahn-SWAH BAYR-nahrt) was the son of a bureaucrat whose appointments took his middle-class Flemish Catholic family to Namur, where he spent his childhood. His early education was undertaken by his mother, a woman of outstanding intelligence. Admitted to the Catholic University of Louvain in 1846, Beernaert received a law doctorate in 1851 with highest honors. Awarded a fellowship, he spent two years studying French and German legal education.

Belgian Political Career

Admitted to the bar in 1853, Beernaert clerked for a prominent lawyer, then established a successful practice in fiscal law. His essays in legal journals earned him a reputation as a scholar. In 1859 he was appointed counsel at the Belgian Supreme Court of Appeals. Surprisingly, he gave up his practice in 1873 to become public works minister in Jules Malou's Catholic Party cabinet. Over the next five years Beernaert proved an able administrator. He improved Belgium's transportation system, established new port facilities at Oostende and Antwerp, and beautified Brussels. However, he failed to end child labor in mines. In June, 1874, he lost a senatorial election but three months later was elected deputy for Thielt, a West Flanders constituency that continued to re-elect him until his death.

Defeated in 1878, the Catholic Party returned to power in 1884. Beernaert was appointed minister of agriculture, industry, and public works. Four months later, King Leopold II entrusted him with the government, naming him prime minister. His ten years as prime minister and finance minister were marked by balanced budgets, protection for the Flemish language, the construction

of fortifications to defend Belgian neutrality, revision of the 1831 constitution, and a tenfold increase in suffrage. The Congo Free State was created in 1885 as Leopold's personal possession. Reforms to protect the welfare of workers were instituted following riots in 1887.

Beernaert's government fell in 1894 on the issue of proportional representation. Although he returned to his law practice, Beernaert was elected president of the Chamber of Representatives, a post he held from 1895 to 1900, and served in the advisory post of minister of state.

Auguste-Marie-François Beernaert *(The Nobel Foundation)*

The International Peace Conference

The International Peace Conference was convoked by Czar Nicholas II of Russia on the invitation of Queen Wilhelmina of the Netherlands. It met at The Hague on May 18, 1899. Meetings continued until July 29 and resulted in agreements on the peaceful settlement of international disputes, the laws of land war, and the adaptation to maritime warfare of the 1864 Geneva Convention. Additional declarations prohibited the use of dum-dums (expanding bullets), the launching of projectiles and explosives from balloons or other new vehicles, and the use of projectiles for the diffusion of poisonous gases. Auguste-Marie-François Beernaert oversaw the conference's commission on arms limitation.

The conference's final act called for a special conference to revise the Geneva Convention and for further discussions on the rights and duties of neutrals, the limitation of land and naval forces, naval bombardment, private property in naval warfare, war budgets, and the development of new types of rifles and naval guns. Criticized for being unrealistic, this conference led to a second series of talks in 1907 and the eventual establishment of international judicial bodies.

The International Peace Conference of 1899 prohibited the use of projectiles to spread poison gas. Nevertheless, fifteen years later, World War I began and gas warfare was practiced. *(Thomas H. Hartshorne/Archive Photos)*

He was active in international efforts to abolish slavery and opposed the brutal exploitation of the Congo, souring his relationship with Leopold.

International Figure

After resigning as prime minister, Beernaert became active in the Interparliamentary Union, presiding over conferences and committees. At the 1899 International Peace Conference in The Hague he oversaw the first commission on arms limitation, and at the 1907 conference, a commission on land warfare. He acted as arbiter of international disputes. A member of the Permanent Court of Arbitration in The Hague, he represented Mexico in a 1902 dispute with the United States, the first case brought before the court. Beernaert was the force behind proposals to unify international maritime law. Conventions dealing with collision and assistance at sea were enacted at a 1910 Brussels conference under his chairmanship. He was president of the Association for the Promotion of International Maritime Law, honorary president of the International Law Association, and member of the Institut de France and Belgian Academy. Also a lifelong patron of the arts, he headed the Commission of Museums and Arts. One of Belgium's leading pacifists, he shared the 1909 Nobel Peace Prize with Baron d'Estournelles de Constant of France. Returning home from a conference on air warfare in Geneva, Beernaert was hospitalized in Lucerne, Switzerland, where he died of pneumonia.

Bibliography
De Lichtervelde, Louis. *Leopold of the Belgians.* New York: Century, 1929.
Ludovici, James L. *Nobel Prize Winners.* Westport, Conn.: Associated, 1957.

Randall Fegley

Menachem Begin

Born: August 16, 1913; Brest-Litovsk, Russia (now Belarus)
Died: March 9, 1992; Tel Aviv, Israel

Prime minister of Israel (1977-1983), winner of 1978 Nobel Peace Prize

Menachem Wolfovitch Begin (meh-NAH-kehm VOHL-fo-vihch BAY-gihn) spent his early life in Brest-Litovsk, one of the regions in eastern Europe in which the growing Zionist movement would influence many of the future leaders of Israel. Begin became an active member of the movement in the early 1930's while studying for his law degree at the University of Warsaw. Although he received his degree in 1933, he never practiced law.

Menachem Begin *(Library of Congress)*

Membership in Zionist Organizations

At the age of ten, Begin joined Ha-Shomer ha-tzair, a left-wing youth organization dedicated to the establishment of a Jewish homeland. Though small in stature, Begin exhibited little fear in responding to the anti-Semitism widespread in Poland. At the age of fifteen, he joined Betar, a revisionist movement, becoming fully immersed in the Zionist movement. Soon after, he fell under the spell of revisionist leader Vladimir Jabotinsky. Betar became a strong advocate for establishment of a Jewish majority in Palestine and creation of a Jewish army for its defense. Begin quickly joined the leadership of Betar, becoming the head of the movement in Poland by 1938. He barely remained ahead of the Nazis following the Nazi invasion of Poland in September, 1939; his parents and brother were not as fortunate, dying in a concentration camp. Begin fled to Vilna, where he was arrested by the Russians and sentenced to eight years of hard labor near the Arctic Circle as "an element dangerous to society."

Begin's years as a disciple of Jabotinsky provided him with the strength to survive Russian prisons and interrogation. When Germany declared war on Russia in June, 1941, Begin was released as a Polish citizen. Ostensibly joining with a Polish army unit to fight the Germans, Begin instead made his way to Palestine, where in 1944 he joined the Irgun Z'vai Leumi (national military organization), an underground movement dedicated to ousting the British from Palestine. As commander of the Irgun, Begin led an organization that became increasingly known for its tactics of terror against both the British army and the Arabs in the region. Many innocent people were killed on both sides in the bitter struggle between the British and outlawed Jewish paramilitary groups.

Establishment of Israel

In May, 1948, David Ben-Gurion announced the establishment of the new state of Israel. Begin, as commander of the Irgun, had in effect already established a state within a state: The Irgun acted according to its own rules. Though it was supposed to be subject to Ben-Gurion's orders, it often carried out its own operations. Begin said that he was willing to merge with the Haganah, the new Israeli army, but only on his own terms. A clash was inevitable, resulting in orders from Ben-Gurion for the shelling of a ship that was bringing arms for the Irgun. Badly needed weapons were lost, but Ben-Gurion established that it was he, and not Begin, who was leading the fight for the new state. Possible civil war was averted.

Israeli prime minister Menachem Begin (left) shakes hands with Egyptian president Anwar el-Sadat upon meeting at Camp David, Maryland, in 1978. *(Archive Photos)*

Politician and Statesman

In 1948, with the establishment of Israel, Begin founded the Herut (freedom) Party, an amalgamation of several radical groups, including the Irgun. As a member of the opposition to the ruling Labor Party of David Ben-Gurion, Begin was known for his radical views with respect to reparations payments to Arabs for the land on which Israel was established (which he opposed), and absorption of territories into a "greater Israel" (which he favored). In the 1960's, he was instrumental in establishment of the Gahal bloc

---

Betar

Betar began as an activist youth organization in Latvia in 1923; among the early founders was Vladimir Jabotinsky. Betar differed from other revisionist movements, advocating the establishment of a Jewish state in its radical advocacy of strong defense. It stressed paramilitary training in addition to its call for support of a Jewish homeland. Menachem Begin joined Betar early in its development, and by 1931 he had become one of its leaders in Poland. By the outbreak of World War II in 1939, Betar included seventy-eight thousand members in twenty-six countries. Many of its members joined in ghetto resistance movements, and they formed a substantial portion of the Jewish Brigade within the British army. In the decades following the establishment of Israel, Betar merged with Israeli sports federations.

Likud

Likud (Likud-Liberalim Leumi, meaning unity-national liberal) is the major right-wing party in Israel. It was founded as a coalition in 1973 between the Gahal bloc (the "freedom" or Herut Party) and the more liberal Miflaget ha-Liberali Party, primarily as a challenge to the Labor Party. The Labor Party had ruled Israel since its inception. Herut had evolved from the Russian Zionism of the 1920's, formally becoming a political party in 1948. Its groups included terrorist organizations such as Irgun Z'vai Leumi, whose leader had been Menachem Begin.

Likud has been a strong advocate of a "greater Israel"—that is, of Israel's retention of occupied territories. On May 17, 1977, the Likud Party won the national elections, and a month later Begin formed a new government with himself as prime minister. Though Begin as head of Likud opposed establishment of an independent Palestinian state, his negotiations with Egyptian president Anwar el-Sadat resulted in the first Middle East peace treaty. In 1983, Begin was replaced by Yitzhak Shamir, who presided over a coalition between Likud and Labor until 1990. In 1993, Benjamin Netanyahu became party leader, becoming prime minister at the head of a Likud administration in 1996. Likud continued its hard-line view toward the Palestinians, its determination to hold on to the occupied territories, and its opposition to a Palestinian state.

Israeli prime minister Menachem Begin meeting in the White House with U.S. president Jimmy Carter in December, 1977, to discuss negotiations with Arab countries and the Palestine Liberation Organization. *(Archive Photos)*

in the Knesset (the Israeli parliament), with the merger of Herut and other smaller liberal parties into the Likud (unity) Party.

In May, 1977, Likud won the national elections, and Begin became prime minister. Though known for his strong views on retention of the West Bank territories and the city of Jerusalem, captured during the 1967 war, Begin was willing, on his own terms, to begin negotiations with Arab states.

In 1978, Begin, Egyptian president Anwar el-Sadat, and U.S. president Jimmy Carter began talks aimed at establishing peace between Egypt and Israel. During most of the year, the negotiations showed little progress, in part because of the failure of both the

United States and Egypt to recognize the strong views held by Begin on the issue of the territories. Begin had spent his life believing in the concept of Eretz Yisrael—the land of Israel—and this remained an issue over which he would never compromise. In a summit convened in September at Camp David in Maryland, an agreement was finally brokered between Begin and Sadat. The treaty was signed on March 26, 1979. It established a semblance of Palestinian autonomy in some occupied territories and mandated the return of the Sinai to Egypt. In 1978, Begin and Sadat were awarded the Nobel Peace Prize.

A Self-Contradictory Figure

Begin's opposition to the establishment of a Palestinian state increasingly split political factions within Israel. The 1982 Israeli invasion of Lebanon, ostensibly aimed at destroying terrorist camps of Yasir Arafat's *fedayeen*, proved disastrous: Casualties mounted, and there were no apparent benefits for Israeli security. In addition, the West's perception of Israel as a beleaguered state suffered greatly as civilian casualties increased and as Lebanon's cities suffered significant damage. The death of Begin's wife, Aliza, in 1982 was an added personal blow, and in 1983 Begin resigned from office. A year later he left the Knesset (the Israeli parliament), retiring from politics. Begin remained a self-contradictory figure, admired for initiating the peace process yet bitterly denounced for leading Israel into a war in Lebanon that seemed to have no end.

Bibliography

Haber, Eitan. *Menachem Begin: The Legend and the Man*. New York: Delacorte Press, 1978.

Sachar, Howard. *A History of Israel*. 2d ed. New York: Alfred A. Knopf, 1996.

Silver, Eric. *Begin: The Haunted Prophet*. New York: Random House, 1984.

Richard Adler

Edvard Beneš

Born: May 28, 1884; Kožlany, Bohemia, Austro-Hungarian Empire
Died: September 3, 1948; Sezimovo Ústí, Bohemia, Czechoslovakia

Czech political leader and diplomat

Edvard Beneš (EH-doo-ahrt BEH-nehsh) was the youngest of ten children of poor peasants. Nonetheless, he received an excellent education. He earned a Ph.D. at the Czech University in Prague, pursued post-doctoral work at the Sorbonne, and received a law degree from the University of Dijon. While in Paris he met Anna Vlčková, whom he married in 1909. Starting the same year, he taught economics at the Commercial Academy in Prague and the Prague Technical School,

Edvard Beneš *(Library of Congress)*

coming under the influence of Tomáš Masaryk. He joined Masaryk's Realist (Progressive) Party and wrote for its journal, *Čas*. After World War I he had a standing appointment to teach sociology at Charles University in Prague.

World War I

With the advent of war in 1914, a leg injury sustained earlier kept Beneš from being drafted into the Austro-Hungarian military. He soon became a leader of the Maffia, an underground organization that worked actively for the downfall of the Habsburg monarchy. He left the empire in September, 1915, for Switzerland, and joined forces with his mentor Masaryk and the Slovak Milan R. Štefanik to work for Czechoslovak independence. Beneš settled in Paris, where he had many contacts, and became the secretary general of the Czechoslovak National Council, a propaganda organization working in Allied capitals for the liberation of the Czechs and Slovaks. His work met with success when the Allies recognized the council as a government-in-exile starting in the summer of 1918. In the autumn of 1918, the Austro-Hungarian Empire collapsed, with Czechoslovak independence being declared on October 28, 1918.

Foreign Minister

With the formation of Czechoslovakia, Beneš began his long career as foreign minister, although he served briefly as prime minister in 1921-1922. He was perhaps the most successful central European statesman between the world wars. He led the Czechoslovak delegation to the Paris Peace Conference in 1919-1920, securing the historic borders of Bohemia and Moravia for his country. A strong supporter of the League of

The Little Entente

This series of treaties was the brainchild of Czechoslovak foreign minister Edvard Beneš in an attempt to fill a power vacuum in central Europe after World War I. It began as an alliance between Czechoslovakia and Yugoslavia in August, 1920, aimed against Hungarian territorial revision after the peace treaties of World War I. Czechoslovakia signed a similar treaty with Romania in April, 1921, while Yugoslavia and Romania signed another accord in June, 1921, directed against Hungary and Bulgaria. This treaty completed the Little Entente. The two-year bilateral treaties were renewed periodically until 1929, when they were replaced by a five-year time limit after which the accords would be renewed indefinitely. France supported the alliance by entering into separate agreements with Czechoslovakia in 1924, Romania in 1926, and Yugoslavia in 1927.

The Little Entente successfully thwarted a Habsburg restoration in Hungary in 1921. Although the alliance was mainly defensive, some attempts were made to coordinate the three countries' economies. After Adolf Hitler's rise to power in Germany, the Little Entente tried to strengthen its organization. It was, however, limited in its effectiveness because the entente made no arrangements for mutual aid in times of attack by countries other than Bulgaria and Hungary. As a result, the Little Entente fell apart with the Munich Agreement in September, 1938.

Czech president Edvard Beneš (left) reviewing Czechoslovakian troops in Prague in 1937. *(Library of Congress)*

Nations, which he believed was the best guarantee for the safety of his small country, Beneš served on its council, being elected as its chairman six times between 1923 and 1927. In 1935 he was appointed president of the League of Nations' assembly. To fill a power void in central Europe with the collapse of Austria-Hungary and to protect his country against revisionist territorial designs by Hungary, Beneš proposed his greatest diplomatic triumph: a series of alliances with Yugoslavia and Romania that became known as the Little Entente. It was strongly supported by France. In 1935, with the rise of Nazi Germany, he negotiated and signed mutual assistance pacts with France and the Soviet Union.

The Munich Agreement

In December, 1935, President Masaryk, now quite old, selected Beneš as his successor. Beneš took office faced with the growing belligerency of Nazi Germany. Immediately following the Nazi takeover of Austria in March, 1938, German chancellor Adolf Hitler started demanding the incorporation of the Sudetenland—Czechoslovak territory that contained a majority German population—into the German Reich. Facing increasingly bellicose threats, and with war seem-

ing imminent in September, 1938, Beneš refused to back down and grant the Nazi demands. He based his stance on the 1935 alliances with the Soviet Union and France. However, rather than facing the prospects of all-out war, the leaders of France and Great Britain decided to appease Hitler by meeting with him and Italian dictator Benito Mussolini in Munich. Without consulting the Czechoslovak government, they agreed to cede the Sudetenland to Germany and to force the settlement upon Beneš. Abandoned by his allies, he relented. He resigned the presidency on October 5, 1938, and went into exile in the United States and England.

World War II

When war broke out in September, 1939, Beneš began a second crusade for the liberation of Czechoslovakia. He moved to London, where he became the president of the Czechoslovak National Committee, quickly recognized as a government-in-exile. Beneš worked among the Allies for the restoration of his country and made numerous radio addresses to occupied Europe. Beneš felt that a strong alliance with the Soviet Union was necessary for the survival of his country. He traveled to Moscow and signed an agree-

The Sudetenland

This region takes its name from an east-west mountain range in northeastern Bohemia and Moravia. The term eventually came to mean a distinct area encompassing most border regions of Bohemia and Moravia that were included in Czechoslovakia after World War I. The vast majority of its population was German, because Czech rulers had invited skilled Germans to settle these regions in the Middle Ages. Many of the three million Sudeten Germans resented being placed in an independent Czechoslovakia after 1918 because of the predominantly Slavic

characteristics of the state and because of economic problems that resulted from the collapse of Austria-Hungary. Backed by Adolf Hitler, the Sudeten Germans, under Konrad Henlein, caused many problems and eventually demanded to be detached from Czechoslovakia. The Munich Agreement of September, 1938, incorporated the region into Germany. After World War II, the Sudetenland was returned to Czechoslovakia, which proceeded to expel virtually all the remaining Germans.

ment in December, 1943, that would become the basis of Czechoslovak foreign policy for decades to come. He returned to Czechoslovakia, as president, with the Red Army and made a triumphal entry into Prague on May 16, 1945.

Communist Coup

Beneš was reelected president in 1946, and he attempted to follow a policy of democracy and independence in national and foreign affairs. His hope was to make Czechoslovakia a bridge between the Soviet Union and the democratic West. He led a precarious coalition government composed of democrats and communists. In February, 1948, the majority of the democratic ministers resigned in protest against increasing illegal activity by the communists. They expected Beneš to call for new elections, which the communists were predicted to lose. The communist leaders, however, threatened civil war if the president did not appoint a new government dominated by communists. Beneš, in poor health after suffering two strokes in 1947, relented a second time, leading to the communist takeover of Czechoslovakia. Beneš temporarily remained in office but resigned on June 7, 1948, rather than sign a new constitution giving legal control of the country to the communists. He retired to his estate in central Bohemia, where died of a stroke in early September, 1948.

Edvard Beneš (with hat raised), visiting New York in the early 1940's, walks beside New York mayor Fiorello La Guardia. Early in World War II Germany had occupied Czechoslovakia, and Beneš at this time was president of the Czech government-in-exile in London. *(AP/Wide World Photos)*

Bibliography

Beneš, Edvard. *Edvard Beneš in His Own Words: Threescore Years of a Statesman, Builder, and Philosopher*. New York: Czecho-American National Alliance, Eastern Division, 1944.

_____. *Memoirs of Dr. Eduard Beneš: From Munich to New War and New Victory*. London: Allen & Unwin, 1954.

Zeman, Z. A. B. *The Life of Edvard Beneš, 1884-1948: Czechoslovakia in Peace and War*. New York: Oxford University Press, 1997.

Gregory C. Ference

David Ben-Gurion

Born: October 16, 1886; Płónsk, Poland, Russian Empire (now Poland)
Died: December 1, 1973; Tel Aviv, Israel

First prime minister of Israel (1948-1953, 1955-1963)

Born David Joseph Gruen (DAH-viht YOH-sehf GREWN), David Ben-Gurion (BEHN-gewr-YOHN) was the sixth child of Avigdor and Sheindel Gruen. His father was an unlicensed legal counsel and a fervent Zionist. Ben-Gurion's family was greatly influenced by the Haskala, the Enlightenment movement that encompassed much of the Judaism of the period. Among the precepts of the movement was the idea that Jews should immigrate to Palestine. This feeling pervaded the Gruen household. David Gruen became an ardent Zionist socialist. He moved to

David Ben-Gurion *(Library of Congress)*

Palestine in 1906, where he survived by working in orange groves and wine cellars. He adopted the name Ben-Gurion, the name of a leader of the Jewish revolt against the Romans.

His agitation for a Jewish state came to the attention of the Turkish authorities, and in 1915 Ben-Gurion had to flee to the United States. There he met Paula Munweis, whom he married in 1917. They had three children, Geula, Renana, and Amos. During World War I (1914-1918), the British began recruitment of Jews for a Jewish Legion to serve in the liberation of Palestine from the Turks, and Ben-Gurion volunteered. In August, 1918, as a member of the legion, Ben-Gurion arrived in Palestine a second time. A year later his wife and young daughter joined him in what would be their permanent homeland.

Early Political Experience

Following the war, Ben-Gurion applied his Zionist fervor as an advocate for the establishment of a Jewish socialist society in Palestine. Further, he argued for the future establishment of a new state of Israel. Often traveling abroad, he established ties with the British Labour Party.

In 1921 Ben-Gurion was elected secretary-general of the General Federation of Jewish Labor (Histadrut), a position he held for twelve years. He was a strong advocate for a workers' society, in which workers would pool their money for establishing both agricultural settlements and industry. As head of the party, Ben-Gurion oversaw organization of strikes, employment for Jews, and aid for the impoverished. In 1923 he traveled to the Soviet Union, hoping for support. However, he quickly became disillusioned with Soviet communism and set about to establish his own socialist state.

The British Jewish Legion

During World War I, Jewish volunteers were recruited to serve as a detachment with the British army to fight for liberation of Palestine from Turkey. The origins of this Jewish Legion were found in the Zion Mule Corps, units of Jewish volunteers who had distinguished themselves in the disastrous Gallipoli campaign. The success of the corps resulted in the idea that similarly motivated units could be used in Palestine. The Jewish Legion initially consisted of two battalions, the Thirty-eighth Battalion, recruited in Great Britain, and the Thirty-ninth Battalion, consisting primarily of American Jews. When David Ben-Gurion, living in exile in the United States, heard of the proposal, he immediately enlisted and began recruitment for the legion. A third battalion, the Fortieth Battalion, served as a reserve unit. Eventually about fifty-six hundred men volunteered.

The Thirty-eighth Battalion reached Palestine in June, 1918, and was assigned to defend positions north of Jerusalem. In September, aided by two companies from the Thirty-ninth Battalion, the legion was instrumental in the capture of the Umm Shart ford across the Jordan. With the end of the war, the Jewish Legion served mostly as police, maintaining order in what was now British Palestine. Demobilization commenced in 1919 and was effectively completed a year later.

During these years, there was strong right-wing opposition to Ben-Gurion's position. Led by Vladimir Jabotinsky, the Revisionists were against the idea of an umbrella organization for socialist workers. Jabotinsky advocated the immediate formation of a Jewish state that would include the area of Transjordan (Jordan). Ben-Gurion wished to accommodate the British; Jabotinsky did not. During the 1920's, both men continually campaigned for the role of leader in the Zionist movement.

In the early 1930's, Ben-Gurion became leader of the new Mapai (Labor) Party. His objective was to establish the party as the leader in the Zionist movement. He strongly urged the immigration of Jews to Is-

Thousands of Jews who fled the Nazis during World War II enlisted in "Jewish Foreign Legion" units to fight against Germany under their own flag. Nazi genocide against Europe's Jews made Zionists more determined than ever to found a Jewish state. *(Library of Congress)*

David Ben-Gurion proclaiming Israel's independence on May 14, 1948, in Tel Aviv. *(Library of Congress)*

rael. At the same time he managed an agreement with Jabotinsky, leader of the more radical wing of Zionists. He also attempted, unsuccessfully, to reach an agreement with nationalistic Arab leaders in Palestine. During World War II (1939-1945), Ben-Gurion advocated aid to the British, at the same time traveling through the United States as a Zionist advocate.

The State of Israel

In the Balfour Declaration of 1917, Britain had expressed sympathy with the Zionist movement and supported other recommendations leading to the establishment of a Jewish state in the Middle East. Despite this historic declaration, it became clear after the war that Britain would provide little aid for Jewish settlement.

Ben-Gurion authorized the Haganah and other armed defense groups to begin stockpiling arms in anticipation of war with the Arabs. He also attempted, with limited success, to rein in the more radical wing of the movement, fearing further antagonism of the British and their American allies. He continued in the role of chief spokesman for Zionism, arguing his cause before the United Nations Special Commission on Palestine in 1947. On May 14, 1948, following the U.N. mandate to partition the area, Ben-Gurion announced establishment of the new state of Israel. Ben-Gurion was the logical choice as first prime minister. He also served as minister of defense for the new government.

Ben-Gurion served two terms as prime minister, from 1948 to 1953, and again from 1955 to 1963. During these years, Israel grew into a viable country, victorious in two major wars. Ben-

The War of Israeli Independence

On May 14, 1948, the establishment of the state of Israel was declared by David Ben-Gurion. The next day, armies from the surrounding Arab states and Iraq invaded Israel. Israel's defense forces were initially overwhelmed by sheer numbers, but within ten days they were able to halt the Arab advance and begin a counterattack. A cease-fire began on June 11. The Israeli army used the time to equip and reorganize themselves.

Fighting resumed the second week in July, at which time the Israeli forces managed victories in both the center and the south. In October, Israel captured Beersheba, opening the road to the south, shortly followed by additional victories in the north. In December, Israeli forces trapped the Egyptian army in the Sinai. Another cease-fire was imposed in January, 1949. On February 24, an armistice was signed between Egypt and Israel that effectively established Israel's independence. Other agreements were later signed with Lebanon, Transjordan (Jordan), and Syria, though no Arab countries were willing to recognize the existence of Israel officially.

Gurion continued to urge Jews worldwide to come to Israel. Many of his ideas were brought to fruition, including free education and the establishment of science and research opportunities in the country. In 1953 he retired, in hopes of living on a kibbutz (an Israeli collective farm). However, the continuing terrorist threat, coupled with the splintering of Israeli political parties, resulted in his recall to the position in 1955. Ben-Gurion recognized the need for outside support, traveling through much of Europe and the United States to enhance Israel's international position. After his final retirement, Ben-Gurion remained a strong symbol of the Jewish state until his death in 1973.

Bibliography

Bar-Zohar, Michael. *Ben-Gurion: A Biography*. New York: Delacorte Press, 1978.

Jabotinsky, Vladimir. *The Story of the Jewish Legion*. New York: Ackerman, 1945.

Kurzman, Dan. *Ben-Gurion: Prophet of Fire*. New York: Simon and Schuster, 1983.

Teveth, Shabtai. *Ben-Gurion and the Holocaust*. New York: Harcourt Brace, 1996.

Zweig, Ronald. *David Ben-Gurion: Politics and Leadership in Israel*. Portland, Oreg.: Frank Cass, 1991.

Richard Adler

Richard Bedford Bennett

Born: July 3, 1870; Hopewell Hill, New Brunswick, Canada
Died: June 26, 1947; Mickleham, Surrey, England

Prime minister of Canada (1930-1935)

Richard Bedford Bennett (RIH-churd BEHD-furd BEH-neht) was born on a farm in Hopewell, New Brunswick, on July 3, 1870. He studied law at Dalhousie University in Halifax, Nova Scotia. He began practicing law in Chatham, New Brunswick, and then he moved to Calgary, Alberta, in 1897. He became wealthy from both his law practice and his investments. By the age of thirty, Bennett had become a millionaire. He never married.

Early Political Career

Bennett soon became involved in the Conservative Party. He served in both the Northwest Territories legislature and the Alberta legislature

Richard Bedford Bennett *(Library of Congress)*

before his election to the House of Commons in 1911. During World War I, he served as the director general of national service, and he became minister of justice in 1921. He impressed people with his personal integrity and commitment to public service. In 1927 his fellow Conservatives selected him to lead their party in the House of Commons. In October, 1929, Wall Street crashed, and the Canadian economy suffered greatly. Prime Minister William Lyon Mackenzie King failed to implement policies to reduce unemployment. He believed that the Depression would not last long, and he saw no reason to approve expensive new social programs. Shortly before the July, 1930, election, King made an incredible blunder. He stated that his government would not provide unemployment assistance to provinces governed by Conservatives. His insensitive remark shocked Canadians and contributed greatly to the Conservative victory in 1930. Richard Bennett argued that because his companies had created so many jobs in Calgary, he would be able to create jobs throughout Canada.

Prime Ministership and Later Years

Winning the election was relatively easy for Bennett, but once in office he did not seem to know how to deal with Canada's severe economic problems. As prime minister, he did not live in the official residence for prime ministers but rather in an elegant suite in Ottawa's fanciest hotel, the Château Laurier. His work ethic had made him wealthy, and he came to believe that hard work and sacrifice would solve Canada's economic problems. Canadians, for their part, came to believe that Richard Bennett did not understand the severity of Canada's social problems. He imposed high tariffs to protect Canadian products from foreign competitors, but this policy backfired because foreigners chose not to purchase expensive Canadian products. Bennett did not seek advice from leading Conservatives, including former prime ministers Robert Borden and Arthur Meighen. He assigned to himself the management of foreign affairs and the ministry of finance.

It became abundantly clear to Canadians that Richard Bennett was inflexible. Most admired his integrity and large personal contributions to charities but came to regret that he was their prime minister. In late 1934, Bennett suddenly made a massive change in his domestic program: He proposed a Canadian version of U.S. president Franklin D. Roosevelt's New Deal. Canadian voters questioned the sincerity of this change in policy, however, and the Liberals easily defeated the Conservatives in 1935. Three years later, Bennett resigned his seat in the House of Commons and emigrated from Canada to England. Thanks to the help of his old friend

Canadian prime minister Richard Bedford Bennett (left) with U.S. president Franklin D. Roosevelt and U.S. secretary of state Cordell Hull in 1933. *(Library of Congress)*

The Canadian New Deal

Richard Bennett did not believe that it was the role of the federal government to spend huge sums of money to deal with the high unemployment and social problems created by the Great Depression. In late 1934 and early 1935, however, he suddenly proposed unemployment insurance, antitrust legislation, minimum wages, and national pensions. He also created a privately owned Bank of Canada entrusted with the power to determine monetary policy in Canada. Although Canadian voters were impressed

that Richard Bennett was finally trying to deal with the Depression in Canada, they suspected that he would modify these new economic policies if he were reelected in 1935. Mackenzie King and his Liberal Party soundly defeated the Conservatives in the October, 1935, national election, then put into effect the same policies that Bennett had espoused. King insisted that the federal government name a majority of the directors of the Bank of Canada.

Lord Beaverbrook, Bennett was appointed to the British House of Lords. He died in his mansion in Mickleham, England, on June 26, 1947.

Bibliography

Bothwell, Robert, Ian Drummond, and John English. *Canada: 1900-1945*. Toronto: University of Toronto Press, 1987.

Hoar, Victor, ed. *The Great Depression: Essays and Memoirs from Canada and the United States*. Toronto: Coop Clark, 1969.

Hutchison, Bruce. *Macdonald to Pearson: The Prime Ministers of Canada*. Don Mills, Ontario: Longmans Canada, 1967.

Edmund J. Campion

W. A. C. Bennett

Born: September 6, 1900; Hastings, Albert County, New Brunswick, Canada
Died: February 23, 1979; Kelowna, British Columbia, Canada

Canadian political leader, premier of British Columbia (1952-1973)

William Andrew Cecil Bennett (WIHL-yuhm AN-drew SEH-sihl BEH-neht), the son of a failed businessman and a devout Presbyterian mother, was named Cecil for Cecil Rhodes, the English business wizard and imperialist. Bennett claimed to be of United Empire Loyalist stock, though his Tory family was among the British who took over lands after expelling the Acadians in the eighteenth century. After his family moved to Saint John, he worked full time in a hardware store after dropping out of school at fifteen. A confirmed teetotaller, he believed in the close relationship between Christianity and conservatism. He moved to Edmonton in 1919, started a partnership in a hardware store in 1927, and that same year married Annie Elizabeth Mary Richards. They had a daughter, Mary, and two sons, Russell and William. After selling his share of the business in 1929, Bennett moved to Kelowna, British Columbia, and created a hardware empire.

Entering Politics

Bennett entered politics as a Conservative, winning election to the British Columbia legislature in 1941. Seven years later, he resigned from the coalition government, then ran unsuccessfully in a federal by-election for a seat that had been held by a Tory for twenty-four years. He tried again in 1949, but the Tories supported someone else. Bennett never forgave this slight. He was reelected a member of the Legislative Assembly in 1948 (for South Okanagan), but in 1951 he broke with the coalition government and sat as an independent. In December, he joined the Social Credit League (the Social Credit Party) and attacked the Liberals' expensive hospital plan, raising political fears about socialism. In the 1952

election, he easily became British Columbia's first Social Credit premier.

Economic Policies

Although nicknamed "Wacky" by detractors, Bennett reigned as premier for two decades. His Bible-thumping Christian fundamentalism fueled his idea of sin-free government. His principal economic policy was "pay-as-you-go" (mockingly called "pave-as-you-go" by critics), whereby the books were balanced by his habit of claiming grants to towns and construction companies as expenses against profits. Bennett took credit for everything he could, particularly the northern extensions of

W. A. C. Bennett *(Library of Congress)*

the Pacific Great System Railway and major hydroelectric projects. While railing against big government and espousing free enterprise, he took over the Black Ball ferry line to create the British Columbia Ferry Corporation in 1958. In 1959, after curbing the power of labor unions, limiting social welfare, and trimming the civil service, he made British Columbia debt-free. He expropriated the largest privately owned hydroelectric firm in 1961, developing the two-river policy, which allowed for a massive Canadian-American development of the northern Columbia watershed and the erection of a huge Peace River dam. He even attempted to establish the Bank of British Columbia, with 25 percent provincial ownership.

Political Clout

Bennett called elections every three years, maintaining his economic expansion by provincial bonds and tax rebates to homeowners. Money was reshuffled to municipal governments. Bennett helped build Simon Fraser University, which, ironically, became a hotbed of radicalism. He quarreled with Lester B. Pearson and Pierre Trudeau over federal-provincial relations, Quebec's status, and offshore mineral rights. He finally lost power in 1972, by a huge margin, to the New Democratic Party's Dave Barrett.

Bennett oversaw the development of British Columbia by exploiting cheap energy sources, investment capital, worker productivity, technological innovations, and the international buoy-

British Columbia premier W. A. C. Bennett arriving in London for an official visit in 1960. *(AP/Wide World Photos)*

Canada's Social Credit Party

The Social Credit Party's name came from the title of a book published in 1924 by English economist C. H. Douglas. Douglas attacked capitalism, especially as practiced by banks, for depriving people of fair compensation for the labor that produced material wealth. He attracted many disciples, and in 1932 Calgary evangelist William Aberhart established the Social Credit League, using radical fiscal reform as his platform. He swept to victory at the polls. Social Credit ran Alberta until 1971, by which time it had spread to other prairie provinces, particularly British Columbia, where W. A. C. Bennett was its main proponent. Federally, it had less power, although it held the balance of power with the New Democratic Party during John Diefenbaker's minority government.

ancy of the 1950's and 1960's. He turned the Social Credit Party into a political force; however, his conflicts with Ottawa and Quebec showed that he put his province ahead of the country

Bibliography

Bowering, George. *Bowering's B.C.: A Swashbuckling History*. Toronto: Viking, 1996.

Mitchell, David J. *W. A. C. Bennett and the Rise of British Columbia*. Vancouver: Douglas & McIntyre, 1983.

Worley, Ronald B. *The Wonderful World of W. A. C. Bennett*. Toronto: McClelland & Stewart, 1972.

Keith Garebian

Theobald von Bethmann Hollweg

Born: November 29, 1856; Hohenfinow, Prussia (now Germany)
Died: January 1, 1921; Hohenfinow, Germany

Chancellor of Germany (1909-1917)

Theobald Theodor Friedrich Alfred von Bethmann Hollweg (TAY-oh-bahlt TAY-oh-dohr FREED-rihk AHL-freht fon BAYT-mahn HOHL-vayk) came from a long line of Frankfurt bankers. He attended a humanistic high school and studied law at Strassburg, Leipzig, and Berlin. He entered the German civil service in 1872 and enjoyed a successful career. In 1909 Bethmann Hollweg became chancellor of Germany, serving under Germany's leader, Kaiser William (Wilhelm) II. Bethmann Hollweg remained in that post until 1917. Some historians have blamed him for giving officials of the Austro-Hungarian Empire a so-called blank check to settle their differences with Serbia during the July, 1914, crisis that led to World War I.

Resistance to Change

Bethmann Hollweg was a conservative who tried throughout his career to maintain the status quo. He resisted change in the political and social systems of Germany, and he tried to ensure that if change had to come, it would come slowly. Consequently, he failed to reconcile the deep social divisions of German society in the years before World War I. He did not wish to abandon the German political system, in which the kingdom of Prussia dominated the German Empire. Nor did he want to change the three-tiered franchise system of Prussia, which gave the wealthy classes much more political power than their numbers warranted. Although he introduced into the German parliament legislation that granted universal male suffrage, he resisted granting similar rights to the rest of the empire because he feared the voting power of the workers and their support for the Marxist Social Democratic Party.

German chancellor Theobald von Bethmann Hollweg in 1917. *(Library of Congress)*

Officers and crew of a German U-boat, U-53, in 1916. *(Library of Congress)*

Outbreak of World War I

Bethmann Hollweg desired to prevent war, but he nevertheless yielded to the demands of the German high command in making political decisions. On the advice of the military leaders of Germany, he sent a telegram to the Austrian government assuring it of Germany's unqualified support for any decisions they made regarding their standoff with Serbia. This standoff was occurring in the aftermath of the assassination of Austrian archduke Francis (Franz) Ferdinand on June 28, 1914. The Austrians subsequently mobilized their military forces and began bombarding the capital city of Serbia. Czar Nicholas II of Russia ordered the mobilization of Russia's armed forces in compliance with a secret alliance his country had with the Serbians. Once the European race to mobilize for war had begun, Bethmann Hollweg did not question the decisions of the military leaders of Germany.

Annexation and Submarine Warfare

Once the war began in August, Bethmann Hollweg reluctantly yielded to the pressure of those in the German government who wanted to annex much conquered territory into the German Empire. Personally, he remained committed to a peace based on restoring the prewar boundaries of Europe. He vociferously opposed the resumption of unrestricted submarine warfare in February, 1917, correctly forecasting that it would draw the United States into the war against Germany. Bethmann Hollweg realized that the economic might of the United States would prove decisive in the war. Nevertheless, he yielded to the pressures of German military leaders and approved the policy. President Woodrow Wilson subsequently asked the U.S. Congress for a declaration of war in April, 1917, citing as grounds the German resumption of unrestricted submarine warfare.

Submarine Warfare in World War I

At the beginning of World War I, the English declared a blockade of the Baltic Sea to prevent neutral vessels from trading with Germany. The Germans retaliated by declaring a submarine blockade of the British Isles to prevent the merchants of neutral countries, especially the United States, from carrying materials of war to Great Britain. After a public outcry in the United States following the sinking of the British liner *Lusitania* in 1915, the Germans agreed to "restricted" submarine warfare in which a submarine would surface, radio the targeted ship that it was about to be attacked, allow the crew to disembark, and only then sink the ship. These restrictions greatly limited the effectiveness of submarine warfare. In 1917, the German high command decided to resume unrestricted submarine warfare. The decision led directly to the entry of the United States into the war in April, 1917.

In July, 1917, Bethmann Hollweg resigned his post as chancellor during the debates in the German parliament concerning a peace resolution. Bethmann Hollweg preferred a resolution based on the status quo before the war—that is, on a peace without annexation of territory. He retired into private life and died at his home in Hohenfinow on the first day of 1921, still convinced that he had followed the correct policies. Historians view his public career as being marked by missed opportunities and ultimately as a failure.

Bibliography

Berghahn, V. R. *Germany and the Approach of War in 1914*. London: Macmillan, 1973.

Bethmann Hollweg, Theobald. *Reflections on the World War*. London: Macmillan, 1920.

Jarausch, Konrad. *The Enigmatic Chancellor: Bethmann Hollweg and the Hubris of Imperial Germany*. New Haven, Conn.: Yale University Press, 1973.

Paul Madden

Bhumibol Adulyadej

Born: December 5, 1927; Cambridge, Massachusetts

King of Thailand (from 1946)

Bhumibol Adulyadej (PEW-mee-pohn ah-DUHN-leh-dayt) (the name means "strength of the land, incomparable power"), the grandson of Thailand's King Chulalongkorn (Rama V), was the third child and second son born to Thai prince Mahidol of Songkhla and Sangwalya Chukramol, a commoner. Upon the death of his physician father in 1929, Bhumibol, along with his mother, sister, and elder brother, was sent to Switzerland to be educated by order of King Prajadhipok. The abdication of King Prajadhipok in 1935 elevated seven-year-old Bhumibol to the status of crown prince. His elder brother, Ananda Mahidol, was king of Thailand.

Rama IX

Bhumibol and his brother, King Ananda, spent World War II in Europe outside Japanese-controlled Thailand. They returned in late 1945 to prepare for Ananda's coronation. However, Ananda was found dead by Bhumibol on June 9, 1946, in the palace from a gunshot wound. Bhumibol Adulyadej was now king. Bhumibol wanted to continue his education before officially being crowned king, so a regency was appointed to attend to the affairs of state. Bhumibol returned to Switzerland. There he studied political science and law at the University of Lausanne and developed an interest in classical and jazz music.

Bhumibol's coronation was further delayed because of an automobile accident in 1949 in Switzerland that severely injured his right eye. In the interim, Bhumibol became engaged to a distant cousin, Mom Rajawongse Sirikit Kitiyakara. Bhumibol was married on April 28, 1950, and crowned King Rama IX on May 5. The royal couple would have three daughters, Ubol Ratana, Sirindhorn, and Chulabhorn, and a son, Vajiralongkorn.

Bhumibol as King

In 1996 King Bhumibol Adulyadej celebrated fifty years on the throne of Thailand, a reign longer than that of any other member of the Chakri Dynasty. During his reign, Bhumibol maintained Thai unity in spite of fifteen constitutions, seventeen coups, and twenty-one prime ministers. Twice he directly intervened in state affairs to halt or avoid bloodshed. In 1973 a television appearance by the king brought an end to violence and student killings. The king arranged the departure of three prominent military leaders. In 1992, when soldiers killed pro-democracy demonstrators, the king summoned the prime minister and the leader of the democracy move-

Bhumibol Adulyadej *(AP/Wide World Photos)*

Thai Independence

The Chakri Dynasty began rule in Thailand in 1782. Each ruler has taken the reign name of Rama from the Brahmanic epic poem *Ramayana*. Thailand maintained its independence during the nineteenth century as France and Britain encroached on Cochin China and Burma, respectively. Thailand managed to do so only by ceding large portions of Thai territory in what is today Cambodia and Laos in the east to the French, and in the south the Malay states to the British. Thailand emerged as an intact sovereign nation, acting as a buffer state between French and British Southeast Asian colonies, the status having been confirmed by an 1896 treaty signed by France and Britain.

ment to the palace. In a televised broadcast he demonstrated his support for increased democracy.

The king's success is in large part a result of a 1957 political collaboration between Bhumibol and Field Marshal Prime Minister Sarit Thanarat. This collaboration made the king the indispensable force of unity among Thailand's commercial, industrial, and financial groups as well as among the military, the intellectuals, and the people at large. Venerated by millions of Thais, King Bhumibol tirelessly traveled the country and sponsored more than eighteen hundred development projects in agriculture, environment, public health, occupational promotion, water resources development, communications, and social welfare.

King Bhumibol became an accomplished saxophone player and jazz composer. In 1996 a compilation of his musical compositions was released, entitled *Forever in Our Hearts: His Majesty the King's Compositions*. In addition, Thailand's king gained recognition as a painter, whose style is distinguished by strong strokes and bold colors, and a photographer who specializes in black-and-white compositions. In 1967 King Bhumibol and his eldest daughter won gold medals for OK class yachting in the Southeast Asian Peninsular Games.

The release of information about Thailand's king and royal family is strictly controlled by the toughest *lese-majeste* laws—laws making it a crime to violate the dignity of a ruler—in the world. Nevertheless, King Bhumibol publicly de-

King Bhumibol Adulyadej opening a session of Thailand's parliament in November, 1996. *(AP/Wide World Photos)*

voted his life to the gradual transformation of Thailand into a united nation intent on improving the welfare of its people.

Bibliography

Crossette, Barbara. "King Bhumibol's Reign." *New York Times Magazine*, May 21, 1989, pp. 30ff.

Fifty Years of Reign. Bangkok: Public Relations Department, 1995.

A Memoir of His Majesty King Bhumibol Adulyadej of Thailand. Bangkok: Office of His Majesty's Principal Private Secretary, 1971 and 1987.

William A. Paquette

Benazir Bhutto

Born: June 21, 1953; Karachi, Pakistan

Two-time prime minister of Pakistan (1988-1990, 1993-1996)

Benazir Bhutto (beh-nah-ZEER BEW-toh) was the first child born to Zulfikar Ali Bhutto and Nusrat Bhutto, a wealthy and politically influential landowning family in the Pakistani province of Sindh. Benazir attended Harvard University and Lady Margaret Hill College, Oxford, in England. In 1987 she married Asif Ali Zardari, with whom she had a son and two daughters.

Political Inheritance

Benazir's father was a major political figure in Pakistan from 1948 until 1977. He established the Pakistan People's Party (PPP) in 1967. From an early age, Benazir took an active part in politics, often accompanying her father to important national and international meetings. Zulfikar Bhutto was president of Pakistan when, in 1977, martial law was established by General Mohammad Zia ul-Haq. Zulfikar Bhutto was accused of complicity in a murder and on April 4, 1979, was executed. Benazir Bhutto assumed leadership of her father's political organization. She and many of her followers were jailed or kept under house arrest for years by the Zia government. In 1984 Bhutto left Pakistan and remained in exile for two years. She was active in the coalition opposing Zia's rule—the Movement for the Restoration of Democracy—from 1984 until 1988. Although promising elections at the time he seized power, Zia did not allow a popular vote until 1988, and that was not under truly democratic conditions.

In 1988 General Zia, who had by then declared himself president, was killed in a plane crash. Benazir was appointed acting head of government. The new government set about liberalizing politics and dismantling the restrictive measures that had been put in place during the Zia years. Elections held in November confirmed the new political order, and Bhutto was named prime minister. She was the first woman ever to be made head of government by popular election in a Muslim country.

Benazir Bhutto in 1989 delivering the commencement address at Harvard University. *(Reuters/Jim Bourg/Archive Photos)*

The First Bhutto Government

Bhutto encountered many difficulties during her tenure in office. The coalition of political forces that had come together to oppose Zia and that carried her to victory in the election began to fall apart. Provincial governments resisted direction from the center. Opposition parties in parliament frustrated government legislative efforts. Islamic fundamentalists refused to accept even the idea, much less the reality, of a woman running the country.

Bhutto's government was also plagued by corruption and mismanagement. Family members, friends, and associates were accused of a variety of financial misdeeds. Bhutto's husband, whom she appointed minister of investments, was a particular target of criticism. The government used its power to harass opposition politicians, a practice that would in turn be used against Bhutto and her followers when the opposition came to power. Bhutto replaced civil servants and judges sympathetic to opposition leader Nawaz Sherif and his Pakistan Muslim League. Her

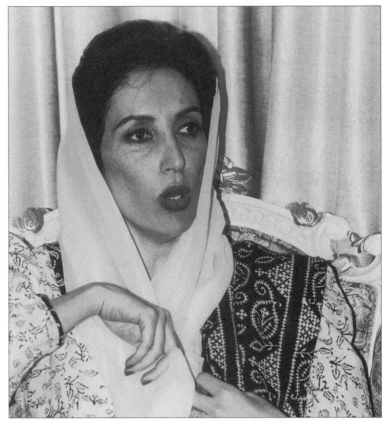

Benazir Bhutto in July, 1993, as opposition leader a few days after Pakistan's president dissolved the government of Nawaz Sherif. In elections three months later, Bhutto was returned to power. *(Reuters/ Muzammil Paha/Archive Photos)*

The Pakistan People's Party

The Pakistan People's Party (PPP) was established by Zulfikar Ali Bhutto in Lahore, Pakistan, on December 1, 1967. The party's manifesto called for a classless society through the application of a socialist agenda guided by the political and social ethics of Islam. Following the general elections of 1970, the PPP was the largest party in West Pakistan. (In 1971, following military intervention by India, East Pakistan seceded from the federation and became Bangladesh.) The PPP pursued a program of democratization that greatly expanded opportunities for most

people, but it also produced confusion and disorder. Under Bhutto's leadership, the PPP dominated Pakistan's politics until 1977, when it was overthrown by the military. All political parties were illegal during the martial-law regime, but when General Zia ul-Haq was killed in a plane crash in 1988, Zulfikar's daughter Benazir was appointed acting head of government. The leadership of the PPP was formally in the hands of Zulfikar's widow, Nusrat. In fact, however, Benazir was in control.

The Attempted Coup of 1995

The military in Pakistan has played an important role in politics since the founding of the country in 1948. On three separate occasions, the military has suspended the civilian government and established martial law. In October, 1995, a conspiracy to overthrow the Benazir Bhutto government and replace it with an Islamic state was revealed. The conspirators included a hundred army officers, twenty-six enlisted men, and several civilians. The accused were strongly committed to Islam and were dissatisfied with the direction the country was taking. Increasingly, Pakistani army officers—who had come from elite families during the British period—were being replaced by men from less privileged backgrounds with a greater commitment to Islam. At first the conspirators were to be allowed to retire, but it was later determined that they would face courts-martial.

government also confiscated passports of prominent opposition politicians. Most troubling was the growing problem of political violence, especially in the important port city of Karachi.

On August 6, 1990, the president of Pakistan, Ishaq Khan, decided that the Bhutto government was incompetent and dismissed it. An interim government was formed, and new elections were held on October 24, 1990. The PPP suffered a serious defeat. The new government under Nawaz Sherif, however, was no more successful in dealing with Pakistan's problems than Bhutto's government had been. The president once again intervened, dismissed the government on July 14, 1993, and called for new elections. The elections of October, 1993, returned Bhutto and the PPP to power.

A Second Government

Bhutto's second experience as prime minister was, if anything, stormier than the first. In 1994 a serious challenge to the government occurred in Northwest Frontier Province when a group of religious fundamentalists demanded the imposition of Islamic law. Civil disorder grew in and around Karachi. The government was unable to achieve progress in economic development, and conditions for the poorest elements of society, those traditionally most supportive of the Bhut-

tos and the PPP, actually worsened. Relations with India were poor and, with the Cold War over, the United States saw little reason to maintain a close relationship with Pakistan.

Split Within the PPP

By the mid-1990's, the movement that had catapulted Bhutto to power was losing strength. The emotional energy generated by the martyrdom of Zulfikar Ali Bhutto had begun to dissipate. To complicate matters, the Bhutto family was sharply divided over control of the party. Benazir Bhutto's leadership was challenged by her brother Murtaza, who had just returned to Pakistan from sixteen years of exile in Damascus. Benazir suspected that her mother, Nusrat, was planning to support Murtaza, so she disbanded the cochair of the PPP and assumed sole control. Murtaza and Nusrat announced the formation of a new wing of the PPP, but it attracted little support.

In September, 1996, Murtaza was killed by police gunfire. Nusrat accused Benazir and her husband of involvement. On November 5, 1996, President Farooq Leghari dismissed the Bhutto government. Benazir had alienated the business community, the judiciary, the military, the president, and the international lending community—and, as the next election would show, the Pakistani public. On February 6, 1997, parliamentary elections all but eliminated the PPP as a national political force.

Assessment

Like Indira Gandhi in India, Benazir Bhutto achieved political power because of the popularity of her father. Zulfikar Bhutto's death created a mystique that carried Benazir and the PPP through a decade of political storms and controversies. Benazir Bhutto's two terms as prime minister produced little substantive progress in solving the political, social, and economic problems of Pakistan. By the end of the 1990's, the Bhutto legacy was politically spent. Following the February 7, 1997, election, Bhutto found herself in the role of a minority opposition leader facing numerous charges of financial corruption and misuse of power.

Bibliography

Bhutto, Benazir. *Daughter of the East*. London: Hamish Hamilton, 1988.

Bouchard, Elizabeth. *Benazir Bhutto, Prime Minister*. Woodbridge, Conn.: Blackbirch Press, 1992.

Lamb, Christina. *Waiting for Allah: Benazir Bhutto and Pakistan*. New York: Penguin Books, 1992.

Shafqat, Saeed. *Civil Military Relations in Pakistan: From Zulfiqar Ali Bhutto to Benazir Bhutto*. Boulder, Colo.: Westview Press, 1997.

Zakaria, Rafiq. *Women and Politics in Islam: The Trial of Benazir Bhutto*. New York: New Horizons Press, 1990.

Louis D. Hayes

Zulfikar Ali Bhutto

Born: January 5, 1928; near Larkana, Sind, India (now Pakistan)
Died: April 4, 1979; Rawalpindi, Pakistan

President (1971-1973) and prime minister (1973-1977) of Pakistan

Zulfikar Ali Bhutto (zewl-fih-KAHR ah-LEE BEW-toh) was born in Sind, the southwestern province of what is today Pakistan, to Shah Nawaz, a low-level Muslim official of the British raj who became Sir Shah Nawaz and a Bombay cabinet member in 1934. His mother, Shah Nawaz's second wife, had been a Hindu dancing girl. Bhutto's prosperous family provided him with a good education and comfortable adolescence in Bombay. When he was thirteen, Bhutto married an older cousin and at her father's death inherited one-third of his large feudal estates. In 1951 he married Nusrat Ispahani, with whom he had four children: Benazir, Murtaza, Sanam, and Shah Nawaz.

Zulfikar Ali Bhutto *(Library of Congress)*

Rise to Power

Educated at the University of California, Berkeley, and Oxford University, Bhutto ascended to power quickly in Pakistan. After graduating from Oxford with honors in law, he returned to Karachi. He quickly ingratiated himself with the ruling elite and in 1957 was named to the Pakistani delegation to the United Nations, where he condemned "economic aggression."

Appointed by President Mohammad Ayub Khan to the coveted post of foreign minister in 1963, Bhutto soon found himself in a pugnacious exchange with India over the Rann (salt marsh) of Kutch. The Rann was 3,500 square miles (9,000 square kilometers), submerged during the rainy months, between Sind and Gujarat. The northern half had traditionally been claimed by Pakistan. Considerable tension on the border led to several weeks of tank skirmishes, with Pakistan claiming a decisive victory.

This contretemps was only a prelude to the crisis that Bhutto provoked by signing a boundary agreement with China. India was already seething after its brief clash with China over the Ladakh region the previous fall. India was therefore immediately angered by Bhutto's ceding to China land that Pakistan did not itself control. Unperturbed, Bhutto insisted that India had no claim to Jammu and Kashmir and asked for a plebiscite overseen by the United Nations. Acting on what he perceived as an advantage in Kashmir, Bhutto promoted an ill-advised guerrilla operation in Kashmir that cost Pakistan several thousand soldiers. Although his policies in Kashmir ultimately proved foolhardy and resulted in an embarrassing military defeat, Bhutto was able to exploit issues there and in the Rann to achieve a considerable popular following.

The Creation of Bangladesh

Friction with Ayub led to Bhutto's dismissal as foreign minister in 1966 and his founding of the Pakistan People's Party in 1967. His socialist demagoguery gave Bhutto so much prominence that in November, 1968, Ayub jailed him for three months before resigning in favor of General Agha Mohammad Yahya Khan. In 1971 Bhutto was complicit in the Pakistani army's brutal suppression of the independence movement in East Pakistan. However, he was embarrassed by India's conse-

Zulfikar Ali Bhutto at the United Nations in 1965, proposing that the organization send international troops into Kashmir. *(Library of Congress)*

quent rout of Pakistani troops in the new country (to be named Bangladesh). This debacle, however, gave Bhutto the chance he wanted to wrest power from the weak Yahya Khan. Bhutto proclaimed himself president and martial law administrator in December, 1971.

The Kashmir Controversy

When Zulfikar Ali Bhutto became Pakistan's foreign minister in 1963, he spoke out against India, sympathized with Palestine, and worked to become a leader in Third World affairs. He was cool toward the United States and signed trade agreements with the Soviet Union. India's problems with insurgency in Kashmir emboldened Bhutto—with help from aggressive generals—to infiltrate Pakistani soldiers into Kashmir in hopes of stirring up revolution. This misadventure culminated on July 25, 1965, in Operation Gibraltar, the invasion of Indian-controlled Kashmir by seven thousand Pakistani guerrillas. They were devastated by Indian forces. Six weeks later India humiliated Pakistan by invading Lahore, and on September 23 General Mohammad Ayub Khan capitulated at the U.N. peace table. Bhutto tried to put a good face on his rashness, blustering about Pakistani patriotism and Indian aggression, but he had obviously committed a great blunder.

The New President

Successfully pushing a new constitution through the National Assembly, Bhutto changed his title in August, 1973, from president to prime minister and enjoyed a cordial meeting with U.S. president Richard Nixon and his secretary of state, Henry Kissinger, in Washington, D.C. Despite his broad following, Bhutto was widely criticized for Pakistan's economic problems. On January 1, 1974, he nationalized all the banks and stopped the flow of hard currency abroad. His harsh "Defense of Pakistan" regulations multiplied and stifled the constitution, making Bhutto at the peak of his power hardly less of a dictator than Romania's Nicolae Ceausescu, whom he welcomed to Karachi in 1975 as part of an effort to become the leader of the Third World.

Decline and Fall

On January 7, 1977, Bhutto announced that general elections would be held in March, prompting his opponents to form the Pakistan National Alliance (PNA) and to offer single opposition candidates. Bhutto campaigned against this nine-party alliance, but his foes, led by former Air Marshal Asghar Khan, could point to many problems in the country. The government had spent lavishly on luxury items, crime had increased sharply, and most of the recently nationalized industries were producing nothing. As the campaign progressed, many opposition candidates were detained by police when they needed to file election papers.

After the elections for the National Assembly on March 7, the PNP was allowed only 17 percent of the seats despite winning more than 35 percent of the popular vote. The PNA boycotted the provincial elections two days later and instigated strikes and street disturbances. At the same time, the shah of Iran refused to guarantee a $300 million loan from Citibank, leaving Bhutto helpless in his struggle against inflation and reduced to jailing thousands of PNA protesters and their leaders. From this point, chaos reigned in the streets until General Mohammad Zia ul-Haq led the July 4 coup that ended Bhutto's tumultuous career.

The Coup of 1977

Despite his enormous popularity as the *Quaid-i-Awam* (leader of the people), Zulfikar Ali Bhutto's scheming and bad judgment led to his overthrow in a military coup led by General Mohammad Zia ul-Haq on the night of July 4, 1977. As prime minister, Bhutto gutted the constitution by manipulating the parliament, packed his government with sycophants and spies, and recklessly nationalized banks and industries. The results of these policies were economic disaster and riots that led to as many as three hundred deaths after rigged elections were held in March, 1977.

Bhutto had named General Zia his army chief of staff in 1976, underestimating him as a servile lackey whom he could publicly humiliate and trust to do as he was told. Zia surprised everyone by imprisoning Bhutto and eventually putting him on trial for the 1974 ambush murder of Nawab Ahmed Khan Kasuri, whose son was a fierce critic of Bhutto. In September, 1978, Zia named himself president of Pakistan, and three months later the High Court pronounced Bhutto guilty. Bhutto was hanged on April 4, 1979. General Zia frequently promised to hold an election but never did. He died in August, 1988, when his plane blew up mysteriously.

Pakistani president Zulfikar Ali Bhutto in December, 1971, the month he took power from Agha Mohammad Yahya Khan. (*AP/Wide World Photos*)

Zulfikar Ali Bhutto was a brilliant man with an apparently genuine desire to alleviate the misery of Pakistan's many sufferers in poverty, and he attracted many followers. Yet he was also an arrogant lover of power who finally could not rise above feudal values and squandered his genius in follies. He was executed in 1979 after being convicted of murdering a political opponent in 1974.

Bibliography

Akhund, Iqbal. *Memoirs of a Bystander: A Life in Diplomacy.* New York: Oxford University Press, 1998.

Raza, Rafi. *Zulfikar Ali Bhutto and Pakistan, 1967-1977.* New York: Oxford University Press, 1997.

Wolpert, Stanley. *Zulfi Bhutto of Pakistan: His Life and Times.* New York: Oxford University Press, 1993.

Frank Day

Hugo L. Black

Born: February 27, 1886; Harlan, Alabama
Died: September 25, 1971; Bethesda, Maryland

U.S. jurist and Supreme Court justice (1937-1971)

Hugo Lafayette Black (HEW-goh la-fih-YEHT BLAK) was born on a farm in rural Alabama. His father, William Black, was a storekeeper and farmer; his mother was Martha Toland Black. Black's early years were spent on the farm. He picked cotton and became a typesetter for the local newspaper. He was educated at the local public schools, which had very limited facilities. After a brief stint in medical school, he entered the law school at the University of Alabama, graduating in 1907. He began practice in Birmingham later that year. He soon became a police court judge for the city of Birmingham. Then, after serving in the army, he returned to practice

Hugo L. Black *(Library of Congress)*

in Birmingham, where he was very successful. In 1921 he married Josephine Foster, with whom he had three children. In 1925 he decided to run for the U.S. Senate. He won easily after a strenuous campaign in which he positioned himself as a Democrat of liberal populist views.

Black's Senatorial Career

Black became a major supporter of the New Deal and ultimately one of President Franklin D. Roosevelt's most effective lieutenants. In his first years in the Senate he allied himself with the liberals, including some progressive Republicans. In his second term, he sponsored the bill that became the Fair Labor Standards Act (1938), which is the basic wage-hour legislation of the United States. He also participated effectively in investigations of merchant marine and airline subsidies and of the utility lobby. By the time of his appointment to the Supreme Court in 1937, Black had developed strong ideas about many issues on which he would later have to vote as a justice.

Black had come to believe that the Supreme Court's practice of deciding what rights are fundamental gave too much power to the judiciary. He was solidly committed to free speech and fairness in criminal procedure. His investigative experiences in the Senate had made him very strongly antimonopoly. His liberalism was widely known when, in August, 1937, President Roosevelt appointed him to the Supreme Court. Although conservatives attacked the nomination, Black's reputation, combined with his popularity in the Senate, brought about a quick confirmation vote of 63 to 16. A few days later Black and his wife went to Europe on a vacation. While they were abroad, a controversy over Black's earlier Ku Klux Klan membership erupted.

Supreme Court justices Hugo L. Black (left) and Robert Jackson at a private film screening in 1942. *(Archive Photos)*

Constitutional Achievements

Black served for thirty-four years as an associate justice of the Supreme Court. He became especially well known for his staunch support of civil rights. He believed that the original purpose of the Fourteenth Amendment was to safeguard the guaranteed liberties of the Bill of Rights against state governments as well as against the

Hugo Black and the Ku Klux Klan

While Hugo Black and his wife were on vacation in Europe after the Senate vote confirming his Supreme Court appointment, the Pittsburgh *Post Gazette* revealed that he had been a member of the Ku Klux Klan from 1923 to 1925. This fact had been well known in Alabama. Attacks were launched on Black, and a few of his supporters changed their positions. Black, whose vacation was ruined by persistent press intrusion, re-mained silent until his return to the United States. On October 1, 1937, he gave a national radio speech saying that indeed he had been a member of the Klan, but that he had resigned years before and had had no further contact with the organization. Public opinion shifted in Black's favor after his speech, and the controversy quickly disappeared.

U.S. Supreme Court justice Hugo L. Black in 1966. Already the oldest member of the Court, he remained on the bench for another five years. *(AP/Wide World Photos)*

ported fairness in criminal prosecutions and was the author of the Court's unanimous opinion in *Gideon v. Wainwright* (1963), holding that indigent defendants have the right to court-appointed counsel in all criminal prosecutions. Black consistently joined with the majority in voting to strike down racial discrimination in and after the Supreme Court's decision in *Brown v. Board of Education* (1954), which outlawed segregated schools. He also wrote for the Court in striking down President Harry S Truman's seizure of the steel mills in 1953, thus helping to define the extent of executive power.

Bibliography

Ball, Howard. *Hugo L. Black: Cold Steel Warrior.* New York: Oxford University Press, 1996.

Black, Hugo L., and Elizabeth Black. *Mr. Justice and Mrs. Black: The Memoirs of Hugo L. Black and Elizabeth Black.* New York: Random House, 1986.

Black, Hugo, Jr. *My Father: A Remembrance.* New York: Random House, 1975.

Frank, John P. *Mr. Justice Black.* New York: Knopf, 1949.

Newman, Roger K. *Hugo Black: A Biography.* New York: Pantheon Books, 1994.

Robert Jacobs

federal government. He believed that the First Amendment rights of freedom of religion and speech are nearly absolute. He strongly sup-

Tony Blair

Born: May 6, 1953; Edinburgh, Scotland

Prime minister of Great Britain (took office 1997)

Anthony Charles Lynton Blair (AN-tho-nee "TOH-nee" CHAHRLZ LIHN-tuhn BLAYR) was the eldest of three children born to Leo Blair, a middle-class attorney with political aspirations, and Hazel, a homemaker. His family moved to Durham, England, when he was ten years old so that his father could run for Parliament as a Conservative. When his father suffered a massive stroke during the campaign, the Blair family had to live under considerably straitened circumstances. Tony Blair attended Fettes College boarding school in Edinburgh on a partial scholarship. In 1972 he entered Oxford. After he graduated in 1975, Blair joined the Labour Party and studied employment and industrial law in London. There he met his wife, a fellow lawyer, Cherie Booth, whom he married in 1980. Together they had three children.

Early Political Life

In his early thirties, Blair decided to enter politics rather than to pursue a career in law. In 1983 he was elected to Parliament from Sedgefield at a time when the Labour Party was facing a crucial decline in influence; it had the fewest seats it had held since World War II. Not discouraged, Blair quickly displayed his ambition to improve aspects of British trade and industry. Throughout the 1980's, Blair increased his political presence as he addressed Parliament on matters of trade and industry.

By 1988 he had been elected to the shadow cabinet (the cabinet of the opposition party, the party not in power) and was appointed shadow secretary of state for energy. A year later, he became the shadow secretary of state for employment. One of his main goals as a moderate reformer was to stop meeting the demands of strong labor unions. In 1992 Labour leader John

Smith appointed Blair shadow home secretary. This position propelled him into the Labour Party's ruling elite, its National Executive Committee, later the same year. In this capacity, Blair pushed for mass party leadership, so that by the late 1990's Labour had the fastest-growing membership in Europe.

At the unexpected death of Smith in 1994, Blair at age forty-one became the youngest leader of the opposition party to date. At his first party conference in September, 1994, he affirmed a program of modernization and change within the

Tony Blair *(Popperfoto/Archive Photos)*

149

New Labour

Britain's Labour Party became known as "New Labour" during the early 1980's under the auspices of Neil Kinnock. It sought to distance itself from the older anticapitalist Labour Party. Since the 1950's, Labour revisionists had attempted to redefine the party's goals and identity while it suffered from political division, inefficient administration, differing philosophical ideals, and mistrust between leaders and members.

Tony Blair and fellow reformer Gordon Brown

were two of the key architects of the new philosophy. New Labour combined a sense of morality and efficiency, and it connected constitutional and political reform to economic reform. Ideologically, the party stressed community, personal responsibility, and cooperation rather than competition. Blair and other New Labour leaders argued that education and skill are imperative for economic vitality and that social reform and government spending must be balanced to maintain an effectively running government.

Labour Party. He sought to minimize the party's attachment to socialism and to emphasize certain radical elements instead. By adjusting the party's membership and reassigning key leaders, Blair

worked to revise the party's goals. In particular, he helped eliminate the much-debated Clause IV of the party's constitution, which had linked the Labour platform to socialist economics. He advocated civil rights, political democracy, and a mixed economy in which the public would control major utilities. He promoted the idea that education, skill, and personal responsibility formed the basis of a strong economy. Although the program met some resistance from some of the larger public-sector unions, Blair's "New Labour" campaign was generally well received by the party and the public. As the power and influence of the Conservative Party declined, the influence of the Labour Party grew steadily with Blair at its helm. In 1996 Blair published *New Britain: My Vision of a Young Country*, a collection of his speeches on social and economic policy, education, and the New Labour agenda.

British prime minister Tony Blair in 1997 visiting British peacekeeping troops in Bosnia. *(Reuters/Ian Waldie/Archive Photos)*

Prime Minister

In 1997 Tony Blair became prime minister of Great Britain. As the leader of government and a self-proclaimed radical, Blair worked to implement the policies of New Labour, promising to refashion British politics, reforge a new coalition in government, and mend Britain's divided society. He and his cabinet created a "welfare-to-work" program to educate welfare recipients and turn them into contributing members of Britain's workforce. To alleviate long-term unemployment among capable young people, his cabinet gave tax breaks to participating employers and withheld social security from people who refused to work. Furthermore, Blair, believing that education is the bedrock of a strong economy, pledged to cut class size in schools and to improve the quality of teaching.

Blair and his ministers also sought to improve domestic accord throughout the nation. Blair pledged tougher measures against crime, asserting that criminals must be punished for their actions regardless of their socioeconomic status. Blair's government also attempted to establish more peaceable relations with Northern Ireland parties, including Sinn Féin, the political wing of the Irish Republican Army (IRA).

Tony Blair's image as a hardworking man of the people catapulted him through the ranks of the Labour Party and into the post of prime minister. While critics called Blair opportunistic and questioned his motives, many Labour Party members and members of the electorate throughout the nation embraced his constitutional reforms and his emphasis on individual responsibility. As prime minister and heir to Labour's revisionist spirit, Blair made tough choices in implementing social policy as he balanced compassion and public funds. Overall, Blair's commitment to social issues and revitalizing the economy fortified and invigorated the Labour Party, transforming it from a fragmented opposition party into an organized, vibrant political force.

The General Election of 1997

On May 2, 1997, Tony Blair and the Labour Party defeated his conservative opponent, incumbent prime minister John Major, in an electoral landslide. For six weeks Blair promised not only a new kind of Labour Party but a new kind of government as well. Ever a savvy politician, Blair had campaigned with little hint that raising interest rates and taxes would be necessary to curtail rising inflation. He also promised to limit public spending as his Tory predecessors had, even though polls indicated that the British public favored raising taxes so that the government could spend more. Instead, Blair made several key pledges in a favorably received ten-point contract with Britain. Some of the constitutional changes he proposed included the creation of a Scottish parliament with the ability to tax and a bill of rights, and the use of proportional representation to determine how many seats each party should have.

Even though both parties asserted that Britain must remain in the European Union (EU) to maintain economic and political viability, neither party actively defended the EU during the campaign. Polls conducted between 1991 and 1997 revealed that initially two-thirds of voters favored Britain's membership, but the proportion had slipped to only half by 1997. Throughout the election Blair cautiously avoided discussions of the merits of the EU; he let others question the value of continued British membership while he focused more on domestic concerns.

British prime minister Tony Blair (center) in Gaza for April, 1998, talks with Palestinian leader Yasir Arafat (to the left of Blair). *(Reuters/David Silverman/Archive Photos)*

Bibliography

Foote, Geoffrey. *The Labour Party's Political Thought: A History*. New York: St. Martin's Press, 1997.

Lloyd, John. "The Blair Story." *New Statesman* 126 (May, 1997): 53-100.

Pelling, Henry, and Alastair J. Reid. *A Short History of the Labour Party*. 11th ed. New York: St. Martin's Press, 1996.

Susanna Calkins

Léon Blum

Born: April 8, 1872; Paris, France
Died: March 30, 1950; Jouy-en-Josas, near Paris, France

French socialist leader, premier of France (1936-1937)

Léon Blum (lay-O BLEWM) was born into a middle-class Jewish family. After studying literature and philosophy at the prestigious Superior Normal School of Paris, he earned a degree in law at the Sorbonne in 1895. Until World War I, he pursued a legal career as a jurist of the Council of State, the highest administrative court of the country, and at the same time wrote highly respected books on literary criticism.

Early Career

Blum first entered the political arena when he became an outspoken opponent of anti-Semitism

Léon Blum *(Library of Congress)*

during the Dreyfus affair of the 1890's. In 1897 he was converted to the humanistic vision of socialism taught by Jean Jaurès, and he became convinced that socialist principles provided a moral foundation for establishing a just society. Although he joined the French Socialist Party in 1902, his political efforts prior to 1914 were generally confined to intellectual circles.

With the outbreak of World War I in 1914, Blum argued that the survival of the French Republic was necessary to the success of socialism, and he worked as cabinet chief of Marcel Sembat, socialist minister of public works. After the war he was elected to the Chamber of Deputies in 1919. He soon became the intellectual spokesman of those democratic socialists who attacked the authoritarian policies of the Russian Bolsheviks.

A believer in unchanging universal values, Blum disagreed with the Marxist thesis that a society's values are determined by its economic system. Rather than violent revolution, he defended the democratic and republican ideals within the traditions of French socialism.

Socialist Leadership

At the 1920 Socialist Party Congress of Tours, the majority of delegates voted to join the new French Communist Party, while Blum was the recognized leader of the minority that remained within the Socialist Party (the SFIO). As director of the party's newspaper, his daily editorial writings demonstrated thoughtful analysis and balanced judgment. Gradually, during the 1920's, Blum helped the SFIO to build a solid base of support.

After the party showed growth in the elections of 1924 and 1932, Blum declined invitations to join center-left coalitions led by the Radical Party.

The Popular Front

During the 1930's, popular fronts were left-wing coalitions that included communist parties. In France, following the riots led by right-wing leagues in 1934, the three major parties of the Left—Socialists, Communists, and Radicals—began to meet together in common demonstrations. For the general elections of 1936, the three parties agreed to a Popular Front coalition, and their common program endorsed more rights for labor unions, a reduction of the work week, an expansion of public works, and an anti-fascist foreign policy.

After the coalition won a parliamentary majority on May 3, 1936, Socialist leader Léon Blum became premier over a Popular Front cabinet. Faced with an unprecedented wave of strikes, Blum negotiated the Matignon agreements, in which workers and unions obtained many of their demands. The three parties, however, strongly disagreed on key issues. Early in 1937, the Radicals pushed Blum to announce a "pause" in new social programs, which infuriated Communists and the unions. Those on the far Left also denounced Blum's policy of nonintervention in the Spanish Civil War. On June 22, 1937, a Radical became premier, soon followed by a rotation of unstable governments. By November, 1938, the Popular Front had completely collapsed.

The French Left usually praised the Popular Front for achieving reforms in labor law, nationalizing the Bank of France and the railroads, and restraining French fascism. The Right responded that these policies damaged the economy, increased social unrest, and did not prepare France for the war.

He explained that the SFIO would seek either a "conquest of power" or an "exercise of power." The party would try to transform society only if it could win a decisive electoral victory. During a national emergency, however, the SFIO would be ready to lead a coalition government if it became the strongest party within a parliamentary majority, and in such a situation it would honor the wishes expressed by the voters and respect the legal requirements of the constitution.

For the election of 1936, Blum's fear of fascism persuaded him to champion the Popular Front coalition, which brought together Communists, Radicals, and Socialists. Because the SFIO emerged as the leading partner within the victorious coalition, Blum was installed as France's first Socialist and first Jewish premier on June 4. Blum's Popular Front government accomplished a number of reforms, including the forty-hour week, collective bargaining, and compulsory arbitration. The government also partially nationalized the Bank of France and the munitions industry.

The coalition was difficult to hold together, however. Blum's decision not to intervene in the Spanish Civil War angered Communist Party members and left-wing socialists. Early in 1937, the Radicals convinced Blum to postpone social legislation, resulting in violent disturbances led by communist unions. He resigned in June after the conservative Senate refused to grant his government special financial powers. In 1938 Blum briefly served as premier for a second time, but with few accomplishments.

Later Career

With the fall of France in 1940, Blum was one of only thirty-six deputies to vote against General Henri Philippe Pétain, premier of unoccupied France. Arrested by the Vichy government (the government installed to cooperate with the German occupation), Blum, a Jew, became a major defendant in the war-guilt trials at Riom. Although his eloquent defense forced a suspension of the trials, he was kept in French and German prisons until liberated by the Americans in 1945. While a prisoner, he supported the Resistance, led by General Charles de Gaulle, and wrote his testament, *For All Mankind*, which defended a humanist view of socialism.

As an elder statesman, Blum continued to be the leader of the Socialist Party and to write for the party's newspaper. Many of his efforts were toward a "third force" which opposed the communists on the Left and General de Gaulle on the Right. In 1946 he negotiated a credit agreement with the United States, and he was premier over a caretaker government that lasted only one month in 1946-1947. This brief premiership occurred during a period of great economic difficulty—it was also during this month that the war in Indochina (later Vietnam) began.

One of the important socialist leaders of the twentieth century, Léon Blum was committed to a democratic and moral conception of socialism, opposing violence and seeking a democratic enlargement of justice and well-being. As prime minister of the Popular Front, often called the French New Deal, his policies established significant re-

Beneath a huge poster of himself, French socialist leader Léon Blum addresses a crowd in Poissy, France, in 1936. *(National Archives)*

The Matignon Agreements

In May, 1936, just before Léon Blum assumed office as premier of the Popular Front government, more than a million French workers participated in sit-down strikes. To end the strikes, the Blum government, on June 7-8, signed the Matignon agreements, which recognized the right of workers to join unions, raised salaries between 7 and 15 percent, and established the forty-hour week and paid vacations. Strikes continued anyway and only gradually ended. The agreements are considered the most significant achievement of the Popular Front, and they became permanent features of labor relations in France. Conservatives argued that the agreements adversely affected the French economy and national defense.

forms in labor legislation and increased the role of the state. Economically, Blum's government was not successful, and military authorities later concluded that he did not do enough to rearm the country in preparation for World War II. Even his critics, however, considered him a man of great integrity and personal courage.

Bibliography

Blum, Léon. *For All Mankind*. Translated by W. Pickles. New York: Viking, 1946.

Colton, Joel. *Léon Blum: A Humanist in Politics*. New York: Knopf, 1966.

Joll, James. *Three Biographical Essays*. London: Weidenfeld and Nicolson, 1960.

Thomas T. Lewis

William E. Borah

Born: June 29, 1865; Jasper Township, Illinois
Died: January 19, 1940; Washington, D.C.

Longtime U.S. senator (1907-1940)

William Edgar Borah (WIHL-yuhm EHD-gur BOH-rah), the son of a strict farmer, had no interest in joining the ministry, the profession his father urged him to follow. Determined to become a lawyer, Borah attended the University of Kansas until tuberculosis forced him to withdraw during his second year of studies. He completed his law studies in his brother-in-law's office, passing the Kansas bar exam in 1887. Because opportunities in Kansas were limited, Borah headed west, establishing a law office in Boise, Idaho, in 1890. Five years later he married Mary O'Connell. They had no children.

Senator Borah

Borah quickly achieved prominence in Idaho's Republican Party. In 1906 the state legislature elected him to the U.S. Senate. He served in the Senate until his death. On domestic issues, Senator Borah advocated progressive reforms, including the direct election of senators and the establishment of a federal income tax. However, he opposed efforts to regulate corporate monopolies on the grounds that government agencies would only perpetuate the existence of the monopolies. After receiving a seat on the Senate Foreign Relation Committee in 1913, Borah became an outspoken critic of President Woodrow Wilson's foreign policy, especially in regard to Mexico. Nonetheless, he voted for the president's request for a declaration of war against Germany in 1917 (thus bringing the country into World War I), maintaining that the United States had to protect its rights as a nation. Although he continued to support American involvement in the conflict, he condemned many wartime measures, such as the Espionage Act, which he regarded as a violation of the First Amendment.

Foreign Policy Leader

Borah's influence over American foreign policy grew during the debate over the Treaty of Versailles, the peace treaty drafted at the end of World War I in 1918. The treaty included provisions for American membership in the League of Nations. As the leader of the "irreconcilables," a group of Republicans adamantly opposed to U.S. participation in any international organization, Borah played a key role in defeating ratification of the treaty in the U.S. Congress. During the

William E. Borah *(Library of Congress)*

157

U.S. senator William E. Borah questioning a witness in a 1938 Senate Judiciary Subcommittee meeting. *(AP/Wide World Photos)*

1920's and 1930's, he also hampered American efforts to join the World Court because it was a subsidiary of the League of Nations. However, Borah's rejection of international associations did not mean that he opposed negotiation and cooperation with foreign nations. A proponent of disarmament as the most effective means of preventing war, Borah advocated international arms talks. At his suggestion, American diplomats convened the Washington Conference in 1921, a meeting that led to arms limitation treaties between the United States, Japan, and several European nations. Throughout the 1920's, Borah urged the United States to offer diplomatic rec-

ognition to the Soviet Union, a cause that did not meet with success until 1933.

In 1924 Borah became chairman of the Senate Foreign Relations Committee, a position which made him a leader in the creation of American foreign policy. Presidents Calvin Coolidge and Herbert Hoover both paid careful attention to Borah's views. His call for a multinational treaty outlawing war resulted in the 1927 Kellogg-Briand Pact (an agreement that contained no measures for enforcement). Borah's power waned after the Democrats won the White House and both houses of Congress in the elections of 1932. In the early days of World War II, Borah

The Isolationists

During the 1920's and 1930's, many Americans believed that the United States should not enter into political or military alliances with other nations. Known as isolationists, the advocates of this policy argued that such alliances would eventually draw the United States into another war. Their opposition to involvement with foreign governments did not extend necessarily to economic and cultural ties, which most isolationists recognized as beneficial to American interests. The isolationists remained a powerful force in American politics until the late 1930's, when the threat to world peace that the Germans represented could no longer be ignored. As a leading isolationist in the senate, William Borah wielded great influence over the conduct of U.S. foreign policy during an era in which the United States failed to offer international leadership.

advocated strict neutrality even as President Franklin D. Roosevelt and the American people gradually turned to the support of Great Britain and France. At the time of his death he remained convinced that American involvement in the European conflict would have disastrous consequences for the nation.

Bibliography

Ashby, Leroy. *The Spearless Leader Senator Borah and the Progressive Movement in the 1920's.* Chicago: University of Illinois Press, 1972.

Maddox, Robert James. *William E. Borah and American Foreign Policy*. Baton Rouge: Louisiana State University Press, 1969.

McKenna, Marian C. *Borah*. Ann Arbor: University of Michigan Press, 1961.

Miller, Karen A. J. *Populist Nationalism: Republican Insurgency and American Foreign Policy Making, 1918-1925*. Westport, Conn.: Greenwood Press, 1999.

Thomas Clarkin

Robert Laird Borden

Born: June 26, 1854; Grand Pré, Nova Scotia, Canada
Died: June 10, 1937; Ottawa, Ontario, Canada

Prime minister of Canada (1911-1920)

Robert Laird Borden (RO-burt LAYRD BOHR-dehn) was descended of English and Scottish ancestors. His father and mother maintained a farm. Robert attended Acacia Villa Seminary. A brilliant student, he was made assistant master at fourteen. Eventually bored with teaching, he studied law and served his apprenticeship as a clerk in a leading Halifax law firm. After being called to the bar in 1878, he practiced in Kentville, Nova Scotia. In 1889 he married Laura Bond and became a senior partner in the firm of Graham and Tupper. He sometimes argued cases before the Supreme Court in Ottawa and attended the Judicial Committee of the Privy Council in Lon-don. His political career began when Prime Minister Charles Tupper, a father of confederation, persuaded him to run as a Conservative in Halifax in the 1896 federal election.

Conservative Politician

The Liberal Party, under the leadership of Wilfrid Laurier, won the 1896 elections, attaining a twenty-eight-seat majority. Borden, however, won his seat, and in Parliament he made a name for himself by attacking government patronage and the corrupt civil service. After becoming Conservative Party leader when Tupper resigned in 1900, Borden promoted a stronger connection with England while also supporting nationalism. He agreed that the Canadian West should control its own resources and lands, just as the East did. Borden proposed a second transcontinental railway, to be owned and run by the government, as competition for the Canadian Pacific. The Canadian Pacific line could not handle the increasing traffic to and from the wheat-rich West.

However, the disorganization of the Conservatives, and Borden's calls for racial selectivity in immigration, gave the 1904 election to the Liberals, who increased their majority in Parliament. Borden lost his own Nova Scotia constituency, but his offer to resign as party leader was turned down. Arrangements were made to win him an easy seat in a by-election in Carleton, Ontario. This win led him to give up his law practice and settle with his family in Ottawa.

Prewar and Wartime Prime Minister

In 1908, after winning two seats (Carleton and Halifax), Borden decided to represent Halifax while participating in House of Commons debates. He argued against Liberal policies, insist-

Robert Laird Borden *(Library of Congress)*

ing that Laurier's Naval Bill was hopelessly inadequate to meet an international emergency. He regarded the Reciprocity Agreement with the United States as a threat to Canadian commercial and financial independence. The 1911 election, in which Borden won the support of business people, manufacturers, bankers, railway men, and influential Liberal Clifford Sifton, returned the Conservatives to power and made Borden prime minister.

Borden fashioned the Naval Aid Bill, which offered three ships to the British navy as part of a permanent system of cooperative control of imperial defense and foreign policy by all members of the commonwealth. The bill was defeated by the Liberal-dominated Senate, but the setback did not deter Borden's efforts to prepare for war.

World War I broke out in 1914, the year Borden was knighted by Britain's King George V. Borden invoked the War Measures Act, putting most of Parliament's power into the cabinet's hands. He also imposed the first direct taxation by Ottawa (the wartime business profits tax of 1916 and the

Robert Laird Borden (left) with Britain's Arthur Balfour at the Washington armament conference of 1922. *(Library of Congress)*

income tax of 1917). The wartime economy thrived because of the taxes and "victory loans," and Borden won servicemen's support by visiting them in England and at the French front and by creating a Ministry of Overseas Military Forces in 1916.

Borden was part of British prime minister David Lloyd George's Imperial War Cabinet and

The Imperial War Cabinet

When David Lloyd George replaced H. H. Asquith as British prime minister in December, 1916, he created a five-man war cabinet for policy discussions. World War I had been raging in Europe for more than two years. The prime ministers of Australia, Canada, New Zealand, and Newfoundland and representatives of India were to serve as equals in an enlarged cabinet to discuss the conduct and conclusion of the war and possible postwar problems. In 1918, Robert Laird Borden spoke at length about incompe-

tence, disorganization, and confusion at the front. His speeches prompted Lloyd George to appoint a special subcommittee whose duty was to obtain information, from every possible source, regarding precisely what efforts would be necessary to win the war. Borden assisted in the preparation of a report, but a month later, this document was irrelevant: The war had abruptly ended. Borden subsequently participated in negotiating peace conditions.

The Women's Franchise Bill of 1918

On March 22, 1918, Robert Laird Borden explained to the House of Commons why a bill to give women the right to vote was necessary. Women had played an important role in the war effort by working in factories, taking jobs usually done by men, and contributing knitted goods and other items deemed necessary for Canadian forces overseas. They were therefore entitled to the franchise—the right to vote—on their own merits. Moreover, as women already had the right to vote in five provinces, it seemed advisable to give them voting rights across the dominion. The Women's Franchise Bill provided that every female British subject of twenty-one or older should be entitled to vote at a dominion election provided she possessed the same qualifications as an entitled male.

the Imperial War Conference. Borden argued that Canada and the other dominions should have autonomous voices in war policy. In return, he enforced conscription (the drafting of men into the Canadian military), which was met with considerable hostility by farmers, organized labor, and French Quebecers. Knowing that the national war effort would be best served by a coalition or union government, he brought one into being in October, 1917, with the help of conscriptionist Liberals. The union government won a resounding majority in the election. It demonstrated its aggressive nationalism through the Military Voters Act and War Times Election Act, which extended voting rights to women relatives of British or Canadian forces but which took away the vote from conscientious objectors.

Postwar Achievements

In 1918, Borden passed a bill eliminating patronage, reformed the civil service, and gave women the right to vote in national elections with the Women's Franchise Bill. In November, after World War I had ended, he led the Canadian delegation to the Paris Peace Conference and exercised Canada's autonomous vote.

Postwar Canada was caught in labor and political unrest. In poor health, Borden resigned from office in 1920. He spent the remaining years of his life representing Canada at the Washington conference on naval disarmament, promoting the League of Nations (he was chief Canadian delegate to its Assembly in 1930), serving as chancellor at McGill and Queen's Universities, delivering public lectures at Oxford and the University of Toronto, and writing his memoirs.

Though he lacked Laurier's eloquence and political cunning and Sir John A. Macdonald's adroit abilities of manipulation, Borden excelled at creating policy. His state papers were always well argued and documented. His high sense of duty served him admirably in his successful attempts to achieve dominion status for Canada and to turn the British Empire into the British Commonwealth of Nations. He always sought to make Canadians accept their national and international responsibilities.

Bibliography

Borden, Robert Laird. *Robert Laird Borden: His Memoirs*. Edited by Henry Borden. Toronto: Macmillan, 1938.

Brown, Robert Craig. *Robert Laird Borden: A Biography*. Vol. 1, *1854-1914*. Toronto: Macmillan, 1975.

English, John. *Borden: His Life and World*. Toronto: McGraw-Hill Ryerson, 1977.

Saunders, Kathleen. *Robert Borden*. Don Mills, Ontario: Fitzhenry & Whiteside, 1978.

Keith Garebian

Louis Botha

Born: September 27, 1862; near Greytown, Natal
Died: August 27, 1919; Pretoria, Transvaal, Union of South Africa

First prime minister of Union of South Africa (1910-1919)

Louis Botha (LEW-ihs BOH-tah) was born near Greytown, Natal (then a British colony, later part of the Union of South Africa), the son of German immigrants. His family was part of the Voortrekkers, the pioneers who settled the inland parts of South Africa. He moved with his family to the Orange Free State (now the Free State) and was educated at a German-language school operated by missionaries. He became a sheep rancher after leaving home and moved to Zululand, where he quickly became involved in politics. He was one of the Boers, South Africans of Dutch or German descent, who fought on the side of the Zulus in tribal wars, and he was recognized for his military skill. In 1884, at the age of twenty-two, he helped found the New Republic, based in Vryheid, a part of Zululand. After the republic failed, he moved to the Transvaal, where he settled permanently.

The Boer War

Botha married an Irish woman, Annie Emmett, and then entered Transvaal politics. Botha was a political moderate, and he tried to reduce the antagonism that was developing between the Boers and the British. He consistently opposed President Paul Kruger's efforts to restrict the growing British presence in the Witwatersrand in the 1890's. In 1895 the South African Republic appointed him as emissary in Swaziland, and in 1897 he won election to the Volksraad, the Transvaal parliament. When the Boer War began in 1899 he was appointed assistant general in Natal and led Boer forces at several major battles. He commanded the southern Boer army, which, although outnumbered, held the Tugela River against British forces until February, 1900, when the British broke through his lines. After the

death of General Piet Joubert in 1900, Botha became commandant-general of the Transvaal forces. In spite of the reversals suffered by the Boers' forces, he distinguished himself as an outstanding leader.

By 1901 Botha realized that the war could not be won and began peace talks with the British. At first they came to nothing. By 1902, however, the Boer leadership realized that the war was lost, and Botha was the main figure in negotiating the peace conference at Vereeniging. It ended the Boer War and produced the Treaty of Vereeniging, signed on May 31, 1902. According to this treaty

Louis Botha *(Library of Congress)*

the Boers recognized British sovereignty, and the Transvaal and the Orange Free State became British Crown Colonies with a promise of representative government in the future. The Transvaal gained responsible government in 1906 and the Orange River Colony in 1907.

Prime Minister

Botha was a conciliator by nature. Once the war had ended, he understood that Boer independence would never be a reality and that it was essential to work within the political structure established by the British. This policy lost him considerable support in the Boer community, but he forged ahead and took the lead in establishing the party known as *Het Volk*. In spite of opposition from the right wing, his leadership skills allowed him to win election as the first prime minister of the Transvaal in 1907. At the national convention in 1909, where the structure of the Union of South Africa was established, he was chosen as the first premier of the Union of South Africa, an office he held until his death in 1919. Botha continued his conciliatory policies. These led to a break with Afrikaaners led by James B. M.

Herzog (1866-1942), who later formed the National Party.

World War I

When Great Britain declared war on Germany on August 4, 1914, most of Britain's self-governing dominions (members of the British Commonwealth) followed suit. South Africa did not, although it was the only dominion that had German troops on its borders—in German Southwest Africa (Namibia). Botha did support the British and the Allied cause against the Germans in World War I, however, a move that aroused much opposition from Afrikaaners who viewed the war as yet another example of British imperialism and hoped that a German victory would bring about independence from Great Britain.

One result of Botha's pro-British policy was the Rebellion of 1914, which lasted from October, 1914, to February, 1915, and included a number of officers and men who were scheduled to invade German Southwest Africa. The Germans had planned to use German Southwest Africa as a base from which to attack South Africa and,

---

The Boer War

In 1877 the British annexed the Transvaal region of southern Africa, a move that aroused much antagonism from the Boers—descendants of Dutch and German settlers—who lived there. The Boers in the Transvaal rebelled against the British and established the South African Republic. On August 3, 1881, the Convention of Pretoria gave the Transvaal self-government. In 1895 Paul Kruger (1825-1904), president of the Transvaal, closed the province's borders to British traders from the Cape Colony. Anti-Boer forces then orchestrated a raid on Johannesburg led by Leander Jameson (1835-1917) that was easily put down. Kruger continued to discriminate against

non-Boers, and on March 24, 1899, the *Uitlanders* (non-Boer residents of South Africa) sent an appeal for help to Queen Victoria.

Negotiations failed, and on October 11, 1899, the Boer War, known in South Africa as the South African War, began between Great Britain and the Transvaal and the Orange Free State. At first the Boers were successful and won easy victories. However, superior British resources ultimately triumphed over the vastly outnumbered Boers. The war was formally ended by the Treaty of Vereeniging on May 31, 1902, in which the Transvaal and the Orange Free State became British Crown Colonies.

The Union of South Africa

South Africa was composed of four constituent territories, the former Boer republics of the Transvaal, the Orange Free State, and the British colonies Cape of Good Hope and Natal. In 1909 a series of meetings took place in Durban, Cape Town, and Bloemfontein to prepare a legal framework for union of the four areas. White delegates from the four areas met under the chairmanship of Chief Justice Baron de Villiers and drafted a bill to be sent to the British Parliament. The South Africa Act, commonly known as the Act of Union, was passed in 1909 and took effect in 1910. Main features of the act included the establishment of three capital cities: Cape Town as the legislative center, Pretoria as the administrative center, and Bloemfontein as the judicial capital. The act made Dutch (later to be replaced by Afrikaans) equal to English, and it established a parliamentary system based on that of Great Britain with local authorities having considerable administrative power. The union's first general election, won by Louis Botha's South African Nationalist Party, was held on September 15, 1910.

they hoped, to support a Boer uprising against the British. Botha suppressed the rebellion and led sixty thousand South African troops in an attack on German Southwest Africa. Germany had only twenty thousand troops stationed in their colony and retreated as the South Africans advanced. They surrendered on July 9, 1915.

General Botha attended the Peace Conference at Versailles in 1919 and signed the Treaty of Versailles on behalf of the Union of South Africa along with Jan Smuts (1870-1950). They signed as representatives of an independent nation. As part of the treaty, South Africa received a League of Nations mandate to govern Southwest Africa.

Bibliography

Muller, C. F. J. *Five Hundred Years: A History of South Africa*. Cape Town, South Africa: H & R Academia, 1981.

Pakenham, Thomas. *The Boer War*. London: Weidenfeld and Nicolson, 1979.

Smith, Iain R. *The Origins of the South African War, 1899-1902*. Essex, England: Longman, 1996.

Warwick, Peter, and S. B. Speis, eds. *The South African War: The Anglo-Boer War, 1899-1902*. Essex, England: Longman, 1980.

C. James Haug

In 1900 Louis Botha became commandant-general of the Transvaal forces in the Boer War. Two years later he was the main figure in the peace conference that ended the fighting. *(Library of Congress)*

Lucien Bouchard

Born: December 22, 1938; Saint-Coeur-de-Marie, Quebec, Canada

Quebec premier (took office 1996) and separatist leader

The son of a truck driver, Lucien Bouchard (lew-see-EH bew-SHAHR) grew up in the Lac-Saint-Jean region of Quebec. He attended Laval University in Quebec City, where he earned two degrees and made friends with Brian Mulroney. Before beginning his political career, Bouchard practiced law for a number of years in Chicoutimi, Quebec, where he was active in various labor relations organizations and public commissions.

A Checkered Political Background

Bouchard's early political sympathies aligned him with the "quiet revolution" and the Quebec Liberal Party of Jean Lesage. He also supported

Lucien Bouchard *(AP/Wide World Photos)*

Pierre Trudeau, who became prime minister of Canada in 1968. The government's crackdown on separatist terrorism in Quebec in 1970 known as the "October crisis" struck Bouchard as excessive, however, and he joined the separatist Parti Québécois soon afterward.

When Brian Mulroney was elected Canadian prime minister in 1984, Bouchard was appointed ambassador to France, a post that he held until 1988. There he played an important role in the creation of regular Francophone Summits. These meetings provide a forum for representatives of 150 million French-speaking people from forty countries around the world. In 1988 Bouchard was invited to run for office and help with the Mulroney reelection campaign. He was appointed to the Mulroney cabinet, serving as secretary for state and then for the environment. He was elected as the Conservative member of Parliament from Lac-Saint-Jean.

The rejection of the Meech Lake Accord by Canada in 1990, however, caused another reversal in Bouchard's politics. This agreement would have redefined the Canadian Constitution in a way more acceptable to Quebec—and to Bouchard. He broke with Mulroney over Meech Lake complications and resigned from both the cabinet and the Conservative caucus.

Separatist Leader

A number of Quebec members of Parliament from both the Conservative and Liberal Parties also felt that Quebec itself had been rejected by the defeat of the Meech Lake Accord. Under the leadership of Bouchard, this group formed a new separatist party called the Bloc Québécois. In the next Canadian election, in 1993, the bloc won fifty-four ridings (electoral districts) in Quebec and became the official opposition in Ottawa.

Meanwhile, in the province of Quebec, the long reign of Robert Bourassa and the Liberal Party came to an end. The Parti Québécois under the leadership of Jacques Parizeau took control of the National Assembly and scheduled a referendum on Quebec independence for October 30, 1995. The Federalist side won by less than one percentage point. Lucien Bouchard had been an effective campaigner for the independence option in the referendum, and he enjoyed an extremely high level of popularity in Quebec. Public pressure practically compelled him to return to Quebec and take the position that Parizeau vacated in the wake of the referendum. He was elected with a comfortable majority as Quebec provincial premier in January, 1996.

As head of the government of Quebec, Bouchard sought to maintain the separatist momentum while reversing a long-established pattern of deficit spending. The provincial

Bloc Québécois leader Lucien Bouchard in 1995, holding a newspaper from 1981 describing a constitutional agreement made without Quebec's consent. *(AP/Wide World Photos)*

The Referendum of 1995

The 1995 referendum on Quebec independence was not the first. In 1980 the issue had come to a popular vote under the Parti Québécois government of René Lévesque and was soundly defeated. The second referendum, in 1995, was also won by the Federalist side, but the outcome was so close that Canada was traumatized by the narrow escape. The seriousness of the threat to Canadian unity could no longer be denied.

Four important reasons can be cited for the surprising strength of the independence forces. First, the Constitution Act of 1982 is perceived by many to have been effected by the Canadian government in a unilateral manner, insulting to the honor of Quebec. Second, the attempt to remedy this perceived insult in the Meech Lake Accord was rejected in 1990. Third, the popularity of Lucien Bouchard reached an almost messianic peak just before the 1995 vote. Fourth, many people in Quebec did not seem to understand the implications of independence. For example, opinion polls revealed that many still expected to use Canadian passports afterward and to continue to be able to work anywhere in Canada.

Days before the 1995 Quebec independence referendum, a Montreal woman surrounded by people who oppose Quebec separation waves a Quebec flag. *(AP/ Wide World Photos)*

debt was growing, eroding Quebec's credit rating and overall economic viability. Bouchard's problem was to make the necessary cuts in government spending without alienating nationalist support.

Bibliography

Bouchard, Lucien. *On the Record*. Toronto: Stoddart, 1994.

Cornellier, Manon. *The Bloc*. Toronto: James Lorimer, 1995.

Martin, Lawrence. *The Antagonist*. Toronto: Viking, 1997.

Steven Lehman

Houari Boumedienne

Born: August 23, 1927; Clauzel, near Goulma, Algeria
Died: December 27, 1978; Algiers, Algeria

President of Algeria (1965-1978)

Before Houari Boumedienne (hew-AH-ree bew-meh-DYEHN), originally called Mohammed Ben Brahim Boukharouba (moo-HAH-muhd bihn BRAH-hihm bew-CHAH-ruh-bah) fought as a rebel soldier in the Algerian war of independence against France during the 1950's, he received his education at the Islamic Institute in Constantine and the al-Azhar University in Cairo. For a short while, he was a schoolteacher.

Algeria Gains Independence

In the 1950's, Algeria, located on the Mediterranean Sea in northwestern Africa and almost entirely desert, was officially known as the Democratic and Popular Republic of Algeria. It had been a French colony since 1830, and its leaders had given up hope of ever achieving independence from France through democratic means. The National Liberation Front (FLN), or the Rejection Front, was dedicated to restoring a sovereign Algerian state. Such a state, the Algerian nationalists decried, could only be realized through open rebellion. In 1960, as chief of staff of the FLN—by then a socialist organization intent on armed insurrection—Boumedienne commanded an Algerian army in Morocco and Tunisia, out of reach of French authorities.

In March, 1962, President Charles de Gaulle of France promoted peace negotiations; the Agreement of Evian stated that independence was to be given to Algeria after a transitional period granting rights of full French citizenship, adequate schools, and medical services for the Muslim population. However, the Algerian war of independence, in which a French army of 500,000 sought to suppress the upstart FLN, soon broke out. Algeria achieved independence from France after eight years of guerrilla warfare in which one million Algerians died. Independence day for Algeria was July 3, 1962.

The French community departed (leaving Algeria with a lack of skilled labor) as the FLN took over the government. Factional infighting quickly began to disrupt the new government as the conservative provisional government struggled against a socialist faction. Governing became chaotic.

Boumedienne Supports Ben Bella

Colonel Houari Boumedienne, chief of the Army of National Liberation, intervened on be-

Houari Boumedienne *(Library of Congress)*

Houari Boumedienne conferring with Egyptian president Gamal Abdel Nasser (left) and Algerian premier Ahmed Ben Bella (right) in 1963. (Library of Congress)

half of Ahmed Ben Bella, Marxist leader of one of the factions, and occupied the capital, Algiers. Victorious, Ben Bella was elected unopposed to the presidency of the first government of a free Algerian republic in 1963. Ben Bella promised a revolutionary Arab-Islamic state based on the principles of socialism and collective leadership within Algeria and on anti-imperialism abroad.

The new president, who steered his country toward a socialist economy, rewarded Boumedienne, naming him minister of defense and vice president. Strongly influenced by French Marxist advisers and by the anti-Zionist Arab states, Ben Bella cultivated cultural and economic relations with France. He established order in a country made chaotic by the departure of the French colonists. He and Boumedienne endeavored to revive the traditional Arabic cultural heritage. Peasants worked on land vacated by the French, and cooperative farms regulated by peasant councils were established.

Ben Bella was intent on introducing major agrarian reform through collectivization of the former colonists' large farms, autonomous industry, and mass education. However, his cultural and social programs failed to produce the results desired. Severe and ongoing conflicts followed. In 1963 and 1964, army revolts broke out. Ongoing civil disorder, coupled with economic stagnation after promises of economic progress and prosperity, made Algerians impatient.

Military Dictatorship

On June 19, 1965, Boumedienne, intent on furthering a program of Algerian Islamic socialism, brought about a successful, nonviolent *coup d'état* against President Ben Bella and established himself as president. He imprisoned Ben Bella for

The Rejection Front

The National Liberation Front (FLN), or Rejection Front, was an Algerian organization committed to revolutionary struggle for independence from France. It sprang up as a result of the failure of an earlier movement, the Algerian Popular Union. The Algerian Popular Union had proposed equal rights for French colonists and native Algerians while preserving the Algerian culture and language and bringing about an end to French colonialism. The Rejection Front condemned French colonial rule. It called for a policy of self-determination and an Algerian constitution granting equality to all inhabitants.

The 1965 Algerian Coup

On June 19, 1965, an Algerian army officer, Colonel Houari Boumedienne, provoked a *coup d'état* against President Ahmed Ben Bella and established himself as the second president of Algeria. Boumedienne was intent on furthering a program of Algerian socialism. Although Algeria had gained independence only three years earlier, many Algerians had become disgruntled and felt that Ben Bella had been unable to fulfill promises of economic prosperity. In a bloodless coup, Vice President Boumedienne took firm control. Boumedienne at first controlled Algeria through a military revolutionary council, but he soon consolidated power for himself. He brought order and increased affluence to Algeria.

fourteen years. Unlike Ben Bella, who had enjoyed immense popular support, Boumedienne controlled Algeria through a revolutionary council. After an attempted military coup failed to oust him in December, 1967, he affirmed absolute control and leadership of Algeria; the country became a military dictatorship. Also in 1967, Algeria declared war on Israel and broke diplomatic relations with the United States.

Boumedienne made economic reconstruction his first priority. He contributed to Algeria's economic growth by encouraging the exploitation of vast deposits of natural gas in the Sahara Desert. Boumedienne presided over the transformation of Algeria from a nearly bankrupt state into a leader among Third World countries. In 1971 Boumedienne ended relations with France when he took control of the Algerian oil industry. Continuing to preside over the Council of Revolution as effective head of state, he formally accepted election as president five years later. In 1976 he proclaimed a new constitution. He also took a leadership position in the nonaligned North African Socialist Federation. Boumedienne chose a politics of nonalliance with either the communist East or capitalist West. This approach made him an influential figure in Third World politics.

Algeria After Boumedienne

Boumedienne ruled Algeria, the second-largest country in Africa, until his death in 1978 from a rare blood disease. He died not having named a successor. During his tenure, the desert country saw a period of steady economic growth and international influence. Algeria became a leading nation among the developing countries, with its large revenues from petroleum extraction.

Following the death of Boumedienne, Colonel Chadli Bendjedid took over and continued Algeria's socialist economy. Although Bendjedid's policies were a continuation of Boumedienne's, he was not able to effect the same political control. In 1989, the FLN was forced to accept a new constitution that allowed multiparty elections. The fundamentalist Islamic Salvation Front (FIS) won the major portion of the vote in 1991. However, the government took military action to keep the fundamentalists from taking over the National People's Assembly. Fundamentalist groups then retaliated violently against the government, immersing Algeria once again into civil war.

Bibliography

Rudy, John. *Modern Algeria: The Origins and Development of a Nation*. Bloomington: Indiana University Press, 1992.

Stone, Martin. *The Agony of Algeria*. New York: Columbia University Press, 1997.

Willis, Michael. *The Islamist Challenge of Algeria: A Political History*. New York: New York University Press, 1997.

M. Casey Diana

Léon Bourgeois

Born: May 21, 1851; Paris, France
Died: September 29, 1925; Château d'Ozer, near Épernay, Marne, France

French politician and diplomat, winner of 1920 Nobel Peace Prize

Léon-Victor-Auguste Bourgeois (lay-O veek-TOHR oh-GEWST bewr-ZHWAH), the son of a Parisian clock maker, was educated in Paris at the Lycée Charlemagne. He entered law school in 1870 but left to serve in an artillery regiment during the Franco-Prussian War (1870-1871). After receiving the doctor of law degree he entered the bar at Paris and began a distinguished career in public service in 1876 as a labor lawyer in the Ministry of Public Works.

Social Reformer

Exposure to labor disputes at the Ministry of Public Works led Bourgeois into a lifelong concern for public welfare. After serving as governor of various departments of northern France, he returned to Paris in 1886 as director of the Ministry of the Interior (1886-1887) and as chief of police. A member of the cabinet in various administrations after 1890, minister of the interior (1890), education (1890-1892), and justice (1892-1893), Bourgeois initiated major reforms of social institutions from public education to the pensioning of workers and the socializing of medicine.

Bourgeois was appointed minister of foreign affairs during an era of widespread government corruption. His reputation was such that the public's confidence was quickly restored after scandals involving the French rail system and the building of the Panama Canal (1891-1893) had brought down previous administrations. He played a major role in imposing a universal income tax and in writing laws that separated church and state. From 1895 to 1896, Bourgeois was premier of France.

Turned out of office by hostile right-wing Chambers of Deputies from time to time, Bourgeois was reappointed to the cabinet by subsequent administrations on the political left. In 1896 his book *Solidarity* formulated a political vision between individualism on the Right and collectivism on the Left. Bourgeois believed in free enterprise within a welfare system. In 1898 he returned as minister of education, was elected president of the Chamber of Deputies from 1902 to 1904, was again minister of state in 1906, and was minister of labor under Raymond Poincaré in 1912. In each office, he reorganized French institutions, notably the curricula of the universities and secondary schools, pensions to workers, and a universal health insurance.

Léon Bourgeois *(Library of Congress)*

172

The League of Nations

The League of Nations (1920-1946) was an international alliance for the perpetuation of world peace following the end of World War I. The organization first convened in 1920 in Geneva, with forty-two nations participating. At its peak it included sixty-three nations, some of which dropped out on the eve of World War II. The League of Nations was divided into three parts: an assembly consisting of three representatives from each member state with one vote to cast, a council composed of permanent members from the major powers (with other members elected by the assembly), and a secretary-general elected by the assembly. This basic structure was passed on to the United Nations in 1946.

Though the league was in many ways the brainchild of U.S. president Woodrow Wilson, the United States never joined, a fact which limited the League of Nations' authority as a peacekeeper. While the league settled some disputes over land rights and helped contain the trade in narcotics and prostitution, it was too weak to prevent World War II.

Long a believer in social planning, Bourgeois wrote widely on the subject of solidarity as an umbrella under which government should manage public affairs—from the raising of taxes to the care of the sick and elderly, from education to job training. The government should also, he wrote, retain regulatory authority over the marketplace. He was the leader of the radical Solidarity Party. Among his studies of public policy are the *Declaration of the Rights of Man* (1903) and *The Politics of Social Planning* (1914). The Solidarity Party stood for three fundamentals of governance: the education of the masses, a minimum wage, and public health and old age insurance.

Solidarity practiced the syncretic school of politics, which believed in the interdependence of the public and private sectors. Syncretism was the "third way" of political ideology after liberal individualism and communism. Its ideals influenced social policy during the Great Depression, including the reforms initiated in the United States under President Franklin D. Roosevelt.

World Peacemaker

At the outbreak of World War I (1914), Bourgeois was appointed minister without portfolio, a post he retained until 1916. He returned to the Ministry of Labor until the end of the war in 1918. A year later, he was appointed to the commission that drafted the rules of the League of Nations, the forerunner of the United Nations. From 1919 to 1924, Bourgeois was the French spokesman in both the Council and the Assembly of the League of Nations. In 1920 he was awarded the Nobel Peace Prize.

Bibliography

Grey, Edward Viscount. *The League of Nations*. New York: Doran, 1918.

Henig, Ruth. *The League of Nations*. Edinburgh, Scotland: Oliver and Boyd, 1973.

Marburg, Theodore. *The League of Nations*. New York: Macmillan, 1918.

Paul Christensen

Boutros Boutros-Ghali

Born: November 14, 1922; Cairo, Egypt

Egyptian diplomat and secretary-general of the United Nations (1992-1996)

Boutros Boutros-Ghali (BEW-tros BEW-tros GAH-lee) was born to Sophie and Youssef Boutros-Ghali. His parents were Copts—members of a Christian denomination originating in Egypt—and their strong religious and ethical standards greatly influenced Boutros Boutros-Ghali. Some of his earliest memories were of his mother preparing her kit for her pilgrimage from Cairo to Jerusalem. He earned diplomas in political science, economics, and public law, as well as a

Ph.D. in international law from Paris University in 1949.

World Statesman

For more than forty years, Boutros-Ghali participated in numerous meetings on international law, human rights, economic and social development, decolonization, conflict in the Middle East, international humanitarian law, the rights of ethnic and other minorities, and development in the Mediterranean region and African-Arab cooperation.

From 1949 to 1977, he served as professor of international law and international relations at Cairo University. From 1974 to 1977, he was a member of the Central Committee and Political Bureau of the Arab Socialist Union. In 1978 he attended the Camp David Summit conference and had a role in negotiating the Camp David Accords between Egypt and Israel, which were signed in 1979. This event thrust him into a prominent place in the public arena. Boutros-Ghali led many delegations of his country to meetings of the Organization of African Unity and the Movement of Non-Aligned Countries, as well as to the summit conference of the French and African heads of state. He also headed Egypt's delegation to the General Assembly sessions in 1979, 1982, and 1990.

Serving as deputy prime minister for foreign affairs of Egypt as of May, 1991, and as minister of state for foreign affairs from October, 1977, until 1991, he became the sixth secretary-general of the United Nations in January, 1992.

International Peace and Security

Boutros-Ghali became the secretary-general of the United Nations in an atmosphere of general complacence over the accomplishments of the

Boutros Boutros-Ghali *(Imapress/Archive Photos)*

United Nations in the new post-Cold War era. However, during his first two years in office, the proliferation of regional conflicts (particularly in Haiti, Somalia, the former Yugoslavia, and Rwanda) gave rise to the need for reform and restructuring of the responsibility of the United Nations' peacekeeping role in the world.

Boutros-Ghali undertook this reform with a focus on "development and international economic cooperation." He declared that development was not only a fundamental human right but also the most secure basis for peace, and that without a fundamental basis in peace, development could not proceed. His agenda involved initiating through the United Nations a peacekeeping/humanitarian aid operation: a situation of sustainable development, along with protection of the environment as a fundamental concept of that development. Boutros-Ghali maintained that among many countries in transition, decades of disregard for the environment had left large areas unable to sustain economic activity in the long term and that among the wealthiest nations, consumption patterns were depleting world resources in ways that jeopard-

U.N. secretary-general Boutros Boutros-Ghali discussing the crisis in Zaire in a 1996 news conference in Rome. *(Reuters/Paolo Cocco/Archive Photos)*

The United States and the United Nations

In the early 1980's, the United Nations was criticized as a vast, sprawling, inefficient bureaucracy. This criticism led to much debate regarding the financial responsibility of the United States to the United Nations. At one time, Congress refused to pay off the United States' $1 billion debt to the organization. This refusal created an unexpected backlash from the U.N. General Assembly, which removed the United States from a key budget committee. Internationalizing its foreign policy through the United Nations—that is, acting through the United Nations instead of on its own—cost the United States an estimated $2 billion in 1996.

Proponents for this approach argue that when the United States intervenes alone, it pays all the costs; when the United Nations acts, the United States pays one-fourth of the costs, and other countries may provide the majority of troops. Nonetheless, there is opposition by many conservatives in Congress not only to U.S. involvement in the United Nations but also to the very existence of the United Nations. Despite the rhetoric of congressional critics, *Time* magazine reported in 1996 that 81 percent of Americans polled believed that the United States should try to strengthen the United Nations.

ized the future of world development. Boutros-Ghali's *Agenda for Peace* (1992) was a hard-line stance on the issue of "sustainable development" and brought a strong reaction from countries and leaders who feared a loss of national control and who were reluctant to provide financial means to achieve agreed-upon results. Many lacked conviction that assessments would benefit their own economic agendas and interests.

Beleaguered U.N. Leader

Management problems within the United Nations under Boutros-Ghali's leadership were an ongoing source of criticism, especially by the United States. A burgeoning budget cost the United States about $2 billion in the year 1996 alone. Boutros-Ghali was willing to tackle seemingly intractable situations, such as those in Bosnia and Somalia, that required multilateral efforts to resolve. Such efforts caused peacekeeping efforts around the world to become burdensome financial and management problems under his leadership. Boutros-Ghali's expectations far outweighed the financial and management abilities of the United Nations to respond. As a result, pressure for budgetary reform, especially from the United States, brought about the suspension of Boutros-Ghali's candidacy for secretary-general in 1996.

Importance

Boutros-Ghali's bold steps to give a stronger voice to developing nations and his commitment to the responsibility of the moral authority of the United Nations provide much to admire. However, it was under his mandate that the United Nations dramatically expanded its peacekeeping mandate, only to find itself rejected on several initiatives. Thus, Boutros-Ghali became a lightning rod for dissatisfaction with the United Nations and, more generally, for widespread frustration at the way nationalist ambitions and ethnic hostilities threatened the order of the post-Cold War world. Through all the controversy, Boutros-Ghali maintained that the success or failure of U.N. peacekeeping is utterly dependent on

Agenda for Peace

In January of 1992, the Security Council of the United Nations requested from Secretary-General Boutros Boutros-Ghali recommendations for ways of strengthening and making more efficient the capacity of the United Nations for preventive diplomacy, for peacemaking, and for peacekeeping. He responded with *Agenda for Peace*, which analyzed the world organization's situation at a time of global transition. It included proposals for changes in the definitions of economic and social progress, which would enable the United Nations to respond more effectively to its members' needs in those areas.

There are four main components to the *Agenda for Peace*. First is peacemaking, or bringing hostile parties to agreement through peaceful means such as negotiation and arbitration. Second is peacekeeping, the deployment of a force to the field, usually with the consent of the parties to the conflict. Peace enforcement—the creation of forces that could respond quickly and forcefully to imminent or outright aggression—is third. Finally, peace building includes action to identify and support structures that will strengthen and solidify peace to avoid a relapse into conflict. These actions include disarming the warring parties, clearing land mines, confiscating and destroying weapons, and repatriating refugees.

Boutros Boutros-Ghali (right) in Istanbul in 1996 after the opening session of the U.N. Conference on Human Settlements (Habitat II). At left is U.N. official Wally N'Dow; Turkish president Suleiman Demirel is in the center. *(AP/Wide World Photos)*

the good faith of contesting parties. Certainly, during his term **as** secretary-general, Boutros-Ghali brought the United Nations' new assertiveness to the forefront, and the world became more aware of and interested in the activities of that body. In 1997 Boutros-Ghali began serving as a professor at Cairo University and as a member of the Egyptian Parliament.

Bibliography

Boutros-Ghali, Boutros. *The Road to Jerusalem*. New York: Random House, 1997.

Ignatieff, Michael. "Alone with the Secretary-General." *The New Yorker*, August 14, 1995, 33-35.

Serrill, Michael. "Under Fire." *Time*, January 18, 1993, 32-34.

Lela Phillips

Omar N. Bradley

Born: February 12, 1893; Clark, Missouri
Died: April 8, 1981; New York, New York

U.S. military leader during World War II

Omar Nelson Bradley (OH-mahr NEHL-suhn BRAD-lee) was the son of a rural teacher and a farmer's daughter. After graduating from West Point, Bradley married Mary Quayle in 1916. They had one daughter, Elizabeth. Bradley learned from his father a sense of justice and respect for his fellows; these would later earn him recognition for being a "soldier's general." After the death of his wife in 1965, Bradley married Kitty Buhler.

The Early Years

In 1911 Bradley entered West Point. In addition to concentrating on his studies, Bradley was a member of the West Point baseball team. Participation in an organized team sport taught him group cooperation in goal achievement. After graduation from the academy in 1915, Bradley served as second lieutenant with the Fourteenth Infantry Regiment in Arizona during the Mexican "border war." His unit, however, saw no battle. When the United States declared war on Germany in 1917, his regiment was sent to Montana to monitor the copper mines. The war ended before Bradley had the chance to serve his country in France.

Bradley spent the next several years alternating between being a student and being an instructor. During this time, he honed his skills in mathematics, tactics, and training and learned strategies of open warfare. These skills helped prepare him for future decision making in life-or-death situations.

Active Duty

Before the beginning of World War II, Bradley was transferred to Washington, D.C., to serve with the War Department and the general staff.

He then went on to the chief of staff's office. After the bombing of Pearl Harbor in December, 1941, Bradley was assigned to the Eighty-second Division, an assignment that earned him a temporary promotion to two-star general.

In 1943 he received orders to join the fighting in Africa. Finally, at the age of fifty, Bradley was going into battle. As commander of the U.S. Army II Corps, he led his troops on a successful campaign to overtake Hill 609, a German stronghold. The success of the II Corps can be attributed to Bradley's plan of sending tanks ahead as mo-

Omar N. Bradley *(Library of Congress)*

bile artillery. This victory enabled the Allied forces to continue advancing and to push the Germans out of Tunisia. Bradley received his third star—and the British forces received the credit.

Bradley led the first amphibious assault during the invasion of Sicily. Against his better judgment, Bradley allowed British general Bernard Law Montgomery to lead his troops in front of II Corps. Had Bradley avoided this slowing down of his men, his troops would have been able to shorten the campaign and thereby save many lives. Bradley was appointed commander of the Twelfth Army Group during the invasion of Normandy. His troops went on to liberate Paris. They seized the first bridgehead over the Rhine River and became the first to establish contact with the Russian allies.

U.S. generals George S. Patton (left) and Omar N. Bradley with British field marshal Bernard Law Montgomery (right) in July of 1944. *(Library of Congress)*

After World War II

After the victory over Germany, Bradley was sent back to the United States to head the Veterans Administration. He served for two years, from 1945 to 1947, revamping the VA to accommodate the increasing population of war veterans. In 1947 Bradley received his fourth star. In 1948 he was appointed army chief of staff. He spent eighteen months in the position before being named the first chairman of the Joint Chiefs of Staff. He served two consecutive terms as chairman, receiving his fifth star in 1950. He also served as the first chairman of the Military Committee of the North Atlantic Treaty Organization (NATO).

The Twelfth Army Group

In order to confuse the Germans as to where the Allied forces would land along the French coastline, the Twelfth Army Group was temporarily called First Army Group, and a fictitious camp was built. Fake buildings, tanks, and aircraft were made from paper, wood, and rubber and set up in England. False messages were sent, indicating that the invasion would take place at Pas de Calais. The deception was successful, and General Omar N. Bradley led the Twelfth Army Group in the invasion of Normandy on D day, June 6, 1944.

After retiring from active duty in 1953, Bradley went to work for the Bulova watch company, first as head of its research and development department and then as chairman of the board.

Bibliography

Bliven, Bruce, Jr. *From Casablanca to Berlin: The War in North Africa and Europe, 1942-1945*. New York: Random House, 1965.

Bradley, Omar Nelson. *A Soldier's Story*. New York: Great Commanders, 1994.

Bradley, Omar N., and Clay Blair. *A General's Life: An Autobiography by General Omar N. Bradley*. New York: Simon & Schuster, 1983.

Lawson, Don. *The United States in World War II*. New York: Abelard-Schuman, 1963.

Reeder, Colonel "Red." *Omar Nelson Bradley*. Champaign, Ill.: Garrard, 1969.

Sweeney, James B. *Army Leaders of World War II*. New York: F. Watts, 1984.

Maryanne Barsotti

Louis D. Brandeis

Born: November 13, 1856; Louisville, Kentucky
Died: October 5, 1941; Washington, D.C.

U.S. jurist and Supreme Court justice (1916-1939)

Louis Dembitz Brandeis (LEW-ihs DEHM-bihtz BRAN-dis) was the son of Adolph Brandeis, a Jewish-Austrian immigrant merchant. Brandeis was raised in Louisville, Kentucky, the seat of the family grain and produce business. Brandeis's mother was Frederika Dembitz, the daughter of an Austrian physician. Brandeis, his brother, and two sisters grew up in a household in which books, music, culture, and political liberty were valued. He was schooled at the Annen-Realschule in Dresden, Germany, from 1873 to 1875. He entered the Harvard Law School on his return to the United States in 1875. He graduated at the top of his class in 1877, a few months before his twenty-first birthday. Brandeis opened his law practice in Boston with Sam Warren. In 1891 he married Alice Goldmark, a second cousin on his father's side. They had two daughters.

Brandeis the Advocate

Brandeis was in private legal practice for thirty-seven years before his appointment to the U.S. Supreme Court. His legal work, which put him at the forefront of the American bar, was particularly notable for its emphasis on labor-management relations during the formative period of the American labor union movement. He also participated in a number of cases that pitted corporations against government, in which he argued for moderation and a broad view of the public interest. He won most of his cases. In 1900 he was a leader in the fight to preserve the Boston subway system. From 1905 to 1913 he represented the Boston and Maine Railroad in its struggle to resist a takeover by the New Haven Railroad. The cases that crowned his career as an advocate and brought wide public notice to his career were the U.S. Supreme Court case *Muller v. Oregon* (1908), which involved a minimum-wage law for women, and his defense of *Collier's Weekly* in the Gifford Pinchot-Richard Ballinger hearings. These hearings involved a complex struggle between the administration of President William Howard Taft and conservation groups. Brandeis was able to expose many of the falsifications of the Taft administration, and Ballinger was ultimately forced to resign as head of the Land Office in the Department of the Interior.

Brandeis's activities increasingly included support for the progressive wing of the Republican Party. His progressivism and the antimonop-

Louis D. Brandeis *(Library of Congress)*

oly strands of his legal and political thought brought him to the attention of President Woodrow Wilson. Wilson sought his advice on a number of matters, and Brandeis assisted him with his reelection campaign. In 1916 Wilson nominated him to the Supreme Court seat that had become vacant when Justice Joseph Lamar died. Brandeis was the first Jewish justice on the Supreme Court, and there was a great deal of overt anti-Semitic opposition to his appointment. After a fierce confirmation struggle, Brandeis took his seat on the court on June 5, 1916.

Brandeis the Justice

The clarity of Justice Brandeis's opinions strengthened the liberal wing of the Supreme Court. He and Justice Oliver Wendell Holmes became especially notable for their powerful and moving dissenting opinions in free-speech cases. In cases having to do with the nation's economic life, Brandeis was also most often found on the liberal side, voting again and again to uphold reform legislation. In *Ashwander v. Tennessee Valley Authority* (1936) and other cases, he argued cogently for judicial self-restraint—that is, he believed that the Court should defer to the opinion of the legislature whenever possible. His opinions supporting welfare capitalism and a humane jurisprudence inspired many government officials of the New Deal era of the 1930's, by whom he was sometimes refereed to as "the prophet" or "Isaiah." Brandeis served on the Supreme Court for twenty-three years, resigning because of ill health in 1939.

Associate Justice Louis D. Brandeis on his way to the U.S. Supreme Court on his eightieth birthday, November 13, 1936. *(AP/Wide World Photos)*

The "Brandeis Brief"

One of Louis D. Brandeis's most important contributions to Supreme Court practice and jurisprudence took place in 1908 while he was still in private practice. In *Muller v. Oregon*, Brandeis defended an Oregon law that established maximum hours that women would be allowed to work. This law was challenged under the due process clause of the Fourteenth Amendment. It was claimed that the law restricted women's liberty to make contracts. Brandeis's innovative brief was based mainly on health and economic data which showed that the Oregon legislature had not acted "unreasonably." The emphasis he placed on evidence showing a factual need for the law was new in Supreme Court practice. Earlier arguments in such cases had emphasized technical legal theory rather than the social conditions that established the need for the statute. Brandeis won the case, and, in the Supreme Court's majority opinion, Justice David Brewer took the unusual step of praising Brandeis's brief. The style and technique of his argument in this case dominated Supreme Court practice thereafter.

Bibliography

Brandeis, Louis Dembitz. *"Half Brother, Half Son": The Letters of Louis D. Brandeis to Felix Frankfurter.* Norman: University of Oklahoma Press, 1991.

Mason, Alpheus T. *Brandeis: A Free Man's Life.* New York: Viking Press, 1946.

Murphy, Bruce Allen. *The Brandeis/Frankfurter Connection: The Secret Political Activities of Two Supreme Court Justices.* New York: Oxford University Press, 1982.

Plummer, Marguerite R. "Louis Brandeis: Pioneer Progressive." In *Great Justices of the U.S. Supreme Court: Ratings and Case Studies.* New York: P. Lang, 1993.

Strum, Philippa. *Louis D. Brandeis: Justice for the People.* Cambridge, Mass.: Harvard University Press, 1984.

Urofsky, Melvin I. *A Mind of One Piece: Brandeis and American Reform.* New York: Scribner's, 1971.

Robert Jacobs

Willy Brandt

Born: December 18, 1913; Lübeck, Germany
Died: October 8, 1992; Unkel, near Bonn, Germany

Chancellor of West Germany (1969-1974), winner of 1971 Nobel Peace Prize

Born Herbert Ernst Karl Frahm (HAYR-bayrt AYRNST KAHRL FRAHM), Willy Brandt (VEE-lee BRAHNT) was the son of an unmarried working-class mother. Influenced by his grandfather, he became an active socialist during his youth. In 1933 he fled Nazi Germany to seek refuge in Norway, where he worked as a journalist under the adopted name "Willy Brandt." After being arrested by the Nazis in 1940, he moved to neutral Sweden, where he continued his journalism and antifascist activities.

Berlin Leader

Returning to Germany after World War II, Brandt first worked as a journalist for the Norwegian military. In 1948 he regained his German citizenship and became the liaison officer of the Social Democratic Party (SDP) in West Berlin. The next year, he was elected a member of the national Bundestag, the lower house of parliament, and he was elected a member of the Berlin city council. During the Soviet invasion of Hungary in 1956, he gained international recognition when he persuaded an angry crowd not to march into East Berlin, and he was elected mayor of West Berlin in 1957.

During his four years as mayor, Brandt was often a symbol of Western determination to resist Soviet expansion. In 1958 Soviet leader Nikita Khrushchev insisted that West Berlin break its ties to West Germany and the North Atlantic Treaty Organization (NATO), a proposal that would have extended the influence of East Germany. Brandt took a firm stand in rejecting Khrushchev's demands. When the Berlin Wall was built in August, 1961, Brandt protested that U.S. president John F. Kennedy's early reaction was too weak, and he encouraged Kennedy to order fifteen hundred American troops to the city.

Brandt had some influence in moving the SDP to accept more moderate policies that increased its appeal among German voters. At the Bad Godesberg conference of 1959, the party approved a platform that renounced strict Marxism and endorsed the principles of private property and free-market economics.

National Leader

In the general elections of 1961 and 1965, Brandt was chosen as the SDP candidate for

Willy Brandt *(The Nobel Foundation)*

Ostpolitik

From its founding in 1949, the Federal Republic of Germany (FRG, or West Germany) refused to recognize the Democratic Republic of Germany (DRG, or East Germany) as an independent country. After 1955 West Germany withheld diplomatic relations from any country that formally recognized the DRG. West Germany was also unwilling to acknowledge the Oder-Neisse line—a new boundary with Poland drawn after World War II—as Poland's western border. These policies promoted fears of German expansionism and increased Cold War tensions.

Between 1966 and 1969, Chancellor Kurt Kiesinger's government initiated a new *Ostpolitik* (or "eastern policy") of normalizing relations between the two Germanies while still refusing full diplomatic recognition. From 1969 to 1974, Chancellor Willy Brandt pursued a more ambitious vision of *Ostpolitik*, and he successfully negotiated several interconnected treaties with Poland, the Soviet Union, Czechoslovakia, and the GDR. The treaties renounced the use of force and accepted all existing boundaries. A controversial treaty with the DRG, ratified in 1973, came close to granting full diplomatic status, based on Brandt's formula of one German nation and two German states.

Brandt received the Nobel Peace Prize of 1971 for his role in reducing East-West tensions. His *Ostpolitik* encouraged President Richard Nixon's policy of détente, and it led to the Helsinki Agreements of 1975. After the fall of communism in East Germany, West Germany reaffirmed recognition of the Oder-Neisse boundary, making peaceful reunification possible.

chancellor, but each time the SDP won less than 40 percent of the votes. In 1966, however, the ruling coalition broke up, and Chancellor Kurt Kiesinger, leader of the conservative Christian Democratic Union (CDU), agreed to include the SDP as part of the Grand Coalition. Brandt was appointed both vice chancellor and foreign minister. Although the coalition did not allow the SDP to advance its domestic agenda, Brandt viewed participation as a historic opportunity for a new *Ostpolitik* (literally "eastern policy") for improving relations between West Germany and East Europe. As foreign minister, he was able to take the first steps toward realizing this vision.

In the general elections of 1969, Brandt's *Ostpolitik* was a major issue, and the SDP won a plurality victory with 42.7 percent of the votes. In order to control a majority of Bundestag seats, Brandt's SDP formed a coalition with the liberal Free Democratic Party (FDP), which supported *Ostpolitik* but opposed socialism.

During his five-year tenure as chancellor, Brandt was able to sign and secure ratification of treaties with Poland, the Soviet Union, Czechoslovakia, and East Germany. As a former journalist, Brandt knew how to use political symbolism effectively—as when he dropped to his knees before the memorial for victims who died in the Warsaw ghetto during World War II. For his work in reducing East-West tensions, Brandt was awarded the Nobel Peace Prize in 1971. The policy was also popular in West Germany, and in the general elections of 1972, the SPD-FDP coalition increased its majority from twelve to forty-eight seats.

In domestic affairs, Brandt's government strengthened the role of labor, introduced a new type of technical education, and reformed the social security system so that pensions became independent of contributions. Although Brandt's tenure showed that the SDP could exercise power responsibly, leftists were unhappy with the non-

Willy Brandt's son (far left) and daughter (right) help unveil a statue of Brandt in 1996 in the new Berlin headquarters of Germany's Social Democratic Party. *(AP/Wide World Photos)*

radical nature of its reforms, and many deserted the party.

Post-Chancellor Years

Brandt appeared to be politically secure until one of his aides, Günter Guillaume, was arrested as a spy in April, 1974. Although Brandt resigned his chancellorship, he did not retire from political life. He continued to win reelection to the Bundestag, and he remained chairman of the SDP until 1987, a position that allowed him to have considerable influence over German politics. While president of the Socialist International from 1976 to 1992, he worked to expand the organization's appeal among the less-developed countries.

By the 1980's Brandt was recognized as a senior statesman in the cause of international peace, and he chaired the North-South Commission, which advocated increased assistance to poor countries. Increasingly associated with the left wing of his party, he vigorously opposed many of President Ronald Rea-

The Guillaume Spy Case

Willy Brandt resigned his position as West German chancellor on May 6, 1974, shortly after it was discovered that his high-level aide Günter Guillaume was a spy for East Germany. Until the scandal, Brandt had appeared politically secure. Despite several warnings, he had done nothing to prevent Guillaume's access to classified mate-

rials. Although the spy scandal resulted in great criticism, some of Brandt's closest associates tried to convince him not to resign. Brandt had often experienced periods of depression, and apparently he resigned to end the painful controversy as quickly as possible. Helmut Schmidt was appointed chancellor on May 9.

gan's Cold War policies, especially the installation of American missiles in Europe.

Brandt's Legacy

As a youth, Willy Brandt showed great courage in his opposition to Nazi Germany. Committed to the cause of democratic socialism, he helped guide the Social Democratic Party to a path of pragmatic moderation. Above all, he was the dominant force in leading West Germany to recognize the existence of East Germany and to accept the Oder-Neisse boundary. (The Oder-Neisse territories had once been part of Germany but were annexed by Poland and Russia in 1945 after World War II.) These policies were almost universally praised for defusing Cold War tensions in Europe.

Bibliography

Binder, David. *The Other German: Willy Brandt's Life and Times*. Washington, D.C.: New Republic Books, 1975.

Brandt, Willy. *My Life in Politics*. London: Viking, 1992.

Prittie, Terence. *Willy Brandt: Portrait of a Statesman*. New York: Schocken Books, 1974.

Zudeick, Peter. "Willy Brandt." In *The German Chancellors*, edited by Hans Klein. Chicago: Edition Q, 1996.

Thomas T. Lewis

Karl Hjalmar Branting

Born: November 23, 1860; Stockholm, Sweden
Died: February 24, 1925; Stockholm, Sweden

Prime minister of Sweden (1920, 1921-1923, 1924-1925), winner of 1921 Nobel Peace Prize

Karl Hjalmar Branting (KAHRL YAHL-mahr BRAHN-tihng) was born into an established upper-class family. His mother was of noble birth. His father, professor Lars Branting, director of the Gymnastic Central Institute for health education, was known for advancing the teaching of physical therapy. Young Branting was educated first at the Beskow School, an exclusive private school in Stockholm. Between 1877 and 1882 he studied at Uppsala University, concentrating on mathematics and astronomy; he intended to become an astronomer. At Uppsala he also grew interested in social, economic, and political issues.

Karl Hjalmar Branting *(The Nobel Foundation)*

When Branting learned, in 1881, that the Stockholm Workers Institute, which provided lectures and courses of study for workers, had been denied funding, he provided the necessary funds himself to keep it open. In 1884 he married Anna Jäderin, a novelist and well-known theater critic. Their only son, Georg, a defense lawyer, became a member of the upper chamber of Parliament. The year before his marriage, Branting traveled extensively through Europe, including Russia, having many discussions with workers and social philosophers. He heard Paul Lafargue, the French socialist, in Paris and Eduard Bernstein, the German revisionist socialist, in Zurich.

Politician and Journalist

After completing his studies Branting worked as a correspondent from 1884 to 1886 for the social liberal newspaper *Tiden* (the times) until its demise. He then became editor in chief for the newspaper *Social-Demokraten*, an organ with an emphasis on educating workers. In 1908 he founded the social democratic magazine *Tiden* and was its editor in chief until 1917, when he resigned from both publications. That year he became finance minister in a liberal coalition government. He was Swedish prime minster three times: 1920, 1921-1923, and 1924-January, 1925, when ill health forced him to step down. He assisted as counselor until his death a month later.

Hjalmar Branting was the Swedish labor movement's greatest leader. When the Social Democratic Party was formed in 1889, he was its uncontested leader. Beginning in 1907 he was party chairman, a post he held until his death. In 1896 he was elected to the lower chamber of Parliament, and until 1902 he was its only Social Democratic member.

Sweden's Social Democratic Party

The Swedish labor movement had its beginning in 1881 when August Palm, a tailor nicknamed "Master Palm," delivered a fiery speech agitating for reform and rights for the workers. In 1889 the Swedish Social Democratic Party was formed, uniting the several trade unions that had developed in various parts of the country. The party is regarded as the most successful social democratic party in the world, having led the government for sixty years either alone or in coalition. The Social Democratic Party has worked closely with trade unions in organizing 85 percent of the labor force, the highest rate of unionization among the industrial democracies. Nonetheless, Sweden is a capitalist society with economic and social power held by large corporations. The ability to avoid confrontation and to work successfully in finding peaceful solutions in labor disputes with corporate Sweden has been the strength of the Social Democratic Party.

Pacifist and Internationalist

Branting's antiwar position was expressed as early as 1895, when he argued for a peaceful separation of Sweden and Norway. Ten years later he mobilized the trade-union movement and the Social Democratic Party in demanding a peaceful breakup of the Norwegian-Swedish union. He sympathized with the Allies during World War I (1914-1918), although he strongly condemned the Treaty of Versailles at war's end. During the war years he took part in several international socialist conferences, and he became a leading figure in the postwar reconstruction of the Socialist International. He advocated Sweden's entry into the League of Nations. In the league, he, as the Swedish delegate beginning in 1920, became known as "the great European." Branting asserted that the only solid foundation on which peace can rest is social justice for all peoples. In 1921 he was awarded the Nobel Peace Prize, jointly with Christian L. Lange of Norway.

Hjalmar Branting's influence remains strong within Swedish social democracy. He is remembered for many things—as a writer, as a fervent speaker, and as promoter of peace. Despite his upper-class origin, his concern for those not as privileged as himself was sincere. His sense of fairness demanded social justice for all.

Bibliography

Berman, Sheri. *The Social Democratic Moment: Ideas and Politics in the Making of Interwar Europe.* Cambridge, Mass.: Harvard University Press, 1998.

Misgeld, Klaus, et al., eds. *Creating Social Democracy: A Century of Social Democratic Labor Party in Sweden.* University Park: Pennsylvania State University Press, 1993.

Scott, Franklin. *Sweden: The Nation's History.* Carbondale: Southern Illinois University Press, 1988.

Tingsten, Herbert. *The Swedish Social Democrats: Their Ideological Development.* Totowa, N.J.: Bedminster Press, 1973.

Elvy Setterqvist O'Brien

Wernher von Braun

Born: March 23, 1912; Wirsitz, Germany
Died: June 16, 1977; Alexandria, Virginia

German rocket engineer, later aerospace scientist with NASA

As a youth, Wernher von Braun (VAYR-nur fon BROWN) read scientific studies as well as the science-fiction accounts of space exploration by Jules Verne and H. G. Wells. He became intrigued with the possibilities of space exploration. In September of 1929, von Braun joined the German Rocket Society, and in 1932 he went to work for the German army to develop rockets and missiles. While engaged in this work, he earned his doctorate degree in aerospace engineering in 1934.

Wernher von Braun *(NASA)*

Developing Germany's Missile Program

In 1936 von Braun was appointed director of Germany's military rocket development program. Under pressure from Adolf Hitler and other German leaders, von Braun's dreams of space travel were subjugated to Germany's demands for weapons. Operating at a secret laboratory at Peenemunde on the Baltic coast, von Braun and other German engineers and scientists built and tested the V-1 cruise missile and the V-2 ballistic missile. When the German war machine collapsed in 1945 at the end of World War II, von Braun disobeyed German orders to destroy all classified rocket documents, hiding them in an abandoned mine in the Harz Mountains of Germany.

The U.S. Rocket Program

On May 2, 1945, under von Braun's direction, the German rocket team surrendered to the American forces. Being vitally interested in German rocket technology, the United States transferred von Braun and his team to Fort Bliss, Texas, along with von Braun's recovered rocket documents and approximately 150 captured V-2 missiles. In 1946 von Braun's team was moved to White Sands, New Mexico, and in 1950 they were sent to the army's Redstone Arsenal in Huntsville, Alabama. There they built the Jupiter ballistic missile. Between 1952 and 1954, von Braun developed one of the first comprehensive space exploration programs in the world. He led the team that put the first American satellite in orbit, the Explorer I, on January 31, 1958. In 1960 von Braun and his team were transferred from the army to the newly established National Aeronautics and Space Administration (NASA). He was given the mandate to build the huge Saturn rockets.

The NASA Years

Von Braun was appointed the director of NASA's Marshall Space Flight Center in Huntsville, serving in that capacity from July, 1960, to February, 1970. In that position, he designed and oversaw the development of the Saturn I, Saturn IB, and Saturn V rockets. On July 16, 1969, a Saturn V launched the crew of Apollo 11 to their successful landing on the moon.

In 1970 von Braun was asked to move to Washington, D.C., to oversee the strategic planning effort of NASA. In less than two years, however, he decided to retire from NASA and became the vice president of engineering and development for Fairchild Industries in Germantown, Maryland. Battling cancer, von Braun retired at the end of 1976. He was awarded the National Medal of Science by President Gerald R. Ford in early 1977.

Wernher von Braun was one of the world's first and foremost rocket engineers and a leading authority on space travel. His intense desire to expand knowledge through the exploration of space led to the development of the Explorer satellites, the Jupiter, Pershing, Redstone, and Saturn rockets, and the world's first space station. His interest in

A V-2 rocket being prepared for test launch at the U.S. Army's proving grounds at White Sands, New Mexico, in 1946. *(Library of Congress)*

The V-2 Ballistic Missile

Wernher von Braun's brainchild, the V-2 (also called the A-4), was the first successful long-range ballistic missile. It is considered to be the ancestor of almost every rocket in operation today. The V-2 was a liquid-propellant missile, 46 feet (14 meters) long, weighing 27,000 pounds (12,000 kilograms), and capable of traveling at speeds greater than 3,500 miles an hour (5,600 kilometers per hour). It could deliver a one-ton warhead to a target 500 miles (800 kilometers) away. Because of its primitive guidance system, however, the V-2's direction was inaccurate. The first successful test of the V-2 occurred on October 3, 1942. From 1942 to 1945, more than thirteen hundred V-2's were fired by the Nazis at London, England, with 518 hits, causing 2,511 deaths.

space exploration led to humankind setting foot on the moon. Von Braun's relentless efforts earned him his legacy as the "Father of the Space Age."

Bibliography

Bergaust, Erik. *Wernher von Braun: The Authoritative and Definitive Biographical Profile of the Father of Modern Space Flight*. Washington, D.C.: National Space Institute, 1976.

Lampton, Christopher. *Wernher von Braun*. New York: Watts, 1988.

Piszkiewicz, Dennis. *The Nazi Rocketeers: Dreams of Space and Crimes of War*. Westport, Conn.: Praeger, 1995.

Alvin K. Benson

William J. Brennan, Jr.

Born: April 25, 1906; Newark, New Jersey
Died: July 24, 1997; Arlington, Virginia

U.S. Supreme Court justice (1956-1990)

William Joseph Brennan, Jr. (WIHL-yuhm JOH-sehf BREH-nuhn JEW-nyur), was the second of eight children born to Irish parents who immigrated to the United States in the 1890's. After receiving a business degree from the Wharton School of the University of Pennsylvania, Brennan attended Harvard Law School, receiving his doctorate of laws in 1931. In 1928, he married Marjorie Leonard, with whom he had three children. (The year after his first wife's death in 1982, he would marry Mary Fowler.) In 1942, during World War II, he interrupted his work with a prominent Newark law firm to join the army, eventually receiving the Legion of Merit for his success in resolving labor disputes arising from the wartime conversion of private businesses.

A Judicial Reformer

Brennan came by his knowledge of the forces governing American business both through his formal education and through his observations of his father's career. After working for many years as a common laborer, William J. Brennan, Sr., eventually became a leader of his local union as well as a member of the Newark board of commissioners.

His father's activist social philosophy informed William J. Brennan, Jr.'s career from its earliest days, when he spearheaded a campaign to revise the New Jersey judicial system. The success of this endeavor brought him to the attention of the governor, who appointed Brennan as a state superior court judge in 1949. Brennan's efforts on behalf of criminal defendants helped to advance him first to the state court of appeals and then to the New Jersey Supreme Court.

Supreme Court Liberal

In October, 1956, President Dwight D. Eisenhower nominated Brennan to the U.S. Supreme Court. The Republican Eisenhower, who was attempting to make a display of bipartisanship on the eve of that year's elections, believed Brennan to be only nominally a Democrat. Eisenhower would soon learn otherwise.

Shortly after he joined the Supreme Court, Brennan joined forces with the liberal voting bloc of justices that would chart a socially active course for the nation as a whole. In particular,

William J. Brennan, Jr. *(Library of Congress)*

193

U.S. Supreme Court justice William J. Brennan, Jr. (left), with his son, William J. Brennan III, as his son was admitted to practice before the Supreme Court in 1967. *(AP/Wide World Photos)*

Brennan became Chief Justice Earl Warren's closest associate, conferring with Warren individually in order to plan strategies to win reluctant justices over to the progressive positions they favored. Brennan proved to be both an eloquent spokesperson for liberal jurisprudence and an excellent politician. Because of his skill in bringing his fellow justices to consensus, he was assigned responsibility for drafting the majority opinion in some of the most important cases to come before the Court during the Warren years.

Even after Warren stepped down in 1969 and the composition of the Supreme Court became more conservative, Brennan remained a powerful force. Some of his most important opinions were drafted during the 1970's and 1980's. He argued on behalf of equal protection under the law in decisions such as *Craig v. Boren* (1976), a

Affirmative Action

Affirmative action in employment was introduced into law by Title VII of the 1964 Civil Rights Act and was confirmed by the U.S. Supreme Court in a series of decisions handed down in the 1970's. Affirmative action in essence involves giving priority in hiring, or in acceptance to a university, to people belonging to minorities who have faced widespread discrimination. In the 1980's, the administration of President Ronald Reagan attempted to check the spread of affirmative action. Justice William J. Brennan, Jr., was among those on the Court who fought this effort. In *Local 28 of the Sheet Metal Workers' International Association v. Equal Employment Opportunity Commission* (1986), for example, Brennan declared for the Supreme Court that "race-conscious class relief" was an appropriate remedy for persistent discrimination. In *United States v. Paradise* (1987), Brennan's majority opinion upheld the principle of racial quotas.

watershed gender-equality case, and *Local 28 of the Sheet Metal Workers' International Association v. Equal Employment Opportunity Commission* (1986), which helped to define the scope of race-based affirmative action programs. Declining health finally forced Brennan to step down from the Court in July, 1990.

Bibliography

Eisler, Kim Isaac. *And Justice for All: William J. Brennan, Jr., and the Decisions That Transformed America.* New York: Simon & Schuster, 1993.

Marion, David E. *The Jurisprudence of Justice William J. Brennan, Jr.: The Law and Politics of "Libertarian Dignity."* Lanham, Md.: Rowman & Littlefield, 1997.

Rosenkranz, Joshua, and Bernard Schwartz, eds. *Reason and Passion: Justice Brennan's Enduring Influence.* New York: Norton, 1997.

Lisa Paddock

Influential U.S. jurist William J. Brennan in his Supreme Court chambers. *(AP/Wide World Photos)*

Leonid Ilich Brezhnev

Born: December 19, 1906; Kamenskoye (now Dneprodzerzhinsk), Ukraine, Russian Empire
Died: November 10, 1982; Moscow, U.S.S.R.

Soviet political leader, head of Soviet Union's Communist Party (1964-1982)

Leonid Ilich Brezhnev (lih-uhn-YEET ihl-YEECH BREHZH-nyehf) was born into a family of Russian ironworkers who had been attracted to Ukraine by its booming foundries. Despite poverty, a working-class background, and the depredations of revolution and civil war (from 1917 to 1921), he completed high school in 1921. With the ascendancy of the Soviets, Brezhnev joined Komsomol (the Young Communist League) in 1923, becoming a party member in 1931. By the outbreak of World War II, he had graduated from Kamenskoye's Metallurgical Institute (1935), married (Victoriya, 1928), and had a daughter

Leonid Ilich Brezhnev *(Library of Congress)*

and son. He also had survived Joseph Stalin's purge of Ukrainian Communist Party officials. Resultant gaps in the bureaucracy hastened his career advancement. These formative years developed the instincts for self-preservation and a yearning for social and political stability that were to guide many of Brezhnev's consequent actions.

Khrushchev Protégé

With the rise of fellow Kursk native Nikita Khrushchev to Ukrainian leadership in 1938, Brezhnev found his patron and protector. He became a party organizer, serving during World War II as a political officer in the Red Army, then resuming his career in Ukraine. In 1950 Khrushchev brought Brezhnev into the Central Party Secretariat, where he served as chief executive of two non-Russian Soviet republics. Both assignments were successful and involved difficult tasks: first, the cession of Bessarabian Czechoslovakia to Moldavia, and second, implementation of Kazakhstan's vast "virgin lands" agricultural expansion. In 1957 Brezhnev was elected to the Politburo, the Soviet Union's highest political body, becoming head of state in 1960. This position, though wielding little actual power, offered opportunities to gather followers and gain international exposure. As dissension increased over Khrushchev's management style and directives, Brezhnev continued to support his mentor. Yet when Khrushchev was removed in October, 1964, Brezhnev sided with the opposition. The very attributes that recommended him as Khrushchev's successor—cautious deliberation and recognition of the importance of "collectivity" in decision making coupled with extensive practical, managerial, and executive experience—had

The Brezhnev Doctrine

Czechoslovakian state socialism, under General Secretary Alexander Dubček, increasingly deviated from that of the Soviet Union in the late 1960's. Czechoslovakia's wide-ranging political and cultural reforms asserted that communism could succeed beyond of the strictures of a ruling Communist Party. Party leadership in Moscow disagreed, however. In the directive of July, 1968, the party proclaimed that relations among socialist states must be based on "socialist internationalism" and "comradely mutual aid." As formulated by Leonid Brezhnev, the statement signified hegemony (dominance) of a single Communist Party with branches in different countries. They were to be guided by the preeminence and experience of the Soviet Union. Only in this way could socialism progress.

Independent action invited intervention, as the Czechs discovered: Warsaw pact countries, under Soviet leadership, invaded Czechoslovakia in August, 1968. The tactic was successful in its specific purpose—suppressing Czechoslovakian autonomy. Its reverberations, however, hastened fragmentation of international communist solidarity. Yugoslavia and Romania, both already pursuing their own courses, denounced the implications of Brezhnev's belief in limited national sovereignty. China, too, condemned the action. Their war of words with the Soviet Union escalated to armed border clashes along the Ussuri River.

appropriately distanced him from his flamboyant predecessor.

Retrenchment, Stability, and Stagnation

Brezhnev's tenure in the Soviet Union's highest political post (general secretary of the Communist Party's Central Committee) can be divided into three phases. The first years, in the 1960's, were dominated by moving away from Khrushchev's policies. A reorganization of ministerial responsibilities increased industrial and agricultural output. Relations with allied Eastern bloc nations were dominated by the "Brezhnev Doctrine," which asserted clearly that Russia was dominant among Soviet states and that other states should follow Moscow's guidelines.

The core of the Brezhnev era (1971-1979) is generally viewed as the most peaceful decade in Soviet history. Material standards of living improved appreciably. The natural sciences, long suppressed, regained intellectual legitimacy. Foreign policy was characterized by détente, a relaxation of tensions. Détente brought a normalization of relations with the West—attested by frequent summit talks with Brezhnev's American counterparts, Presidents Richard M. Nixon, Gerald R. Ford, and Jimmy Carter. The success in 1972 of the Strategic Arms Limitation Talks (SALT I), personally negotiated by Brezhnev, acknowledged the legitimacy of nuclear parity (equivalence) with the United States. The signing of the Helsinki Accords of 1975 formally recognized the Soviet Union's post-World War II boundaries. These agreements, however, were laden with potential causes of discord. Human rights provisions in the Helsinki documents increased tension between Brezhnev and the United States over U.S. "meddling" in internal Soviet Union issues of Jewish emigration and treatment of dissidents. Many in the U.S. government continued to distrust the Soviet Union under Brezhnev, and his use of foreign proxies to expand Soviet influence, especially the sending of Cuban troops to Angola, confirmed their suspicions. Internally, decentralization of the Soviet bureaucratic apparatus bought party loyalty at

The Invasion of Afghanistan

Afghanistan's links to Russia grew stronger in the 1970's, culminating with the coming to power of the Marxist-oriented People's Democratic Party. The extremism of the country's new leaders, however, was distrusted by Moscow. The Afghani government was unable to control factional fighting, which resulted in a hundred Soviet advisers being killed in the Herat uprising of spring, 1979. Leonid Brezhnev decided to intervene with an armed force of eighty thousand. The resulting situation was similar in some ways to the earlier U.S. involvement in Vietnam. The conflict's unpopularity increased with mounting casualties (thirteen thousand dead, thirty-five thousand wounded) and expenses. The diplomatic liability of fighting a protracted, unwinnable war also proved costly. Yet nearly ten years passed before radical changes in Soviet leadership (the ascension of Mikhail Gorbachev) led to a Soviet withdrawal.

the price of cronyism, corruption, and disillusionment with the basic tenets of the communist system.

The invasion of Afghanistan in December, 1979, marked the beginning of Brezhnev's final three years in power. The misguided invasion brought rapid international condemnation. The United States led a boycott of the 1980 Moscow Olympics and refused to ratify the SALT II accords. Election of U.S. president Ronald Reagan (1980), with his conception of the Soviet Union as an "Evil Empire" and escalation of the arms race, threatened a full-fledged renewal of the Cold War. In Poland, the Solidarity union defied Brezhnev's imposition of martial law (December, 1981), while other Eastern bloc countries increasingly strayed from the tenets of the Brezhnev Doctrine without retribution. Plagued by deteriorating health, Brezhnev surrounded himself with companions who bedecked one another—and especially their leader—with medals, awards, and the privileges of power. Grandiose heroic projects such as Siberia's rail line continued to make headlines, while social services, especially in the countryside, deteriorated.

Leonid Brezhnev (bottom right) and other Soviet delegates signing a joint communique at a Warsaw Pact conference. *(Library of Congress)*

It was under Brezhnev's leadership that the Soviet Union invaded Afghanistan in 1979. Here Afghan resistance fighters return to a village destroyed by Soviet troops. *(U.S. Department of Defense)*

Brezhnev was never overly ambitious, nor did he particularly crave power, yet he rose to command supreme authority. His success lay in his fidelity to a form of bureaucratic humanism previously unknown in the Soviet Union. Brezhnev's preference for peaceful, orderly, hierarchical coexistence extended into international relations. Underlying this principle, however, was a belief in the rightfulness of the status quo that left many others, both at home and abroad, dissatisfied and disillusioned.

Bibliography

Brown, Archie, Michael Kaser, and Gerald S. Smith, eds. *The Cambridge Encyclopedia of Russia and the Former Soviet Union*. New York: Cambridge University Press, 1994.

Dornberg, John. *Brezhnev: The Masks of Power*. London: Andre Deutsch, 1974.

Murphy, Paul J. *Brezhnev: Soviet Politician*. Jefferson, N.C.: McFarland, 1981.

Michael W. Tripp

Aristide Briand

Born: March 28, 1862; Nantes, Breton, France
Died: March 7, 1932; Paris, France

French foreign minister and eleven-time premier (prime minister), winner of 1926 Nobel Peace Prize

Aristide Pierre Henri Briand (ah-rih-STEED pee-AYR o-REE bree-O), the son of a Breton innkeeper, studied Greek and Latin in high school and went on to study law in Paris. As a young boy he took regular Sunday walks with novelist Jules Verne. By the age of thirty, Briand had become active in syndicalist politics and union activity. The syndicalists were virulently anticlerical (opposing the clergy's influence in politics) and supported violent action by workers. Briand opposed the rampant militarism and nationalism evident at the end of the nineteenth century. While his suave social manner led friends to refer

Aristide Briand *(The Nobel Foundation)*

to him as the "Breton charmer," Briand was reclusive in his personal life. He never married.

Rise in Politics

Briand, after several failed attempts, was elected to the Chamber of Deputies (France's parliament) for Loire in 1902. He served in the chamber for the rest of his life. Briand was a member of the French Socialist Party, which he had cofounded. The French Socialist Party opposed doctrinaire Marxist socialism, preferring to advance socialist causes within a capitalist system. Within a short time of his election, Briand established his reputation for superior oratory and debating skills. He spoke without notes.

In 1905 Briand accelerated his political prospects through his leadership in passing a law mandating the separation of church and state. Although an atheist, Briand won praise from Catholics for his moderation during debates of the issue. He talked extensively with leading clerics of all faiths before endorsing the legislation. His superb performance led to an offer of a cabinet post (minister of public worship and education), which he accepted in March, 1906. In 1908 he was made minister of justice, and in 1909 he became the first socialist premier (prime minister) in French history. In the topsy-turvy world of French politics, Briand was premier on eleven different occasions between 1909 and 1932.

During his first premiership, Briand confronted a serious railway strike that threatened Paris's food supply and the national economy. His handling of this crisis cost him support from socialist parties in the Chamber of Deputies and he had to step down on February 27, 1911. He became premier again during World War I in October, 1915, but was forced to resign in March,

Aristide Briand (second from right, front) and other delegates to the 1921 Washington disarmament conference. Charles Evans Hughes is to the left of Briand. *(Library of Congress)*

1917, after French forces performed poorly in southeastern Europe. He played virtually no role in the Paris peace negotiations which led to the Versailles Treaty of 1919.

Cooperation with Germany

After another brief premiership in 1921-1922, Briand became foreign minister in 1924 and remained in that position through a succession of

The Railroad Strike of 1910

The 1910 railroad strike began when the Northern Railroad Company of France fired the chairman of the Federation of Mechanics and Locomotive Engineers in October. Paris was the major city affected. The strike occurred during Aristide Briand's first premiership and placed him in a difficult position: The strike was not illegal, and Briand had a long and close association with French unions.

Briand instructed his minister of war to provide military protection for workers who did not wish to strike. This led the National Railroad Syndicate to urge a general strike by all railway workers throughout France. The effort failed when only a small number of workers participated. It is ironic that it was Briand who, at a Nantes union congress in 1894, had passionately persuaded union leaders to adopt the general strike as an appropriate action. On that occasion, Briand gained support from socialist and radical organizations. In 1910, however, socialists and radicals attacked him for protecting capitalists. He was called a "dictator." Briand defended his decisive use of the military on the grounds that railroads were essential to the well-being of the nation.

The Kellogg-Briand Pact

Signed on August 27, 1928, the Kellogg-Briand Pact was an attempt to outlaw war. The pact arose from an April, 1927, proposal by French foreign minister Aristide Briand for a bilateral treaty of friendship between the United States and France. The administration of U.S. president Calvin Coolidge did not desire a bilateral agreement, but Secretary of State Frank B. Kellogg suggested a multilateral treaty that forbade all countries signing the document from going to war.

Briand feared that such an agreement would diminish what already had been achieved by the 1928 Locarno Treaty, but he consented to further discussions with Kellogg. In 1928 they produced the pact that bore their surnames. It eventually was signed by sixty-two nations. They agreed to resolve all international disputes without resorting to warfare.

The Kellogg-Briand Pact was filled with loopholes and exceptions. Every nation reserved the right to self-defense, and existing alliances and mutual military guarantees remained in effect. Moreover, the agreement included no provision for sanctions against a country violating the terms. While the Kellogg-Briand Pact gave hope to the world for a lasting peace—and earned for Kellogg a Nobel Peace Prize—it was an ineffective instrument for achieving that goal.

left-center cabinets, some of which he led himself, into 1931. He believed that lasting peace in Europe could come only if other countries extended a hand of friendship to Germany. With the assistance of German foreign minister Gustav Stresemann, Briand led the undertaking to restore a spirit of cooperation in western Europe. His most honored achievement was the Treaty of Locarno, initialed on October 16, 1925, and officially signed in London on December 1, 1925. Locarno represented a series of agreements by which Germany, France, Belgium, England, and Italy mutually guaranteed peace in Europe.

Shortly after negotiations were held in Locarno, Switzerland, Briand invited Stresemann to join him for secret talks in the little mountain village of Thoiry. They discussed certain future adjustments to the Versailles Treaty that would ease German resentments over the harsh conditions imposed by the treaty. Briand gave his full support to German entrance into the League of Nations, which became a reality in September, 1902. In recognition of their efforts, Briand and Stresemann were named cowinners of the 1926 Nobel Peace Prize.

Last Years

In 1927, Briand suggested a bilateral treaty with the United States that would outlaw war as a means of achieving foreign policy objectives. That proposal led to the multilateral Kellogg-Briand Pact, signed on August 27, 1928. The agreement denounced war. In the late 1920's Briand began to advance the possibility of creating a European federal union, popularly known as the United States of Europe. Stresemann gave his support to this notion, but the idea did not gain widespread backing at the time.

Although he had been in poor health for some time, early in 1932 Briand decided to run for the presidency of the French Republic. Concerned friends had urged him to abandon the campaign, but he persisted. While in Paris, on March 7, 1932, Briand died from heart failure.

Briand's Contributions

Briand's easy charm and his determination to

maintain post-World War I European cooperation made him an extremely popular international statesman. The Locarno Treaty was his major achievement, but he added to his renown through the Kellogg-Briand Pact and his early vision of an integrated Europe.

Bibliography

Ferrell, Robert. *Peace in Their Time: The Origin of the Kellogg-Briand Pact.* New York: Norton, 1969.

Jacobson, Jon. *Locarno Diplomacy: Germany and the West.* Princeton, N.J.: Princeton University Press, 1972.

Kellen, Emery. *Peace in Their Time: Men Who Led Us in and out of War, 1914-1945.* New York: Alfred A. Knopf, 1963.

Ludwig, Emil. *Nine Etched from Life.* Reprint. Freeport, N.Y.: Books for Libraries Press, 1969.

Ronald K. Huch

Alan Francis Brooke

Born: July 23, 1883; Bagnères de Bigorre, France
Died: June 17, 1963; Harley Wintney, Hampshire, England

British military leader during World War II

Born and educated in France, Alan Francis Brooke (A-luhn FRAN-sihs BROOK) was the ninth and youngest child of parents from northern Ireland. He attended Woolwich Military Academy, and during World War I he joined the Royal Artillery. At the Battle of the Somme (July, 1916), Brooke introduced the first "creeping barrage" to support attacking infantry. Brooke's abilities and accomplishments marked him as an officer of considerable promise, and he rose from lieutenant to lieutenant colonel during the war. He was promoted to major general in 1935 and to lieutenant general in 1938.

Alan Francis Brooke *(Library of Congress)*

Battlefield Commander

In 1939 Brooke commanded the Second Corps of the British Expeditionary Force (BEF), sent to France at the start of World War II. During the Battle of France (May, 1940), Brooke displayed considerable skill in waging a fighting retreat across northern France.

Appointed commander in chief, home forces, Brooke was responsible for rebuilding the British army to face the expected German invasion. Fortunately for Brooke and Great Britain, the invasion never came. In December, 1941, Brooke replaced Sir John Dill as chief of the imperial general staffs. In March, 1942, he was made chairman of the chiefs of staff committee, the group responsible for British war planning. Brooke played an equally important role as the closest military adviser to Prime Minister Winston Churchill.

Strategic Adviser

One of Brooke's prime contributions to the Allied cause was his willingness to argue against Churchill's more outlandish plans. Brooke also accompanied the prime minister to all the major wartime conferences with the other Allied leaders. Always well prepared, highly articulate, and very intelligent, Brooke presented the British case clearly and persuasively. Like Churchill, he favored an indirect strategy against the Axis forces (led by Nazi Germany) in Europe, preferring to attack the periphery of the enemy. By contrast, the Americans favored a direct assault as quickly as possible.

During the early months of the United States' involvement in the war in 1942, Brooke exerted considerable influence over the U.S. Joint Chiefs of Staff (the American counterpart of the British group). The U.S. joint chiefs respected Brooke's abilities but often found him cold and difficult as an individual. Later, as the Americans became more experienced, they were more forceful in presenting their views of how the war should be waged.

Brooke longed for active field command. He had hoped to be named supreme Allied commander for the invasion of France and had even been promised the position by Churchill. When U.S. general Dwight D. Eisenhower was named, Brooke was extremely disappointed. Nevertheless, he continued to perform in an outstanding fashion as chief of the imperial general staffs.

Brooke was knighted in 1940, and in 1944 he was promoted to the rank of field marshal. When the war ended in the spring of 1945, he received

Brooke in 1944, flanked by Winston Churchill (left) and U.S. general Dwight D. Eisenhower. *(Library of Congress)*

a number of awards and honors from the various Allies. In September, 1945, he was raised to the peerage as Baron Alanbrooke of Brookeborough; he was made a viscount when he resigned as

The British Expeditionary Force

When World War II began in September, 1939, the British Expeditionary Force (BEF) was sent to France under Field Marshal Lord Gort. Lieutenant General John Dill commanded the First Corps, and Lieutenant General Alan Brooke the Second Corps. Stationed on the left of the Allied line, the BEF planned an advance into Belgium to meet the anticipated German thrust. However, when the Germans unexpectedly attacked through the dense forest of the Ardennes and raced toward the English Channel, the BEF was in danger of being cut off.

The BEF began a fighting retreat toward the Channel ports. On May 16, six days after the

German offensive had begun, the BEF began evacuating troops from Dunkirk. For reasons never completely explained, German dictator Adolf Hitler halted his troops before they crushed the British, allowing their escape by sea. Other elements of the BEF had retreated to the south. Brooke was sent to Cherbourg with reinforcements to establish a British stronghold there. This mission proved to be impossible, and the last remnants of the BEF were evacuated to Britain by mid-June. Although most of the troops of the BEF escaped, the bulk of the army's equipment, including its vehicles and heavy weapons, was lost.

chief of staff in 1946. Brooke died in 1963. He was one of the ablest of British soldiers during the war, and his service was essential to the Allied victory. His most important contribution was the links of respect and cooperation he helped forge with Britain's American allies.

Bibliography

Dear, I. C. B., ed. *The Oxford Companion to World War II*. New York: Oxford University Press, 1995.

Dupuy, Trevor N., ed., with Curt Johnson and David L. Bongard. *The Harper Encyclopedia of Military Biography*. New York: HarperCollins, 1992.

Fraser, David. *Alanbrooke*. New York: Atheneum, 1982.

Keegan, John. *The Second World War*. New York: Viking, 1990.

———, ed. *Who Was Who in World War II*. New York: Crowell, 1978.

Michael Witkoski

Stanley Bruce

Born: April 15, 1883; Melbourne, Australia
Died: August 25, 1967; London, England

Prime minister of Australia (1923-1929)

Though born in Australia, Stanley Melbourne Bruce (STAN-lee MEHL-burn BREWS) was sent to England for his university education, which he received at Cambridge University. He then worked for a London business firm in which his father was the controlling partner. In World War I, he fought for the British army on the western front. He received several medals for distinguished service.

Businessman Turned Politician

Bruce experienced several combat wounds during the war and was given leave to return to Australia. Once there, he took over the family business interests and, in a short time, revitalized their sagging fortunes. In 1918 he entered politics as a Nationalist. He impressed many in the Australian political establishment with his combination of cultivated manners and practical know-how. He was at once an insider and an outsider. At the end of 1921 Bruce became treasurer in the government of Prime Minister William Morris Hughes. Even as Hughes's continued preference for government intervention in the economy alienated his more right-wing supporters, Bruce's efficiency and caution won for him a sizable constituency. When the Nationalists had to depend on the conservative Country Party for support, Hughes was ousted in 1923 and replaced by Bruce. Bruce's aristocratic demeanor was the polar opposite of his predecessor's populism.

Coalition Leader

The Nationalist and Country parties agreed to form a coalition government with Bruce as leader. Each party was to hold a defined number of seats in the cabinet. The Bruce era was characterized as one of "men, money, markets." Australia's economy was oriented toward exports, with the country supplying agricultural products and other raw goods for foreign consumption. War veterans were given land grants; these increased a general sense of prosperity and heightened productivity. Bruce also funded scientific research that assisted farmers. In foreign policy, Bruce was a strong supporter of the League of Nations, though the generally peaceful 1920's did not present any overt challenges to the postwar order.

Stanley Bruce *(Library of Congress)*

Bruce's policies helped maintain the high price of farm products and other raw materials, but they forced wages down. This situation occasioned labor-union protests, and the Bruce era became the defining period in Australian workers' consciousness. A series of dockworkers' strikes created panic and occasioned repressive government measures against organized labor. Opponents charged that, while disciplining labor, the Bruce government gave tax breaks to wealthy landowners. When the economy began to decline in the late 1920's, Bruce ignored any warnings of hard times and continued with his antilabor policies. On October 12, 1929, the Nationalists lost to the Labor Party by a wide margin, and Bruce's term as prime minister ended.

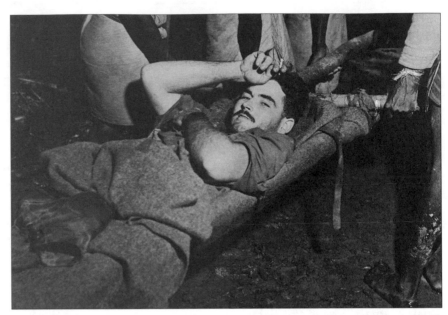
An Australian soldier injured in fighting on the Pacific island of New Guinea in 1943. *(Library of Congress)*

Bruce was reelected to Parliament in 1931. In 1932, Bruce was appointed as Australian high commissioner (representative) in London. In 1939, he was urged to return to Australia as prime minister. His agreement to return was contingent

---

Australian Troops in World War II

The United States was brought into World War II by the December, 1941, Japanese surprise attack on Pearl Harbor. Nevertheless, American and British leaders jointly decided to give the European theater of war a higher priority than the Pacific theater. Most Australian troops had been placed in the Mediterranean theater, where they served valiantly in Greece and North Africa. Australia asked the Allied High Command to redeploy some of these troops to Australia; the British countered with a proposal to put an Australian division in Burma. Stanley Bruce's ties to the British leadership were crucial in helping the British understand that Australia needed the troops back home for its psychological morale as well as for its military defense. There was also tension between the U.S. military and Australian general Thomas Blamey. Blamey noted that American troops were given spectacular assignments that garnered headlines, whereas Australian troops were assigned to mop up isolated garrisons, assignments that did nothing to win them military glory. Nevertheless, Australia remained a faithful and cooperative member of the Allied coalition until war's end in 1945.

upon Labor agreeing to join an all-party coalition. Labor refused, however, so Bruce remained in England. There he influenced British conduct of World War II and mediated between Australian and British concerns regarding troop deployment. Bruce was eventually ennobled as Viscount Bruce of Melbourne. He remained in England until his death in 1967.

Between Britain and Australia

Like his American contemporary Herbert Hoover, Bruce was a talented man who had done well in nonpolitical spheres and who was respected as an outsider free from any political taint. Like Hoover as well, however, Bruce was faced with changing socioeconomic conditions that he could not handle. In addition, his strong British associations have meant that Bruce has not fared especially well in Australian political memory.

Bibliography

Cumpston, I. M. *Lord Bruce of Melbourne*. Melbourne: Longman Cheshire, 1989.

Edwards, Cecil. *Bruce of Melbourne: Man of Two Worlds*. London: Heinemann, 1966.

Rickard, John. *Australia: A Cultural History*. New York: Longman, 1988.

Ward, Russel. *The History of Australia: The Twentieth Century*. New York: Harper, 1977.

Nicholas Birns

Gro Harlem Brundtland

Born: April 20, 1939; Oslo, Norway

First woman prime minister of Norway (1981; 1986-1989; 1990-1996)

Gro Harlem Brundtland (GROH HAHR-lehm BROONT-lahnd) was born Gro Harlem in Oslo, a year before Norway was to suffer the traumatic five-year occupation by Nazi Germany. She attended high school in Oslo, and she married Arne Olav Brundtland, a conservative journalist, in 1960. During Gro Harlem Brundtland's years in power, her husband often opposed her policies in print, a situation that amused some Norwegians watching the progress of her government.

Gro Harlem Brundtland *(AP/Wide World Photos)*

Social Policy Expert

Brundtland was educated at Oslo University, after which she went to the United States to earn a master's degree in public health from Harvard University. She then worked as an assistant medical director for the Oslo Board of Health from 1968 until she decided to run for election to the Norwegian parliament, the Storting, and to accept the offer of a government position from the Labor Party. Brundtland served as environmental minister from 1974 to 1979. For most of those years, she also served as deputy leader of the Labor Party. In 1981 she became prime minister, the first woman to hold that position in any of the Scandinavian countries except Iceland, where Vigdís Finbogadóttir had served as interim president a year earlier.

Brundtland came to office not as a seasoned politician who had a surface familiarity with a number of issues but as a technical expert in the environment and public health fields. Her depth of knowledge in these areas would prove helpful to her as she shepherded Norwegian social policy through the increasingly free-market economic currents of the 1980's. Brundtland's first tenure was short, as she was in essence only a caretaker who had to call elections quickly. Her party lost to the Conservatives led by Kaare Willoch. In 1986, though, she won election in her own right and served in office during years in which the Cold War ended and Norway's traditional strategic position as the northern bulwark of the North Atlantic Treaty Organization (NATO) was made far less essential. It was domestic social policy, however, that dominated her agenda.

Norwegian Leader, World Spokesperson

Brundtland's interest in health and the environment quickly was accorded world notice. In

1987 she chaired a U.N. panel on the environment and development, a duty that brought her wide notice. Unlike the best-known European woman leader of the twentieth century, Margaret Thatcher, Brundtland positioned herself as a center-left political figure. Her theories on economic development won her an international reputation, leading her to be termed "the mother of sustainable development." Brundtland's popularity enabled her to be returned to office in 1990 after the Conservative Party had managed to gain power for a brief interval the year before. Some Norwegians, though, accused her of cultivating too many international connections and neglecting basic social needs such as medicine. In the mid-1990's, for example, Norway was forced to import thousands of doctors from other countries because of a dire shortage.

On the World Stage

Brundtland's domestic reputation was diminished after Norway's refusal to join the European Union (EU). She abruptly resigned in October, 1996, turning over the prime ministership to Thorbjørn Jagland. There was speculation that

Norwegian prime minister Gro Harlem Brundtland delivers the concluding address at the fourth U.N. World Conference on Women, held in Beijing, China, in 1995. *(AP/Wide World Photos)*

The European Union Debate in Norway

With the end of the Cold War, many nations that had been neutral decided to apply for membership in the European Union (EU). (The European Community, or EC, became the European Union in 1993.) Austria, Finland, and Sweden joined the union, a situation that led the Norwegian government, historically an ally of most of the EU countries, to follow suit. Gro Harlem Brundtland emerged early as the leader of the pro-EU contingent; the anti-EU forces were also led by a woman, Anne Enger Lahnstein of the Center Party. Brundtland argued that entry into the EU would be good for business and that Norway would be influenced by EU policies anyway, considering its geographical position in Europe. Opponents to entry argued that Norway's natural resources, especially in fishing and farming, made it more self-reliant than many other countries. Opponents also exploited the fact that the word "union" reminded many Norwegians of their country's earlier subjugation to Sweden. Moreover, the strong German presence in the EU had unpleasant overtones of the Nazi occupation from 1940 to 1945. There was an 88 percent turnout for the referendum on November 28-29, 1994, in which Norwegian voters chose not to apply for membership in the European Union by a vote of 52.5 percent to 47.5 percent.

Gro Harlem Brundtland holding her first press conference as the head of the U.N.'s World Health Organization (WHO) in 1998, promising a new "unity of purpose" for the WHO. *(AP/Wide World Photos)*

Brundtland was advancing herself as a candidate for the U.N. secretary-generalship, which eventually went to Kofi Annan of Ghana. Again, some observers accused Brundtland of heavily promoting herself for the position. In March of 1998, Brundtland was named head of the World Health Organization. She thus became a pioneer for women on the international stage much as she had been in Norwegian politics.

Bibliography

Geyer, Robert. *The Uncertain Union: British and Norwegian Social Democrats in an Integrating Europe.* Brookfield, Vt.: Avebury, 1997.

Kiel, Anne Cohen, ed. *Continuity and Change: Aspects of Contemporary Norway.* New York: Oxford University Press, 1993.

Liswood, Laura A. *Women World Leaders: Fifteen Great Politicians Tell Their Stories.* San Francisco: Pandora/HarperCollins, 1995.

Nicholas Birns

William Jennings Bryan

Born: March 19, 1860; Salem, Illinois
Died: July 26, 1925; Dayton, Tennessee

U.S. political figure and three-time presidential candidate

William Jennings Bryan (WIHL-yuhm JEH-nihngz BRI-uhn) was born on the eve of the U.S. Civil War, but into a family that was not much affected by that conflict. His father was a political figure and later a state circuit judge whose decisions were influenced by his deep religious convictions. After graduating from Illinois College in Jacksonville and Union College of Law, Chicago, Bryan practiced law in Illinois. He later moved to Nebraska, where he was elected as a Democrat to the U.S. House of Representatives in 1890 and 1892. In Congress Bryan gained a reputation for oratorical eloquence.

Presidential Campaigns

In 1894 Bryan sought to be chosen a U.S. senator. At the time senators were elected by state legislatures. Bryan's hopes ended when the Republican Party gained control of the Nebraska legislature. However, by 1896 he had nonetheless become a national leader in the Democratic Party and was the major spokesman for agrarian unrest throughout the Midwest. One of the major changes advocated by Bryan and the agrarian movement was the coinage of silver as well as gold. This move, it was argued, would put more money into circulation and would help farmers survive the periodic financial panics of the late nineteenth century.

At the Democratic Party Convention in 1896, Bryan delivered the most famous speech of his career, his "cross of gold speech" in defense of free silver (silver coinage). After impressing the delegates with the virtues of his issue and with the possible international intrigue backing the gold standard, Bryan delivered his famous conclusion:

> [W]e will answer their demand for a gold standard by saying to them: You shall not press down upon the brow of labor this crown of thorns, you shall not crucify mankind upon a cross of gold.

The result of this speech was that Bryan received the Democratic nomination for president at the convention. In the November election he lost to Republican nominee William McKinley.

In 1900 William Jennings Bryan again received the Democratic nomination and was again defeated by McKinley. Bryan's weekly newspaper,

William Jennings Bryan *(Library of Congress)*

213

Three-time U.S. presidential candidate William Jennings Bryan was renowned for his oratorical skill. *(Library of Congress)*

1896 free-silver position. He saw the two as inseparable, since the gold standard was favored by eastern financial leaders who had strong international ties. Bryan differed from more conservative anti-imperialists such as former Democratic president Grover Cleveland and businessman Andrew Carnegie in his support of domestic issues such as free silver and in his attempt to define the United States' world mission. The major opportunity for William Jennings Bryan to influence the entire world came in 1912 with the election of Democratic president Woodrow Wilson. Like Bryan, Wilson was a Progressive Democrat and a reformer. In December, during a visit by Bryan to Wilson's home in Trenton, New Jersey, the president-elect offered Bryan the position of secretary of state. Bryan accepted the offer.

Commoner, founded in Lincoln, Nebraska, in 1901, promoted Progressive issues and led to a third presidential nomination for Bryan in 1908. He lost the November election to Republican nominee William Howard Taft.

Secretary of State

During the 1900 presidential campaign Bryan added a strong anti-imperialism argument to his

Although both Wilson and Bryan were a bit uncertain how well they would work together, Bryan soon became a trusted adviser to the presi-

Progressivism

The Progressive movement of the early twentieth century in the United States attempted to correct political, social, and economic problems of the time. There were Progressives in both political parties. Theodore Roosevelt led Progressives in the Republican Party. In the Democratic Party, a major leader was William Jennings Bryan. Most Progressives favored primary elections, controls on big business, women's suffrage, an end to child labor, and the adoption of a national social insurance. For Bryan and other more religiously motivated Progressives, prohibition of alcoholic beverages became a major issue as well. The 1912 presidential campaign marked the peak of Progressivism. The victor, Woodrow Wilson, chose Bryan as his first secretary of state.

The Scopes "Monkey" Trial

In March of 1925, the Tennessee state legislature passed the Butler Act, which prohibited the teaching of evolution in Tennessee schools. Two weeks later the American Civil Liberties Union offered to finance a court case that would test the constitutionality of the law. In April, several citizens of the small eastern Tennessee town of Dayton convinced John Scopes, a young biology teacher, to agree to stand trial for violating the Butler Act.

The trial was held in July in the courthouse in Dayton. It attracted worldwide interest. The atmosphere was described as half circus, half revival meeting. The defense was headed by Clarence Darrow, the best-known trial lawyer in the nation, whose plan was to have the defendant plead guilty, then put the law on trial. William Jennings Bryan, three times a presidential candidate and a former secretary of state, agreed to lead the prosecution and to defend the biblical account of creation. Scopes was convicted, but the verdict was overturned on technical grounds by the state supreme court. The heat and strain of the trial had a profound effect on Bryan, who died only five days later. The Butler Act remained on the books of Tennessee until 1967 but was never again tested or enforced.

dent and a useful part of the administration. Both men thought that foreign policy would be second to domestic policy in the coming years. Events in Europe soon changed that perception. As World War I drew nearer, U.S. foreign policy became a matter of worldwide interest, and it led to a break between Wilson and Bryan. Both were committed to U.S. neutrality and world peace, but Bryan's stronger commitment to the traditional U.S. policy of isolation led to Bryan's resignation as secretary of state in 1915. His two years in that position had been devoted to the cause of world peace; he negotiated thirty treaties in behalf of that cause.

Last Years

Bryan believed that he could do more for the cause of peace as a private citizen than he could as secretary of state. He considered but rejected a personal trip to Europe in an effort to end the war. However, when the United States entered the war in 1917, he pledged his full support to the war effort. When the armistice was signed in November, 1917, Bryan renewed his campaign for permanent peace in the world.

In his later years Bryan decided that he had been concentrating more on politics than on serving God. Especially after the war, he tried to weld his deep religious and moral convictions to his program for political and social change. From 1916 to 1925 he wrote more on religious topics than on political issues. His syndicated Sunday School lessons were read by millions throughout the United States.

Part of Bryan's attempt to serve God was his strong opposition to the teaching of biological evolution as fact instead of theory. As a firm believer in the divine inspiration and infallibility of the Bible, Bryan rejected evolution in favor of the Genesis account of the creation of humankind by God. The climax of this battle, the last battle of his career, was the famous Scopes trial (the Scopes "monkey" trial) in Dayton, Tennessee, in 1925. As depicted in a play about the trial, *Inherit the Wind* (1955), Bryan's arguments against evolution were exposed as illogical by defense lawyer Clarence Darrow, who publicly humiliated the aging statesman. On July 26, 1925, five days after the end of the trial, William Jennings Bryan died in Dayton, Tennessee.

Bibliography

Anderson, David. *William Jennings Bryan*. Boston: Twayne, 1981.

Bryan, William Jennings, and Mary Baird. *The Memoirs of William Jennings Bryan*. Chicago: John C. Winston, 1925.

Clements, Kendrick. *William Jennings Bryan: Missionary Isolationist*. Knoxville: University of Tennessee Press, 1982.

Coletta, Paolo. *William Jennings Bryan*. Vol. 3 in *Political Puritan, 1915-1925*. Lincoln: University of Nebraska Press, 1969.

Kaplan, Edward S. *U.S. Imperialism in Latin America: Bryan's Challenges and Contributions, 1900-1920*. Westport, Conn.: Greenwood Press, 1998.

Springen, Donald K. *William Jennings Bryan: Orator of Small-Town America*. New York: Greenwood Press, 1991.

Glenn L. Swygart

Zbigniew Brzezinski

Born: March 28, 1928; Warsaw, Poland

Cofounder of the Trilateral Commission (1973), U.S. national security adviser (1977-1981)

Zbigniew Kazimierz Brzezinski (ZBIHG-nyehf kah-ZEEM-yesh breh-ZHIHN-skee) was the son of a Polish diplomat. His father took a post in Canada in 1938, moving the family with him. The next year saw the beginning of World War II, with Nazi Germany and the Soviet Union invading Poland. When the war ended in 1945, Poland was occupied by the Soviet army, and soon the country was made a communist satellite of the Soviet Union. The invasion and communist takeover of his homeland made a deep impression on Brzezinski. He remained in Canada, earning his bachelor's and master's degrees at McGill University. He then moved to the United States, where he earned his Ph.D. at Harvard University in 1953.

Early Academic Career

After graduating from Harvard, Brzezinski remained there for seven years, teaching political science at the university. His teaching and research focused on the Soviet Union and on communism more generally. Brzezinski quickly developed a reputation as an astute analyst of international affairs, a proponent of the United States' hard line toward the communist bloc, and a prolific writer of books and articles.

In 1960 Brzezinski joined the faculty at Columbia University. He became increasingly involved in politics, serving as an adviser to Democratic candidates for president. He also wrote a number of influential books, including *The Soviet Bloc: Unity and Conflict* (1960) and *Ideology and Power in Soviet Politics* (1967). In 1973 Brzezinski helped found the Trilateral Commission, an international nongovernmental organization created to promote cooperation among the countries of North America, Western Europe, and Japan. Brzezinski served as the commission's director from 1973 to 1976.

The Carter Administration

A longtime politically involved Democrat, Brzezinski was selected by President Jimmy Carter to serve as his national security adviser in 1977. In this capacity Brzezinski also served as the head of the National Security Council. Although his hard-line attitude toward the Soviet Union had moderated somewhat over time, Brzezinski continued to advocate firm responses to Soviet activities in Africa and Afghanistan. He also was instrumental in negotiating several important treaties signed between the Soviet Union and the United States, including the Stra-

Zbigniew Brzezinski *(Library of Congress)*

The Trilateral Commission

In 1973 a group of prominent private citizens in North America, Western Europe, and Japan established the Trilateral Commission, with the express purpose of improving economic cooperation among their countries. The commission was a response to the perceived inability of the United States unilaterally to lead the industrialized, democratic countries of the West in the bipolar environment of the Cold War.

Although it was originally intended to exist for only a few years, the Trilateral Commission's mission and institutional existence were continually renewed (in three-year increments) through the end of the twentieth century. It re-mains an influential nongovernmental organization with more than three hundred participants from the member countries. Each of the three regions is represented in the commission's executive leadership. The work of the Trilateral Commission generally takes the form of publications, task-force reports, and conferences designed to highlight important international issues and to suggest policy responses. Research teams typically include representatives from all three regions. The commission also holds annual meetings in locations that rotate among the three regions.

U.S. security adviser Zbigniew Brzezinski (far left) was instrumental in procuring the SALT II nuclear arms treaty, here being signed by U.S. president Jimmy Carter and Soviet leader Leonid Brezhnev in 1979. *(AP/Wide World Photos)*

tegic Arms Limitation Talks (SALT II) treaty in 1979.

Soviet-American relations deteriorated toward the end of Carter's term, and the spirit of détente inherited from the Nixon years gave way to a renewed arms race and increased activity by Soviet proxies in the Middle East and Africa. The perceived malaise of American foreign policy helped pave the way for Republican Ronald Reagan's election as president in 1980. Brzezinski lost his position upon Carter's defeat, and he returned to academic life at Columbia University.

Elder Statesman

The collapse of communism and the disintegration of the Soviet Union in the late 1980's and early 1990's provided Brzezinski the opportunity to renew and refine his arguments about communism as an ideology, an economic system, and a political force. In general he considered his earlier positions to have been vindicated by events. From his new academic bases at the Center for Strategic and International Studies and The Johns Hopkins University's School of Advanced International Studies, Brzezinski wrote numerous books, articles, and essays evaluating the collapse of the communist world and offering suggestions for founding a new international order. Brzezinski emerged as a respected elder statesman of post-Cold War international affairs.

Zbigniew Brzezinski helped found the Trilateral Commission in 1973 and was its director until 1976. Here cofounder David Rockefeller (left) and Italian foreign minister Lamberto Dini confer at the organization's twenty-fifth annual meeting, held in Berlin in 1998. *(AP/Wide World Photos)*

Bibliography

Adrianopoulos, Gerry Argyris. *Kissinger and Brzezinski: The NSC and the Struggle for Control of U.S. National Security Policy*. New York: St. Martin's Press, 1991.

Brzezinski, Zbigniew. *The Grand Chessboard: American Primacy and Its Geostrategic Imperatives*. New York: Basic Books, 1997.

_____. *The Grand Failure: The Birth and Death of Communism in the Twentieth Century*. New York: Collier Books, 1990.

Steve D. Boilard

Nikolai Ivanovich Bukharin

Born: October 9, 1888; Moscow, Russia
Died: March 15, 1938; Moscow, U.S.S.R.

Soviet political leader and supporter of revolutionary Vladimir Ilich Lenin

Both parents of Nikolai Ivanovich Bukharin (nyih-kuh-LI ih-VAH-nuh-vyihch bew-KAHR-yeen) were Moscow public schoolteachers, and he grew up in a cultivated atmosphere. Always an intellectual, Bukharin joined the Bolsheviks of the Russian Social Democratic Party when he was only eighteen. From 1911 to 1917 he lived in exile in Austria, Switzerland, Sweden, Norway, England, and the United States. When he hurried home to Russia in 1917—the time of the Russian Revolution—he was a sophisticated socialist revolutionary.

Nikolai Ivanovich Bukharin *(AP/Wide World Photos)*

The Years with Lenin

The Bolsheviks, under Vladimir Ilich Lenin, seized power in Russia in November, 1917. They spent the next three years fighting a civil war in order to maintain power. Bukharin remained close to Lenin until Lenin's death in 1924, despite several major disagreements. Bukharin argued early that capitalist states were organizing national economies and becoming so powerful that they would thwart the transition to socialism predicted by Karl Marx in the nineteenth century.

Thus, he believed, before a socialist revolution could triumph throughout the world, capitalism had to be destroyed to create a new proletarian state which would dissolve into communism. Lenin originally disputed this thesis but soon came to accept it. Bukharin also disagreed with Lenin about the crucial role that nationalism would play in fighting imperialism. Later he came to appreciate the vitality of nationalist revolutions. The two leaders also differed significantly on capitalism's power to maintain order within the national boundaries of capitalist states. Bukharin was much more apprehensive about the capitalist state's organizational ability. In all these issues, Bukharin revealed his fear of the all-powerful state, whether capitalist or socialist, and he advocated moving away from state power toward a communal economy.

Russia's destructive civil war led to a harsh program of "war communism," a regimen of rationing, centralization, and mass terror. Whereas this brutal policy served effectively during the national crisis, the Bolshevik leaders—including Bukharin—mistook the forced compliance of a people under stress with a system that would foster the highest ideals of communism. By 1920 Lenin realized that "war communism" had

Pravda

Nikolai Bukharin was the editor of *Pravda*—the official Communist Party newspaper—almost uninterruptedly from December, 1917, until April, 1929, when a series of three articles led to his dismissal. In "Notes of an Economist" (September 30, 1928), Bukharin promoted ideas about economic policies that prompted immediate rebuttals from Stalin and Trotsky. In two other pieces in January, 1929, Bukharin elaborated what he said was Lenin's plans for the party's future. Although seemingly innocent, these essays were deliberately provocative because Stalin and Trotsky had already set a different course for the Soviet Union. Most significantly, Bukharin warned the faithful—accurately, as it turned out—of the grave consequences of implementing Stalin's program.

On June 30, 1929, after leaving his editorship, Bukharin published another essay, entitled "The Theory of Organized Chaos." While purporting to be a simple discussion of recent developments in capitalism, this clever piece had a hidden intention: exposure of the awkward industrial bureaucracy that was encumbering Russia itself. The Russian reading audience knew this style as "Aesopian language"—a means of expressing ideas covertly, a mode of expression that Russian writers had learned well under the czars.

Bukharin made one more important appearance in *Pravda*. On August 3, 1934 (he was now editor in chief of *Izvestia*), *Pravda* devoted several pages to Bukharin's speech on the National Writers Congress in which he voiced opinions about literature quite unorthodox for their time. Radical expression was forbidden soon afterward, and in four years Bukharin was dead.

created great problems in the agricultural sector. He then inaugurated the New Economic Policy (NEP).

The New Economic Policy

Lenin's NEP had numerous aspects. Previously, food had been forcibly requisitioned from the peasantry; now they were to pay taxes rather than pay in food. Also, peasant farmers were allowed to sell some of their food locally, providing an impetus for increased production. The NEP loosened restrictions on market mechanisms, stressed cooperation, and reconsidered the goals of socialism. Bukharin supported these policies from the beginning.

After Lenin's death in 1924, Joseph Stalin consolidated his power in the government until, in a few years, he was in control. Bukharin was loosely aligned with Joseph Stalin on most issues. Central to all government debates over Russian economic policies was the role of the peasantry in a socialist state. Historians debate the breadth and intensity of the split on this issue, but two broad factions evolved. The leftists, led by Leon Trotsky, stressed rapid industrialization at heavy cost to the peasants. The rightists followed Bukharin in urging fewer demands on the countryside. Throughout the controversies generated by the NEP, Bukharin generally supported Lenin's ideas. In the two years following Lenin's death, Bukharin had no substantive recommendations on the urgent need to industrialize.

In his study *The Road to Socialism and the Worker-Peasant Alliance* (1925), Bukharin argued for the Left's cooperation with the peasants in building socialism, and in 1926 he became chair of the executive arm of the Communist International (the Comintern). In 1927 he was at the height of his influence in the party and leaned toward the leftist viewpoint on industrialization. In 1928, however, he joined two other high-ranking Politburo members in an inner-party struggle against

The Third International

The Communist International (or Comintern) held its Third World Congress in Moscow from June 22 through July 12, 1921. The two previous congresses—in 1919 and 1920—had been dominated by Russia, and Lenin had written the Twenty-one Conditions for a party's membership in the Comintern. The Third International found Germans and Italians concerned about Moscow's dominance over other parties and about Lenin's opposition to a broad alliance of socialists and communists for the purpose of fighting fascism. Lenin insisted on holding to his conditions, which called for a core of loyalists united for a world revolution. He thereby forced a split between his die-hard followers and those Italian socialists and communists who wanted to resist Benito Mussolini. Lenin prevailed, and Mussolini jailed many left-wing Italians. The same sequence of events was repeated in Germany under Adolf Hitler.

Sergei Kirov, assassinated in 1934. The event led Joseph Stalin to move against his opponents, and Nikolai Ivanovich Bukharin was executed in 1938. *(Archive Photos)*

Stalin's plan for accelerated industrialization, a plan that Bukharin warned against in a series of *Pravda* articles.

Fall from Grace

With the triumph of Stalin and his plan for rapid industrialization, Bukharin was shunted to the sidelines. His last major scholarly effort followed from his post as head of the Institute of History of Science and Technology and resulted in an important presentation in 1931 at an international conference in London on science policy. Many details of the last eight years of Bukharin's life are missing. They were years of struggle between Stalin and his enemies in the Politburo (the executive committee of the Communist Party). Bukharin was usually in the opposition, and matters came to a head with Stalin's assassination of Sergei Kirov on December 1, 1934. Moderates in the Politburo had engineered Kirov's election to Stalin's inner Secretariat, and with his murder Stalin moved to crush his opposition.

Bukharin had warned against Stalin from the beginning, and Stalin's devastating agricultural policies and his antihumanism confirmed Bukharin's fears. By 1936 Stalin's great terror was under way with the trial of sixteen defendants. Bukharin himself was arrested in 1937 and put on trial on March 2, 1938. The grim farce of a trial led swiftly to Bukharin's execution on March 15, 1938. Bukharin's death symbolized the end of the old Bolsheviks, among whom Bukharin had been a favorite of Lenin's and a highly regarded thinker.

Bibliography

Bukharin, Nikolai. *How It All Began*. Translated by George Shriver. New York: Columbia University Press, 1998.

Cohen, Stephen F. *Bukharin and the Bolshevik Revolution: A Political Biography, 1888-1938*. New York: Knopf, 1973. Reprint with new Introduction. New York: Oxford University Press, 1980.

Kemp-Welch, A., ed. *The Ideas of Nikolai Bukharin*. Oxford, England: Clarendon Press, 1992.

Larina, Anna. *This I Cannot Forget: The Memoirs of Nikolai Bukharin's Widow*. New York: W. W. Norton, 1993.

Lewin, Moshe. *Political Undercurrents in Soviet Economic Debates. From Bukharin to the Modern Reformers*. Princeton, N.J.: Princeton University Press, 1974.

Frank Day

Bernhard von Bülow

Born: May 3, 1849; Klein-Flottbeck, Holstein
Died: October 28, 1929; Rome, Italy

Chancellor of Germany (1900-1909)

Bernhard Heinrich Martin von Bülow (BAYRN-hahrt HIN-rihk MAHR-tihn fon BEW-loh) was the son of a Prussian diplomat. His mother was of middle-class origins and created for her children a warm and supportive home. After completing his secondary education largely in the company of other sons of the aristocracy, Bülow studied law at Lausanne, Switzerland, and the universities of Berlin and Leipzig. He entered the diplomatic service in 1874 and served in a variety of diplomatic posts in most of the capitals of eastern Europe. In 1886 he married, in Vienna,

Bernhard von Bülow *(Library of Congress)*

Maria Anna, the daughter of Prince Domenico Bocadelli of Bologna; she was a distant cousin of Lord Acton, the British historian. The couple were childless.

Bülow served in the Secretariat of the Congress of Berlin in 1878, and in 1897 he was named state secretary of the German Foreign Office. Now located in Berlin, he became part of the entourage of Emperor William II. He was one of the emperor's favorite advisers, distinguished by his urbane charm and ability to soothe the mercurial character of the monarch.

Chancellor of the German Empire

In October of 1900, on the resignation of Prince Hohenlohe, Bülow (now a count, later a prince) became chancellor of the German Empire as well as minister-president of Prussia. (This dual position was necessary because of the effective control of the empire by the government of Prussia.) Bülow saw himself as the heir of chancellor Otto von Bismarck and of Bismarck's policy of dealing with the European great powers to the advantage of Germany and Prussia. His task was, however, substantially more difficult than that of his distinguished predecessor, in large part because of the gradual division of Europe into two large, competing alliances: the Triple Alliance of Germany, Austria-Hungary, and Italy (created by Bismarck in the early 1880's), and the Triple Entente, composed of Britain, France, and Russia. The Triple Entente was in the process of formation during Bülow's tenure, and his failure to prevent its formation constitutes the principal failing of his chancellorship.

Like Bismarck, though with substantially less success, Bülow pressed for greater recognition of Germany's status as a great power. He stressed the need for the acquisition of colonial properties. During his tenure in the Foreign Office, Germany had successfully acquired a ninety-nine-year lease on Kiaochow in China, purchased the Mariana Islands, and acquired by treaty most of Samoa in the western Pacific. In the 1880's Germany had acquired Togoland and Cameroon in western Africa and a colonial holding in eastern Africa, and had taken over from a private company a concession in southwest Africa in the early 1890's. Many of these holdings involved the Germans in policing conflicts among African tribes.

The Germans introduced considerable efficiency into the administration of their colonial possessions; at least temporarily, this efficiency counted in their favor as colonial administrators. However, the costs of these operations put a severe strain on Germany's budget. Bülow regarded these possessions as an acknowledgment of Germany's status as a world power, and he believed that the costs associated with them were necessary expenses. However, they were to play a part in his downfall as chancellor.

Since by 1900 most of the world had already been divided into colonial holdings, Bülow's goal of securing Germany's status through acquiring colonial assets could best be met by economic endeavors. One area where German economic penetration seemed possible was in the Ottoman

Otto von Bismarck, Germany's "iron chancellor." Bernhard von Bülow saw himself as following in Bismarck's footsteps. (*Archive Photos*)

Empire, the predecessor of modern Turkey. Such a policy was not without risk, as it invited resistance from those great powers that already had a stake in parts of the Turkish Empire, notably

The Baghdad Railway

The *Deutsche Bank* secured a preliminary concession to build a railway from Anatolia, Turkey, to the Persian Gulf by way of Baghdad in 1898. The concession was confirmed in 1902. However, Bernhard von Bülow was unable to secure British approval for the project; this approval would be necessary for the *Deutsche Bank* to be able to raise international capital for the construction costs. The British feared the impact on their link to India. In addition, the Russians,

seeking to control Persia (Iran), were adamantly opposed. Though the first section of the railroad was built, largely with German funds, the second portion, through the mountains of western Anatolia, would have entailed major construction expenses that could not have been met from German sources alone. Bülow's inability to secure great-power approval prevented the completion of the Baghdad Railway.

The Algeciras Conference

France, which had acquired Algeria in the 1830's, sought to expand its influence in North Africa in the early twentieth century. France surrendered its interest in Egypt to the British in 1898 and its interest in Libya to Italy in 1900, in both cases in return for a free hand in Morocco. France therefore pushed ahead to expand its control of Morocco. Bernhard von Bülow sought to block this expansion by pressing for an international conference that would guarantee equal economic opportunities to all powers. Under German pressure, the great powers agreed to meet at Algeciras, in Spain, in January, 1906.

When the conference met, only Austria supported the German position unconditionally. Yet because the close ties developing between Britain and France were still secret, the powers agreed to the Act of Algeciras in April of 1906. It guaranteed equal economic access to Morocco, though parts of Morocco's government were to be subjected to French and Spanish supervision. Although Algeciras appeared to be a victory for Bülow, in actuality it did not prevent growing French dominance in Morocco.

Great Britain. It also evoked opposition from Russia, which was seeking to expand its influence in northern Iran (Persia). Another area where Bülow hoped at least to preserve the opportunities for German business interests was Morocco. In both Turkey and Morocco, Bülow used diplomatic negotiations to advance German interests. He was largely unsuccessful in the long run, a consequence of the hardening of great-power relationships in the competing alliance systems.

Internal Policy

Bülow sought to build good relationships with the party leaders in the Reichstag, the legislature of the empire, so that they would approve his various proposals. He was only partially successful. He won support from conservative elements for his renewal of agricultural protection, but the mounting costs of his foreign policy, particularly his pursuit of colonial possessions, required additional tax revenue. His tax proposals met strong opposition in the Reichstag. Nevertheless, as long as he retained his close relationship with the emperor his position as chancellor was secure.

During a visit to England in 1908, Emperor William gave an indiscreet interview to an English journalist that was printed in the *Daily Telegraph*. The interview aroused a storm of opposition in Germany, during which Bülow failed conspicuously to defend the emperor. In not defending the emperor, he lost his support. When his tax increases went down to defeat in the Reichstag in July of 1909, Bülow submitted his resignation as chancellor, and it was accepted by the emperor. Bülow later served briefly as ambassador to Italy in 1914. He tried to prevent Italy from throwing its support to the Allies in World War I, but he failed. He then lived in retirement in a villa in Rome until his death in 1929.

Bibliography

Hull, Isabel V. *The Entourage of Kaiser William II, 1888-1918.* Cambridge, England: Cambridge University Press, 1982.

Langhorne, Richard. *The Collapse of the Concert of Europe: International Politics, 1890-1914.* New York: St. Martin's Press, 1981.

Lerner, Katherine Ann. *The Chancellor as Courtier: Bernhard von Bülow and the Governance of Germany, 1900-1909.* Cambridge, England: Cambridge University Press, 1990.

Wolf, John B. *The Diplomatic History of the Baghdad Railway.* New York: Octagon Books, 1973.

Nancy M. Gordon

Ralph Bunche

Born: August 7, 1904; Detroit, Michigan
Died: December 9, 1971; New York, New York

U.S. diplomat, winner of 1950 Nobel Peace Prize

Ralph Johnson Bunche (RALF JON-suhn BUHNCH) grew up in Albuquerque, New Mexico, and Los Angeles, California. He was the son of a barber and amateur musician who died when he was twelve. Raised by his maternal grandmother, Lucy Johnson, and heavily influenced by a white schoolteacher in Albuquerque named Emma Belle Sweet, Bunche (an American of African descent) overcame the racial prejudice prevalent in the United States at the time to become an internationally acclaimed statesman and the winner of the Nobel Peace Prize. He received a bachelor's degree from the University of California at Los Angeles (UCLA) in 1927 summa cum laude, a master's degree in 1928, and a Ph.D. in 1934, both from Harvard University. During World War II he served with the U.S. Joint Chiefs of Staff, the Office of Strategic Services, and the Department of State.

Athletic and Academic Career

Bunche was an outstanding athlete in high school and college. He was also a scholar of considerable talent. Convinced by his maternal grandmother that he was as good as anyone else and could accomplish whatever he chose to work for, he refused to acquiesce to the racial discrimination of the time. He once ran alongside a streetcar in Los Angeles while his grandmother rode because he refused to sit at the back of the car, as then required by California law. He did not become embittered at the prejudice he encountered because of a schoolteacher in Albuquerque, Emma Belle Sweet, who had encouraged him to excel at academics and convinced him that not all white people were racists.

After graduating from UCLA in 1927 (he attended on an athletic scholarship and played on a championship basketball team), Bunche went on to receive a doctorate in political science from Harvard and did postgraduate work at Northwestern University and the London School of Economics. He traveled widely in Africa and became a professor of political science and chairman of the department from 1928 to 1950 at Howard University in Washington, D.C.

Diplomat

During World War II Bunche performed valuable services for several agencies of the U.S. gov-

Ralph Bunche *(The Nobel Foundation)*

U.S. president Harry S Truman congratulates Ralph Bunche on his receipt of a national Outstanding Citizenship Award in 1949. *(AP/Wide World Photos)*

ernment, including the Joint Chiefs of Staff, the Office of Strategic Services (OSS), and the State Department. After the war he joined the United Nations (U.N.) Secretariat as director of the division of trusteeship. He was assisting Count Folke Bernadotte mediate the Jewish-Arab conflict in Palestine when Bernadotte died at the hands of assassins in 1948. Bunche proceeded to supervise an armistice agreement between the Jews and Arabs. For his efforts, Bunche received the Nobel Peace Prize for 1950, the first person of African descent to win the award. He became the principal director of the U.N. Department of Trusteeship from 1948 to 1954 and U.N. undersecretary for special political affairs from 1958 to 1969. He also headed a U.N. delega-

The United Nations Palestinian Commission

After the assassination of Count Folke Bernadotte in 1948 by Jewish terrorists, Ralph Bunche became the principal arbiter for the United Nations in the seemingly insoluble dispute between Palestinians and Jews over the creation of a Jewish state in Palestine. During eighty-one days of nonstop negotiations, Bunche worked his staff and the often-obstinate Jewish and Palestinian diplomats to the brink of exhaustion. At one point during the negotiations

he locked himself and the diplomats of the two states in a room for twenty hours, refusing to adjourn until a particularly difficult problem had been resolved. This sort of hard work and refusal to admit defeat epitomized Bunche's life. The agreements hammered out by Bunche and the Arab and Palestine delegations established a peace in the region that endured for six years—as long as its terms were observed by both sides.

tion to study water development projects in the Middle East, including the disputed diversion of Jordan River waters in Palestine.

Ralph Bunche practiced what many others preached. He evaluated individuals on their merits, not the color of their skin or their ethnic or religious heritage. He possessed a sure formula for success: an incredible capacity for hard work and a refusal to admit defeat. He had little patience for racial prejudice, but he did not become aggressive when he encountered it, even in the capital city of his own nation. During his life he received many awards, academic scholarships, and prizes, including the Medal of Freedom (American's highest civilian award), presented to him by President John F. Kennedy in 1963.

Ralph Bunche in his U.N. office in 1954; he headed the U.N. Department of Trusteeship. *(AP/Wide World Photos)*

Bibliography

Bunche, Ralph. *The Political Status of the Negro in the Age of Federalism.* Chicago: University of Chicago Press, 1973.

————. "United Nations Intervention in Palestine." In *Colgate Lectures in Human Relations.* Hamilton, N.Y.: Colgate University, 1949.

Haskins, Jim. *Ralph Bunche: A Most Reluctant Hero.* New York: Doubleday, 1974.

Keppel, Ben. *The Work of Democracy: Ralph Bunche, Ida Lupino, Kenneth B. Clark, Lorraine Hansberry, and the Cultural Politics of Race.* Cambridge, Mass.: Harvard University Press, 1995.

Kugelmass, J. Alvin. *Ralph J. Bunche: Fighter for Freedom.* New York: Messner, 1952.

Urquhart, Brian. *Ralph Bunche: An American Life.* New York: W. W. Norton, 1993.

Paul Madden

Warren E. Burger

Born: September 17, 1907; St. Paul, Minnesota
Died: June 25, 1995; Washington, D.C.

Chief Justice of the United States (1969-1986)

Warren Earl Burger (WAH-rehn URL BUR-gur) was the fourth of seven children born to Charles and Katharine Burger. After high school, he completed extension courses with the University of Minnesota for two years and enrolled in the St. Paul College of Law (renamed Mitchell College of Law) in 1927. Burger graduated magna cum laude with his LL.B. in 1931. In 1933 he married Elvera Stromberg, with whom he had two children.

Warren E. Burger *(Library of Congress)*

Career Path

Warren Burger was admitted to the Minnesota bar in 1931 and joined a St. Paul law firm that same year. In 1935 he became a partner, establishing a successful civil practice lasting twenty-two years. Burger was a member of numerous civic organizations and became active in the state Republican Party in the 1930's. As a Minnesota delegate to the 1952 Republican National Convention, he played a key role in securing the delegation's support for presidential candidate Dwight D. Eisenhower.

In 1953 Burger was appointed assistant attorney general in charge of civil litigation in the U.S. Department of Justice. Although not known as a trial lawyer, he handled a number of major cases; one of the most controversial involved the dismissal of a part-time employee on loyalty grounds. Burger was nominated by President Eisenhower to fill a vacancy on the U.S. Court of Appeals for the District of Columbia in 1955. The Senate confirmed his appointment the following year.

For thirteen years Burger served as an appeals judge and became known for his conservative views, especially regarding criminal defendants, on an otherwise liberal court. He also developed a reputation as a critic of the U.S. Supreme Court and particularly of Chief Justice Earl Warren. His dissatisfaction with the Warren Court arose not only from the nature of its rulings but also from the Court's activism in tackling new legal issues. Burger believed that courts should exercise restraint in the use of judicial power and leave policy making to other governmental branches.

Chief Justice Burger

When Chief Justice Warren announced his retirement in 1969, President Richard M. Nixon's nomination of Burger as his replacement was an attempt to fulfill a campaign promise. Nixon, a Republican, had pledged to appoint federal judges supportive of "law and order" and a willingness to interpret laws narrowly. Burger's nomination was embraced by conservative senators, and within a month he was sworn in as the fifteenth chief justice on June 23, 1969.

The Supreme Court, despite three more Nixon appointees, never realized what most observers predicted under Burger's leadership. The Burger Court did become increasingly conservative regarding criminal procedures and defendant rights, but it never completely overturned major Warren Court decisions. In other legal areas, the Court demonstrated considerable activism and produced significant decisions regarding abortion, capital punishment, alien rights, school busing, and affirmative action. One important case decided by the Supreme Court concerned the use of executive privilege by Richard M. Nixon in 1974. In a unanimous ruling, the Court held that presidential tape recordings were not protected from an investigation the Watergate special prosecutor was conducting. President Nixon announced his resignation in the days that followed.

Burger is probably best remembered for his efforts to improve the administration of justice and to bring attention to the management issues confronting courts. During Burger's tenure, federal court budgets and support staffs grew, new technologies were introduced, and managerial procedures and practices were strengthened. Even the Supreme Court experienced change as he developed an administrative structure that resulted in increased efficiency, professionalism, and diversity.

The Burger Record

Burger was a hard-working individual from a modest background who ascended to occupy one of the world's most prestigious positions. Under his leadership for seventeen years, the Supreme Court proved willing to exercise its authority and defied the attachment of any specific ideological label. In 1986 he retired to chair the Commission on the Bicentennial of the American Constitution.

Capital Punishment

Most observers assumed that the four "law and order" Supreme Court justices appointed by President Richard Nixon, including Chief Justice Warren Burger, would be supporters of capital punishment. Thus, the Court surprised the country in 1972 when it ruled in *Furman v. Georgia* that the death penalty, as it was then applied by the states, was unconstitutional. This ruling effectively commuted the sentences of more than six hundred inmates on death row. The five justices forming the majority did not agree on the legal reason, although three were troubled by arbitrary procedures associated with sentencing. The four Nixon appointees dissented in separate opinions. The *Furman v. Georgia* ruling did not prohibit capital punishment outright, and states responded by passing new laws delineating procedures to be followed. The Court revisited the issue in 1976 and, in a 7-2 vote, upheld a new Georgia statute. Burger and the other Nixon appointees joined the majority. Over the next decade, the Burger Court continued to clarify when and how the death penalty could be imposed. Burger remained a strong defender of capital punishment and expressed frustration with litigation delaying executions.

U.S. president Richard M. Nixon bidding his staff farewell after his resignation in August, 1974. The Supreme Court had unanimously decided that Nixon's private tape recordings, which showed his involvement in the Watergate cover-up, could not be withheld by Nixon under "executive privilege." *(Archive Photos)*

Bibliography

Friedman, Leo, and Fred L. Israel, eds. *The Justices of the United States Supreme Court, 1789-1969: Their Lives and Major Opinions.* Vol. 4. New York: Chelsea House, 1969.

Lamb, Charles M., and Stephen C. Halpern, eds. *The Burger Court: Political and Judicial Profiles.* Urbana: University of Illinois Press, 1991.

Lee, Francis Graham, ed. *Neither Conservative nor Liberal: The Burger Court on Civil Rights and Liberties.* Malabar, Fla.: Krieger Publishing Company, 1983.

Schwartz, Bernard. *The Ascent of Pragmatism: The Burger Court in Action.* Reading, Mass.: Addison-Wesley, 1990.

Schwartz, Herman, ed. *The Burger Years: Rights and Wrongs in the Supreme Court, 1969-1986.* New York: Penguin Books, 1988.

Woodward, Bob, and Scott Armstrong. *The Brethren: Inside the Supreme Court.* New York: Simon and Schuster, 1979.

William A. Taggart

George Bush

Born: June 12, 1924; Milton, Massachusetts

President of the United States (1989-1993)

George Herbert Walker Bush (JOHRJ HUR-burt WAH-kur BOOSH), the son of wealthy investment banker Prescott Bush, who served as Republican senator from Connecticut from 1953 to 1963, enjoyed a privileged childhood, attending prestigious private schools. Upon graduation from Phillips Academy in Andover, June, 1942, Bush enlisted in the U.S. Navy and served as a bomber pilot during World War II. In 1945 he married Barbara Pierce, the daughter of a magazine publisher; they had six children. He graduated Phi Beta Kappa from Yale University with a B.A. in economics in 1948. With assistance from his family, Bush entered the oil business in Texas. By 1964 he had become a millionaire in his own right. He retired from active business in 1966 to devote himself to politics.

Early Political Career

Bush won the Texas Republican nomination for U.S. senator in 1964 but lost in the general election. In 1966 and 1968 he was elected to Congress, the first Republican to represent Houston in the House of Representatives. Bush supported the policies of President Richard M. Nixon, including his escalation of the Vietnam War. Bush tried again for the Senate in 1970 but failed.

Nixon rewarded Bush's loyalty by appointing him ambassador to the United Nations, where he served from 1971 to 1973. Although the appointment was criticized because Bush had little foreign-policy experience, he proved to be an effective spokesman for his country and enjoyed the world of diplomacy. In 1973 Nixon asked Bush to become chairman of the Republican National Committee. During the Watergate scandal, Bush strongly defended Nixon against accusations of his involvement in the cover-up of illegal activities.

President Gerald R. Ford appointed Bush to head the U.S. Liaison Office in Communist China in 1974. In 1975 Ford called Bush home to become director of the Central Intelligence Agency; Bush defended the agency against criticism of its questionable activities during the previous decades. After Ford was defeated in 1976, Bush returned to private life and began to plan a campaign for the presidency.

Vice President

Bush formally entered the race for the Republican presidential nomination in May of 1979, taking a moderate stance on most issues. In contrast, the leading conservative candidate, Ronald

George Bush *(Library of Congress)*

233

U.S. president George Bush was highly popular after the conclusion of Operation Desert Storm in 1991; here U.S. troops march in a welcome-home parade in New York City. *(Frances M. Roberts)*

thing of an embarrassment when Reagan won the nomination and asked Bush to be the vice presidential candidate. Bush accepted, and the Republican ticket easily defeated President Jimmy Carter, who had been unable to free American hostages held captive in Iran.

Reagan assigned important duties to his vice president. Bush headed task forces on crime, terrorism, and drug smuggling. He also traveled to more than sixty countries as the representative of the United States. When Reagan was briefly incapacitated after an assassination attempt in 1981, and again when he underwent surgery for colon cancer, Bush was acting president.

Reagan, promised to cut taxes, greatly increase spending on the military, and still balance the budget. Bush denounced the program as "voodoo economics," a phrase that came to be some-

The main scandal of the Reagan presidency was the Iran-Contra affair, in which the Reagan ad-

The Distinguished Flying Cross

George Bush was awarded the highest honor for bravery in aviation in World War II. He enlisted in the Navy on his eighteenth birthday, and when he completed flight training in June, 1943, he was the youngest commissioned pilot in the Navy. Assigned to the aircraft carrier USS *San Jacinto*, Bush joined the Pacific war early in 1944.

On September 2, 1944, Bush's bomber ran into intense antiaircraft fire while attacking a Japanese radio installation on the island of Chichi Jima. As he began his approach, Bush's plane suffered a direct hit and the engine caught fire.

Although the smoke was so thick that he could hardly see, Bush completed his attack and successfully released his bombs on target. Bush managed to fly out over the ocean and parachute into the open sea. Neither of his two crewmen survived: One jumped with Bush but his chute failed to open; the other went down with the plane. To prevent the tide from carrying him back to the island, Bush paddled his life raft for three anxious hours before he was rescued by a submarine. For his heroism during the attack on the radio installation, Bush was awarded the Distinguished Flying Cross.

The Persian Gulf War

The invasion and takeover of oil-rich Kuwait by Iraqi dictator Saddam Hussein in August, 1990, created a major international crisis. World leaders worried that Hussein might next try to attack Saudi Arabia. George Bush and others feared the consequences for Western countries dependent on Middle East oil if a large proportion of the world's oil production were to be controlled by a ruthless dictator. He began a diplomatic and public-relations campaign to convince the American public and America's allies to use force against Iraq. The U.N. Security Council condemned Iraq and ordered economic sanctions. Bush persuaded Saudi Arabia to permit the stationing of hundreds of thousands of troops on its territory. Through personal diplomacy, he organized an international coalition including Britain, France, and even several Arab countries that was ready to use military force if deemed necessary.

With the consent of the U.S. Congress, Bush launched a massive air assault on Iraq in January, 1991—Operation Desert Storm—that devastated military and civilian targets. A land attack in February, lasting only one hundred hours, drove the Iraqi army from Kuwait. Later Bush was criticized for ordering a cease-fire before the tanks of the elite Iraqi Republican Guard had been captured and for making no attempt to remove Saddam Hussein from power. Hussein later used the guard effectively in suppressing postwar revolts.

ministration secretly sold arms to Iran and illegally used the profits to support guerrillas attacking the government of Nicaragua. Because Bush had chaired the National Security Council crisis management team, critics were skeptical when Bush denied having knowledge of Iran-Contra.

The Presidency

Bush captured the Republican nomination for president in 1988, running as the heir of the two-term Reagan administration. He promised that there would be "no new taxes," that the capital gains tax would be cut, and that military spending would be increased. Bush carried forty states, but the Democrats retained control of both the House of Representatives and the Senate. Bush was therefore unable get the cuts in the capital gains tax he sought. In 1990 he abandoned his no-new-taxes pledge in order to prevent the federal budget deficit from soaring to more than $300 billion.

Bush's main interest was foreign affairs, an area in which his administration witnessed a se-

ries of triumphs for American policy. In 1989 the Berlin Wall fell; the next year Germany was reunited after forty-four years of division between communist and noncommunist halves. In December, 1989, Bush ordered the invasion of Panama by the U.S. military, which succeeded in removing the Panamanian dictator, Manuel Noriega, from power. Negotiations with Soviet president Mikhail Gorbachev produced a series of agreements on nuclear and conventional arms reductions, relieving Cold War tensions. The collapse of communist governments in Eastern Europe and the breakup of the Soviet Union in 1991 marked the end of the Cold War.

Bush's effective diplomacy and spectacularly successful victory in the Persian Gulf War raised his standing in public opinion polls to an all-time high. His reelection seemed assured. However, a serious recession in 1991-1992 and rising unemployment aroused public fears concerning the American economy. Bush seemed unable to deal with the problem or even, some felt, to understand its seriousness for the average American.

George Bush puts on headphones at a 1989 joint press conference with Soviet president Mikhail Gorbachev (right). They are aboard a Soviet cruise ship. *(Reuters/Gary Hershorn/Archive Photos)*

Despite Bush's diplomatic and military triumphs, Governor Bill Clinton of Arkansas defeated Bush in November, 1992.

Bibliography

Duffy, Michael. *Marching in Place: The Status Quo Presidency of George Bush*. New York: Simon and Schuster, 1992.

Green, Fitzhugh. *George Bush: An Intimate Portrait*. New York: Hippocrene Books, 1989.

Hyams, Joe. *Flight of the Avenger: George Bush at War*. San Diego: Harcourt Brace Jovanovich, 1991.

Parmet, Herbert. *George Bush: The Life of a Lone Star Yankee*. New York: Scribner's, 1997.

Woodward, Bob. *The Commanders*. New York: Simon and Schuster, 1991.

Milton Berman

Mangosuthu Gatsha Buthelezi

Born: August 27, 1928; Mahlabatini, Natal, South Africa

South African political leader and anti-apartheid activist

Mangosuthu Gatsha Buthelezi (mahn-goh-SEW-tew GAHT-shah bew-teh-LAY-zee) was born in the part of South Africa known as Zululand, the grandson of an *ingonyama* ("great chief") and the son of a chief of the Zulu nation. He attended Adams College, a Christian secondary school, and then Fort Hare University College and the University of Natal. During his college years, he participated in his first political demonstrations against the white rule of mostly black South Africa. He took his father's place as hereditary chief of the Buthelezi clan of the Zulu nation in 1953.

Resisting Apartheid

In the late 1950's, under a new law called the Promotion of Bantu Self-Government Act, the white government of South Africa created ten separate territories, called *Bantustans*, in which black South Africans were to live. The black residents, who had no choice in the matter, would have some measure of independence but would have no rights as South African citizens. The Zulus were granted a Bantustan named KwaZulu. It consisted of thirty dry and rocky parcels of land that overlapped but were smaller than the traditional Zululand.

Buthelezi, who had been accepted by the government as the official leader of the Zulus, resisted the creation of these black homelands. He refused to work with the government to organize and regulate his people, even though leaders of other groups accepted the new system. In 1968, pressure from the government and from the Zulus themselves forced Buthelezi to give in and allow the government to form a territorial bureaucracy. A few years later, he agreed to accept appointment as chief minister of KwaZulu, but his position did not mean he supported the government's efforts to keep white and black South

Africans separate and unequal. Buthelezi was a popular leader, and when KwaZulu held its first election in 1978, the Zulu people voted to retain him as chief minister.

By the mid-1970's, South Africa had drawn the disapproval of the international community because of apartheid, its rigid system of racial segregation. Within the country, black opposition to white rule was becoming stronger. Other nations imposed economic sanctions on South Africa, refusing to do business with the country until it ended apartheid. A number of multinational cor-

Mangosuthu Gatsha Buthelezi *(Archive Photos/Express Newspapers)*

237

The *Mfecane*

In the early part of the nineteenth century, most of South Africa was populated by different clans and tribes of Nguni and other Bantu-speaking peoples. Under the leadership of Shaka, a strong and intelligent chief, the Zulus emerged as the most powerful military force in the area that is now known as Natal. For about ten years, beginning in 1818, Shaka's armies swept over the open plains, conquering other tribes and making them flee Natal. This massive migration came to be called the *mfecane* ("crushing" or "forced wanderings") or *difaqane*. As a result of the *mfecane*, much of Natal was cleared of residents and burned. Refugees from these wars formed new nations on the relatively secure high veld of South Africa's interior. When the Boers (descendants of Dutch settlers) who left the Cape of Good Hope settlements in the Great Trek came upon this fertile land in the 1830's, they found it so disordered that they settled there themselves and founded the Orange Free State and South African (Transvaal) Republics.

porations began to divest themselves of their holdings in South Africa. They were spurred on by stockholders who did want to make a profit by supporting racial oppression in South Africa. Buthelezi opposed both sanctions and divestiture, believing that they would harm South Africans more than they would help end apartheid.

South Africa's leading black political movement, the African National Congress (ANC), supported both policies. The ANC also was not opposed to using violence to bring about racial equality, while Buthelezi favored working with the government to create communities with shared power. The ANC accused Buthelezi of conspiring with the government to limit black participation. Buthelezi and the ANC began to struggle between themselves while both struggled against white rule.

After Apartheid

With the dismantling of apartheid, signaled by anti-apartheid leader Nelson Mandela's 1990 release from prison and the government's lifting of its ban against the ANC, Mandela was the clear favorite to lead black South Africans. Buthelezi was his only serious challenger. His Inkatha Freedom Party and the

Mangosuthu Gatsha Buthelezi at a 1994 rally in Soweto, South Africa, where he protested that upcoming South African elections would not be free and fair. *(Reuters/Juda Ngwenya/Archive Photos)*

ANC stepped up their conflict, leading to violence and the death of thousands in the early 1990's. When negotiations were held between black and white leaders to plan for multiracial elections and multiracial government, Buthelezi joined adamant segregationists in refusing to participate. In the 1994 national elections, in which blacks were for the first time granted the vote, Mandela was elected president. Buthelezi received only about 10 percent of the vote nationwide but more than 50 percent in his home province.

President Mandela appointed Buthelezi to the position of minister of home affairs in an attempt to unify the government and the nation. However, in 1995, Buthelezi launched a campaign to reestablish the Zulu nation as a separate entity, with himself as leader. He did so partly because he realized that the new national government was reducing the power of tribal and territorial authorities, and therefore of the Zulu people. Buthelezi announced that the Inkatha Freedom Party would not participate in drawing up the new post-apartheid constitution.

Although most of the Zulu chiefs supported Buthelezi's plan, most of the Zulu people and their elected officials did not. Political violence within the new province claimed more lives. The next year, when local elections were held in the newly named KwaZulu-Natal province, Buthelezi spoke in favor of national unity. However, distrust between Inkatha and the ANC continued. In 1998, South Africa's Truth and Reconciliation Commission (TRC) heard allegations that Buthelezi had collaborated with the apartheid government to set up assassination squads in the 1980's. The allegations threatened to increase the alienation of Buthelezi and Inkatha from the mainstream post-apartheid government.

Caught in the Middle

Buthelezi's leadership was marked by compromise between two difficult positions. On one hand, he had to deal with one of the most oppressive and racist governments of the modern world; he had to find a way for his people to survive, if not to thrive, under the oppression. On the other hand, he was accused by more radical black leaders of being too willing to cooperate—even collaborate—with the white government. These two pressures, along with his own ego and desire for power, made him an influential leader under apartheid. Once apartheid ended, however, he soon found himself outside the mainstream of South African politics.

Bibliography

Bradley, Catherine. *Causes and Consequences of the End of Apartheid*. Austin, Tex.: Raintree Stech-Vaughn, 1996.

Mzala. *Gatsha Buthelezi: Chief with a Double Agenda*. Atlantic Highlands, N.J.: Zed Books, 1988.

Pratt, Paula Bryant. *The End of Apartheid in South Africa*. San Diego, Calif.: Lucent, 1995.

Temkin, Ben. *Gatsha Buthelezi, Zulu Statesman: A Biography*. New York: Purnell, 1976.

Cynthia A. Bily

Richard E. Byrd

Born: October 25, 1888; Winchester, Virginia
Died: March 11, 1957; Boston, Massachusetts

U.S. aviator and explorer known for Antarctic expeditions

Richard Evelyn Byrd (RIH-churd EE-veh-lihn BURD) was born into a distinguished family in Winchester, Virginia. His mother, Eleanor Bolling Byrd, was a direct descendent of Lord Delaware, and his father, Richard Evelyn Byrd, Sr., was a lawyer and a direct descendent of William Byrd II, the founder of Richmond. Young Byrd attended the Shenandoah Valley Military Academy, and when he was thirteen his parents gave him a trip around the world alone. Byrd later attended Virginia Military Institute and the University of Virginia; then, upon graduating from the U.S. Naval Academy in 1912, he joined the battleship fleet and saw active service suppressing revolutions in Haiti and Santo Domingo. He was later placed on a retired list because of earlier sports injuries sustained as a naval cadet.

Aviator

Byrd, however, protested and was permitted to attend flight training at Pensacola, Florida. He took his wings as a naval aviator in 1918. Dedicated to aviation, Byrd pioneered the technique of nighttime landings of seaplanes as well as long-range over-water navigation. He also developed the artificial-horizon bubble sextant, known as the Byrd sextant, the drift indicator, and other types of navigational instruments for aviation, including equipment for the newly built three-engine amphibious NC-1 flying boats. During the early 1920's Byrd successfully introduced legislation to establish a Navy Bureau of Aeronautics, established the Naval Reserve Air Force, and organized an air station at the Great Lakes Training Station.

In 1924 Byrd was appointed navigator for the proposed transpolar flight of the Navy's dirigible *Shenandoah* from Alaska to Spitzbergen, Norway, a venture that was cancelled by President Calvin Coolidge. Disappointed, Byrd began to organize his own Navy flight expedition to the Arctic but was forced to forgo his plans. However, in 1925 he commanded a small naval flying detachment that accompanied Commander D. B. MacMillan's Arctic expedition. Under the sponsorship of the National Geographic Society, the expedition explored approximately 30,000 square miles (78,000 square kilometers) of northern Greenland and Ellesmere Island.

Richard E. Byrd *(Library of Congress)*

In September of 1933, Admiral Richard E. Byrd arrived in Boston to make final preparations for his second Antarctic expedition. *(Library of Congress)*

In 1926 Byrd took leave from the Navy and organized a private expedition to the Arctic, financially supported by *The New York Times*, John D. Rockefeller, Jr., and Edsel Ford. On May 9, 1926, he and Floyd Bennett flew a Fokker trimotor over the North Pole in a 15.5-hour round trip from Spitzbergen. For this feat they both received the Congressional Medal of Honor and were ac-

Science and Antarctica

Since the early 1920's, scientists have used the Antarctic to study the effects of extreme cold weather on human physiology and nutrition in stress environments, as well as testing transportation, equipment, shelter, and clothing. Participating nations have also conducted extensive research concerning meteors, seismographic profiles of the ice cap, the earth's magnetism, geomagnetism, deposits of valuable minerals, cosmic rays, glaciology, climate, and weather. Scientists are concerned with the causes of an alarming reduction in the populations of krill, penguins, and other forms of life, particularly seals and whales, which utilize food resources of the region. Further concerns are the immediate and future effects of pollution that humans are creating by their presence in this environmentally fragile area. Studies are also being conducted to identify and understand earlier forms of now extinct life as well as reconstructing the dynamics of geological change.

claimed as national heroes. Byrd was promoted to the rank of commander. However, some scholars have since argued that Byrd and Bennett did not actually reach the pole, contending that they were approximately 150 miles (240 kilometers) short of their goal. These findings are based on a distance and time discrepancy, an in-flight oil leak, and review of Byrd's diary and flight log.

Thirty days after Charles Lindbergh's successful transatlantic solo flight, Byrd accomplished the same feat in the Fokker trimotor *Trans-Atlantic Flight of America*. With three companions he reached his destination in 42 hours, making a crash landing in bad weather on June 29, 1927, at Ver-sur-Mer on the coast of Brittany, France. In recognition, the French made Byrd a Commandant of the French Legion of Honor. This flight is described in his book *Skyward* (1928).

Antarctica

Byrd made five expeditions to Antarctica for exploration and mapping, in 1928-1930, 1933-1935, 1939-1941, 1946-1947, and 1955-1956. His first expedition established the Little America Base on the Ross Ice Shelf at the Bay of Whales,

and he conducted numerous studies in addition to aerial surveys of vast areas. On November 28-29, 1929, with Bernt Balchen, who was chief pilot to the Ellsworth-Wilkins Expedition, Byrd made the first flight over the South Pole, a flight of 800 miles (1,290 kilometers). Congress recognized this feat by promoting him to rear admiral on the retired list. He was recognized as a national hero. Byrd's main purpose on his third expedition was to establish the first permanent American colony in the Antarctic and to substantiate American territorial claims.

Byrd participated in the organization of the U.S. Navy Antarctic Developments Project in 1946-1947, when he returned to Antarctica. He was made officer in charge of the expedition Operation Highjump, a large naval exercise that conducted extensive aerial mapping and tested military equipment under polar conditions. In 1955 he was nominally in charge of the U.S. Antarctic programs, supervising Operation Deepfreeze, coordinating government supported logistical, scientific, and political work in Antarctica and directing the U.S. Antarctic program for the International Geophysical Year

Byrd's Second Antarctic Expedition

Richard E. Byrd's privately financed second Antarctic expedition of 1933-1935 explored and charted approximately 200,000 square miles (518,000 square kilometers) of the continent. Byrd conducted extensive aerial mapping, including Marie Byrd Land (named after his wife) and the Edsel Ford Mountains, using aircraft, mechanical land vehicles, and dogs. He also claimed areas of Antarctica for the United States. Byrd spent most of the winter (five months) of 1934 alone at an isolated weather station named Bolling Advance Base. He stayed there with only his dog, Igloo, in a meteorological hut approximately 123 miles (198 kilometers) south of the

Little America II base. He recorded weather observations, conducted other scientific studies, and had contact with his support camp only by radio. Byrd nearly lost his life before he was rescued, after having suffered severe frostbite and carbon monoxide poisoning from a defective oil stove. Byrd wrote two autobiographical accounts of these experiences in *Discovery* (1935) and *Alone* (1938), both best-sellers. A notable accomplishment of this expedition was the use of wireless communication in which more than 300,000 words of newspaper accounts were successfully transmitted to *The New York Times* from Byrd's base in Little America.

(IGY) of 1957-1958. In recognition of Byrd's work, the American Geographical Society presented him with the prestigious Livingstone Medal for achievement in geography. He was also acknowledged by the American Association for the Advancement of Science.

Bibliography

Hoyt, Edwin P. *The Last Explorer: The Adventures of Admiral Byrd*. New York: John Day, 1968.

Mountfield, David. *A History of Polar Exploration*. New York: The Dial Press, 1974.

Roberts, David. *Great Exploration Hoaxes*. San Francisco: Sierra Club Books, 1982.

Rodgers, Eugene. *Beyond the Barrier: The Story of Byrd's First Expedition to Antarctica*. Annapolis, Md.: Naval Institute Press, 1990.

Steinberg, Alfred. *Admiral Richard E. Byrd*. New York: G. P. Putnam's Sons, 1960.

John Alan Ross

James Callaghan

Born: March 27, 1912; Portsmouth, England

Prime minister of Great Britain (1976-1979)

The father of Leonard James Callaghan (LEH-nurd JAYMZ KA-la-han), a naval man, died when James was nine, reducing the family to poverty. At sixteen, Callaghan secured a safe clerical job with the Inland Revenue and became involved in the local trade union. In 1936 he was appointed its assistant general secretary.

A Career in Politics

After enlistment and commission in the Royal Navy in 1943, he stood for Parliament as the Labour Party candidate for Cardiff South, in South Wales. The Labour Party landslide of 1945 swept him with it, thus beginning a career in Parliament that was to continue uninterrupted for forty-two years and was to include most of the major offices of state.

In the postwar government led by Clement Attlee, Callaghan held two junior ministerial posts. He had achieved enough notice for himself that, after the loss of the 1951 election to the Conservative Party, he was elected to Labour's shadow (opposition) cabinet, becoming shadow transport minister. He held this until Attlee's res-

James Callaghan *(Express Newspapers/Archive Photos)*

British prime minister James Callaghan meeting with U.S. president Jimmy Carter. *(Library of Congress)*

ignation following the 1955 election defeat. Under the new leader, Hugh Gaitskell, he became shadow colonial secretary. His politics moved to the center-right. However, he maintained close links with the Trades Union Congress (TUC). In 1957 Callaghan became a member of the National Executive Council of the Labour Party, its main policy-making body. Labour suffered further defeat in 1959. The next year, Callaghan topped the party conference poll for the shadow cabinet, and Gaitskell appointed him shadow chancellor of the Exchequer in 1961. He held this post until Labour was victorious in the elections of 1964.

Senior Government Minister

Under Prime Minister Harold Wilson, Callaghan had his first taste of real political power as chancellor. Wilson was also a professional economist, however, so Callaghan hardly had a free run. After the devaluation of sterling in 1967, he offered Wilson his resignation, exchanging jobs with Home Secretary Roy Jenkins. This was a post more suited to his interests. At that time, Northern Ireland was in the midst of civil rights unrest. Callaghan managed to keep his good name despite having to send British troops into the province.

After the 1970 Labour defeat, Callaghan continued as shadow home secretary, opposing Britain's entry into the European Common Market (the European Economic Community, or EEC). He was also involved in a new "social contract" policy. In 1973 he switched jobs to become shadow foreign secretary.

The 1967 Devaluation of the Pound

The newly elected Labour government of 1964 inherited a mounting balance-of-trade deficit. British industry was uncompetitive, and many believed that the British currency (sterling) was overvalued. However, Prime Minister Harold Wilson and his chancellor of the Exchequer, James Callaghan, made it their financial policy not to devalue. Wilson felt that for the Labour government to use devaluation to counter economic crises would only increase speculation. They took other measures—higher interest rates and reduced government expenditure—to bring economic stability. Such measures were backed by the London financial institutions and by the United States, whose own currency was also having difficulties. However, they worked against Callaghan's plans for expansion.

These measures met with some apparent success until 1966, when a slump in exports made the position of British sterling untenable. On November 18, 1967, the value of the pound was cut from $2.80 to $2.40, as measured against the U.S. dollar. Callaghan resigned immediately. Although more positive domestic measures could now be implemented, the Labour Party was unable to reap any electoral advantage.

Labour was reelected in 1974 after the Conservatives' failure to curb industrial unrest. As foreign secretary, Callaghan helped renegotiate Britain's membership in the EEC and took the issue successfully through a referendum. In 1976 Harold Wilson suddenly announced his resignation. Callaghan emerged as the overall winner for leader, collecting the votes of the right and center.

As prime minister, Callaghan inherited a deteriorating economic situation, with extremely high inflation and serious unemployment. He agreed on a policy to regulate incomes with the TUC, cut government spending, and took out international loans. By 1978 these measures were stabilizing the economy, but in the same year both the Party Conference and the TUC rejected any further income policy. Callaghan insisted on a five percent ceiling for wage increases. A "winter of discontent" followed. Labour's tiny majority in Parliament collapsed, and the Labour government fell in the spring of 1979. In the subsequent election, the Conservative Party under Margaret Thatcher came to power. Callaghan continued as Labour leader till 1980. From 1983 to 1987 he was "father of the House of Commons" as its longest-serving member. On his retirement he was honored as Baron Callaghan of Cardiff, enabling him to continue his political career in the House of Lords.

Callaghan's lack of any doctrinaire position kept him in the center of the many left-right conflicts within the Labour Party. He helped keep the party together, and himself influential, aided by his avuncular manner and his sense of the working man. He was the last of Britain's old-style Labour leaders to maintain a social contract between government and unions.

Bibliography

Derbyshire, J. Dennis, and Ian D. Derbyshire. *Politics in Britain from Callaghan to Thatcher.* Edinburgh, Scotland: Chambers, 1990.

Kellner, Peter, and Christopher Hitchens. *Callaghan: The Road to Number Ten.* London: Cassell, 1976.

Morgan, Kenneth O. *Callaghan: A Life.* London: Oxford University Press, 1997.

David Barratt

Plutarco Elías Calles

Born: September 25, 1877; Guaymas, Sonora, Mexico
Died: October 19, 1945; Mexico City, Mexico

Mexican revolutionary, president of Mexico (1924-1928)

Plutarco Elías Calles (plew-TAHR-koh ay-LEE-ahs KAH-yays) was born the illegitimate son of María Jesús Campuzano and Plutarco Elías Lucero, a Sonoran landowner of moderate means. His mother died when Calles was only three. His maternal aunt, Josefa, and her husband, Juan Bautista Calles, adopted and raised their nephew. Calles's father, an alcoholic, played only a minor role in his son's life. Calles adopted his uncle's name and added that of his father to it only in later life.

Although trained as a teacher, Calles pursued a variety of occupations in his early years—writer, farmer, mill operator, and store owner, to name a few. None proved to be successful enterprises. In 1911 he entered public service as chief of customs in the border town of Agua Prieta.

The Revolution

When the Mexican Revolution broke out in 1910, Calles played no initial role in it. He became active when he joined the ranks of Mexico's first chief, Venustiano Carranza, in his effort to overthrow General Victoriano Huerta. Huerta was responsible for the imprisonment and murder of Mexico's popularly elected president, Francisco Madero. When Carranza triumphed, he made Calles the interim governor and military chief of the Mexican state of Sonora. Later President Carranza named Calles to his cabinet as secretary of industry, commerce, and labor.

The Sonoran Dynasty

When Carranza attempted to control the selection of his successor, Calles resigned his position and returned to Sonora. He supported the bid of his fellow Sonoran, Alvaro Obregón, to oust Carranza. Obregón's forces triumphed, and Carranza was assassinated during his attempt to escape to Veracruz. In 1920 Obregón was elected president, and he named Calles secretary of the interior. In 1923 Obregón sought to duplicate Carranza's strategy of selecting his successor. While Carranza failed, Obregón succeeded. He chose Calles, who became Mexico's president in 1924. Calles and Carranza had to put down a revolt by another Sonoran, Adolfo de la Huerta, before Calles's position was secure.

Plutarco Elías Calles *(Library of Congress)*

247

Mexican president Venustiano Carranza, ousted by Plutarco Elías Calles and Alvaro Obregón. *(Popperfoto/Archive Photos)*

The Calles administration (1924-1928) was handicapped by Obregón's plan to take over the presidency once more in 1928. Moreover, Calles had to contend with a rebellion by the country's Catholics, who opposed Calles's move to limit their temporal power. The president had no choice but to back his former chief's bid for the presidency. Obregón won the election.

The Maximato

The assassination of President-elect Obregón on July 17, 1928, threw Mexican politics into total confusion. The country's constitution made no provision for a vice president, and the question of who would succeed Calles at the end of his term on November 30 became a critical issue. Calles had many supporters who believed that he should continue in office, if only on a temporary basis. However, there was also a large group of his detractors who were against it.

In a statesmanlike address to Congress, Calles declared that he would not remain in office beyond the November date and called on the legislature to name an interim president and set the date for new national elections. Calles's move drew nearly unanimous support, and the president's popularity reached its highest level. However, for the next six years Calles ran the country behind the scenes through the formation of a new organization, the National Revolutionary Party, and a powerful political machine. This period in Mexican history is called the Maximato.

With the election of Lázaro Cárdenas in 1934, Calles's influence came to an end. Accused by the new president of interference, Calles was exiled

Agrarian Reform

Plutarco Elías Calles had a strong interest in land reform, from the viewpoints of both a former teacher and a landholder. He saw in Mexico the potential for becoming a leading agricultural nation, capable of improving its balance of trade through the export of agricultural surplus. He sought to educate Mexico's peasant farmers to produce commercial crops rather than simply pursuing subsistence farming. Calles established agricultural schools throughout the country for this purpose.

to the United States in 1936. He remained out of the country until 1941, when he returned under a general amnesty declared by President Manuel Avila Camacho. Calles remained in Mexico City, totally inactive in politics, until his death there in 1945.

Bibliography
Aguilar Camin, Héctor, and Lorenzo Meyer. *In the Shadow of the Mexican Revolution*. Austin: University of Texas Press, 1993.

Dulles, John W. F. *Yesterday in Mexico*. Austin: University of Texas Press, 1961.

Marcoux, Carl Henry. *Plutarco Elías Calles and the Partido Nacional Revolucionario: Mexican National and Regional Politics in 1928 and 1929*. Ann Arbor: University of Michigan Press, 1995.

Carl Henry Marcoux

Kim Campbell

Born: March 10, 1947; Port Alberni, British Columbia, Canada

First woman to serve as Canada's prime minister (1993)

Avril Phaedra (Kim) Campbell (AYV-rihl FEED-rah "KIHM" KAM-behl), Canada's nineteenth prime minister and the first woman to hold the position, was born in 1947 in British Columbia. She had a troubled family life, with her mother leaving the family when Avril was twelve. It was at that age that she decided to change her name to Kim. She attended the University of British Columbia and was elected student council presi-

Kim Campbell in 1993, shortly before being elected leader of Canada's Progressive Conservative Party. *(AP/ Wide World Photos)*

dent. She continued her education in the early 1970's at the London School of Economics but did not finish her degree there.

First Taste of Politics

After teaching at various educational institutions in British Columbia, Campbell began her political career as an elected member of the Vancouver School Board. She served in this capacity until 1985, when she became involved in provincial politics as an adviser to the premier of British Columbia. In 1986 she was elected to the provincial legislature as a member of the conservative Social Credit Party. In that same year she lost in a bid for the party's leadership. Always an independent thinker, Campbell clashed with the new party leader over the issue of abortion. He favored a restrictive policy; she did not. By 1988 she was ready for a political change.

Federal Politics

The Progressive Conservative government of Brian Mulroney convinced Campbell to run for their party in the 1988 federal election. Campbell won a close battle in her Vancouver riding (district). She arrived in Ottawa and was soon appointed to the federal cabinet, first in a junior position and then, from 1990 to 1993, as Canada's first female minister of justice. In this role, Campbell introduced controversial measures related to gun control and the testimony of rape victims. In 1993 she became the first woman to be the minister of national defence. Once again she had to deal with controversy. First, she advocated the purchase of new helicopters, which opposition parties criticized as too expensive. Second, a Somali man was murdered by Canadian peacekeepers, and the military leadership attempted to cover up the crime.

Legacy as Prime Minister

By 1993 the government of Brian Mulroney was extremely unpopular with the Canadian electorate. Early in the year Mulroney announced his resignation. A party leadership convention to replace him was scheduled for June. Because Campbell was new to the federal political scene, and because her gender and background made her unique, she became a popular choice to succeed Mulroney. More experienced candidates withdrew rather than fight Campbell's momentum. On June 13, 1993, that surge of support won Campbell the Conservative leadership and the position of prime minister in a second-ballot victory over fellow cabinet minister Jean Charest.

With only a matter of months before an election had to be called, Campbell had little time to build a record of leadership for herself. She reorganized the federal cabinet, shrinking it in the process, but could not introduce a substantial legislative agenda before calling an election

Canadian prime minister Kim Campbell on a hay ride at a 1993 barbecue. *(Reuters/Phil Stringer/Archive Photos)*

The 1993 Election

After two months in power, Prime Minister Kim Campbell called an election for October 25, 1993. Heading into the election Campbell and her Progressive Conservative Party were tied in the public opinion polls with their main opponents, the Liberal Party under Jean Chrétien. Campbell was also the most popular choice as political leader. Several critical mistakes, however, were made during the Conservative campaign. During a leaders' debate, Campbell was unable to respond to charges that she was with-

holding poor economic results. Then a comment by her that nothing could be done about high unemployment was perceived by many as showing insensitivity toward unemployed Canadians. Finally, her campaign ran television ads that seemed to ridicule a facial disfigurement of Jean Chrétien. Election day proved to be the worst defeat for a governing party in Canadian history: Campbell and her party won only 2 seats out of 295.

Kim Campbell (far right) with other participants in the First Annual Summit of the Council of Women World Leaders, held at Harvard University in 1998. Seated at left is Violeta Barrios de Chamorro of Nicaragua; standing third from the right is Benazir Bhutto of Pakistan. *(AP/Wide World Photos)*

for October 25, 1993. That election campaign ended with a historic and devastating defeat for Canada's first female prime minister. She began the election campaign with 150 seats in the Canadian parliament. The election left her with two seats. Even more embarrassing, Campbell was decisively defeated in her own riding. Shortly after the loss, she left politics. She returned to teaching and later was appointed to a diplomatic position.

Campbell's legacy is brief but significant. Many celebrated her position as Canada's first female prime minister as an important symbolic step toward greater equality between men and women. On the other hand, some argued that Campbell's defeat demonstrated that Canadians still had considerable trouble accepting women in positions of power.

Bibliography

Campbell, Kim. *Time and Chance: The Political Memoirs of Canada's First Woman Prime Minister*. Toronto: Doubleday Canada, 1996.

McLaughlin, David. *Poisoned Chalice: The Last Campaign of the Progressive Conservative Party?* Toronto: Dundurn Press, 1994.

Newman, Peter Charles. *The Canadian Revolution, 1985-1995: From Deference to Defiance*. Toronto: Viking, 1995.

Steve Hewitt

Henry Campbell-Bannerman

Born: September 7, 1836; Glasgow, Scotland
Died: April 22, 1908; London, England

Prime minister of Great Britain (1905-1908)

Henry Campbell was the son of Scottish aristocrats Sir James Campbell and his wife. In 1871 he changed his name to Henry Campbell-Bannerman (HEHN-ree KAM-behl-BA-nur-muhn) by adding his mother's maiden name in accord with the requirements of a will. He was educated at Glasgow University and Trinity College, Cambridge.

Emergence as Liberal Leader

Campbell-Bannerman entered the House of Commons in 1869 as member of Parliament for Stirling and was soon recognized as a talented Liberal Party member. He served in a series of increasingly responsible positions in the ministries of Prime Ministers William Gladstone and the fifth earl of Roseberry. Campbell-Bannerman served twice (1871-1874 and 1880-1882) in the War Office as finance secretary. He also served as finance secretary and Parliamentary liaison at the Admiralty (1882-1884), as chief secretary for the Irish Office (1884-1885), and twice (1886; 1892-95) as secretary of state for war. His experiences with finance and both the army and navy served Britain well during the 1890's and 1900's, when the nation's need for military reorganization and reform reached a crisis and Britain's position on the high seas was challenged by Germany and the United States.

In 1895 Campbell-Bannerman arranged for the retirement of the duke of Cambridge as commander in chief of the armed forces. Cambridge, a member of the royal family, had held that position for thirty-five years and was adamantly opposed to any reform of the army. While the Royal Navy had sustained its reputation and capacity for combat, the British army was one of the most ineffective military forces in Europe: in its organization, leadership, strategic and tactical values, and training, it more reflected the military thinking of the Napoleonic era than the increasingly technical society of the late nineteenth century. Queen Victoria applauded Campbell-Bannerman's achievement and knighted him in 1895 in appreciation of his having removed her cousin from office. However, through parliamentary procedures, the Conservative Party manipulated the political situation and brought down Prime Minister Roseberry's government. During the second ministry of Lord Salisbury, Campbell-

Henry Campbell-Bannerman *(Corbis/Hulton-Deutsh Collection)*

British soldiers fighting in World War I. Henry Campbell-Bannerman engineered the removal of the duke of Cambridge as head of Britain's armed forces in 1895, which allowed a reorganization of the army into an effective fighting force. *(American Stock/Archive Photos)*

Bannerman in 1899 assumed the leadership of the Liberal Party, which was factionalized on the issues of the Boer War and Irish home rule. These divisive issues continued to plague the Liberal Party for several years; Campbell-Bannerman pursued moderate or centrist positions that, on occasion, increased the disunity.

Prime Minister

In December, 1905, Prime Minister Arthur Balfour (a Conservative) resigned but did not dissolve Parliament. Campbell-Bannerman became prime minister, and King Edward VII invited him to form a government by appointing a cabinet. Campbell-Bannerman constructed a renowned cabinet comprising many of the most talented leaders in British politics. The nation endorsed this Liberal ministry in the general election of January, 1906. Campbell-Bannerman's government formulated and approved extensive social and economic legislation, but almost all of it was vetoed by the House of Lords. However, some notable objectives were achieved. Domestically, the most substantive measure to be enacted was the Trade Disputes Act of 1906, which recognized organized labor's

The Liberal Return to Power in 1906

The Conservative government led by Prime Minister Arthur Balfour alienated many sectors of British society between 1902 and 1905. Balfour made a series of unrelated policy errors and decisions, including importing Chinese laborers to the British Transvaal colony in South Africa, the Education Act of 1902 (it drew protests from religious nonconformists), and Balfour's position in the debate over tariff reform. Balfour's ineffective leadership led to dissension within his own party. In December, 1905, Balfour resigned without dissolving Parliament. Sir Henry Campbell-Bannerman formed a new Liberal cabinet that unified the Liberal Party and was supported overwhelmingly in the general election of January, 1906. The principal ministers in this Liberal cabinet were H. H. Asquith, Edward Grey, Richard Haldane, John Morley, David Lloyd George, and John Burns.

right to strike. In foreign affairs, the Anglo-Russian Entente resolved colonial differences with czarist Russia over Persia, Afghanistan, and Tibet. Finally, Campbell-Bannerman circumvented the opposition of the House of Lords and obtained self-government for two British colonies in Africa, the Transvaal and Orange River Colony. Campbell-Bannerman became ill in 1907 and resigned in early April, 1908; H. H. Asquith became prime minister. Campbell-Bannerman died later that same month.

Campbell-Bannerman's ministry focused on needed domestic legislation to eliminate abuses in Edwardian England. His confrontations with the House of Lords led his successor, Asquith, to bring about a fundamental constitutional change in 1911: The Parliament Act of 1911 eliminated the veto power of the House of Lords and extended democratic principles in Britain.

Bibliography

Bernstein, George L. *Liberalism and Liberal Politics in Edwardian England*. Winchester, Mass.: Allen and Unwin, 1989.

Russell, A. K. *Liberal Landslide: The General Election of 1906*. Hamden, Conn.: Archon, 1973.

Spender, John Alfred. *The Life of the Right Hon. Sir Henry Campbell-Bannerman, G.C.B.* 2 vols. London: Hodder and Stoughton, 1923.

Wilson, John. *CB: A Life of Sir Henry Campbell-Bannerman*. London: Constable, 1973.

William T. Walker

Lázaro Cárdenas

Born: May 21, 1895; Jiquilpan, Michoacán (now Mexico)
Died: October 19, 1970; Mexico City, Mexico

President of Mexico (1934-1940)

Lázaro Cárdenas del Río (LAH-thah-roh KAHR-thay-nahs dehl REE-oh) was born in western Mexico, the son of poor parents in the state of Michoacán. He lacked a broad education, partly because he joined revolutionary peasants fighting for Emiliano Zapata at the age of fifteen. Years later, as president of Mexico, Cárdenas was sympathetic toward socialism but never thought of it as a realistic model for Mexican development.

Rise to Power

Cárdenas was a shrewd insurrectionary during the civil war that shook Mexico between 1910 and 1920, and he always managed to side with the winning faction. An excellent soldier, he was promoted to general for his loyalty and became governor of the state of Michoacán in 1929. After the Great Depression hit Mexico, Cárdenas once again sided with those who favored militant reformism. Once the inner circle began mentioning his name as a presidential candidate, nonofficial peasant and worker groups favored Cárdenas.

Only thirty-nine years old, Cárdenas took his campaign seriously even though there was almost no doubt that he would win. Traveling 18,000 miles (about 29,000 kilometers) throughout Mexico, Cárdenas often visited small villages on the back of a burro. Many people were impressed because Cárdenas listened to them with genuine sincerity and obviously represented a change from previous administrations. In the presidential election of 1934, of four candidates, he received 2.2 million votes. The other three received a combined total of forty thousand votes.

After his inauguration, Cárdenas decided to mobilize the masses to achieve better working conditions in the factories and the fields. Cárde-

nas wanted to educate and reshape citizens by means of socialist education and civic festivals. However, he also maintained a catastrophic policy of persecution of Catholics that had begun in 1931. The destruction of religious symbols, expulsion of priests, and burning or closing of churches alienated many. Women took the lead in waging a campaign against religious persecution, often reopening churches by force.

Former Mexican president and behind-the-

Lázaro Cárdenas *(Library of Congress)*

scenes power figure Plutarco Elías Calles had assumed that he could manipulate Cárdenas after the 1934 presidential election. He was resisted by Cárdenas, however, and he began criticizing Cárdenas and preparing for a showdown. Finally, Cárdenas exiled Calles and many of his supporters in 1936, thus consolidating his regime. The crisis with Calles resulted in the establishment of conservative governors who opposed the president's mass mobilization.

Land and Labor Reforms

In 1937 and 1938, Cárdenas decided to pursue a strongly populistic course of action to mobilize workers and peasants. His major weapons were the Confederation of Mexican Workers, a national labor union, and the National Confederation of Campesinos (peasants), both created in 1938. These groups attracted a mass following, several thousand of whom received weapons and military training. Although Cárdenas deposed fourteen state governors, many resisted his reforms anyway. Meanwhile, a severe economic slump hit Mexico in 1938. Half the country's mine workers were unemployed. After Cárdenas seized foreign oil holdings in Mexico in March, 1938, he faced new opposition from the international community. At that point, Mexican moderates and conservatives agreed to work out

General Lázaro Cárdenas in uniform in the mid-1930's. *(Archive Photos)*

The Six-Year Plan

In 1933 President Plutarco Elías Calles promised a six-year plan so that Lázaro Cárdenas, the regime's presidential candidate in the 1934 election, would be more attractive to voters. The Great Depression indicated that traditional economic ideas were no longer workable; therefore, socialistic ideas had gained in popularity. Delegates met in December of 1933 to formulate the six-year plan. Radicals took control of the meeting and established militant provisions: Twelve thousand new rural schools that would teach socialist ideas, collective bargaining for unionized workers, stimulation of agricultural and industrial cooperatives, simplified and accelerated land reform, and construction of public works—roads, railways, and highways—in order to rejuvenate the economy and provide work. In 1934 Cárdenas campaigned extensively, expounding on the six-year plan as the basis for his future reforms.

The six-year plan on which Lázaro Cárdenas campaigned in 1934 included proposals for accelerated land reform. Here land is being parceled out to Mexican peasants. *(Library of Congress)*

their differences within the political system. The result was that Cárdenas curtailed his reforms and agreed to name a moderate army officer the new president in 1940. Afterward, Cárdenas organized Mexico's defenses as commander of the Pacific Defense Zone during World War II.

Bibliography

Ashby, Joe. *Organized Labor and the Mexican Revolution Under Lázaro Cárdenas*. Chapel Hill: University of North Carolina Press, 1964.

Bantjes, Adrian. *As If Jesus Walked on Earth: Cardenismo, Sonora, and the Mexican Revolution*. Wilmington, Del.: Scholarly Resources, 1998.

Becker, Marjorie. *Setting the Virgin on Fire: Lázaro Cárdenas and the Redemption of the Mexican Revolution*. Berkeley: University of California Press, 1995.

Townsend, William C. *Lázaro Cárdenas: Mexican Democrat*. Ann Arbor, Mich.: George Wahr, 1952.

Douglas W. Richmond

Pat Carney

Born: May 26, 1935; Shanghai, China

Canadian political figure, minister for international trade (1986-1988)

Born in Shanghai, China, Patricia "Pat" Carney (pa-TRIH-shah "PAT" KAHR-nee) became one of the most powerful women in the history of Canadian politics. Her early career choice was journalism, which she practiced from 1955 to 1970. During this period she attained a postsecondary education, graduating from the University of British Columbia with a bachelor of arts degree in 1960. In 1977 she obtained an M.A. from the same institution.

In 1970 she left journalism to become a financial consultant, a career she followed throughout the 1970's. By the end of that decade she had become interested in politics. She decided to seek the nomination of the Progressive Conservative Party for a Vancouver-area riding (district). She subsequently captured the riding in the general election of 1980. Unfortunately for Carney, the Conservatives lost the 1980 election to the Liberals under Pierre Trudeau.

In the Parliament

Carney took an active role in her party's opposition to the Trudeau government. She served in several different opposition roles, including as critic of the government's financial and energy policies, the latter a sensitive issue to western Canadians in the early 1980's.

In 1984, Carney was reelected as part of a landslide victory for her party under the leadership of Brian Mulroney. Carney was one of several women appointed to important positions in the cabinet. Her first job was as minister of energy, mines, and resources, the last position she had occupied as a critic in opposition. In all her cabinet positions, Carney was the first woman to occupy the position. In 1986, she occupied a more significant position, as minister for international trade. In 1988, negotiations between Canada and the United States resulted in the signing of the 1989 Free Trade Agreement between the Mulroney government and the U.S. administration of President Ronald Reagan. The deal proved extremely controversial among Canadians, especially since only a few years earlier Mulroney had completely ruled out such a step. As minister of international trade, and later as president of the Treasury Board, a prominent fi-

Pat Carney on a visit to Japan in 1987 as Canada's minister for international trade. *(AP/Wide World Photos)*

Economic Development and the Canadian Environment

The issue of sustainability became increasingly important in Canada in the 1980's. Specifically, many people wondered whether the environment could be protected while economic development was being promoted. The issue peaked in 1988 in debates over the Free Trade Agreement, signed in 1989 between the government of Brian Mulroney and the administration of Ronald Reagan. One of the main areas of criticism was that the agreement threatened Canada's environment. It did so, argued the agreement's opponents, because it created a "level playing field"—meaning that the lower environmental standards of some American states would overturn tougher Canadian regulations. Proponents of the agreement countered that the agreement would raise standards, not lower them. The agreement went ahead. Three years later, Canada signed the Air Quality Agreement with the United States. It compelled both sides to reduce the industrial air pollution that produced acid rain. The Mulroney government argued that the latter agreement demonstrated that economic development did not necessarily prevent efforts to protect the environment.

nancial position in the cabinet, Carney was called upon to try to convince a large number of skeptical Canadians that the agreement was a positive step. Ultimately, the Mulroney government called an election, and the trade agreement quickly became the top issue during the campaign.

Out of Politics

The 1988 election was fought without Pat Carney's participation. Troubled by health problems and tired of the political life, she announced that she would not seek reelection. She was replaced in her riding by Kim Campbell, who would win the seat and experience a meteoric rise through the cabinet all the way to the prime ministership in 1993 before seeing her government crushed in the 1993 election. Carney, on the other hand, initially turned away from politics, spending her time working on her law degree.

Return to Politics

Carney did not stay out of politics forever, however. Her return was not as an elected member of Parliament but as a political appointment to the Canadian Senate. Unlike the Australian and American senates, selection of members of the Canadian equivalent had always been made by the party holding power. Usually those people appointed to the Senate reflected the politics of the party in power. Carney's appointment was no exception. Carney gained even greater publicity as a senator than she had as a cabinet minister. First she publicly speculated that her home province, British Columbia, might be prepared to separate if the Canadian federation did not become more equitable. Then she complained after a senatorial perk, a free breakfast, was removed. This publicity somewhat overshadowed her genuine accomplishments.

Bibliography

Frizzell, Alan Stewart, Jon H. Pammett, and Anthony Westell. *The Canadian General Election of 1988*. Ottawa: Carleton University Press, 1989.

Kome, Penney. *Women of Influence: Canadian Women and Politics*. Toronto: Doubleday Canada, 1985.

Newman, Peter C. *The Canadian Revolution, 1985-1995: From Deference to Defiance*. Toronto: Viking, 1995.

Steve Hewitt

Jimmy Carter

Born: October 1, 1924; Plains, Georgia

President of the United States (1977-1981)

James Earl Carter, Jr. (JAYMZ URL KAHR-tur JEW-nyur), who always preferred to be called Jimmy, was the son of a Georgia farmer and businessman. In 1946, Jimmy Carter graduated from the U.S. Naval Academy and married Rosalynn Smith. The Carters had three sons and one daughter. During his Navy service, Carter worked with Hyman Rickover and others in developing the nuclear submarine program. He then served on the crew of the nuclear submarine *Sea Wolf*. After his father died in 1953, Carter resigned from the Navy and returned to Georgia to run the family farm and business interests. His success in this work soon led him into a life of public service.

Georgia Politics

Jimmy Carter's public career coincided with the beginning of the modern Civil Rights movement, to which his career would be inseparably linked. The U.S. Supreme Court's decision in *Brown v. Board of Education* (1954), mandating desegregation of U.S. public schools, began a period of social change throughout the nation. Carter's own racial views were more liberal than those of most southerners. As chairperson of his county school board, he refused to join the White Citizens Council, and he led an unsuccessful attempt to consolidate and integrate the local public schools. Carter then ran for and won a new seat in the Georgia state senate. His four years in the legislature were marked by the unusual combination of social liberalism and fiscal conservatism, with education as his major area of interest.

Carter's first gubernatorial race, in 1966, was unsuccessful. However, the 1970 election thrust him into the governor's office and, to some extent, into the national spotlight. In his inaugural address, he called for an end to racial segregation and discrimination, and he was heralded by the media as blazing a trail for more moderate social and racial attitudes in the South.

Carter's commitment to racial balance led to a large number of African American appointments to state positions. In an unprecedented move, he also placed a portrait of Martin Luther King, Jr., in the Georgia state capitol.

Carter reorganized the state government, instituted zero-based budgeting, and led the way to opening government meetings to the public. He also supported a variety of environmental programs, including a major expansion of the state park system and the protection of rivers. Governor Carter gained public support by favoring

Jimmy Carter *(Library of Congress)*

261

U.S. president Jimmy Carter at the 1978 Camp David peace talks with Egypt's Anwar el-Sadat (left) and Israel's Menachem Begin (right). *(National Archives)*

The Camp David Accords

On September 17, 1978, Israeli prime minister Menachem Begin and Egyptian president Anwar el-Sadat signed two documents. This historic event was the conclusion of a meeting held at the U.S. presidential retreat at Camp David, Maryland. The host of the meeting was President Jimmy Carter. In 1948, when Israel was declared a nation, Egypt and other Arab nations declared war on Israel. The following thirty years witnessed three additional wars, the most significant being the Six-Day War in 1967. The state of war between Israel and Egypt did not officially end until March 26, 1979, when a formal treaty based on the Camp David accords was signed.

The events leading up to the Camp David meeting began in November, 1977, when Egyptian president Sadat made an unprecedented visit to Israel and addressed the Israeli parliament, the Knesset. The negotiations that followed, designed to end the state of war, eventually became deadlocked. When President Jimmy Carter invited Sadat and Israeli prime minister Begin to meet at Camp David, they both accepted the invitation. In the treaty in 1979, Israel agreed to withdraw from land occupied in the 1967 war, and normal diplomatic relations were established between the countries. President Carter classified the Camp David accords as the most significant accomplishment of his administration.

The Iranian Hostage Crisis

In 1979, Muslim fundamentalists in Iran overthrew the pro-Western regime of Shah Mohammad Reza Pahlavi. Since Iran under the shäh had been an important client state of the United States, the Muslims, led by the Ayatollah Ruhollah Khomeini, demanded an end to all ties with the United States. Later in the year, President Jimmy Carter allowed the shah into the United States for medical treatment.

In November of that year, militant Iranian students seized the U.S. embassy in Tehran, Iran's capital. They took the embassy personnel hostage and demanded the return of the shah.

They held their hostages captive for more than a year despite Carter's ongoing diplomatic attempts to end the crisis. Carter also approved a covert military rescue attempt that proved an embarrassing failure. The hostages, and the Carter presidency, suffered humiliation for 444 days. The militants hated Carter as a symbol of the United States. They held the hostages until after Carter lost the 1980 election and Ronald Reagan was inaugurated as president. The hostages were released January 20, 1981, a few hours after Carter had left office.

stiffer penalties for convicted criminals, especially for drug violations, and by supporting the reinstatement of the death penalty. Being constitutionally barred from a second term, Carter left office in January, 1975. Almost immediately, he began seeking the 1976 Democratic nomination for president.

The 1976 Presidential Election

Jimmy Carter faced an uphill battle in his quest for the White House. He was virtually unknown outside Georgia, and no full-fledged southerner had been elected president since the Civil War. The major theme of his campaign was that, as an outsider with no previous connection to Washington, he would bring with him a new perspective on national issues. Carter also promised an administration based on truth, compassion, and moral leadership.

Victory in the Iowa caucuses and the early primaries gave Carter the momentum he needed. He secured a first-ballot victory at the Democratic National Convention in New York. To balance the ticket, he chose a northern liberal, Senator Walter Mondale from Minnesota, as his vice-presidential running mate. Carter's early

lead in the polls has been attributed largely to a nationwide desire for change: The United States had withdrawn from Vietnam only a few years before, and, more important politically, the Republican Party was badly tarnished by the Watergate scandal that had forced President Richard Nixon to resign in 1974. Carter's lead lessened considerably as the campaign issues became clear, but he won a narrow victory over the incumbent, President Gerald Ford.

President of the United States

The domestic policies of the Carter administration focused on economic issues. The nation was in the last stages of a major recession, and Carter had criticized President Ford for not controlling inflation and unemployment. However, the problems did not disappear, and by the end of Carter's term the inflation rate was more than double the 1976 rate. The unemployment rate and the federal budget deficit were also considerably higher.

In foreign affairs, the Carter administration strongly advocated human rights. This emphasis put a strain on relations with the Soviet Union. The Strategic Arms Limitation Talks (SALT II)

Jimmy Carter (left) in the White House with Soviet foreign minister Andrei Gromyko in 1977. Gromyko was in Washington for negotiations regarding the expiring Strategic Arms Limitation Talks (SALT) Treaty. *(AP/Wide World Photos)*

from winning a second term, was the Iran hostage crisis of 1979-1981.

Carter ran for reelection in 1980. In August, 1980, although opinion polls showed that he had the lowest recorded approval rating of any president, Carter survived a strong challenge in the Democratic primaries from Senator Edward Kennedy of Massachusetts. Carter was nominated by the Democratic Party for a second term. In the general election he lost in a landslide to Ronald Reagan.

After returning to Georgia, Jimmy Carter remained active in public affairs. He served as a peacemaker and as a good-will ambassador on several occasions. He also became involved in the Habitat for Humanity program, building low-cost housing for those in need. He wrote several books, including *Keeping the Faith: Memoirs of a President* (1982), *The Blood of Abraham* (1985), and *The Virtues of Aging* (1998). The most positive contribution of President Carter was his attempt to provide much-needed moral leadership to the nation.

treaty was signed in 1979, but President Carter could not secure Senate ratification of the agreement. Foreign-policy victories for the Carter administration included the controversial Panama Canal treaties, which returned the canal to Panama, and the 1978 Camp David accords between Israel and Egypt. The most difficult foreign-policy issue, and one that helped prevent Carter

Bibliography

Hargrove, Erwin. *Jimmy Carter as President: Leadership and the Politics of the Public Good.* Baton Rouge: Louisiana State University Press, 1988.

Jones, Charles. *The Trusteeship Presidency: Jimmy Carter and the United States Congress.* Baton Rouge: Louisiana State University Press, 1988.

Morris, Kenneth. *Jimmy Carter: American Moralist.* Athens: University of Georgia Press, 1996.

Troester, Rod. *Jimmy Carter as Peacemaker: A Post-Presidential Biography.* Westport, Conn.: Praeger, 1996.

Glenn L. Swygart

René Cassin

Born: October 5, 1887; Bayonne, France
Died: February 20, 1976; Paris, France

French diplomat, winner of 1968 Nobel Peace Prize

The son of a Jewish merchant, René-Samuel Cassin (reh-NAY sahm-WELL kah-SA) studied humanities and law at Aix-en-Provence and earned a doctorate from the Faculty of Law at Paris. Serving in the infantry in World War I, he was severely wounded by German shrapnel. An amazing coincidence saved his life: He was taken to a field hospital for hopeless cases where his mother was a nurse, and she convinced the doctors to save her son.

Victims' Rights Advocate

After the war, Cassin began to fight on behalf of its victims. He advocated compensation for damages, artificial limb banks, retraining programs, small-business loans, and orphans' rights. In 1918 Cassin formed the Federal Union of Associations for Disabled War Veterans and served as vice president of the High Council for Wards of the Nation. In 1921 he arranged conferences of veterans from Italy, Poland, Germany, Czechoslovakia, and in 1926 established an international organization of disabled veterans.

Cassin was a French delegate to the League of Nations from 1924 to 1936. Through the league's International Labor Organization, he encouraged veterans from opposing sides to demonstrate together for disarmament. During World War II, Cassin joined French president Charles de Gaulle in London to serve as minister of justice in the French government-in-exile. He drafted the agreement between de Gaulle and Winston Churchill that became the charter of the French Free Forces.

The United Nations

With the war's end in 1945, the world became aware of the atrocities that had been perpetrated in Adolf Hitler's Germany. The League of Nations had been disbanded. World leaders drafted the charter for a new organization, the United Nations, which was to include a Commission on Human Rights. This represented the first time that a supranational organization would address nations' treatment of their citizens. Eleanor Roosevelt, former first lady of the United States, chaired the commission, with Cassin as vice chairman.

René Cassin *(The Nobel Foundation)*

French diplomat René Cassin in 1970, two years after being awarded the Nobel Peace Prize. *(AP/Wide World Photos)*

Cassin worked arduously on the Universal Declaration of Human Rights. He served as mediator between the Western emphasis on the civil and political sphere and the Eastern concern for economic, social, and cultural rights. Cassin was also author of the charter of the United Nations Educational, Scientific, and Cultural Organization (UNESCO).

Later Career

From 1950 to 1960, Cassin was a member of the Court of Arbitration at The Hague, and from 1965 to 1968 he presided over the European Court of Human Rights at Strasbourg. After retiring as professor of law at the University of Paris in 1960, he participated in many juridical and diplomatic federations and institutes.

In 1968, the year that the Covenants of the Universal Declaration were officially accepted by the international community, Cassin was awarded the Nobel Peace Prize. At age eighty-one, he was among the prize's oldest recipients. He

The U.N. Universal Declaration of Human Rights

In 1947 the newly formed U.N. Commission on Human Rights decided to articulate a statement of principle on human rights and then to draft covenants—conventions regarding standards, implementation, and enforcement. A drafting committee was appointed, with representatives from several nations. René Cassin was vice chairman of the commission and worked hard on the declaration.

The text of the Universal Declaration of Human Rights was sent to the U.N. General Assembly in 1948. It asserted the universal right to life, personal security, equality before the law, freedom of conscience, religion, expression and assembly, the right to work at a fair wage, reasonable working hours, and free education. The General Assembly adopted the declaration on December 10, 1948. The commission then turned to the covenants. Mechanisms for enforcement and controversy over encroachment on national sovereignty posed the greatest problems. Ultimately, the commission took six years to submit two covenants to the General Assembly, and it took the General Assembly thirteen years to consider them.

accepted his award on December 10, 1968, the twentieth anniversary of the adoption of the Universal Declaration. With the Nobel Prize money, Cassin established the International Institute of Human Rights at Strasbourg as a center for human rights documentation, communication, and research.

Cassin was a pioneer in the difficult field of standardizing and legislating human rights on the international level. While the Universal Declaration, the Covenants, and the various organizations connected with them have limited effectiveness in practical terms against real despots or atrocities, they represent the high ideals for which Cassin and his colleagues always stood.

Bibliography

Frankel, Marvin E., with Ellen Saideman. *Out of the Shadows of Night: The Struggle for International Human Rights*. New York: Delacorte Press, 1989.

Nickel, James W. *Making Sense of Human Rights: Philosophical Reflections on the Universal Declaration of Human Rights*. Berkeley: University of California Press, 1987.

Tolley, Howard, Jr. *The U.N. Commission on Human Rights*. Boulder, Colo.: Westview Press, 1987.

Wintterle, John, and Richard S. Cramer. *Portraits of Nobel Laureates in Peace*. London: Abelard-Schuman, 1971.

Barry Stewart Mann

Fidel Castro

Born: August 13, 1926 or 1927; near Birán, Oriente province, Cuba

Cuban revolutionary and communist premier of Cuba (from 1959)

Fidel Castro Ruz (fee-THEHL KAHS-troh REWS) was born the son of a Spanish immigrant landowner and his Cuban maid. Raised in relative comfort, Fidel was educated in Jesuit schools. He attended the University of Havana from 1945 to 1950, graduating with a degree in law. It was during his college days that Castro first became politically active, protesting government interference in the law school. In 1948 he married Marta Diaz-Balart, a union that produced one son but was dissolved in 1954.

Launching the Revolution

Army general Fulgencio Batista y Zaldívar seized power in Cuba in a *coup d'état* in March of 1952; Batista had been a powerful figure in the Cuban government since the early 1940's. The coup convinced Castro, then a practicing lawyer and candidate for congress, that only an armed uprising could restore constitutional order to Cuba. His political program at that time called for little more than a return to democratic government and moderate land reform.

In league with his brother Raúl and a band of more than one hundred fighters, Castro planned to seize control of the Moncada army barracks in his home province of Oriente on July 26, 1953, and call for a national uprising against Batista. The attack failed miserably, generating only feeble popular response, and Castro and his colleagues were captured and sentenced to long prison terms. However, two years later, Ba-

tista bowed to public pressure and decreed an amnesty for the rebels. Castro soon fled to Mexico to plot a return to Cuba.

Seizure of Power

As an exile in Mexico, Castro gathered around him a new squad of followers, most notably the Argentine-born physician Ernesto "Che" Guevara. He also kept in touch with the anti-Batista underground in Cuba. After months of secretly training his men in guerrilla warfare, Castro set sail for Cuba in December of 1956, landing on an obscure beach in Oriente. The peasants of the area, long exploited by the local landowners and Batista's soldiers, rallied to the side of the guerrillas. In the cities, student organizations and trade unions that were under the control of the Communist Party instigated demonstrations, strikes, and sabotage actions on behalf of Castro.

Cuban president Fidel Castro enjoying a cigar in 1978. *(AP/Wide World Photos)*

268

Disgusted with government human rights violations and corruption, the middle class also began to desert Batista. The United States, initially supportive of Batista, placed an arms embargo on Cuba. The Cuban army, ill-prepared to fight a counterinsurgency war, lost one battle after another. On December 31, 1958, Batista fled the country and Castro proclaimed the triumph of the revolution.

The Road to Socialism

Castro assumed the post of premier of Cuba in January of 1959. His goals in power proved far more radical than those he had pronounced during the insurrection against Batista. He staffed the Cuban government with key allies from the Communist Party. A far-reaching land reform program decreed in 1960 cost him the support of the middle class, thousands of whom left for the United States. The expropriation of American-

Revolutionary leader Fidel Castro and followers in the 1950's at his base in the mountains in the Cuban province of Oriente. *(Library of Congress)*

The Bay of Pigs Invasion

Under President Dwight D. Eisenhower, the Central Intelligence Agency (CIA) carried out sabotage and limited military actions against the Castro regime in 1959 and 1960. By the time John F. Kennedy became president in January of 1961, the CIA had organized an invasion of Cuba using anti-Castro exiles trained in Guatemala. The initial landing was to take place at the Bay of Pigs on the southern end of the island in mid-April.

The American planners of the invasion, through wishful thinking, misread the mood of the Cuban people. Almost all those who were seriously dissatisfied with the revolution had already departed for the United States. Moreover, the bombing of Cuban airfields by the exile air force rallied public opinion behind Castro. The national uprising—on which the CIA was counting to coincide with the debarkation of the invasion force—never occurred. The Cuban army and militia remained loyal to the revolutionary government, and between April 15 and 17 they killed or captured several thousand of the invaders.

The Cuban Missile Crisis

Fearing a recurrence of the Bay of Pigs invasion, Fidel Castro secretly agreed with Soviet Premier Nikita S. Khrushchev to place nuclear missiles in Cuba in the fall of 1962. For Castro, the missiles represented a military and diplomatic guarantee for the survival of his revolution. For Khrushchev, they were a way to keep pace with the United States in the nuclear arms race by threatening the American homeland as well as a way to extend Soviet influence into Latin America.

The discovery of the missiles by U.S. spy planes in October of 1962 led to the most frightening showdown of the Cold War. President John F. Kennedy demanded an immediate withdrawal of all Soviet offensive weapons in Cuba, and when Khrushchev failed to respond, Kennedy placed a naval blockade around the island. After thirteen days, during which the world approached nuclear war, the Soviet leader agreed to remove the missiles in return for a U.S. pledge never to invade Cuba again. Castro proved the genuine loser of this confrontation: His reputation as an independent statesman was compromised, as Kennedy and Khrushchev negotiated the future of Cuba without him.

owned properties, particularly large sugar plantations, led president Dwight D. Eisenhower to instruct the Central Intelligence Agency (CIA) to plan Castro's ouster. Cuba drew close to the Soviet Union and fomented revolution in other parts of Latin America. After Castro nationalized American oil refineries, which had refused to process deliveries from the Soviet Union, the United States broke off diplomatic relations with Cuba in January, 1961. In April, Castro utilized the victory of his forces at the Bay of Pigs to openly proclaim himself a Marxist-Leninist. The next year he secretly invited the Soviet Union to install nuclear weaponry in Cuba, instigating the Cuban Missile Crisis of October, 1962.

Cementing the Revolution

Cuba assumed many of the trappings of a Soviet-style socialist regime. A new Communist Party was established in 1965, with Castro as first secretary. Most remaining private holdings in land and industry became state-owned enterprises or cooperatives. "Mass organizations" of trade unions, neighborhood committees, and

Fidel Castro (left) meeting with Egyptian president Gamal Abdel Nasser at the New York office of the United Arab Republic in 1960. *(AP/Wide World Photos)*

women's groups mobilized the population on behalf of Castro. Cuba stepped up efforts to overthrow pro-American regimes in Latin America, Asia, and Africa. Soviet subsidies for sugar and easy credit for oil and other commodities helped keep the Cuban economy afloat.

Castro and the Crisis of Communism

In the 1980's, Cuba faced daunting challenges. Pro-Castro governments in Nicaragua and Grenada fell—the former voted out of office after relentless economic pressure from the United States, the latter after a U.S. invasion ordered by President Ronald Reagan. Worse, the ongoing political and economic turmoil in the Soviet Union threatened Cuba's economic pipeline. The collapse of communism in Eastern Europe in 1989 and the dissolution of the Soviet Union in 1991 meant the end of Cuba's beneficial trade relationship with the socialist bloc. Castro vowed "Socialism or Death!" yet the dramatic contraction of the Cuban economy during the 1990's forced him to look to foreign investment and the limited use of market mechanisms at home as the only way to revive a seemingly moribund regime.

Cuba's Indispensable Man

Worshiped by millions, detested by just as many others, both on and off the island, Fidel Castro had made himself Cuba's indispensable man. No decision in domestic or foreign affairs could be made without his consent, and he was determined to preserve his brand of socialism no matter what the price. His victories—weaning Cuba away from the diplomatic orbit of the United States, guaranteeing a minimum of education, shelter, and health care to the Cuban people—were as monumental as his failures. These included Cuba's continued dependence on sugar exports, a crumbling industrial infrastructure, and the denial of freedom of expression and political dissent.

In January, 1998, Pope John Paul II made an unprecedented visit to Cuba. He conducted open-air masses attended by hundreds of thousands of Cubans, including Castro. The pope criticized both the U.S. embargo of the island and the Cuban government's stance toward abortion, divorce, and contraception (all legal). As a result of the pope's visit, some political prisoners were released, and the United States ended its ban on humanitarian flights and cash remittances. In the government elections, 95 percent of the Cuban populace returned Castro to the presidency with a 99 percent victory.

Bibliography

Balfour, Sebastian. *Castro*. New York: Longman, 1995.

Lockwood, Lee. *Castro's Cuba, Cuba's Fidel*. Boulder, Colo.: Westview Press, 1990.

Quirk, Robert E. *Fidel Castro*. New York: W.W. Norton, 1993.

Szulc, Tad. *Fidel: A Critical Portrait*. London: Hutchinson, 1987.

Julio César Pino

Nicolae Ceausescu

Born: January 26, 1918; Scornicesti, Romania
Died: December 25, 1989; near Bucharest, Romania

Autocratic president of Romania (1967-1989)

Nicolae Ceausescu (nee-ko-LI chow-CHEHS-kew) was born of a peasant family in Scornicesti, a village of the type that he would later attempt to raze. As was not uncommon, he received only four years of formal education. At some stage in the 1930's

Ceausescu became involved in the Romanian Communist Youth Movement, and he was arrested and imprisoned in 1936 for his political activities. He allegedly met Elena Petrescu in 1939 and was again incarcerated in 1940. Upon

Nicolae Ceausescu *(Library of Congress)*

his release (or escape, depending on which account is accurate) in August, 1944, he married Elena. Ceausescu's resistance activities during World War II are subject to much debate; it has been alleged that much of what was later assigned to his credit in this respect was actually the work of his older brother Marin.

Party Functionary

Ceausescu's first notable official position under the Romanian Workers' (Communist) Party was that of secretary for the Union of Communist Youth, 1944-1945. In 1947, King Michael abdicated the throne under Soviet pressure. Ceausescu's former cellmate, Gheorghe Gheorghiu-Dej, who was first secretary of the Romanian Communist Party, became, in effect, head of state. From 1948 to 1950, Ceausescu was minister for agriculture; he was deputy minister for the armed forces with the (honorific) rank of major general from 1950 to 1954. He subsequently rose to the Party Politiburo and Secretariat, acquiring a repututation as the first secretary's most unswervingly loyal supporter.

Until 1958 Gheorgiu-Dej was rigidly subservient to the wishes of the Soviet leadership in Moscow in both the foreign and domestic spheres. In that year Soviet troops were withdrawn from Romanian soil as a partial reward for Gheorghiu-Dej's diligence in repressing the Hungarian minority in Transylvania during the Hungarian Revolt of 1956. Thereafter, Romania embarked on a highly independent path in its conduct of foreign affairs. Gheorghiu-Dej refused to take sides during the ideological disputes between Russia and China, and he kept open relations with the People's Republic of China and Albania—both against the Moscow leaders' wishes. The Roma-

The 1965 Romanian Constitution

Following the death of Romanian leader Gheorghe Gheorgiu-Dej in March of 1965, his sucessor Nicolae Ceausescu had the Romanian Communist Party vote a new constitution into being. The redesignation of Romania as a "socialist state" rather than a "people's republic," as under the Gheorgiu-Dej regime, indicated a new direction that would be dictated by Ceausescu.

A significant feature of the 1965 constitution was the endorsement of racial homogeneity in the form of a uniquely Romanian language and culture. This policy was directed against Jews, Gypsies, Germans, and, above all, the Hungarians of Transylvania. The Hungarians formed the largest and most vigorous grouping of non-Romanians within the state. Ethnic resistance to the policies pursued under this provision would spark uprisings among the Hungarian population that in December, 1989, escalated into the Winter Revolution.

nian leader categorically rejected the Soviet Union's grandiose Council for Mutual Economic Assistance (CMEA) scheme of 1962, which called upon the Soviet republics and their Eastern satellites to integrate their economies. Under this plan Romania was to have been designated as a major supplier of agricultural produce. Conversly, Gheorghiu-Dej envisioned heavy industrialization in Romania after the Stalinist Soviet model.

The Balkan Maverick

Gheorghiu-dej died on March 19, 1965, and Ceausescu was elected party first secretary. As though to underline the changeover, Ceausescu engineered the renaming of the party from the Romanian Workers' Party to the Romanian Communist Party. He also had the country's name changed from the Romanian People's Republic to the Socialist Republic of Romania. The constitution of 1965 consolidated the new regime after Ceausescu's own image and foreshadowed many of his later policies.

The first phase of Ceausescu's rule, 1965-1971, seemed to promise gradual liberalization. Ceausescu himself hinted at opening the political process, allowing divergent, uncensored views within the cultural realm, and some measure of free-market capitalism. On the international level, it was Ceausescu's refusal to conform to the hard line taken by Soviet premier Leonid Brezhnev that earned him attention and acclaim. Ceausescu broke with all other Warsaw Pact countries by refusing to condemn Israel during the Six-Day War of 1967.

In August of 1968 Romania won praise from the Western press by openly defying the Soviet call for action to suppress the Czechoslovakian Prague Spring. Ceausescu's refusal to allow the Warsaw Pact's military units transit across Romanian frontiers (the Bulgarian contingent had to be airlifted into Czechoslovakia), and his fiery anti-Russian speeches asserting that his country would fight, raised his international prestige. Ceausescu exploited his legend as the liberal, nonconforming Communist in his dealings with the United States, the Western allies, and China, to his material advantage.

Despotism

In 1971 liberalization was permanently shelved after a trip taken by the Ceausescus to China and North Korea. Ceausescu was attracted to the unbending Stalinism and personality cults in these two countries and decided to emulate Mao Zedong and Kim Il Sung. Ceausescu imposed strict censorship and transformed the arts and media into vehicles for his public adoration.

Romanian president Nicolae Ceausescu in 1968, on a balcony in Prague, Czechoslovakia, with Czech president Ludvik Svoboda (left) and Alexander Dubček (right). *(Archive Photos)*

The Securitate, a well-indoctrinated secret-police force, carried out mass arrests, intimidation, torture, and murders of suspected dissidents. Next to Albania, Romania developed into the most repressive of the communist states of the Eastern bloc. Abroad, however, Ceausescu still managed to maintain his reputation as the underdog who had dared to buck Moscow, and he was able to continue receiving aid from the Western powers.

One of Ceausescu's pet projects, "systemization," called for the bulldozing of centuries-old country villages and their replacement with concrete apartment blocks. Others included the construction of sumptuous villas where the Ceausescu family, which now included a son, Nicu, and a daughter, Zoia, could dwell in palatial splendor, and ostentatious government buildings to advertise the glory of the Ceausescu regime.

Ceausescu's obsession with racial exclusivity precipitated his downfall. Riots in Timisoara in December of 1989

The Winter Revolution of 1989

By December, 1989, Father Laszlo Tokes, a priest in the Hungarian Reformed Church and one of Romanian dictator Nicolae Ceausescu's most outspoken critics, had become one of the goverment's special targets. With foreknowledge of the priest's impending arrest, thousands of residents in Tokes's hometown of Timisoara stood outside his door, confronting the authorities. On December 16, the army was ordered to fire on the crowd. Throughout that day and the next, hundreds were killed.

Ceausescu's heavy-handed attempts to char-acterize the growing protests as products of foreign conspiracies backfired during a speech on December 21, and fighting broke out in Bucharest itself. On December 22, the army defected to the side of the rebels, and vicious block-by-block battles were waged by desperate Securitate units. The capture and December 25 executions of Nicolae and Elena Ceausescu effectively ended opposition to the revolution, though some diehard Securitate held out in Bucharest's sewers until they were starved into surrendering on January 10, 1990.

arising from his mistreatment of the Hungarian minority were met with such violent measures of repression that feelings of revulsion spread throughout the country. Attempting to harangue a Bucharest crowd into submission on December 21, Ceausescu lost control of the populace: Revolt broke out in the capital. They attempted to flee by helicopter, but Nicolae and Elena Ceausescu were apprehended, tried, and summarily executed on December 25, 1989.

Bibliography

Brown, J. F. *Surge to Freedom: The End of Communist Rule in Eastern Europe.* Durham, N.C.: Duke University Press, 1991.

Crampton, R. J. *Eastern Europe in the Twentieth Century.* New York: Routledge, 1994.

Stokes, Gale. *The Walls Came Tumbling Down: The Collapse of Communism in Eastern Europe.* New York: Oxford University Press, 1993.

Raymond Pierre Hylton

Austen Chamberlain

Born: October 16, 1863; Birmingham, Warwickshire, England
Died: March 16, 1937; London, England

British statesman and diplomat, foreign secretary (1924-1928), winner of 1925 Nobel Peace Prize

Joseph Austen Chamberlain (JOH-sehf OS-tehn CHAYM-bur-lihn) was the son of Joseph Chamberlain and his first wife, Harriet Kendrick, who died in childbirth. His father remarried twice and had six children altogether. Neville Chamberlain, prime minister from 1937 to 1940, was Austen's half-brother. The family was Unitarian. Joseph Chamberlain had had a successful career as a businessman in Birmingham, enabling him to retire from business in 1873. He entered local politics in 1873 and Parliament in 1876 where he became widely known as a sponsor of local government reform. He then became a leader of the segment of the Liberal Party that broke away over the issue of Irish home rule.

Austen attended Rugby School and Trinity College, Cambridge, from which he received a degree in 1885. He also studied at the École des sciences politiques in Paris and spent a year in Germany completing his education. His studies abroad gave him a more thorough understanding of European politics than many of his contemporaries. In 1906 he married Ivy Muriel Dundas. They had two sons and one daughter.

Early Political Career

Austen Chamberlain entered Parliament in 1888 representing a constituency arranged for him by his father. In 1892 he switched to a county seat near his hometown of Birmingham, and immediately thereafter he became junior whip of the Liberal Unionists, the party of which his father was a leading light. In 1895 he was appointed to the office of civil lord of the Admiralty, serving five years. In 1900 he became financial secretary to the treasury, transferring shortly thereafter to the office of postmaster-general, a post that brought him into the cabinet of the Conservative-Liberal Unionist government. In 1905 most Liberal Unionists transferred to the Conservative Party, but they remained out of office until the coalition governments of World War I.

In 1915 Chamberlain joined the wartime coalition government as secretary of state

Austen Chamberlain *(The Nobel Foundation)*

for India. He resigned in July, 1917, taking responsibility (though the failure was more military than political) for the mistakes of the military campaign in Mesopotamia against the Turks.

Major Role in Postwar Governments

Chamberlain rejoined the cabinet in 1918, and in January, 1919, following the first postwar election, he became chancellor of the Exchequer. He successfully carried three budgets through Parliament. By the spring of 1921 he had advanced to Conservative Party leader, taking a leading part in negotiations over the separation of Ireland from

British foreign secretary Austen Chamberlain and the delegates of six other nations in 1925 signing the Treaty of Locarno. *(Library of Congress)*

Chamberlain and the Locarno Treaties

In October of 1924, following the restructuring of German reparations under the Dawes Plan and the withdrawal of the French occupying forces, European leaders met in Locarno, Switzerland, to negotiate treaties that would reduce international tension. British participation in the Locarno Treaties was a major achievement of Austen Chamberlain. The German government, led by its foreign minister, Gustav Stresemann, had adopted a policy of accepting and carrying out the terms of the Treaty of Versailles. This policy was matched by a conciliatory government in France, anxious to normalize its relations with Germany.

A treaty guaranteeing the borders between France and Germany and Belgium and Germany was signed by Germany, France, and Bel-

gium, and was guaranteed by Great Britain (represented by Chamberlain as foreign secretary) and Italy. France signed treaties of mutual assistance with Poland and Czechoslovakia in case of attack by Germany. For five years, until the beginning of the Great Depression, a conciliatory tone dominated international relations in Europe on the basis of the Locarno Treaties. It was the guarantee of mutual assistance signed by France and Poland that triggered France's entrance into World War II following Hitler's attack on Poland in 1939. Chamberlain's contemporaries in England and elsewhere recognized the importance of his work at Locarno, and for his part in designing the treaties he was knighted by King George V.

Britain. However, Chamberlain lost the support of the Conservative Party in 1922 over the issue of continuing the coalition with the Liberals. He remained out of office until 1924, when the Conservatives won a majority in a general election. Chamberlain became foreign secretary in the first Stanley Baldwin government, where he played a leading role in making possible the Locarno Agreements, settling major differences between France and Germany. For his services he was knighted. Chamberlain also stabilized the British position in China.

Chamberlain became ill in 1928, and when the Conservatives were defeated in May he lost his office. He served briefly as first lord of the Admiralty in 1931 in an all-party government, but thereafter he declined office. He served on a Select Committee of Parliament created in 1932 to consider constitutional reform in India. In his last years he spoke out frequently in Parliament about the rising menace of Nazism in Germany.

Bibliography

Busch, Briton Cooper. *Britain, India, and the Arabs, 1914-1921*. Berkeley: University of California Press, 1971.

Marks, Sally. *The Illusion of Peace: International Relations in Europe, 1918-1933*. New York: St. Martin's Press, 1976.

Petrie, Charles. *The Chamberlain Tradition*. London: L. Dickson, 1938.

Thomson, David. *England in the Twentieth Century*. Baltimore: Penguin, 1966.

Nancy M. Gordon

Neville Chamberlain

Born: March 18, 1869; Birmingham, Warwickshire, England
Died: November 9, 1940; Highfield Park, Heckfield, Hampshire, England

Prime minister of Great Britain (1937-1940)

Arthur Neville Chamberlain (AHR-thur NEH-vihl CHAYM-bur-lihn) was the son of Joseph Chamberlain, a famous politician. After being educated at Rugby school, Neville prospered as a manufacturer in Birmingham. He married Anne Vere Cole in 1911.

Election to Office

As a Unionist, Chamberlain was elected City Council member and then Lord Mayor of Birmingham. He worked to preserve open spaces and to improve public health and public housing. In 1916 he became minister of national service, a thankless task consisting mostly of administering a new conscription law. When his policies failed, he resigned. In 1918, with the support of the Birmingham Unionists, Chamberlain was elected to Parliament by a landslide.

As a supporter of the Liberal-Conservative coalition, Chamberlain promoted bills to protect illegitimate children and to promote public health. Prime Minister Bonar Law made him postmaster-general in 1922 and minister of health in 1923. When Stanley Baldwin succeeded Bonar Law, Chamberlain briefly became chancellor of the Exchequer. Later he became Baldwin's minister of health.

As minister of health from 1924 to 1929, Chamberlain's achievements were great. He promoted health insurance and pensions for widows, orphans, and the elderly. His ministry was also concerned with housing for the poor, hospitals, medical education, smoke abatement, and establishing a green belt of land to encircle London.

Chancellor of the Exchequer

In the national coalition government of Ramsay MacDonald in 1931, Chamberlain became chancellor of the Exchequer, the second most powerful post in the government. Through the Great Depression, Chamberlain stuck by traditional economic principles and did not advocate extensive borrowing or public works projects (as did President Franklin D. Roosevelt in the United States). Chamberlain revived the British economy by raising protective tariffs on many imported goods. He built more houses, extended benefits to more of the unemployed, and created a national commission to administer these benefits.

Neville Chamberlain *(Library of Congress)*

British prime minister Neville Chamberlain (left) shaking hands with German dictator Adolph Hitler after signing the Munich Agreement in September, 1938. *(Library of Congress)*

Chamberlain became involved in foreign affairs, particularly issues of disarmament. Under Labor and Liberal Party influence, the British armed forces had been allowed to deteriorate. Many in the MacDonald government hoped that disarmament would bring world peace. Although Chamberlain realized that Adolf Hitler was rearming Germany, he hoped that international agreements could restrain Hitler. Yet in 1934 Chamberlain moved to build up British air forces. During the new national coalition under Prime Minister Stanley Baldwin (1935-1937), the situation in Europe worsened. In the face of widespread opposition, Chamberlain continued to urge rearmament. Toward Germany and Italy, the government mixed somewhat empty threats with gestures of conciliation.

Chamberlain as Prime Minister

When Chamberlain became prime minister in May, 1937, he relaxed some tariffs between Britain and the United States and recognized Jews as a protected minority in Palestine. Knowing that England could deal with Hitler effectively only from strength, he continued to rearm. Chamberlain's position was undercut by antiwar sentiment at home. The policies of successive French governments and isolationism in the United States made it weaker still.

Even though Hitler was becoming increasingly belligerent, Chamberlain favored a policy of appeasement. That is, he continued to negotiate in the hope that, if concessions were made to Germany, war could be avoided—or at least to gain time for Britain to prepare. Chamberlain's

The Unionist Party

The Unionist Party began in 1886 as a group opposing home rule for Ireland. These "Liberal Unionists" worked so closely with Conservative party members that the names became almost interchangeable. The Unionists themselves split in 1903 over proposals by Joseph Chamberlain, a cabinet minister from Birmingham, to erect a "tariff wall" around the British Empire.

Joseph Chamberlain's sons, Austen and Neville, became the new Unionist leaders. In 1914 Neville fused Unionists and Conservatives into a single organization in Birmingham, and in 1918 he was elected to Parliament. When Austen became the national Unionist leader, Neville supported him, even though he disagreed with some of his brother's policies. Neville Chamberlain represented the somewhat radical Unionists within Conservative ranks through the 1920's.

efforts culminated in the Munich Agreement of 1938, through which he sincerely hoped to ensure peace. When Hitler occupied all of Czechoslovakia in March, 1939, however, Chamberlain began to prepare his nation for war and announced that Britain would support Poland if Germany attacked. He still thought that Germany might realize that peace was in its best interest.

War

On August 21, 1939, Germany and the Soviet Union signed a mutual nonaggression pact. On September 1, Germany invaded Poland, and World War II began. Chamberlain was devastated. He told the nation that the efforts of a lifetime had "crashed into ruins." He invited Winston Churchill to join his cabinet. Chamberlain continued in office until the German army took over Norway. In May, 1940, Chamberlain resigned in the interest of a government of national unity, and Churchill became prime minister. Chamberlain stayed on briefly in the cabinet, but in the middle of Britain's darkest days, he discovered that he had a cancerous growth. An operation followed, but Chamberlain died on November 9, 1940.

A political cartoonist's view of the signing of the Munich Agreement, with Hitler looking smugly satisfied and Chamberlain appearing happy but foolish. *(Library of Congress)*

The Munich Agreement

On September 30, 1938, leaders from Great Britain, France, Germany, and Italy met in Munich, Germany. They agreed that Germany could occupy part of Czechoslovakia. Many people have called this a sell-out and labeled Neville Chamberlain, the British prime minister, a coward. The truth is more complicated. In 1919 the Treaty of Versailles, signed after World War I, created Czechoslovakia. Millions of Germans lived in the Sudeten region of Czechoslovakia, near the German border. By the 1930's, these people were claiming that the Czechs were discriminating against them, and they wanted the Sudetenland to be incorporated into Germany. Chamberlain pursued a double policy. First, he hoped to maintain peace by redressing the harsh terms of the Versailles treaty, which made Germans resentful. This policy was called "appease-ment." On the other hand, though many British citizens opposed rearmament, Chamberlain was rearming England. At the very least, he hoped that Britain could delay war until it was ready.

In September, 1938, Chamberlain flew to Germany to talk with the German leader, Adolf Hitler. His purpose was not to keep the Sudeten-land from Germany but to make sure that Europe did not go to war. Although the Munich Agreement gave the Sudetenland to Germany, Germany renounced war and any further claims to European territory. Chamberlain declared that he had achieved "peace for our time." Hitler did not keep his word. In March, 1939, Germany occupied the rest of Czechoslovakia, and Chamberlain announced that appeasement was over. The Munich Agreement became a symbol of the futility of the appeasement policy.

The Scapegoat

The figure of Neville Chamberlain has come to symbolize the lackluster and uncomprehending leadership whose cowardly policy of appeasement allowed Hitler to start and almost win World War II. The truth is much different. Chamberlain may have been diffident and uncharismatic, but he was an intelligent and wise leader of unshakable integrity who had great concern for his nation. Even though he knew that his party could not stay in office if it seemed too warlike, he pressed for rearmament. Yet he never lost sight of the possibility of averting war. He also knew that appeasement would buy precious time in which Britain could prepare. His fault, if it was a fault, was that he hoped too fervently for peace when, in retrospect, it is apparent that peace was a lost cause.

Bibliography

Charmley, John. *Chamberlain and the Lost Peace*. Chicago: Ivan R. Dee, 1990.

Dilks, David. *Neville Chamberlain*. Vol. 1. Cambridge, England: Cambridge University Press, 1984.

Feiling, Keith. *The Life of Neville Chamberlain*. London: Macmillan, 1946.

MacLeod, Iain. *Neville Chamberlain*. London: Frederick Muller, 1961.

Parker, R. A. C. *Chamberlain and Appeasement: British Policy and the Coming of the Second World War*. New York: St. Martin's Press, 1993.

Rock, William R. *Chamberlain and Roosevelt: British Foreign Policy and the United States, 1937-1940*. Columbus: Ohio State University Press, 1988.

George Soule

Chen Duxiu

Born: October 8, 1879; Huaining (now Anqing), Anhui Province, China
Died: May 27, 1942; Chiangchin, near Chongqing, China

Cofounder of Chinese Communist Party (1921)

Chen Duxiu (CHUHN DEW-SHYEW), also written Ch'en Tu-hsiu, was the fourth child of a well-to-do family. His father died soon after his birth, and he was raised by his mother and grandfather; the latter was also his first teacher. He passed the lowest level imperial examinations in 1896 but failed the next level of exams in the following year. He then went to a modern school in Hangzhou to study French, English, and naval architecture. Later he studied in Japan, graduating from the Tokyo Higher Normal School and attending Waseda University. Between 1907 and 1910 Chen studied in France and became an ardent admirer of French culture. He took part in the 1911 revolution but refused to join Sun Yatsen's United League. His marriage was an arranged one, and he and his wife had three sons; he and his wife later became estranged.

Writer and Teacher

Soon after returning from France, Chen founded a magazine called the *New Youth*. He used it as a vehicle for advocating social and cultural regeneration along Western lines and criticizing the traditional Confucian social order. It became an important mouthpiece of the Chinese literary renaissance. In 1917 the new chancellor of National Beijing University made Chen the dean of its College of Letters. Other prominent scholars and educators such as Hu Shih and Li Dazhao also joined its faculty. Together, they encouraged the bright young students to pursue intellectual enquiry.

On May 4, 1919, students of Beijing University led other college students in a demonstration against China's loss of Shandong (Shantung) at the Treaty of Versailles. (At this treaty following World War I, U.S. president Woodrow Wilson and other Allied leaders agreed to hand over former German possessions in Shandong province to Japan, denying China the right of national self-determination.) The demonstration, called the May Fourth Movement, became the catalyst for the Chinese intellectual renaissance. Chen joined in the demonstrations, was arrested by the Beijing authorities and was jailed for three months. He resigned as dean after being released and left Beijing for Shanghai.

Founder of the Chinese Communist Party

In Shanghai Chen became the center of a Marxist study group and was converted to Marxism.

Chen Duxiu *(Kim Kurnizki)*

283

At the same time Li Ta-chao established a Marxist study group in Beijing, and Mao Zedong, who had been a library assistant at Beijing University, set up a Marxist study group in Changsha. Chen, although he was at Canton (Guangzhou) at the time, was considered the leader. He was unanimously elected secretary of the Chinese Communist Party (CCP) at its founding in Shanghai in July, 1921. He remained general secretary of the CCP until being ousted in 1927.

Chen opposed the formation of an alliance between the CCP and the Nationalist Party (the Kuomintang, or KMT) because he feared the larger KMT. However, he was overruled by the Comintern (the international communist organization based in Moscow) and had to implement its decisions. In 1927 Chiang Kai-shek, leader of the KMT and successful commander in chief of the Northern Expedition to unify China, purged the CCP from its ranks. Chen was held responsible for this debacle, which had resulted from the policy he had opposed. Soviet leader Joseph Stalin and Chen's opponents within the CCP censured him for his so-called opportunism and replaced him with new leader Qu Qiubai. Chen was formally expelled from the CCP in 1929.

Chen moved to Shanghai after his ouster, where he bitterly attacked Stalin's leadership and its failures in China. He turned to Stalin's rival Leon Trotsky. It is not certain whether Chen's conversion to Trotskyism was due to a genuine intellectual conversion or to political expediency. He did establish contact with Trotsky, then in exile in Istanbul, Turkey. Trotsky, however, denounced him and his supporters for their internal quarrels. Chen also failed in his attempts to regain influence within the CCP.

Arrest, Jail, and Final Years

Chen was arrested in October, 1932, on charges of endangering the republic. He underwent a highly publicized trial by the Jiangsu provincial high court; he was found guilty and sentenced to fifteen years in prison. He was released in a general amnesty in August, 1937, in the wake of Japan's invasion of China; the amnesty was a move to garner public support for the government. Chen declared his support for a united front of all political parties and persons in a patriotic war against Japan, despite which the CCP accused him of being pro-Japanese.

In failing health, Chen spent his last years in

The Communists and Nationalists in the 1920's

Chen Duxiu and most of the Central Committee of the Chinese Communist Party (CCP) opposed the forming of an alliance with the Kuomintang (KMT), or Nationalist Party. They considered the KMT the party of the bourgeoisie. (Their own CCP was seen as the party of the proletariat—the working class.) Chen feared that the infant Chinese Communist Party would be absorbed or crushed by the larger, dominant KMT. However, the Comintern, located in the Soviet Union, decided that the CCP should form a united front with the KMT. The Comintern's aim was to control the KMT from within. As loyal party general secretary, Chen implemented the united-front policy despite his misgivings. The KMT purged the Communists from its ranks in 1927, killing many of them, marking the failure of the Comintern's policy in China. In the Soviet Union this failure became part of the power struggle between Joseph Stalin and Leon Trotsky. Stalin would not back down from supporting the alliance with the KMT, because Trotsky opposed it. When the KMT purge came, Stalin blamed Chen Duxiu for the failure, accused him of surrendering to the KMT, and had him expelled from the CCP.

Peita

Peita is the shortened name for National Beijing University, the oldest and most prestigious modern university in China. Cai Yuanpei (1876-1940), modern China's most famous educator, became chancellor of Peita in 1916. Cai implemented academic freedom and hired famous scholars of all opinions to join its faculty. Among them was Chen Duxiu. Peita held entrance exams for students nationwide and attracted the best young men of that generation (women were also admitted after 1920). Chen supported Peita students who published an avant-garde journal called the *New Tide*. Peita students led in the May Fourth Movement that shaped modern Chinese nationalism. The movement was a catalyst in the formation of the Chinese Communist Party and the reorganization of the Kuomintang (the Nationalist Party). The *New Tide* and the *New Youth* were the standard-bearers of the Chinese intellectual renaissance.

Chiangchin, a small town near China's wartime capital Chongqing (Chungking). His writing during his last years, both in jail and after release, were devoted to two subjects. The first group was ancient Chinese language, phonetics, and philology. The second was politics. He reconsidered his earlier opinions on Marxism, now denouncing it as leading inevitably to dictatorship by a small minority. He concluded that democracy was necessary to guarantee political rights. He died in 1942 at the age of sixty-three.

Chen Duxiu had widespread influence on twentieth-century China. His magazine *New Youth* was a standard-bearer of the new cultural movement and the intellectual renaissance. As dean of the College of Letters of Beijing University, he inspired and was admired by the brightest Chinese students of that generation. Finally, as founder and early leader of the Chinese Communist Party, he helped mold a movement that ruled China from 1949.

Bibliography

Fei, Jin Lee. *Chen Duxiu: Founder of the Chinese Communist Party*. Princeton, N.J.: Princeton University Press, 1983.

Kuo, Thomas C.T. *Ch'en Tu-hsiu (1879-1942) and the Chinese Communist Movement*. Princeton, N.J.: Princeton University Press, 1969.

Schwarcz, Vera. *The Chinese Enlightenment: Intellectuals and the Legacy of the May Fourth Movement*. Berkeley: University of California Press, 1986.

Jiu-Hwa Lo Upshur

Chiang Kai-shek

Born: October 31, 1887; Chikow, Fenghua County, Chekiang Province, China
Died: April 5, 1975; Taipei, Taiwan

Chinese military and political leader, head of Nationalist Party from 1925, president of Taiwan (1950-1975)

Born into a wealthy family, Chiang Kai-shek (CHYONG KI-SHEHK), also known as Chiang Chieh-shih, Chung-Cheng, and, officially, Chiang, received a private education until 1904, when he went to Paoting Military Academy in North China. In 1906 he went to Japan to study for two years at the Tokyo Military Academy. While there he met Sun Yat-sen, who would found the Republic of China. The young military student joined the T'ung Meng Hui, later known as the Kuomintang (KMT) or Nationalist Party, which Sun Yat-sen had started a few years earlier. The older man recognized Chiang's capabilities and served as his mentor. In 1927 Chiang married

Chiang Kai-shek *(Library of Congress)*

Mayling Soong, the daughter of a well-known Protestant minister. She would be of great assistance in his career, particularly in his relations with the United States.

Building a Nation

When Sun Yat-sen led a successful revolution against the corrupt Qing (or Ching) Dynasty in 1911, Chiang played an important role. For more than a decade he worked with the Republic's leader to unite a nation ruled, in large part, by warlords. In 1924 Sun appointed Chiang president of the Whampoa Academy, where he trained an army. After the unification of China in 1928, Chiang held various military and government posts. In 1932 he became a member of the Central Committee of the Kuomintang and president of the National Military Commission, making him the most powerful man in China.

Chiang's political philosophy sprang from three sources. First was his early study of China's traditional culture and literature. Second was his commitment to Sun Yat-sen's revolutionary teachings. Third, Chiang read the writings of many foreign experts. While studying in Japan, for example, he paid close attention to that nation's reforms in the late nineteenth century and its military training and management. After he became China's military leader, he invited foreign advisers to assist him in establishing China's army. He protected traditional Chinese culture, but he also promoted modernization.

Fighting Japanese Aggression

Japan had invaded China without consequences several times in the past, but when Japan attacked in July, 1937, China resisted. Shortly after the invasion, Chiang became director-general of the KMT. During the struggle against Japan and throughout World War II, he led China's military, government, and ruling political party. Under extremely difficult conditions and with inferior forces, China fought alone for four years. Then, on December 7, 1941, Japan attacked the United States, and China's war became part of World War II. Chiang served as supreme commander of Allied forces in China. The area he supervised included Indochina, Vietnam, and Thailand. He promoted cooperation among Asian peoples. After the war ended in August, 1945, Chiang supported Korea, India, and Vietnam in their drives for independence from European colonial powers.

During World War II Chiang participated as an equal in international meetings with the other leaders of the Allies, including U.S. president Franklin D. Roosevelt and British prime minister Winston Churchill. When the Allies and other nations established the United Nations, China

Chiang Kai-shek rallying his Kuomintang (Nationalist) supporters. *(Library of Congress)*

was one of five countries given a permanent seat on the U.N. Security Council.

The Communist Challenge

Chiang had opposed communism since 1926. By 1936 he had succeeded so well in limiting communism that the Chinese Communists faced

---

Mayling Soong, Madam Chiang Kai-shek

Chiang Kai-shek's wife was a great asset to his political career. Mayling Soong was born in 1897, the daughter of a Protestant minister. She went to the United States in 1908 and graduated from Wellesley College in Massachusetts, where she majored in English literature. She then returned to China and studied Chinese history and culture. In 1927 she married Chiang Kai-shek. She focused her attention on social and women's issues and, unofficially, on foreign relations. Her

skill in working with people helped her husband unite others and solve problems. She also organized numerous charitable organizations. Madam Chiang lectured often, both in China and in the United States. During World War II her command of English and her knowledge of Western cultures were vital. Among her most famous speeches in the United States were two given February 18, 1943, one to the Senate and one to the House of Representatives.

destruction. In December, 1936, however, Hsueh Liang Chang took Chiang captive and forced him to cooperate with the Communists to fight against Japan. The war against Japan gave the Communists new life.

With Japan ousted in 1945, the Chinese Communists were strong enough to wage war against the Republic of China government. China's National Assembly elected Chiang Kai-shek head of the government in 1948. In 1949 the Communists took over China. They forced Chiang to move to Taiwan, which had just been returned to China by Japan and declared a province. In Taiwan, Chiang established an anticommunist stronghold.

Defending Taiwan

An island off the coast of southeastern China, Taiwan had been ceded to Japan in 1895. One of the Kuomintang Party's main purposes had been to work for its return to China. In 1943 in a meeting of Allies in Cairo, Chiang brought up Taiwan's return to China after the war. Roosevelt and Churchill immediately agreed.

When Chiang took the government of the Republic of China to Taiwan, its economy was devastated, and it faced attack by the superior forces of the communist mainland. The world paid little attention and offered no aid, but Chiang decided to defend Taiwan. He defeated the communist army at Quemoy, a small island a few miles from

Chiang Kai-shek (center) at the tomb of Sun Yat-sen, former leader of the Kuomintang, in 1946, for a ceremony honoring Sun's birth. *(National Archives)*

The Republic of China

In 1911 Sun Yat-sen led a revolution that overturned China's Qing Dynasty. On January 1, 1912, he established the government of the Republic of China (ROC), the first republic in Asia. The system of government was based on three principles: by the people, of the people, for the people. This system changed an autocratic style of government that had lasted thousands of years. Many local Chinese warlords refused to accept the change. In 1926, to unify the country, Chiang Kai-shek led a military force in the two-year Northern Expedition. He destroyed the warlords, and the country was unified in 1928. The Communist Party, however, had gained strength.

In 1937 Japan invaded the struggling country. For eight years China fought the invaders. Peace and prosperity did not follow victory at the end of World War II: The Communist Party began a civil war. In 1949 it defeated the Republic of China, and that government moved to Taiwan. Chiang Kai-shek headed the government, which succeeded in holding off Communist forces. With the support of its former World War II allies, the Republic of China managed to retain China's seat at the United Nations until 1971. In 1979 the United States withdrew recognition of the Republic of China. In the 1990's, thirty countries had diplomatic relations with the Taiwan-based Republic of China, and two hundred countries maintained cultural and economic relationships with it.

the mainland. In 1950 U.S. naval forces came to the aid of Chiang in defending Taiwan. The island went from danger to safety. Chiang began to develop Taiwan's economy, improve the standard of living, and establish a democratic government. In 1950 the average annual income in Taiwan was $50. By the 1990's it had risen to more than $12,000.

Chiang Kai-shek occupies an important place in China's long history. He unified the country, led it through the most destructive invasion it had ever faced, reinstated China as a world power, and turned Taiwan into a modern, prosperous, democratic island.

Bibliography

Dolan, Sean. *Chiang Kai Shek*. Broomall, Pa.: Chelsea House, 1988.

Hedin, Sven A. *Chiang Kai-shek, Marshal of China*. New York: Da Capo Press, 1975.

Lattimore, Owen. *China Memoirs: Chiang Kai-shek and the War Against Japan*. Tokyo: University of Tokyo Press, 1991.

Loh, Pichon P. Y. *The Early Chiang Kai-shek: A Study of His Personality and Politics*. New York: Columbia University Press, 1971.

George C. Y. Wang

Joseph Benedict Chifley

Born: September 22, 1885; Bathurst, New South Wales (now Australia)
Died: June 13, 1951; Canberra, Australian Capital Territory, Australia

Prime minister of Australia (1945-1949)

Joseph Benedict Chifley (JOH-sehf BEH-neh-dihkt CHIHF-lee), widely known as Ben Chifley, was the son of a blacksmith in the provincial city of Bathurst. For much of his childhood, he was brought up on his grandfather's farm and was educated two or three days per week by a country teacher. He was largely self-taught, although he attended the Patrician Brothers' School for about two years and took classes at a local night school. In 1914 he married Elizabeth Gibson McKenzie.

Joseph Benedict Chifley *(Library of Congress)*

Chifley and the Labor Movement

Chifley joined the New South Wales Railways in 1903 and worked his way up through the ranks, becoming a fully qualified engine driver in 1914. He became active in trade union affairs and was dismissed from employment by the railways during the great transport strike of 1917. Although he was later reemployed, he was demoted for his part in the strike. In 1920 he helped to found a new union under federal rather than state law, the Australian Federated Union of Locomotive Engineers.

Political Career

In the early 1920's, Chifley made two unsuccessful bids for preselection by the Australian Labor Party to contest state elections. In 1925 he stood unsuccessfully for the federal seat of Macquarie, but he won the seat in 1928. He held it until 1931, then from 1940 to 1951. In 1931 he was made minister for defense and assistant to the treasurer, but he lost his seat in the election of that year. The Labor Party lost office as a result of the Depression and a serious split in its own ranks.

Back in Parliament, Chifley was federal treasurer (1941-1949), minister for postwar reconstruction (1942-1945), and prime minister (1945-1949). During World War II he worked diligently to meet the enormous demands of the war effort while introducing social security initiatives and urging wartime economic austerity. In 1942, he introduced the system of "uniform taxation," by which the federal government took a monopoly on income tax, absorbing the income taxes formerly levied by the states. This greatly increased the commonwealth's financial power at the states' expense.

Shortly after the death of prime minister John

Curtin in July, 1945, Chifley was named prime minister by his party, and he won an election in his own right in September, 1946. His government supported a policy of full employment and increased social services. It also encouraged a large-scale immigration program. In 1947, Chifley had legislation passed nationalizing the private banks, but the law was declared unconstitutional by the High Court in the following year.

Trade unions became unhappy with Chifley's government, and strikes were called by coal miners, shipbuilders, and waterside workers. In 1949, Chifley employed troops to work at mines during a coal strike, a move that generated considerable controversy. His government was defeated in the election of December, 1949, and Liberal Party leader Robert Gordon Menzies came to power. Chifley then led the federal opposition until his death in 1951.

Place in History

In a speech he delivered in November, 1949, that continues to be an inspiration to the Australian labor movement, Chifley referred to it as the "light on the hill." He

On a visit to London, Australian prime minister Joseph Benedict Chifley (left) receives a sprig of rosemary from a World War I veteran at a 1946 ceremony marking ANZAC Day. It was the thirty-first anniversary of the landing of Australian and New Zealand troops at Gallipoli. *(AP/Wide World Photos)*

The Campaign to Nationalize Banks

In 1945, Prime Minister Ben Chifley attempted to introduce reforms that would give the federal government control over national monetary policy and banking. In 1947, the Melbourne City Council challenged a key provision that required government instrumentalities to do business solely with the Commonwealth Bank. The High Court found that this section was unconstitutional because it imposed a burden on the states that breached the federal character of Australia's constitution. Fearful that other provisions would be struck down by legal challenges, Chifley responded in August, 1947, by announcing that his government would legislate to nationalize banking. The banks then challenged this legislation. In 1948, a High Court judgment found that the legislation was unconstitutional. This judgment was upheld by the Privy Council in the following year.

is regarded as having been a great treasurer and Labor leader, though lacking predecessor Curtin's vision and political adroitness. He was a hardworking prime minister, acknowledged even by his opponents as a first-class administrator, though also criticized by some of them as a doctrinaire socialist.

Bibliography

Bennett, Scott. *J. B. Chifley*. Melbourne, Australia: Oxford University Press, 1973.

Crisp, L. F. *Ben Chifley: A Political Biography*. London: Angus & Robertson, 1977.

Johnson, Carol. *The Labor Legacy: Curtin, Chifley, Whitlam, Hawke*. Sydney: Allen & Unwin, 1989.

Russell Blackford

Shirley Chisholm

Born: November 30, 1924; Brooklyn, New York

First African American woman to serve in U.S. Congress (1969-1983)

Shirley Anita St. Hill Chisholm (SHUR-lee a-NEE-tah saynt-HIHL CHIH-zuhm) was the daughter of Charles St. Hill, a West Indian immigrant factory worker, and Ruby Seale St. Hill, a seamstress from Barbados. When she was three years old, she and her sisters were sent to live in Barbados while their parents worked to save for their children's education. At the age of eleven she returned to Brooklyn, where she finished grade school and high school and earned a scholarship to Brooklyn College.

After graduating from Brooklyn College in 1946, she taught at Mount Calvary Nursery School and earned a master's degree in education at Columbia University. In 1949 she married Conrad Chisholm, a private investigator. From 1953 to 1959 she worked as director of the Hamilton-Madison Settlement House, the largest day-care center in New York. In 1959 she began work as a consultant with the Bureau of Child Guidance for the New York City Board of Education, where she set up day-care centers for working women and took an active interest in politics.

New York State Assemblywoman

In 1964 Chisholm was elected to the New York State Assembly representing the fifty-fifth district. During her four years of service in the state legislature, she supported SEEK, a program designed to get more black and Puerto Rican students into the City University. She introduced legislation to establish publicly supported day-care centers and supported unemployment insurance for domestic workers. She worked to restrict the use of weapons by policemen and fought for the repeal of the state's abortion law.

First African American Congresswoman

In November, 1968, Shirley Chisholm was elected to the U.S. House of Representatives, defeating civil rights leader James Farmer. Chisholm was the first African American woman elected to Congress and served as a member of the House of Representatives from 1969 to 1983. Her home district included the Bedford-Stuyvesant and Bushwick sections of Brooklyn.

Because of her twenty years of experience in the field of education, Chisholm hoped to be assigned to the Education and Labor Committee. However, she was assigned to the Subcommittee

Shirley Chisholm *(Library of Congress)*

293

U.S. congresswoman Shirley Chisholm giving her supporters the victory sign. *(Archive Photos)*

Chisholm was a strong proponent of the Equal Rights Amendment (ERA), passed by Congress in 1970 (though it was never ratified by the states). She was a founding member of the National Women's Political Caucus (1971) and founded the National Political Congress of Black Women in 1984. While in the state legislature, Chisholm fought to legalize abortion, and she continued that fight in Congress. She cosponsored a measure to establish a national commission on consumer protection and product safety and worked for the repeal of the Internal Security Act of 1950. She cosponsored the Adequate Income Act of 1971, guaranteeing an annual income to families. Chisholm proposed funding increases for day-care centers and expanded services for working mothers. In the foreign affairs area she called for the end of British arms sales to South Africa and spoke out against the war in Vietnam.

on Forestry and Rural Villages. Chisholm fought the seniority system by refusing the assignment and was reassigned to the Veteran Affairs Committee, where she investigated discrimination in veterans' groups and worked for better benefits for veterans. At the time of her retirement she was a member of the prestigious House Rules Committee and secretary of the House Democratic Caucus.

The Congressional Seniority System

Early in her career as a congresswoman, Shirley Chisholm fought the seniority system that assigned members to committees. Every member of Congress belongs to a committee that studies and votes on proposed laws. Membership on major committees is reserved for senior members of Congress who have served for many years. New members are assigned to less important committees. When Chisholm was assigned to the Agriculture Subcommittee on Forestry and Rural Villages, she filed an amendment to the assignment asking that her name be removed from the list. She protested that "the forestry subcommittee has no relevancy whatever to the needs of my constituency. Apparently, all the gentlemen in the Congress know about Brooklyn is that a tree grew there." Chisholm won her battle and was reassigned to the Veteran Affairs Committee.

Shirley Chisholm, second from right, with other members of the Congressional Black Caucus in 1980 announces the caucus's support of Senator Edward Kennedy's presidential candidacy. *(AP/Wide World Photos)*

The 1972 Presidential Campaign

Chisholm campaigned for the 1972 presidential nomination, but her share of the vote never exceeded seven percent. She lost the nomination to Senator George McGovern. In *The Good Fight* (1973) she tells the story of that presidential campaign. Chisholm was a champion of equal rights for people of color and support for cities. Always outspoken in her struggle to reform American politics, Chisholm's slogan was "unbought and unbossed," the title of her 1970 autobiography. She was reelected five times, serving in Congress for twelve years. In 1977, after her marriage to Conrad Chisholm ended in divorce, she married businessman Arthur Hardwick. Jr. She retired to devote her time to lecturing and teaching, and she taught at Mount Holyoke College from 1983 to 1987.

Bibliography

Chisholm, Shirley. *The Good Fight*. New York: Harper & Row, 1973.

_____. *Unbought and Unbossed*. Boston: Houghton Mifflin, 1970.

Duffy, Susan. *Shirley Chisholm: A Bibliography of Writings by and About Her*. Metuchen, N.J.: Scarecrow Press, 1988.

Hicks, Nancy. *The Honorable Shirley Chisholm, Congresswoman from Brooklyn*. New York: Lion Books, 1971.

Judith Barton Williamson

Jean Chrétien

Born: January 11, 1934; Shawinigan, Quebec, Canada

Prime minister of Canada (took office 1993)

Joseph-Jacques Jean Chrétien (zhoh-SEHF ZHOK ZHO kray-tee-EH) was born in Shawinigan, Quebec, the son of a paper-mill machinist. He received a B.A. degree in 1955 from St. Joseph Seminary in Trois-Rivières and a law degree from Laval University in 1958. He practiced law in Shawinigan, serving as the director of the bar in Trois-Rivières in 1962-1963. In 1957 Chrétien married Aline Chaîné of Shawinigan, and they had three children: France, Hubert, and Michel.

Canadian prime minister Jean Chrétien recording a radio message in January, 1998, for Canadians suffering the effects of a devastating ice storm. *(AP/Wide World Photos)*

The Cabinet Years

Jean Chrétien was first elected to the Canadian House of Commons in 1963 as a Liberal Party member for the riding (district) of Saint-Maurice-Laflèche. He was reelected in 1965 and was then appointed parliamentary secretary to Prime Minister Lester B. Pearson. He served in several different cabinet posts during the Pearson Liberal government: as minister of finance in 1966; minister of state in 1967; and as the minister of national revenue in 1968. From 1968 to 1984, Chrétien continued to gain valuable political and administrative experience in a number of cabinet posts within the Liberal Party led by Pierre Elliott Trudeau. He served as the minister of Indian affairs and northern development (1968-1974), establishing ten new national parks in Canada and drafting a major policy paper (a "white paper") on native issues.

He later became president of the treasury board (1974-1976), minister of industry, trade, and commerce (1976), minister of finance (1976-1979), minister of justice and attorney general of Canada (1980-1982), and minister of energy, mines, and resources (1982-1984). In a specially created post as the minister responsible for constitutional negotiations (1980-1982), Chrétien played an important role in both the 1980 and 1995 referendums on Quebec sovereignty that affirmed that province's place within the Canadian federation. As minister of justice in 1982, Chrétien oversaw the passage of the Constitution Act, which both repatriated Canada's constitution from Britain to Canada and entrenched basic human rights within that guiding document.

In 1984 Chrétien was unsuccessful in an attempt to be elected Liberal Party leader. This was partly because of the desire for "new blood" within the party (Chrétien was closely associated with Trudeau as a leader) and partly because the Liberal Party traditionally alternated between English-Canadian and French-Canadian leaders (both Trudeau and Chrétien were of French-Canadian heritage). The Liberals went on to lose the September, 1984, election, but Chrétien was reelected. In 1985 he wrote a best-selling autobiography, *Straight from the Heart*.

Liberal Party Leadership

In 1986 Chrétien resigned from the House of Commons to practice law. In 1990, however, he reentered political life by being elected Leader of the Liberal Party of Canada. In the 1993 election, the Liberal Party won an overwhelming majority of seats in Parliament, and Chrétien was sworn in as prime minister of Canada on November 4, 1993. The Progressive Conservative Party (traditional rivals of the Liberal Party) won only two seats, and two relatively new parties (the right-wing Reform Party of Canada and the separatist Bloc Québécois party) shared official opposition status almost equally. Chrétien had a clear man-

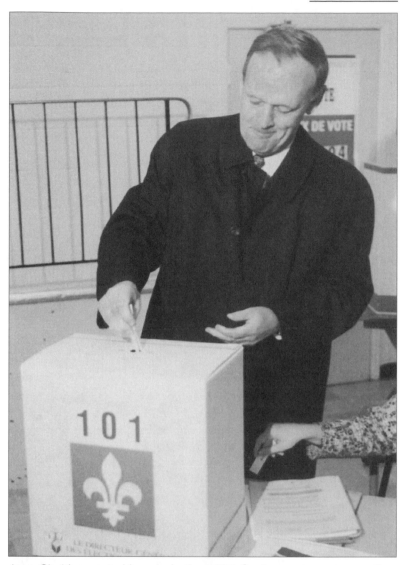

Jean Chrétien casts his vote in the 1995 Quebec vote on separation. *(Reuters/Archive Photos)*

The North American Free Trade Agreement

On January 1, 1994, the North American Free Trade Agreement (NAFTA) between Canada, Mexico, and the United States came into effect, creating the world's largest free-trade zone. NAFTA was a natural extension of the 1989 Free Trade Agreement between Canada and the United States. Both these agreements were intended to bring mutual benefit to the signing countries by encouraging free exchange of goods and labor products, with an end to all tariffs in fifteen years.

The Election of 1997

On June 2, 1997, the Liberal Party of Canada won reelection with a bare majority of seats (154 seats out of 301). The Reform Party of Canada (60 seats) became the official opposition party in the House of Commons, with the Bloc Québécois (45 seats), the New Democratic Party (21 seats), and the Progressive Conservative Party (20 seats) all achieving official party status in Parliament.

The 1997 results reflected a regionalist splintering of votes across the country. The New Democratic Party for the first time made gains in economically hard-hit Atlantic Canada, reflecting that region's dissatisfaction with the Liberal Party's extensive cutting of social programs. The Reform Party, while replacing the Bloc Québécois as the official opposition, did not win hoped-for support in Eastern Canada and remained a Western-based political movement. The right-wing and anti-Quebec views of the Reform Party did not appeal to voters in Ontario, where about one-third (103) of the seats in Parliament are located. The Bloc Québécois remained a Quebec-based party, adding a third region to the mix of interests in Canada's central parliament. The reduction of the Liberal majority in the 1997 election reflected voter anger about an unnecessary election (the Liberals had a year left before an election was mandatory) and about the government's mixed record regarding budget cutting and national unity issues.

Jean Chrétien finishing his address to a pro-unity rally on October 27, 1995, three days before residents of Quebec vote on whether to separate from Canada. Secession was narrowly voted down. *(AP/Wide World Photos)*

date for leadership from Canadian voters, but he had to lead a Parliament with very mixed and conflicting political agendas.

Cutting the Deficit

From 1993 to 1997, the Chrétien government worked to cut the national deficit, mainly through a series of cuts to social, cultural, and research programs. These cuts proved popular with some segments of Canadian society while arousing anger from those who felt that Canada's social welfare system was being destroyed. During Canada's deep economic recession in the mid-1990's, Chrétien (with other Canadian bureaucrats and business leaders) undertook a series of "Team Canada" trade missions to encourage sales of Canadian goods and technical expertise abroad. Similarly, the North American Free Trade Agreement (NAFTA) in 1994 strengthened economic ties between Canada, Mexico, and the United States.

In 1995 Quebec held a second referendum to determine whether that province would remain within the Canadian federation of provinces. Although the "yes" side in favor of remaining in Canada won (by a narrow margin), many Canadians blamed Chrétien for not being proactive and assertive enough in promoting the federalist cause. Chrétien's popularity was also harmed by the introduction of controversial gun control legislation and by his failure to eliminate the unpopular goods and services tax first introduced by the Progressive Conservative government in 1989.

Reelection

In 1997, Chrétien again led the Liberal Party to victory, but with only a slim majority of seats in Parliament. The widening range of political opinion in Canada was shown by the fact that five different parties (the Liberals, the Political Conservatives, the Reform Party, the Bloc Québécois, and the New Democratic Party) all won enough seats to claim official party status in Parliament. With an improved economy and a smaller deficit, federal spending on basic social programs and research infrastructure increased.

Chrétien remains best known for his deep commitment to Canadian federalism and for his efforts to restore the Canadian economy to health by balancing the budget and promoting Canadian trade interests.

Bibliography

Chrétien, Jean. *Straight from the Heart*. Toronto: McClelland and Stewart-Bantam, 1986.

Martin, Lawrence. *Chrétien*. Toronto: Lester, 1995.

Mowers, Cleo, ed. *Towards a New Liberalism: Recreating Canada and the Liberal Party*. Victoria, British Columbia, Canada: Orca, 1991.

Helen Bragg

Winston Churchill

Born: November 30, 1874; Blenheim Palace, Oxfordshire, England
Died: January 24, 1965; London, England

British military and political leader, prime minister of Great Britain during World War II (1940-1945)

Sir Winston Leonard Spencer Churchill (WIHN-stuhn LEH-nurd SPEHN-sur CHUR-chihl) was the son of Randolph Churchill, Conservative Party leader, and Jenny Jerome, an American. He was a descendant of the dukes of Marlborough. Winston was educated at Harrow, an exclusive school, where he did not excel, and Sandhurst, Britain's equivalent of West Point, where he was very successful. He became a commissioned officer in the cavalry in 1895 and served in India.

Winston Churchill *(The Nobel Foundation)*

When his father died prematurely, the young Churchill had to earn his own living. He became a journalist and author while attached to military units. He also took heroic part in several imperial wars. He gained national attention for a daring escape from a prisoner of war camp in South Africa.

Political Beginnings

Churchill entered Parliament in 1900 as a Conservative but switched to the Liberal Party. He became noted for bringing about legislation to improve conditions for working people. Nevertheless, some Labour Party leaders became his enemies when Churchill, as home secretary, suppressed strikes vigorously.

Appointed to be in charge of the British navy in 1911, he worked energetically to prepare the British fleet for war before the onset of World War I. Unfortunately for his career, he became the scapegoat for the failure of the war's Gallipoli campaign, in which large numbers of British troops lost their lives. Thereafter he left the government to fight in France. After the war he held several other cabinet posts. By that time he had left the Liberals and rejoined the Conservative Party. It is rare for a British politician to desert a party, and almost unheard of to do it twice.

A Time of Crisis

Churchill became an isolated figure in Parliament after he left office over a disagreement in 1931. During this period he warned about the growing menace of Adolf Hitler's Germany. His detractors discounted him as a militaristic has-been and ignored his calls for rearmament. Meanwhile the government of Neville Chamberlain gave in to Hitler's demands for more territory. Churchill warned that yielding to bullying only increases the aggressor's appetite, leading inevitably to greater demands and eventually to war. He was the one leader who understood Hitler's menace from the beginning, and when Britain went to war in September, 1939, Churchill was invited back into the government to take charge of the navy again. As disasters befell British troops, people turned to Churchill as the man who could provide resolute leadership in time of war.

The Finest Hour

Winston Churchill became prime minister at a

U.S. president Franklin D. Roosevelt (left) and British prime minister Winston Churchill in Casablanca, Morocco, for a World War II conference in January of 1943. *(National Archives)*

The Gallipoli Campaign

The campaign at Gallipoli, in Turkey, was Winston Churchill's plan to shorten World War I. It ended in disaster, and he became the scapegoat for the failure, losing his position as first lord of the Admiralty. In 1915 the massive and hopeless slaughter in the trenches of France and Belgium led Churchill to propose a daring end run around Germany and its allies. The plan was to break through the Dardanelles, the waterway connecting the Black Sea with the Mediterranean. Britain's then floundering ally, czarist Russia, would be helped directly if the Dardanelles could be forced open.

The Gallipoli campaign was fraught with dif-

ficulties from the beginning, in large part because of a lack of cooperation from other government and armed forces leaders. The admiral in charge of the navy, for example, did not want to risk British ships, and the army was reluctant to release sufficient troops. As a result the campaign went too slowly, giving the enemy enough time to reinforce the landing zone and butcher the invaders. Churchill took the blame for the whole campaign, and when the cabinet government was reshuffled in 1915 Churchill was asked to resign. Many observers thought that a promising career was over.

Churchill's Wartime Speeches

Winston Churchill used the English language effectively and richly throughout his life in countless speeches, articles, and books. His most important compositions were his wartime speeches, which were beamed over radio to millions throughout the world. His rich prose granted hope and a vision of grand purpose in the struggle. Listeners today are sometimes unimpressed by his steady, clear, calm voice and his complicated, exact sentences. For those tossed on the stormy seas of war, however, his voice was the voice of the steady captain defying the waves.

Some of the phrases Churchill coined will live in the language forever, such as "Never in the field of human conflict was so much owed by so many to so few," a tribute to the Royal Air Force during the Battle of Britain. When he first became prime minister he uttered these famous words: "I have nothing to offer but blood, toil, tears and sweat." As he expressed it himself, his voice gave the roar to the British lion.

desperate time in World War II, May of 1940. Soon all of continental Europe would be under Nazi domination. Meanwhile, the Soviet Union was collaborating with the Nazis, and the United States was still neutral. Therefore, Britain stood alone as the underdog against an undefeated and vicious power. An armada of German war planes and a fleet of submarines were aimed at forcing

Winston Churchill in 1946, delivering the speech in which he coined the term "Iron Curtain" to describe the communist bloc, at Westminster College in Missouri. *(Courtesy Winston Churchill Memorial and Library in the United States)*

Britain's surrender. These were indeed the darkest days of the war for the British people. In a famous defiant speech, Churchill turned the tables and declared it to be "their finest hour." When the Royal Air Force won the Battle of Britain in the summer of 1940, German plans to invade Britain were cancelled. Even so, the German air force continued to pound Britain at night all through the fall of 1940 and into the spring of 1941, a period that has been called "the Blitz." Churchill provided calm, determined, courageous, unfaltering leadership throughout this ordeal. He projected his spirit in the government and to the nation at large via the radio. His V-for-victory signal, determined face, and jaunty cigar became symbols of British defiance and resolve. Churchill picked able and energetic men to run key departments. He also visited damaged areas and brought comfort to victims. Even his most unsympathetic political enemies agreed that he was truly a great war leader.

Later Career

After Russia and the United States entered the war in 1941, Churchill became one of three major Allied leaders; the other two were U.S. president Franklin D. Roosevelt and Russian leader Joseph Stalin. Churchill's close friendship with Roosevelt helped direct Allied efforts toward victory. While American leaders wanted an early direct invasion of occupied France, Churchill called for campaigns in the Mediterranean theater. He was suspicious of Stalin, but he was able to keep the Allies working toward common goals. Churchill encouraged Roosevelt to take a firmer line with the Russian dictator. A year after the war was over, much of Eastern Europe was under communist control. Churchill declared that an "iron curtain" had come down across that part of Europe.

A bitter disappointment in Churchill's career occurred when the Labour Party ended the wartime coalition government in 1945, just before the war was over. The Labour Party then defeated him despite his heroic wartime leadership. He was out of office while the Labour Party introduced the many new social programs that comprised the welfare state from 1945 to 1951. Churchill returned to power as prime minister in 1951, accepting much of what Labour had passed into law. He resigned in 1955 at the age of eighty-one. Nevertheless, he continued to write voluminously. Honors came to him from all directions, including a Nobel Prize in Literature. Churchill died in 1965 at the age of ninety and was given a magnificent state funeral.

If Winston Churchill had died before World War II he would still have been remembered as an important figure. Nevertheless, his greatest fame came from his confrontation with Nazi Germany. Because he was the leader of a united Britain in its desperate struggle to survive in 1940-1941, he as been revered as the indomitable Englishman who preserved Western civilization at the moment of its greatest peril.

Bibliography

Churchill, Winston. *My Early Life: A Roving Commission*. New York: Charles Scribner's Sons, 1987.

Gilbert, Martin. *Churchill: A Life*. New York: Henry Holt, 1991.

Payne, Robert. *A Portrait of Winston Churchill*. New York: Coward, McCann and Geoghegen, 1974.

Rose, Norman. *Churchill: An Unruly Life*. New York: Simon & Schuster, 1994.

Young, John W. *Winston Churchill's Last Campaign: Britain and the Cold War, 1951-1955*. New York: Clarendon Press, 1996.

Henry G. Weisser

Joe Clark

Born: June 5, 1939; High River, Alberta, Canada

Prime minister of Canada (1979-1980)

Charles Joseph "Joe" Clark (CHAHRLZ JOH-sehf "JOH" KLAHRK) grew up in a small farming community, the son of a politically active newspaperman and a gifted schoolteacher. Clark attended the University of Alberta, obtaining a B.A. in history (1960) and later an M.A. in political science (1973). During the period 1961-1971, he served a rigorous political apprenticeship, working in a variety of provincial and federal Progressive Conservative (PC) Party offices as organizer, strategist, campaigner, and speech writer. He became a practicing politician in 1972, when he was elected a member of Parliament (MP). Clark was an MP for twenty-one years,

Joe Clark *(AP/Wide World Photos)*

representing the Alberta riding (district) of Rocky Mountain (1972-1979) and later the riding of Yellowhead (1979-1993). In 1973 he married Maureen McTeer, a health-care lawyer and writer; they have one daughter, Catherine.

Prime Minister

Clark maintained his seat in the July, 1974, general election, but the PC Party generally lost ground to the Liberals, led by Pierre Elliott Trudeau. Having lost his third consecutive election as leader of the PC Party, Robert Stanfield announced that he would step down. Clark ran for the leadership, and—to the surprise of many in the party—he emerged from the Ottawa Progressive Conservative Convention in February, 1976, as the new leader. Campaigning on the theme of Canada as a "community of communities," a country sufficiently decentralized to accommodate a variety of regional and organizational interests, he defeated the Liberals (led by Trudeau) in the May, 1979, general election. Clark formed a minority government and became the sixteenth prime minister of Canada. At age thirty-nine, he was the youngest person ever to hold the office.

Clark was adroit at parliamentary debate and a good organizer. However, the media generally ignored or misunderstood what he said and lampooned him as a weak, ineffectual leader. This image undermined his credibility. After only seven months in power, he was forced to fight another general election. In the February, 1980, general election, the Liberals (under Trudeau) won 148 seats and the PCs 101. As leader of the opposition from 1980 to 1983, Clark delayed the Trudeau constitutional plan until a judicial review was achieved and a federal-provincial compromise was reached. Even though he had received support at two national party meetings, a sizable minority of PCs still considered Clark too "progressive" and thus an electoral liability. Clark decided to settle the question of his leadership at a convention, held in June, 1983. He eventually lost on the fourth ballot to Brian Mulroney, who went on to lead the PCs to a great victory in the September, 1984, general election, winning 211 out of 282 seats.

Secretary of State for External Affairs

Mulroney appointed Clark secretary of state for external affairs, an office the latter held for the years 1984-1991. Many regard him as one of the most effective secretaries of state in the history of the department. For example, he played a leading role in Canada's—and the world community's—efforts to bring an end to apartheid in South Africa. With the end of the Cold War, he formulated a new policy toward Europe, proposing far-reaching reforms of NATO and the Conference on Security and Cooperation in Europe (the CSCE). He chaired (in Ottawa) the opening round of groundbreaking arms control talks that became the first post-Cold War arms control agreement.

At the United Nations, Clark advanced a new concept of "cooperative security," building on

Joe Clark speaking before the Canadian House of Commons in 1986. *(AP/Wide World Photos)*

Canada's long-standing belief in multilateral diplomacy and international law. As well, he took initiatives to increase dialogue in the Pacific Rim region, recognizing Canada's growing economic

Clark's Minority Government

In 1979 the Joe Clark government made a rash decision to govern as if it were a majority government. Clark spent much of his tenure (1979-1980) dealing with matters left over from the previous administration. He also found it difficult to establish smooth relations with powerful premiers Peter Lougheed (Alberta) and Bill Davis (Ontario), who were locked in a disagreement over energy prices. Consequently, only three bills moved past first reading, and only one of these became law. In particular, Clark concentrated on reforming government spending. John Crosbie, the Progressive Conservative Party's finance minister, introduced a budget that included a number of tax increases, such as an excise tax of 18 cents on a gallon of gasoline at the pump, the privatization of Petro-Canada, and a mortgage tax credit. He failed to win support from the other parties, especially the New Democratic Party (NDP), for key parts of his "austerity" program. On December 13, 1979, the opposition defeated the government on a no-confidence vote of 139 to 133.

and security interest in that area. He proposed a North Pacific security dialogue, in which countries of the region have subsequently shown new interest. He also presided over Canada's joining of the Organization of American States (OAS) in 1989. During the Persian Gulf crisis, Clark worked to ensure that the world's response proceeded under the auspices of the United Nations.

Constitutional Affairs Minister

After the collapse, in June, 1990, of the Meech Lake (Constitutional) Accord, which attempted to bring Quebec back into the Canadian "constitutional fold," Mulroney appointed Clark constitutional affairs minister, an office he held for the years 1991-1993. (Quebec had refused to sign the 1982 constitution because it failed to accommodate its aspirations as a "distinct society.") As constitutional affairs minister, Clark was able to produce an apparent solution to Canada's constitutional crisis, one that included agreement on Senate reform and Aboriginal self-government. Although the people of Canada rejected the accord in a national referendum in 1992, he arguably brought Canadians closer to true national unity than any person in the second half of the twentieth century. On referendum night, October 26, 1992, Clark was gracious yet somewhat defiant in his speech: He accepted the verdict of the Canadian people but rejected what he regarded as the cynical and divisive tactics of Preston Manning, leader of the Reform Party. Exhausted after the long constitutional debate, Clark retired from Canadian politics as of the fall, 1993, general election.

In many ways, Clark was ahead of his time. For example, his government produced Canada's first austerity budget. As opposition leader, he led what has been called "the most effective parliamentary opposition in Canadian history." Clark is widely viewed as a man of integrity, honesty, and honor. He persevered in the face of many obstacles and maintained an understanding of Canada's regional diversity and the spirit of compromise required to keep Canada together. In 1998 Clark returned to politics (as a matter of duty) and ran for the leadership of the PC Party, which ranked fifth of five in the House of Commons.

Joe Clark, serving as Canada's minister of external affairs, at a news conference at the United Nations in 1990. *(AP/Wide World Photos)*

Bibliography

Bliss, Michael. *Years of Change, 1967-1985.* Toronto: Grolier Limited, 1986.

Clark, Joe. *A Nation Too Good to Lose: Renewing the Purpose of Canada.* Toronto: Key Porter, 1994.

Humphreys, David L. *Joe Clark: A Portrait.* Toronto: Deneau and Greenberg, 1978.

Simpson, Geoffrey. *Faultlines: Struggling for a Canadian Vision.* Toronto: Harper Perennial, 1993.

Robert M. Seiler

Georges Clemenceau

Born: September 28, 1841; Mouilleron-en-Pareds, France
Died: November 24, 1929; Paris, France

Two-time premier of France (1906-1909, 1917-1920)

Georges Clemenceau (ZHOHRZH klay-mo-SOH) was born in a remote part of the Vendée, a poor and conservative area in western coastal France. Georges absorbed his father's ideals and decided to continue family traditions by studying medicine. In 1862 Clemenceau was arrested for organizing an anti-Napoleonic demonstration in Paris. After release from seventy-three days in prison, he continued his contacts with radicals, completed his medical degree, and decided in 1865 to go to the United States to become a journalist. He also became a French teacher at a girls' school in Connecticut. In 1869 he decided to marry one of his students and to return to France as a country doctor serving in his native Vendée. In 1870, as France rushed into a disastrous war with Germany, Clemenceau returned to Paris to be in the midst of one of France's great cataclysms.

Politics

Clemenceau was in Paris on September 4, 1870, when the radical Léon Gambetta declared that Republican France would continue the war effort against Germany. The following day, Clemenceau was appointed mayor of Montmartre. By February, 1871, he also represented the Seine department in the National Assembly. He was caught up in the violent events of the Paris Commune, established by Radical Republicans and Socialists who hoped that it would form the basis of a new national government. Efforts to mediate between the Commune and the government failed to prevent a bloodbath, and the government crushed the Commune in May of 1871. The mediation did, however, cause Clemenceau to break with the extreme Left. From 1871 to 1875, he practiced medicine, reentering parliament in

1876 as a leftist Republican deputy for Montmartre. He also ran *La Justice*, the principal Radical Republican newspaper, in which he consistently opposed French colonial expansion. His brilliant, fact-filled speeches in Parliament gained him credit for bringing down Jules Ferry's government in 1885. This event launched Clemenceau's reputation as a destroyer of ministries.

Alleged involvement in the Panama Canal scandal caused Clemenceau to lose his parliamentary seat in 1893. His marriage ended, and *La Justice* folded into bankruptcy. Life reached a low

Georges Clemenceau *(Library of Congress)*

307

French premier Georges Clemenceau with other leaders at the Paris Peace Conference in 1919. The so-called Council of Four, left to right, are British prime minister David Lloyd George, Italian premier Emanuele Orlando, Clemenceau, and U.S. president Woodrow Wilson. *(Library of Congress)*

ebb, and Clemenceau returned to writing. It was the Dreyfus affair that again made Clemenceau important to Radical Republicans. In April, 1902, they convinced him to accept a Senate seat, which he held until 1920. By March, 1906, Clemenceau had been given his first cabinet position. As minister of the interior, he was in the vortex of action, having to come to grips with labor unrest and Catholic Church agitation over a new law separating church and state. His strong independent actions earned him the nickname "the Tiger" and an invitation to form his own ministry.

The Miners' Strike of 1906

In 1906 Georges Clemenceau became minister of the interior several days after a horrific mine disaster at Courrières near Lens killed more than a thousand miners. Miners' rage was first directed at mine owners and engineers for a long legacy of safety neglect, but it soon turned to demands for higher wages. The anger provided a golden opportunity for the main trade union syndicate, the Confédération Générale du Travail (CGT), to organize miners. The CGT had long preached that direct action through a general strike would produce revolutionary changes. Clemenceau's policy during the strike was a mixture of firmness and conciliation. He personally visited the disaster scene and spoke

to strikers, telling them that he supported their right to strike but also warning them not to interfere with the rights of others who wanted to work. He made it clear that the army would be on the scene but would remain out of sight as long as order was maintained. Violence did break out, but Clemenceau held the army back, preferring instead to build up forces. Eventually twenty thousand troops were in place (one soldier for every two strikers), and leaders of the strike were arrested. The miners gradually returned to work. Clemenceau gained the permanent enmity of the CGT and Socialists, but he soon gained the premiership as a result of his hard stand.

The Treaty of Versailles

After the end of World War I, the victors met at the Paris Peace Conference to draft a peace treaty with Germany in the winter of 1919. The treaty, signed that year, was known as the Treaty of Versailles. Ignoring extremist demands for the dismemberment of Germany, Georges Clemenceau sought a peace that would maintain Allied unity in the postwar era. He negotiated with British prime minister David Lloyd George and idealistic U.S. president Woodrow Wilson. Negotiations were carried out in English, a situation that left Italy's Vittorio Orlando as a lesser and oft ignored member of the Big Four (the victorious powers). Clemenceau accepted a British proposal to limit the German army to 100,000, as it was stricter than he himself would have demanded. His own proposal for an independent Rhineland to serve as a buffer state was blocked. Clemenceau conceded to an Anglo-American guarantee of a demilitarized Rhineland. The territory of Alsace-Lorraine, long disputed, was returned to France without any difficulty.

Clemenceau firmly demanded Article 231, which placed responsibility for the war on Germany's shoulders, in order to gain reparations (payment for war damages). He also insisted that the treaty be signed in the Hall of Mirrors at Versailles, the same place where, half a century before, France had been forced to sign a humiliating peace treaty. For his part in the treaty, the French Right attacked Clemenceau for weakness, while the Left attacked him as a nationalist extremist. Clemenceau himself viewed the treaty as deeply flawed and as a product of compromise. He considered Allied unity of purpose more important than the treaty in guaranteeing the future security of France.

Leadership

The Clemenceau ministry managed to stay in power for three years. In May, 1908, he took another strong stand against worker violence when a strike in the gravel pits of Seine-et-Oise turned violent. A national workers' association threatened a general strike. Clemenceau called in the army, and the workers responded by setting up barricades. Violence caused Clemenceau to arrest seven labor leaders. The threatened general strike did not materialize, and the Seine-et-Oise strike ended. Clemenceau's success in suppressing unrest produced lasting animosity from the Left. In July of 1909, Clemenceau's ministry fell over clumsily handled questions about naval affairs. During the next two years, he wrote and toured. By 1911 he had settled into an important role as a member of the Senate Commission for Foreign Affairs and the Army. He soon founded a popular paper, *L'Homme libre* (the free man), in which he warned of Germany's desire for war and French unpreparedness. At the outbreak of World War I in 1914, Clemenceau took the familiar role of critic of a succession of cabinets. He attacked the lack of munitions, troops, and adequate battlefield medical attention. Early in the war his newspaper was suppressed, but it reemerged as *L'Homme enchaîné* (the chained man), which was subject to less censorship because its criticism was aimed at bolstering the war effort.

In the fall of 1917, two French governments quickly fell apart, and in November Clemenceau was asked to form a new ministry. He took control of the war effort, and in the span of a year the Tiger became known as Father Victory. Clemenceau rallied French morale with dynamic speeches. His lifelong identification with republicanism produced scant suspicion about the strong authoritarian measures he took. He appeared at the front, proving that he shared risks. Double agents were shot and peace advocates arrested. By the time an armistice was declared in 1918, Clemenceau took a realistic view about the trials ahead, making it known to the war allies that France was a devastated nation needing to guarantee its future.

Peace for France brought the return of labor unrest. Clemenceau soon decided that he could best serve France in the largely symbolic role as president. However, he was not elected. His last years were spent in continued writing and worldwide travel. He commuted between a simple cottage in the Vendée and his Paris apartment. Clemenceau died in 1929, requesting that he be buried in a simple grave, without ceremony, next to his father.

Bibliography
Dallas, Gregor. *At the Heart of a Tiger: Clemenceau and his World, 1841-1929*. New York: Carroll & Graf, 1993.
Holt, Edgar. *The Tiger: The Life of Georges Clemenceau, 1841-1929*. London: Hamish Hamilton, 1976.
Newhall, David. *Clemenceau: A Life at War*. Lewiston, N.Y.: Mellen, 1991.
Watson, David R. *Georges Clemenceau: A Political Life*. London: Eyre Methuen, 1974.

Irwin Halfond

BIOGRAPHICAL ENCYCLOPEDIA OF
20th-Century
World Leaders

Index

In the following index, volume numbers and those page numbers referring to full articles appear in **bold face** type.

Abdulla, Farooq, **2:** 545

Abdul Rahman, **1: 1-3**

Abernathy, Ralph David, **1: 4-6**

Abuja, Nigeria, establishment as Nigerian capital, **1:** 87

Acheson, Dean, **1: 7-10**

Acquired immunodeficiency syndrome (AIDS), Zaire and, **4:** 1080; Zimbabwe and, **4:** 1106

Act of European Unity, **2:** 388

Adams, Gerry, **1: 11-13**; **4:** 1314

Addams, Jane, **3:** 892

Adenauer, Konrad, **1: 14-17**

Affirmative action, **1:** 194

Afghanistan, Soviet invasion of, **1:** 198

Aflaq, Michel, **1:** 60

African Democratic Assembly, **3:** 724

African National Congress (ANC), **1:** 238; **3:** 948, 985, 989

African socialism, **3:** 830; **4:** 1159

Afrika Corps, **4:** 1315

Afro-Asian Bandung Conference, **5:** 1453

Agenda for Peace (Boutros-Ghali), **1:** 176

Agrava Commission, **4:** 1279

Aguinaldo, Emilio, **1: 18-20**

Airpower in the 1920's, **4:** 1073

Akihito, **1: 21-23**; **3:** 694

Albright, Madeleine, **1: 24-26**; **4:** 1137

Algeciras Conference, **1:** 226

Algerian coup of 1965, **1:** 171

Alianza Popular Revolucionaria Americana, **2:** 645

Allenby, Edmund Henry Hynman, **1: 27-29**; **2:** 498

Allende, Salvador, **1: 30-33**; **4:** 1236-1237

Alliance Party of Malaysia, **1:** 3

All-India Muslim League, **3:** 775

American Expeditionary Force (AEF), **4:** 1229

Americo-Liberians, **2:** 411

Amin, Idi, **1: 34-37**; **4:** 1160, 1163

Anarchism, **5:** 1631, 1642

ANC. *See* African National Congress (ANC)

Andropov, Yuri, **2:** 574

Anglican Church, South Africa and, **5:** 1519

Anglo-French Entente, **1:** 98

Anglo-Iranian Oil Company (AIOC), **4:** 1094

Anglo-Iraqi Treaty, **2:** 500

Anglo-Japanese Alliance, **4:** 1056

Angolan Revolt, **5:** 1373

Annan, Kofi, **1: 38-40**

Anschluss, **4:** 1306

Antarctica, exploration of, **1:** 242

Anti-Ballistic Missile Treaty, **5:** 1417

Antitrust legislation, U.S., **3:** 814

ANZUS Pact, **4:** 1065

Apartheid, **1:** 237; **3:** 947, 985, 989; **5:** 1518, 1520; ending of, **2:** 385

Appeasement of Nazi Germany, **1:** 72, 93, 280; **2:** 464, 562

Aprista movement, **2:** 644-645

Aquino, Benigno, **1:** 41; **4:** 1030

Aquino, Corazon, **1: 41-43**; **4:** 1031, 1279

Arab Federation, **3:** 745

Arab-Israeli wars. *See* Six-Day War; Yom Kippur War

Arab Revolt, **2:** 498; **3:** 904

Arab socialism, **4:** 1130

Arafat, Yasir, **1: 44-48**; **4:** 1137

Arbitration, **3:** 886

Arias Sánchez, Oscar, **1: 49-51**

Aristide, Jean-Bertrand, **1: 52-54**

Arms Race, The (Noel-Baker), **4:** 1154

Arras, Battle of, **1:** 27

Arusha Declaration, **4:** 1159

Asquith, H. H., **1: 55-58**; **3:** 901, 932

Assad, Hafez al-, **1: 59-62**

Asser, Tobias Michael Carel, **1: 63-64**

Astor, Nancy, **1: 65-67**

Astor, Waldorf, **1:** 65

Aswan High Dam, **4:** 1130

Atatürk, Kemal, **1: 68-71**; **2:** 482; **3:** 755

Atlantic, Battle of the, **2:** 418

Atomic bomb. *See* Hiroshima and Nagasaki, bombing of

Atoms for Peace program, **2:** 475

Attlee, Clement, **1: 72-75**

Australian Commonwealth, establishment of, **1:** 103; **4:** 1294

Australian Council of Trade Unions (ACTU), **2:** 642
Australian Labor Party (ALP), **2:** 642; **3:** 810
Australian mining boom, **2:** 344
Australian navy, **2:** 505
Austria, German takeover of, **4:** 1306
Austro-Hungarian Empire, **2:** 514; ethnicity issues in, **2:** 512
Authenticité, **4:** 1078
Authoritarianism, **5:** 1630
Axworthy, Lloyd, **1: 76-78**
Aydeed, Muhammad Farah. *See* Aydid, Muhammad Farah
Aydid, Muhammad Farah, **1: 79-81**
Ayub Khan, Mohammad, **1:** 142
Azikiwe, Nnamdi, **1: 82-85**
Azócar, Patricio Aylwin, **4:** 1238

Babangida, Ibrahim, **1: 86-88**
Baby Doc. *See* Duvalier, Jean-Claude
Badoglio, Pietro, **2:** 380
Baghdad Pact, **4:** 1082
Baghdad Railway, **1:** 225
Bajer, Fredrik, **1: 89-90**
Bakr, Ahmed Hassan al-, **3:** 748
Baldwin, Stanley, **1: 91-94**
Balfour, Arthur, **1: 95-98,** 254
Balfour Declaration, **1:** 97, 124; **5:** 1561
Balkan Wars, **2:** 482; **3:** 755; **5:** 1534
Ballinger, Richard, **5:** 1465
Banerjea, Surendranath, **1: 99-101**
Bangladesh, establishment of, **1:** 143; **3:** 776
Bantu Education Act, **5:** 1518
Barak, Ehud, **4:** 1139, 1213
Barbot, Clement, **2:** 451
Barre. *See* Siad Barre, Muhammad
Barthou, Jean-Louis, **3:** 897
Barton, Edmund, **1: 102-104**
Ba'th Party, **1:** 60
Batista y Zaldívar, Fulgencio, **1: 105-108,** 268
Batlle Doctrine, **1:** 110
Batlle y Ordóñez, José, **1: 109-110**
Bay of Pigs invasion, **1:** 269; **3:** 821
Beer-hall putsch, **2:** 581; **3:** 695, 944
Beernaert, Auguste-Marie-François, **1: 111-113**
Begin, Menachem, **1: 114-117,** 262; **5:** 1365
Belfast peace negotiations of 1997, **1:** 12
Ben Bella, Ahmed, **1:** 170-171
Bendjedid, Chadli, **1:** 171

Benelux Charter, **5:** 1427
Benelux Economic Union, **5:** 1426
Beneš, Edvard, **1: 118-121; 4:** 1043
Bengalee, The, **1:** 100
Ben-Gurion, David, **1:** 115, **122-125; 3:** 680; **5:** 1570
Bennett, Richard Bedford, **1: 126-128**
Bennett, W. A. C., **1: 129-131**
Berber Dahir, **4:** 1107
Berlin, Battle of, **5:** 1624
Berlin Crisis, **3:** 820
Berlin Wall, **3:** 712, 820; **5:** 1525; fall of, **1:** 235; **2:** 577
Bernadotte, Folke, **1:** 228
Bernstein, Eduard, **5:** 1642
Besant, Annie, **5:** 1482
Betar, **1:** 115
Bethmann Hollweg, Theobald von, **1: 132-134**
Bhopal poison-gas disaster, **2:** 545
Bhumibol Adulyadej, **1: 135-137**
Bhutto, Benazir, **1: 138-141**
Bhutto, Murtaza, **1:** 140
Bhutto, Zulfikar Ali, **1:** 138, **142-145; 5:** 1626
Biafra secession from Nigeria, **1:** 85
Biko, Steve, **5:** 1519
Bill 101, **3:** 919
Bimini, Adam Clayton Powell and, **4:** 1258
Bismarck, Otto von, **1:** 224; **5:** 1577
Black, Hugo L., **1: 146-148**
Black and Tan War, **2:** 352, 394
Black and Tans, **2:** 341
Black Muslims, **3:** 979
Black Panther Party, **3:** 857
Black Star Line, **2:** 552
Black Thursday and Black Tuesday, **3:** 717
Blair, Tony, **1: 149-152**
Blamey, Thomas, **1:** 208
Blitz, the, **1:** 303, **2:** 563
Blitzkrieg, **2:** 582, 598; **3:** 835; **4:** 1232
Bloc Québécois, **1:** 166, 297
Bloody Sunday, **2:** 340, 648; **3:** 831; **4:** 1141; **5:** 1495
Bloomsbury Group, **3:** 837-838
Blum, Léon, **1: 153-156; 4:** 1075
Boer War, **1:** 163-164; **3:** 870; **5:** 1419; Canada and, **3:** 895
Bolshevik Revolution, **3:** 915. *See also* Russian Revolution
Bolsheviks, **1:** 220; **3:** 808, 831, 982; **5:** 1495
Bolshevism, **3:** 927
Borah, William E., **1: 157-159**

Borden, Robert Laird, **1: 160-162**
Bormann, Martin, **3:** 682
Boston police strike of 1919, **2:** 346
Botha, Louis, **1: 163-165**, **5:** 1420
Botha, P. W., **2:** 383, 385
Bouchard, Lucien, **1: 166-168**
Boumedienne, Houari, **1: 169-171**
Bourgeois, Léon, **1: 172-173**
Boutros-Ghali, Boutros, **1: 174-177**
Boxer Rebellion, **3:** 716, **5:** 1522, 1600
Bradley, Omar N., **1: 178-180**
Branch Davidians, FBI confrontation with, **4:** 1299
Brandeis, Louis D., **1: 181-183**
Brandt, Willy, **1: 184-187**
Branting, Karl Hjalmar, **1: 188-189**
Brasília, building of, **3:** 880
Braun, Wernher von, **1: 190-192**
Brazilian New State, **5:** 1530
Brazzaville Conference, **2:** 462
Brennan, William J., Jr., **1: 193-195**
Brest-Litovsk, Treaty of, **3:** 944
Bretton Woods Conference, **3:** 839
Brezhnev, Leonid Ilich, **1: 196-199**
Brezhnev Doctrine, **1:** 197
Briand, Aristide, **1: 200-203**; **2:** 652
Britain, Battle of, **2:** 563, 582
British Commonwealth, **2:** 479; **3:** 862
British East India Company, **4:** 1234
British Eighth Army, **4:** 1089
British Empire, Canada and, **4:** 1206
British Expeditionary Force, **1:** 205
British monarchy, **2:** 478
British navy, **2:** 559
Brooke, Alan Francis, **1: 204-206**
Brown, Elaine, **3:** 857
Brown, Willie, **3:** 764
Brown v. Board of Education, 1954, **4:** 1037; **5:** 1557
Bruce, Stanley, **1: 207-209**
Brundtland, Gro Harlem, **1: 210-212**
Brüning, Heinrich, **3:** 690
Bryan, William Jennings, **1: 213-216**
Brzezinski, Zbigniew, **1: 217-219**
Bugandan Rebellion, **4:** 1164
Bukharin, Nikolai Ivanovich, **1: 220-223**
Bulge, Battle of the, **4:** 1200, 1335
Bull Moose Party, **4:** 1326
Bülow, Bernhard von, **1: 224-226**; **2:** 485
Bunche, Ralph, **1: 227-229**

Burger, Warren E., **1: 230-232**; **4:** 1291
Burma, British colonialism and, **5:** 1472
Burma campaign, World War II, **1:** 35; **4:** 1098; **5:** 1403
Burnham, Forbes, **3:** 766
Bush, George, **1: 233-236**; **2:** 334, 415; **4:** 1156, 1226
Bustamante y Rivero, José Luis, **2:** 645
Buthelezi, Mangosuthu Gatsha, **1: 237-239**
Byng, Julian, **3:** 861; **4:** 1057; **5:** 1527
Byrd, Richard E., **1: 240-243**

Cairo Accord, **3:** 800
Callaghan, James, **1: 244-246**
Calles, Plutarco Elías, **1: 247-249**, 257; **4:** 1166; **5:** 1538
Cambodia, killing fields of, **4:** 1251
Campbell, Kim, **1: 250-252**, 260; **2:** 527; **4:** 1114
Campbell-Bannerman, Henry, **1:** 55, **253-255**
Camp David Accords, **1:** 116, 174, 262
Canada Council, **5:** 1440
Canadian Bill of Rights, **2:** 406
Canadian Medical Association (CMA), **2:** 528
Canadian New Deal, **1:** 127
Capital punishment, United States and, **1:** 231
Capitalism, **5:** 1638, 1641
Caporetto, **3:** 943
Cárdenas, Lázaro, **1: 256-258**
Carney, Pat, **1: 259-260**
Carranza, Venustiano, **1:** 247; **2:** 401; **4:** 1165, 1191; **5:** 1537, 1607
Cartel des Gauches, **3:** 676
Carter, Jimmy, **1:** 217, **261-264**; **3:** 864; **4:** 1104, 1196, 1287
Cassin, René, **1: 265-267**
Castillo, Ramón, **4:** 1223
Castro, Fidel, **1:** 106, **268-271**; **2:** 451, 601; **4:** 1177
Caudillismo, **5:** 1631
Ceausescu, Nicolae, **1: 272-275**
Central African Federation, **3:** 804
Central American Peace Accord, 1987, **1:** 50
Central Intelligence Agency (CIA), **1:** 32, 270; **3:** 821, 966; **4:** 1082, 1095
Central Treaty Organization, **4:** 1082
Chaco War, **5:** 1362, 1445
Chamber of Deputies, French, **3:** 676
Chamberlain, Austen, **1: 276-278**, 281
Chamberlain, Joseph, **1:** 281; **2:** 540
Chamberlain, Neville, **1:** 72, **279-282**; **2:** 464
Chamorro, Emiliano, **5:** 1422
Chamorro, Violeta, **4:** 1179

Chanak crisis, **3:** 935

Chao Tzu-yang. *See* Zhao Ziyang

Charles, Prince of Wales, **2:** 397

Charlottetown Agreement, **4:** 1112

Charter of Rights and Freedoms, **5:** 1502

Charter 77, **2:** 639

Chen Duxiu, **1: 283-285**

Cheney, Dick, **2:** 493

Ch'en Tu-hsiu. *See* Chen Duxiu

Chernenko, Konstantin, **2:** 575

Chernov, Victor, **3:** 833

Chiang Ch'ing. *See* Jiang Qing

Chiang Kai-shek, **1: 286-289; 2:** 606; **3:** 921; **5:** 1458

Chiang Tse-min. *See* Jiang Zemin

Chifley, Joseph Benedict, **1: 290-292**

Chiluba, Frederick, **3:** 805

China, Republic of, establishment of, **1:** 289

China, U.S. opening of relations with, **4:** 1147

Chinese Communist Party (CCP), **1:** 284; **2:** 605; **3:** 770, 929; **4:** 1028, 1208; **5:** 1615

Chinese Red Army, **5:** 1616, 1619

Chirac, Jacques, **4:** 1076

Chisholm, Shirley, **1: 293-295**

Chou En-lai. *See* Zhou Enlai

Chrétien, Jean, **1:** 251, **296-299; 2:** 527

Christian Democratic Party, Italian, **2:** 381

Christian Democratic Union (CDU), German, **1:** 15

Churchill, Winston, **1:** 72, **300-303; 2:** 562

Chu Teh. *See* Zhu De

CIA. *See* Central Intelligence Agency (CIA)

Ciudad Juárez, Treaty of, **3:** 964

Civil Rights Act of 1964, **3:** 786, 825

Civil Rights movement, U.S., **1:** 4, **3:** 762, 856

Cixi. *See* Tz'u-hsi

Clark, Joe, **1: 304-306; 5:** 1501

Clemenceau, Georges, **1: 307-310**

Cliche Commission, **4:** 1111

Clinton, Bill, **2: 333-336**, 337, 415; **4:** 1137, 1226

Clinton, Hillary Rodham, **2:** 333, **337-339**

Cliveden set, **1:** 67

Clodumar, Kinza, **2:** 429

Coalition for a Democratic Majority, **3:** 864

Coalition governments, **5:** 1643

Cold War, **2:** 595, 631; **3:** 820, 846; arms race and, **4:** 1123; containment policy and, **1:** 10; Haiti and, **2:** 451. *See also* Berlin Wall

Collins, Michael, **2: 340-342**, 352

Colorado Party, Paraguayan, **5:** 1446

Columbus, New Mexico, Pacho Villa's raid on, **5:** 1538

Common law, **3:** 707

Common Law, The (Holmes), **3:** 706

Common Market. *See* European Economic Community (EEC)

Communism, **5:** 1642

Communist International (Comintern), **1:** 222; **3:** 956

Communist Party, Chinese. *See* Chinese Communist Party (CCP)

Communist Party, French, **3:** 703; **4:** 1075

Conakat Party, Congolese, **5:** 1509

Confédération Générale du Travail (CGT), **1:** 308

Congo Crisis, **2:** 623

Congregation of the Missionaries of Charity, **5:** 1469

Congress of Racial Equality (CORE), **3:** 762, 857

Congress Party, Indian, **4:** 1133

Conservativism, **5:** 1638

Constantine, **5:** 1534

Constitution Act, Canadian, **1:** 296

Constitutional monarchism, **5:** 1632, 1637

Consumer Pricing Act, **3:** 789

Containment, **1:** 10; **3:** 787

Contra movement, **4:** 1178. *See also* Iran-Contra scandal

Cook, Joseph, **2: 343-344**

Coolidge, Calvin, **2: 345-348; 5:** 1435

Co-operative Commonwealth Federation (CCF), **2:** 420

Copps, Sheila, **2: 349-351**

CORE. *See* Congress of Racial Equality (CORE)

Corporatism, **4:** 1120

Cosgrave, William T., **2: 352-354**

Coubertin, Pierre de, **2: 355-357**

Council of Economic Advisers (CEA), **2:** 592

Council of Europe, **5:** 1426

Cremer, William Randal, **2: 358-359**, 567

Cross of gold speech, Bryan's, **1:** 213

Cuban Constitutional Army, **1:** 107

Cuban Missile Crisis, **1:** 270; **2:** 548; **3:** 822, 847; **5:** 1434, 1472

Cuban Revolution, **1:** 107, 268; **2:** 602

Cultural Revolution, **2:** 392; **3:** 767, 931; **4:** 1027; **5:** 1617, 1621

Curtin, John, **2: 360-363**, 509

Curzon, George Nathaniel, **2: 364-366**

Cyprus, **3:** 975; **4:** 1188; independence of, **3:** 799, 976

Cyprus Crisis, **3:** 799, 976; **4:** 1188

Czechoslovakia, dissolution of, **2:** 641
Czechoslovakia, establishment of, **4:** 1042
Czechoslovakia, Soviet invasion of, **1:** 197

Dáil Éireann, **2:** 341, 352; **4:** 1173
Dalai Lama, The, **2: 367-370**
Daugherty, Harry M., **2:** 625
Dawes, Charles G., **2: 371-373**
Dawes Plan, **2:** 372, 651; **5:** 1443
Dawson, Anderson, **2:** 504
Dawson, Geoffrey, **1:** 67
Dayan, Moshe, **2: 374-377**
Deakin, Alfred, **2: 378-379**
December Revolution of 1905, Russian, **4:** 1141
Defferre, Gaston, **4:** 1076
Defferre Law, **4:** 1076
De Gasperi, Alcide, **2: 380-382**
de Gaulle, Charles. *See* Gaulle, Charles de
de Klerk, F. W., **2: 383-385**; **3:** 987
Delors, Jacques, **2: 386-388**
Demirel, Suleyman, **4:** 1180-1181
Democracy, **5:** 1632
Democratic Unionist Party (DUP), Northern Irish, **4:** 1185
Deng Xiaoping, **2: 389-392**; **3:** 925, 930; **5:** 1612
Department of Health, Education, and Welfare, **2:** 474
Depression. *See* Great Depression
Desai, Morarji, **2:** 539
Descamisados (shirtless ones), **4:** 1222
Desert Storm, **1:** 235; **2:** 493; **4:** 1261. *See also* Persian Gulf War
De-Stalinization, **3:** 846
Détente, **1:** 197; **2:** 535
de Valera, Eamon, **2:** 341, 352, **393-396**
Dewey, Thomas, **5:** 1508
Dia, Mamadou, **5:** 1391
Diana, Princess of Wales, **2: 397-399**
Díaz, Porfirio, **2: 400-403**; **3:** 964; **5:** 1537, 1606
Diefenbaker, John G., **2: 404-407**
Dien Bien Phu, French defeat at, **5:** 1541
Diouf, Abdou, **5:** 1391
Djilas, Milovan, **2: 408-409**
Doe, Samuel K., **2: 410-413**
Dole, Robert, **2: 414-416**
Dole-Mondale vice-presidential debate, **2:** 415
Dollar diplomacy, **5:** 1437
Domino theory, **4:** 1252

Dönitz, Karl, **2: 417-419**
Douglas, Helen Gahagan, **4:** 1146
Douglas, Tommy, **2: 420-422**
Douglas, William O., **2: 423-424**
Douglas-Home, Alexander, **2: 425-427**; **5:** 1583
Downer, Alexander, **2: 428-430**
Duarte, José Napoleon, **2: 431-433**
Du Bois, W. E. B., **2: 438-441**; **4:** 1151
Dubček, Alexander, **2: 434-437**
Ducommun, Elie, **1:** 90
Due process of law, **3:** 707
Dulles, John Foster, **2: 442-445**
Dumbarton Oaks Conference, **2:** 594, 596
Duplessis, Maurice, **2: 446-448**
Duvalier, François, **2: 449-452**
Duvalier, Jean-Claude, **1:** 52; **2: 453-455**

Easter Rebellion, **2:** 341, 393
East Timor, Indonesian invasion of, **5:** 1450
Eban, Abba, **2: 456-459**
Éboué, Félix, **2: 460-462**
EC. *See* European Community (EC)
Ecumenism, **3:** 781
Eden, Anthony, **2: 463-466**; **3:** 963
Edward VII, **2: 467-470**
Edward VIII, **1:** 94; **2: 471-472**, 561
Efendi, al-. *See* Karami, Rashid
Egyptian Expeditionary Force (EEF), **1:** 28
Eichmann, Adolf, trial of, **5:** 1575
Eisenhower, Dwight D., **2: 473-476**; **5:** 1433
El Alamein, **4:** 1316
Elizabeth II, **2: 477-480**
El Salvador, civil war in, **2:** 432
El Salvador Peace Pact, **4:** 1216
Engels, Friedrich, **3:** 807; **5:** 1640
Enrile, Juan, **1:** 42
Entebbe airport hostage rescue, **3:** 679; **4:** 1212
Entente Cordiale, **2:** 469-470; **4:** 1235
Enver Pasha, **2: 481-483**
Equal Rights Amendment (ERA), **1:** 294
Erzberger, Matthias, **2: 484-486**; **5:** 1442
Ethiopia, Italian invasion of, **2:** 616, 618
Ethiopian Revolution, **2:** 617
Ethnic cleansing, **4:** 1069
EU. *See* European Union (EU)
European Atomic Energy Community (Euratom), **5:** 1427
European Coal and Steel Community, **1:** 16; **2:** 382

European Commission, **2:** 386-387
European Community (EC), **2:** 386; Greece and, **4:** 1187; Turkey and, **4:** 1182
European Economic Community (EEC), **5:** 1427; Britain and, **1:** 246; **2:** 648
European Recovery Program (ERP), **4:** 1034
European Union (EU), **2:** 387; **3:** 876; Britain and, **1:** 151; Norway and, **1:** 211
Evangelium Vitae, **3:** 784
Evatt, Herbert Vere, **2: 487-488**
Evian, Agreement of, **1:** 169
Evita. *See* Perón, Eva
Evren, Kenan, **4:** 1180
Executive privilege, **1:** 231

Fadden, Arthur William, **2: 489-490**
Fahd, **2: 491-493**
Fahd Plan, **2:** 492
Fair Labor Standards Act, **1:** 146
Faisal (Saudi Arabia), **2: 494-497**; **5:** 1592
Faisal I (Iraq), **2: 498-500**
Falangists, **2:** 519
Falkenhayn, Erich von, **4:** 1232
Falkland Islands, **4:** 1063
Falkland Islands War, **5:** 1475
Fall, Albert B., **2:** 627
Farabundo Martí Front for National Liberation (FMLN), **2:** 433; **4:** 1216
Fard, Wallace D., **3:** 979
Fascism, **4:** 1118, **5:** 1644
Fashoda Crisis, **1:** 96
FBI. *See* Federal Bureau of Investigation (FBI)
Fedayeen, **3:** 746
Federal Bureau of Investigation (FBI), **3:** 719; confrontation with Branch Davidians, **4:** 1300
Federal Parliamentary Labour Party, Australian, **5:** 1386
Federal Reserve Board, **2:** 591
Federal Reserve System, U.S., **2:** 593
Federation of Rhodesia and Nyasaland. *See* Central African Federation
Ferraro, Geraldine, **2: 501-503**
Fez Plan, **2:** 492
Fianna Fáil, **2:** 394; **4:** 1172
Field, Winston, **5:** 1412-1413
Fifth Amendment, **3:** 707
Fifth Republic, French, **2:** 556
Figueres, José, **1:** 49

Final Solution, **3:** 686, 899
Fine Gael, **2:** 353
Finnish civil war, **4:** 1020
Fisher, Andrew, **2: 504-505**; **3:** 733
Foch, Ferdinand, **3:** 778
Ford, Gerald R., **2: 506-508**
Forde, Francis Michael, **2: 509-510**
Fortress Europe, **3:** 697
Four Modernizations, **2:** 390
Fourteen Points, Woodrow Wilson's, **2:** 516; **4:** 1133; **5:** 1587
Fourth Red Army, **5:** 1620
Fourth Republic, French, **2:** 555
France, Battle of, **1:** 204
Francis Ferdinand, **2: 511-513**
Francis Joseph I, **2: 514-517**
Franco, Francisco, **2: 518-521**; **3:** 792
Frankfurter, Felix, **2: 522-523**
Franz Joseph I. *See* Francis Joseph I
Fraser, Malcolm, **2: 524-526**, 643
Free French movement, **2:** 460, 462, 554
Free German Youth (FDJ), **3:** 713
Free Officers' Organization, Egyptian, **5:** 1363
Free trade movement, Australian, **4:** 1295
FRELIMO. *See* Front for the Liberation of Mozambique (FRELIMO)
French Equatorial Africa, **2:** 461
Friendship, Treaty of, Soviet-Egyptian, **5:** 1365
Front for the Liberation of Mozambique (FRELIMO), **3:** 959
Fry, Hedy, **2: 527-528**
Fujimori, Alberto, **2: 529-532**
Fulbright, J. William, **2: 533-535**
Fulbright scholarships, **2:** 534
Fusion Party, Australian, **2:** 344

Gallipoli campaign, World War I, **1:** 68, 97, 301; **3:** 734
Galvao, Henrique, **5:** 1373
Gandhi, Indira, **2: 536-539,** 546
Gandhi, Mahatma, **2: 540-543**; **4:** 1132-1133, 1197
Gandhi, Rajiv, **2:** 539, **544-546**
Gandhi, Sanjay, **2:** 539, 544
Gang of Four, **3:** 768; **5:** 1617
García Robles, Alfonso, **2: 547-549**
Garvey, Marcus, **2: 550-552**
Gaulle, Charles de, **2:** 460, **553-556**; **3:** 916; **4:** 1074, 1253

Gaullism, **4:** 1255

General Agreement on Trade and Tariffs (GATT), **2:** 333

General strike of 1926, British, **1:** 92

General Theory of Employment, Interest, and Money, The (Keynes), **3:** 839

Geneva Conference (1954), **2:** 445; **3:** 705; **5:** 1540-1541, 1617

Geneva Convention, **1:** 112

Geneva Protocol, **4:** 1154

George V, **1:** 56; **2: 557-560**

George VI, **2: 561-563**

Germany, division into East and West, **5:** 1524

Germany, reunification of, **3:** 875, 877

Getty, Don, **3:** 873

Ghana, establishment of, **4:** 1150

Ghana, 1966 coup in, **4:** 1152

Gheorghiu-Dej, Gheorghe, **1:** 272

Giap, Vo Nguyen. *See* Vo Nguyen Giap

Glasnost, **2:** 575

Glenn, John H., Jr., **2: 564-565**

Gobat, Charles Albert, **2: 566-567**

Goddard, Robert H., **2: 568-570**

Goebbels, Joseph, **2: 571-573**

Golan Heights, **1:** 61

Goldman, Nahum, **5:** 1570

Good Neighbor Policy, **3:** 739

Goods and services tax (GST), Canadian, **2:** 351; **4:** 1113

Gorbachev, Mikhail, **2: 574-577; 5:** 1392

Gore, Al, **2: 578-580**

Göring, Hermann, **2: 581-583; 3:** 835

Gorton, John Grey, **2: 584-585; 4:** 1054

Gothic Line, **3:** 836

Gouin, Paul, **2:** 447

Government of India Acts, **3:** 774; **4:** 1198

Gramsci, Antonio, **2: 586-588**

Grand Trunk Pacific, **3:** 896

Grau San Martín, Ramón, **1:** 105

Gray, Herbert, **2: 589-590**

Gray Report, **2:** 590

Great Depression, **3:** 717, 839; **4:** 1321; Canada and, **2:** 421; Germany and, **3:** 695; Hitler and, **3:** 690

Great Leap Forward, **2:** 392; **4:** 1027

Great Proletarian Cultural Revolution. *See* Cultural Revolution

Great Society, **3:** 786

Green Book, The (Qaddafi), **4:** 1268

Green Line, Cypriot, **3:** 977

Greenspan, Alan, **2: 591-593**

Grey, Edward, **1:** 55

Griffith, Arthur, **2:** 352

Gromyko, Andrei Andreyevich, **2: 594-597**

GST. *See* Goods and services tax (GST)

Guderian, Heinz, **2: 598-600**

Guevara, Che, **1:** 268; **2: 601-604**

Guillaume spy case, **1:** 186

Gulf of Tonkin Resolution, **2:** 535

Gulf War. *See* Persian Gulf War

Guo Moruo, **2: 605-607**

Gustav Line, **3:** 836

Guyana, independence of, **3:** 766

Habsburgs, **2:** 515

Habyarimana, Juvénal, **2: 608-611**

Haganah, **1:** 124; **2:** 374-375; **3:** 678

Hague Conference, 1899, **4:** 1297

Hague Conference, 1907, **1:** 64; **4:** 1297

Haig, Alexander M., **2: 612-614**

Haile Mengistu Mariam, **5:** 1398

Haile Selassie I, **2: 615-618**

Haiti, 1986 revolt in, **2:** 454

Halsey, William F., **2: 619-620; 4:** 1145

Hammarskjöld, Dag, **2: 621-624**

Hanson, Pauline, **3:** 726, 811

Harding, Warren G., **2: 625-628**

Harriman, William Averell, **2: 629-631**

Hassan II, **2: 632-634**

Hassan, Mulay, **4:** 1108

Haughey, Charles James, **2: 635-637**

Havel, Václav, **2: 638-641**

Hawke, Robert, **2:** 524, **642-643; 3:** 810

Hay, John, **5:** 1436

Haya de la Torre, Víctor Raúl, **2: 644-645**

Health-care reform, U.S., **2:** 338

Heath, Edward, **2: 646-649; 5:** 1583

Hebron Agreement, **4:** 1137

Helfferich, Karl, **2:** 485

Henderson, Arthur, **2: 650-652**

Herriot, Édouard, **3: 675-677**

Hertzog, James Barry Munnik, **5:** 1421

Herzl, Theodor, **5:** 1559

Herzog, Chaim, **3: 678-681**

Hess, Rudolf, **3: 682-684**

Hewson, John, **3:** 811

Hill, Anita, **5:** 1479

Himmler, Heinrich, **3: 685-687**

Hindenburg, Paul von, **3: 688-691**, 695, 942;
   4: 1190

Hirohito, **1:** 21; **3: 692-694**

Hiroshima and Nagasaki, bombing of, **5:** 1437,
   1506-1507

Hiss, Alger, **4:** 1051, 1146

Hitler, Adolf, **2:** 464, 571; **3: 695-698**; Sudetenland
   and, **1:** 120. *See also* Nazi Party; World War II,
   Germany and

Hoare, Samuel, **3:** 898

Hoare-Laval Agreement, **3:** 898

Hobby, Oveta Culp, **3: 699-701**

Ho Chi Minh, **3: 702-705**; **5:** 1617

Ho Chi Minh Trail, **5:** 1542

Hoffa, Jimmy, **3:** 824

Hohenzollern Dynasty, **5:** 1578

Holmes, Oliver Wendell, Jr., **3: 706-708**

Holocaust, **3:** 686, 698; **5:** 1571, 1575. *See also* Jews,
   Nazi genocide against

Holt, Harold, **3: 709-711**

Home, Lord. *See* Douglas-Home, Alexander

Honecker, Erich, **3: 712-714**

Hong Kong, return to China of, **3:** 771

Hoover, Herbert, **3: 715-718**; **5:** 1410

Hoover, J. Edgar, **3: 719-721**

Hoover Commission, **3:** 717

Houphouët-Boigny, Félix, **3: 722-724**

Hourani, Akram, **1:** 60

House Committee on Education and Labor,
   4: 1257

House Committee on Un-American Activities,
   4: 1052

House of Lords, British, **2:** 426

Howard, John, **2:** 428; **3: 725-727**

Hsuan-tung. *See* Pu-yi

Huerta, Adolfo de la, **4:** 1167

Huerta, Victoriano, **1:** 247; **3: 728-729**, 965; **4:** 1165,
   1191; **5:** 1537, 1606

Hughes, Charles Evans, **3: 730-732**

Hughes, William Morris, **3: 733-736**

Huk Rebellion, **3:** 967

Hull, Cordell, **3: 737-740**

Hull House, **3:** 892

Humanae Vitae, **4:** 1203

Hume, John, **1:** 12

Humphrey, Hubert H., **3: 741-743**

Hungarian revolt, **4:** 1125, 1127

Hussein I, **3: 744-747**

Hussein, Saddam, **1:** 235; **3: 748-751**; **4:** 1261

Hutus, **2:** 611

Hutu-Tutsi conflict, **2:** 609

Ibn Saud, **2:** 494

Ideology, definition of, **5:** 1633

Ikeda, Hayato, **3: 752-754**; **5:** 1377

Il duce. *See* Mussolini, Benito

Immigration Restriction Act of 1901, Australian,
   3: 710

Imperial Conference of 1926, **3:** 862

Imperial War Cabinet, **1:** 161

Imperialism, **5:** 1638

Imperialism, the Highest Stage of Capitalism (Lenin),
   3: 914

Inchon landing, Korean War, **3:** 951

India, independence of, **2:** 563; **4:** 1097

India, state of emegency in, 1975-1977, **2:** 537

Indian Home Rule Leagues, **5:** 1482

Indian National Congress, **1:** 100; **4:** 1133, 1197

India-Pakistan War, **2:** 537

Indochina War, **3:** 704

Industrial Relations Act, British, **2:** 648

Inkatha Freedom Party, **1:** 238

İnönü, İsmet, **3: 755-757**

Institutional Revolutionary Party (PRI), Mexican,
   5: 1609

Intermediate Range Nuclear Forces Treaty, **4:** 1260

International Arbitration League, **2:** 359

International Atomic Energy Agency, **2:** 475

International Disarmament Conference, **2:** 652

International Olympic Committee, **2:** 356

International Peace Bureau, **1:** 90; **2:** 567

International Peace Conference, **1:** 112

Interparliamentary Union, **1:** 90; **2:** 359, 567; **3:** 890

Intifada, **1:** 48; **4:** 1274

Inukai, Tsuyoshi, **3:** 692

IRA. *See* Irish Republican Army (IRA)

Iran, Islamic revolution in, **3:** 842; **4:** 1275; OPEC
   and, **5:** 1594

Iran-Contra scandal, **1:** 234; **4:** 1289; **5:** 1424

Iranian hostage crisis, **1:** 263

Iran-Iraq War, **3:** 751, 843; **4:** 1276

Iraq, U.N. sanctions against, **1:** 39

Irgun Z'vai Leumi, **1:** 114

Irish arms-smuggling scandal of 1970, **2:** 635-636

Irish Free State, **2:** 342, 394

Irish Land Purchase Act of 1903, **1:** 96
Irish Republic, establishment of, **2:** 395
Irish Republican Army (IRA), **2:** 341, 352, 394. *See also* Sinn Féin
Irish Volunteers, **2:** 393; **4:** 1171
İsmet Pasha. *See* İnönü, İsmet
Isolationists, U.S., **1:** 159
Israel, establishment of, **1:** 124
Israeli independence, war of, **1:** 125
Israeli Intelligence Service, **3:** 680
Itaipú Dam, **5:** 1446
Italian Communist Party (PCI), **2:** 588
Italian Popular Party, **2:** 381
Italian Socialist Party (PSI), **2:** 586
Italian Somaliland, **5:** 1397
Itō Hirobumi, **3: 758-761**

Jabotinsky, Vladimir, **1:** 123
Jackson, Jesse, **3: 762-764**
Jagan, Cheddi, **3: 765-766**
Janata Front, **2:** 538
Jaruzelski, Wojech, **5:** 1548
Jaurès, Jean, **1:** 153
Jeanneney, Jules, **3:** 677
Jewish Documentation Center, **5:** 1573-1574
Jewish Legion, British, **1:** 123
Jews, Nazi genocide against, **3:** 686, 698, 899. *See also* Holocaust
Jiang Qing, **3: 767-769**
Jiang Zemin, **3: 770-773**
Jinnah, Mohammed Ali, **3: 774-776; 4:** 1097
Joffre, Joseph-Jacques-Césaire, **3: 777-778; 4:** 1232
John XXIII, **3: 779-781**
John Paul II, **3: 782-784**
Johnson, Lyndon B., **3:** 741, **785-788**
Jones, Paula, **2:** 336
Jordan, Barbara, **3: 789-791**
Juan Carlos I, **3: 792-794**
Juárez, Benito, **2:** 400
Judicial activism, **2:** 424
Judiciary Act of 1925, **5:** 1465
July Agreement of 1936, **4:** 1306
July 26 movement, **1:** 106-107
Jutland, Battle of, **2:** 562

Kabila, Laurent, **4:** 1080
Kádár, János, **3: 795-797**
Kagera Basin Organization (KBO), **2:** 610

Kagera River Basin, **2:** 610
Kanakas, **1:** 103
Kapp, Friedrich, **5:** 1387
Kapp putsch, **3:** 944; **5:** 1387, 1442
Karamanlis, Constantine, **3: 798-799; 4:** 1187
Karami, Rashid, **3: 800-802**
Karmal, Babrak, **5:** 1369
Kasavubu, Joseph, **2:** 623; **3:** 945; **5:** 1510
Kashmir, Pakistani invasion of, **1:** 143
Kashmir, unrest in, **2:** 545
Katanga, **2:** 624; secession of, **3:** 946; **5:** 1509
Katangan Republic, **5:** 1510
Katipunan, **1:** 18
Katzenbach, Nicholas, **5:** 1552
Kaunda, Kenneth, **3: 803-806**
Kautsky, Karl, **3: 807-809**
Keating, Paul, **3: 810-812**
Keeler, Christine, **3:** 961
Keiretsu, **3:** 753
Kellogg, Frank B., **1:** 202; **3: 813-815**
Kellogg-Briand Pact, **1:** 158, 202; **3:** 813; **5:** 1444
Kennan, George F., **3: 816-818**
Kennedy, John F., **3: 819-822**
Kennedy, Robert F., **3:** 720, **823-826**
Kenya, independence of, **3:** 828
Kenyatta, Jomo, **3: 827-830; 4:** 1162
Keppler, Wilhelm, **4:** 1306
Kerensky, Aleksandr Fyodorovich, **3: 831-834**
Kerensky government, **3:** 955
Kerr, John, **5:** 1569
Kesselring, Albert, **3: 835-836**
Keynes, John Maynard, **3: 837-840**
Khan, Ishaq, **1:** 140
Khartoum, **3:** 870
Khmer Rouge, **2:** 508; **4:** 1250; **5:** 1401
Khomeini, Ayatollah. *See* Khomeini, Ruhollah
Khomeini, Ruhollah, **1:** 263; **3: 841-844; 4:** 1084, 1275
Khrushchev, Nikita S., **1:** 196, 270; **3: 845-848**, 983, **4:** 1086; **5:** 1624
Kiesinger, Kurt, **1:** 185
Kikuyu, **3:** 827
Killing fields, Cambodian, **4:** 1251
Kim Il Sung, **3: 849-852**
Kim Jong-p'il, **4:** 1194
King, Charles, **5:** 1512
King, Ernest Joseph, **3: 853-855**
King, Martin Luther, Jr., **1:** 4; **3: 856-859**; J. Edgar Hoover and, **3:** 721

King, William Lyon Mackenzie, **1:** 126; **3: 860-862;**
    4: 1056; **5:** 1439
King-Byng affair, **3:** 861
Kinkaid, Thomas, **2:** 620
Kinneret Operation, **2:** 457
Kirkpatrick, Jeane, **3: 863-865**
Kirov, Sergei, **5:** 1431
Kissinger, Henry A., **3: 866-869,** 908; **4:** 1104
Kitchener, Horatio Herbert, **3: 870-872**
Klaus, Václav, **2:** 641
Klein, Ralph, **3: 873-874**
Kleindienst, Richard, **4:** 1291
Kohima, Battle of, **5:** 1403
Kohl, Helmut, **3: 875-878**
Konoye, Fumimaro, **5:** 1491
Korean Commission, **4:** 1302
Korean War, **1:** 9; **3:** 851, 951-952; **4:** 1303, 1310;
    China and, **4:** 1208; settlement of, **2:** 443
Koresh, David, **4:** 1299
Kosovo, **4:** 1068
Kreisky, Bruno, **5:** 1575
Kristallnacht, **2:** 572
Kruger, Paul, **1:** 164; **5:** 1419
Kubitschek, Juscelino, **3: 879-880**
Kuomintang (KMT), **1:** 286; **2:** 605; **3:** 921; **5:** 1458
Kuo Mo-jo. *See* Guo Moruo
Kuroki, Tamesada, **4:** 1230
Kuwait, invasion of, **1:** 235; **2:** 493; **3:** 749
Kwangtung Army, **3:** 850; **5:** 1492
Kwasniewski, Aleksander, **5:** 1550

Labor Party, Australian, **2:** 361
Labour Party, British, **2:** 651; first government of,
    3: 957
La Follette, Robert M., Jr., **3: 881-884**
La Fontaine, Henri-Marie, **3: 885-886**
La Guardia, Fiorello Henry, **3: 887-889**
Lancaster House Agreement, **4:** 1104
Land for peace agreements, **4:** 1137
Land mines, **1:** 77; **2:** 398
Lange, Christian Lous, **3: 890-891**
Lansdowne, Lord. *See* Petty-Fitzmaurice, Henry
Lansdowne letter, **4:** 1235
Lateran Treaty, **4:** 1119, 1241
Lathrop, Julia C., **3: 892-893**
Laurier, Wilfrid, **1:** 160; **3:** 860, **894-896**
Lausanne Conference of 1932, **2:** 652; **4:** 1193
Lausanne Peace Conference of 1923, **3:** 756

Laval, Pierre, **3:** 677, **897-900**
Law, Bonar, **1:** 91; **3: 901-902**
Lawrence, T. E., **1:** 28; **3: 903-905**
League of Nations, **1:** 173; **4:** 1153; **5:** 1587
Lebanese Civil War, **3:** 801
Lebensraum, **3:** 682
Le Duc Tho, **3:** 868, **906-908**
Lee Kuan Yew, **3: 909-911**
Leghari, Farooq, **1:** 140
Lend-Lease Act, **2:** 630
Lend-lease program, **1:** 8; **2:** 630
Lenin, Vladimir Ilich, **1:** 220; **3: 912-915; 5:** 1428,
    1495
Leopard Battalion, **2:** 455
Leopold II, **1:** 111
Le Pen, Jean-Marie, **3: 916-918**
Lerdo de Tejada, Sebastian, **2:** 400
Lévesque, René, **3: 919-920**
Lewinsky, Monica, **2:** 336
Leyte Gulf, Battle of, **2:** 620
Liberal Party, Australian, **2:** 525; **4:** 1066
Liberal Party, Canadian, **5:** 1500
Liberal socialism, **2:** 409
Liberalism, **5:** 1635
Liberia, U.S. aid to, **2:** 412
Likud, **1:** 116
Limann, Hilla, **4:** 1283
Lin Biao, **3: 921-922**
Lin Piao. *See* Lin Biao
Li Peng, **3: 923-925**
Little Entente, **1:** 119
Litvinov, Maksim Maksimovich, **3: 926-928;**
    4: 1086
Liu Shao-ch'i. *See* Liu Shaoqi
Liu Shaoqi, **3: 929-931**
Lloyd George, David, **1:** 55, 161; **2:** 366; **3:** 902,
    932-935
Locarno, Treaty of, **1:** 202, 277; **3:** 691; **5:** 1444
Lodge, Henry Cabot, **3: 936-938**
Löhr, Alexander, **5:** 1545
Long, Huey, **3: 939-941**
Long March, **3:** 922; **4:** 1025; **5:** 1615, 1619
L'Ordine Nuovo, **2:** 587
Lougheed, Peter, **3:** 874
Ludendorff, Erich, **3:** 688, **942-944**
Luftwaffe, **2:** 582
Lumumba, Patrice, **2:** 623; **3: 945-946; 5:** 1509
Lusitania, sinking of, **1:** 134

Luthuli, Albert. *See* Lutuli, Albert
Lutuli, Albert, **3: 947-949**
Lynching, **5:** 1564

Maastricht Treaty, **3:** 876, 973
MacArthur, Douglas, **3: 950-953**
MacDonald, Ramsay, **1:** 72; **2:** 650-651; **3: 954-957**
Machel, Samora Moisès, **3: 958-959**; **4:** 1104
Macmillan, Harold, **2:** 646; **3: 960-963**
Madero, Francisco, **2:** 401; **3:** 728, **964-965**; **5:** 1537, 1606
Madrid Peace Conference, **4:** 1138
Maginot Line, **4:** 1233
Magloire, Paul E., **2:** 449
Magsaysay, Ramón, **3: 966-967**
Mahathir bin Mohamad, Datuk Seri, **1:** 2; **3: 968-970**
Major, John, **3: 971-974**
Makarios III, **3:** 799, **975-977**
Malaysia, founding of, **3:** 910
Malaysian currency crisis of 1997, **3:** 969
Malcolm X, **3: 978-981**
Malenkov, Georgi M., **3: 982-984**
Manchukuo, **3:** 693; **4:** 1264
Manchuria, Japanese invasion of, **3:** 693; **5:** 1436
Mandela, Nelson, **1:** 238; **2:** 385; **3: 985-988**, 989; release from prison of, **2:** 385
Mandela, Winnie, **3:** 986, **989-991**
Manhattan Project, **4:** 1308
Mankiller, Wilma P., **3: 992-994**
Manley, Michael, **4: 1017-1019**
Mannerheim, Carl Gustaf, **4: 1020-1022**
Mannerheim Line, **4:** 1021
Manning, Preston, **1:** 306; **4: 1023-1024**
Mao Tse-tung. *See* Mao Zedong
Mao Zedong, **2:** 389; **3:** 767, 921; **4: 1025-1028**, 1208
March on Washington (1963), **3:** 858
Marcos, Ferdinand E., **1:** 41; **4: 1029-1031**, 1279
Marcos, Imelda, **4:** 1029
Marne, Battles of the, **3:** 778
Marshall, George C., **2:** 473; **4: 1032-1035**
Marshall, Thurgood, **4: 1036-1038**; **5:** 1478
Marshall Plan, **2:** 621, 629; **4:** 1034; **5:** 1507
Martin, Paul, **4: 1039-1040**
Marx, Karl, **3:** 807, 912; **5:** 1640
Marxism, **1:** 153; **2:** 587; **3:** 807, 912; **5:** 1640; Lenin and, **3:** 914
Marxism, revisionist, **5:** 1641
Marxist-Leninism, **5:** 1642

Masaryk, Tomáš, **1:** 118; **4: 1041-1043**
Massé, Marcel, **4: 1044-1045**
Massey, Vincent, **4: 1046-1047**
Massey, William Ferguson, **4: 1048-1049**
Massey Commission, **4:** 1047
Matignon Agreements, **1:** 155
Mau-Mau Uprising, **1:** 34; **3:** 827
Mauriac, François, **5:** 1571
Maximato, **1:** 248
Mayaguez incident, **2:** 508
May Fourth Movement, **1:** 283
Mayling Soong, **1:** 287
McCarthy, Eugene, **3:** 743, 788, 825; **4:** 1175
McCarthy, Joseph R., **4: 1050-1053**; **5:** 1417
McCarthyism, **4:** 1051
McFarlane, Robert, **4:** 1289
McGovern, George, **4:** 1149
McMahon, William, **2:** 524; **4: 1054-1055**
McVeigh, Timothy, **4:** 1299
Meech Lake Accord, **1:** 166, 306; **4:** 1112
Meighen, Arthur, **4: 1056-1057**
Meiji Constitution, **3:** 760
Meiji Restoration, **3:** 759
Mein Kampf (Hitler), **3:** 696; **4:** 1306
Meir, Golda, **4: 1058-1061**
Menem, Carlos Saúl, **4: 1062-1064**
Mengele, Josef, **5:** 1575
Mensheviks, **3:** 808, 831; **5:** 1495
Menzies, Robert Gordon, **2:** 489; **3:** 735; **4:** 1054, **1065-1067**
Mexican Civil War, **3:** 728
Mexican peso crash, 1995, **5:** 1610
Mexican Revolution, **1:** 247; **2:** 401-402; **3:** 965; **4:** 1165; **5:** 1537, 1606
Mexico, U.S. invasion of, **3:** 729
Mfecane, **1:** 238
Midway, Battle of, **4:** 1145
Militias, private, in U.S., **4:** 1299
Milner, Lord, **5:** 1604
Milošević, Slobodan, **4: 1068-1071**
Miners' strike of 1906, French, **1:** 308
Minto-Morley Reforms, **4:** 1198
Mitchell, William, **4: 1072-1073**
Mitterrand, François, **4: 1074-1076**
Mobutu Sese Seko, **4: 1077-1080**
Mohammad Reza Pahlavi, **1:** 263; **4: 1081-1084**, 1094, 1275
Molina, Arturo, **2:** 431

Molotov, Vyacheslav Mikhailovich, **4: 1085-1087**
Monarchical absolutism, **5:** 1635
Mondale, Walter F., **2:** 503; **4:** 1289
Mondlane, Eduardo, **3:** 959
Monnet, Jean, **5:** 1427
Montagu-Chelmsford Reforms, **4:** 1198
Montevideo Conference, **3:** 740
Montgomery, Bernard Law, **1:** 179; **4: 1088-1090**, 1201
Montgomery Bus Boycott, **1:** 4; **3:** 856
Morgenthau, Henry, Jr., **4: 1091-1092**
Morgenthau Plan, **4:** 1092
Moro Islamic Liberation Front, **4:** 1280
Moro National Liberation Front (MNLF), **4:** 1031
Mosaddeq, Mohammad. *See* Mossadegh, Mohammad
Moscow Conference of Foreign Ministers, **3:** 740
Mossadegh, Mohammad, **4:** 1081, **1093-1095**
Motherland Party, Turkish, **4:** 1181
Mother Teresa. *See* Teresa, Mother
Mountbatten, Louis, **2:** 563; **4: 1096-1098**
Mubarak, Hosni, **4: 1099-1102**
Mugabe, Robert, **4: 1103-1106**; **5:** 1413
Muhammad V, **4: 1107-1108**
Muhammad, Elijah, **3:** 978
Muldoon, Robert, **4: 1109-1110**
Mulroney, Brian, **1:** 166, 250, 259, 305; **4: 1111-1114**
Munich Agreement, **1:** 120, 282; **2:** 464
Museveni, Yoweri Kaguta, **4: 1115-1117**
Mussolini, Benito, **2:** 380; **3:** 898; **4: 1118-1121**, 1241
Mutesa II, **4:** 1164
Muzorewa, Abel, **4:** 1104; **5:** 1414
Myrdal, Alva, **4: 1122-1123**
Myrdal, Gunnar, **4:** 1122

NAACP. *See* National Association for the Advancement of Colored People (NAACP)
NAFTA. *See* North American Free Trade Agreement (NAFTA)
Naguib, Muhammed, **5:** 1364
Nagy, Imre, **4: 1124-1127**
Nalundasan, Julio, **4:** 1029
Nasser, Gamal Abdel, **1:** 45; **2:** 465; **4: 1128-1131**; **5:** 1363, 1365
Nation of Islam, **3:** 978-979
National Aeronautics and Space Administration (NASA), **1:** 190
National Association for the Advancement of Colored People (NAACP), **2:** 439; **4:** 1036-1037

National Democratic Party (NDP), Rhodesian, **4:** 1103
National Front, French, **3:** 917
National government, British, **1:** 93
National Guard, Nicaraguan, **5:** 1423
National Health Service, British, **1:** 74
National Insurance Act of 1911, British, **1:** 56; **3:** 935
National Insurance Bill, Israeli, **4:** 1060
National Liberation Front (FLN), Algerian, **1:** 169
National Liberation Front (NLF), Vietnamese, **3:** 705
National Party of Australia, **2:** 525
National Party of New Zealand, **4:** 1110
National Resistance Movement (NRM), Ugandan, **4:** 1116
National Security Council (NSC), **2:** 613; **3:** 869; **4:** 1289
National Socialist Party, German. *See* Nazi Party
National Socialists, German. *See* Nazi Party
National union government, French, **4:** 1247
Nationalism, **2:** 516; **5:** 1637
Nationalist Party, Australian, **3:** 735
Nationalist Party, Chinese. *See* Kuomintang (KMT)
NATO. *See* North Atlantic Treaty Organization (NATO)
Nautilus, USS, **4:** 1309
Nazi Party, **2:** 581; **3:** 685, 691, 695; propaganda of, **2:** 571. *See also* Hitler, Adolf
Nazi-Soviet Nonaggression Pact, **4:** 1086, 1306
Négritude, **5:** 1391
Negro World, **2:** 550
Neguib, Muhammad, **4:** 1128
Nehru, Jawaharlal, **4: 1132-1135**
Neoconservative movement, **3:** 863
Netanyahu, Benjamin, **4: 1136-1139**
Netanyahu, Jonathan, **4:** 1136, 1212
New Deal, **3:** 732, 951; **4:** 1091, 1322; **5:** 1460
New Democratic Party, Canadian, **2:** 421
New Economic Policy (NEP), Soviet, **1:** 221; **3:** 913
Newfoundland, **5:** 1407, 1440
New Guinea, **2:** 362; Australia and, **2:** 362
New State, Portuguese, **5:** 1372
Newton, Huey, **3:** 857
Niagara Movement, **2:** 439
Nicholas II, **3:** 831; **4: 1140-1143**
Night (Wiesel), **5:** 1571
Nimitz, Chester W., **3:** 854; **4: 1144-1145**

Nixon, Richard M., **1:** 231; **2:** 612; **3:** 820, 867; **4: 1146-1149**, 1273; pardon of, **2:** 507. *See also* Watergate scandal
Nkomo, Joshua, **4:** 1103; **5:** 1413
Nkrumah, Kwame, **2:** 440; **4: 1150-1152**
Nkumbula, Harry, **3:** 803
Nobel Institute, **3:** 891
Nobel Peace Prize, **3:** 891
Noel-Baker, Philip John, **4: 1153-1154**
Nol, Lon, **5:** 1401-1402
Nonalignment, **4:** 1134
Noriega, Manuel, **4: 1155-1157**, 1260
Normandy invasion, **1:** 179; **2:** 474; **4:** 1089
Norris-La Guardia Act, **3:** 887
North, Oliver, **4:** 1289
North African Socialist Federation, **1:** 171
North American Free Trade Agreement (NAFTA), **1:** 297; **2:** 333; **4:** 1113; **5:** 1610
North Atlantic Treaty Organization (NATO), **1:** 9; Bosnia and, **4:** 1070; Canada and, **5:** 1441; establishment of, **4:** 1207
Northern Expedition, **2:** 606
Nuclear Arms Reduction Treaty (INF treaty), **4:** 1290
Nuclear Nonproliferation Act, **2:** 565
Nuclear Test Ban Treaty, **2:** 595, 630
Nuremberg Trials, **2:** 418, 582; **3:** 683; **4:** 1193, 1307
Nyerere, Julius, **4: 1158-1161**

Obote, Milton, **1:** 34; **4:** 1115, **1162-1164**
Obregón, Álvaro, **1:** 247; **4: 1165-1167**; **5:** 1537
O'Connor, Sandra Day, **4: 1168-1170**
Oder-Neisse line, **1:** 185
Official Languages Act, Canadian, **5:** 1517
Ogaden War, **5:** 1396
Oil embargo, 1973, **5:** 1592
O'Kelly, Seán T., **4: 1171-1173**
Oligarchy, **5:** 1630
Olympic Games, **2:** 356
Omdurman, Battle of, **3:** 871
O'Neill, Thomas P., Jr., **4: 1174-1176**
One Nation Party, Australian, **3:** 726, 811
One Nation policy, Australian, **3:** 811
OPEC. *See* Organization of Petroleum Exporting Countries (OPEC)
Operation Breadbasket, **3:** 762
Operation Overlord, **2:** 474
Opus Dei, **2:** 521

Orange Free State, **5:** 1420
Organization of African Unity (OAU), **4:** 1152
Organization of American States (OAS), **1:** 306
Organization of Petroleum Exporting Countries (OPEC), **2:** 496; **5:** 1592-1593
Orozco, Pascuál, **3:** 728; **4:** 1165; **5:** 1537
Ortega, Daniel, **4: 1177-1179**
Oslo Accords, **1:** 47; **4:** 1136-1137
Ostpolitik, **1:** 185
Otlet, Paul, **3:** 885
Ottawa Agreement, **1:** 93
Ottawa Treaty, **1:** 77
Ottoman Empire, **1:** 27, 68, 225; **3:** 755
Ouchy Convention, **5:** 1427
Özal, Turgut, **4: 1180-1183**

Pahlavi. *See* Mohammad Reza Pahlavi
Paisley, Ian, **4: 1184-1185**
Pakistan, establishment of, **3:** 776; **4:** 1097
Pakistan People's Party (PPP), **1:** 138-139
Palestine Liberation Organization (PLO), **1:** 45; **3:** 746; **4:** 1137
Palestinian National Congress, **1:** 46
Pan-African Congress, **3:** 828, 986; **4:** 1151
Pan-Africanism, **4:** 1151
Panama, U.S. invasion of, **4:** 1156
Panama Canal, **4:** 1327
Pan-American Conferences, **3:** 739
Panjat Sila (five principles), **5:** 1452
Papa Doc. *See* Duvalier, François
Papandreou, Andreas, **3:** 799; **4: 1186-1189**
Papandreou, George, **3:** 799
Papen, Franz von, **4: 1190-1193**
Papua, **2:** 362
Paris Peace Conference, **1:** 309; **3:** 934. *See also* Versailles, Treaty of
Paris Peace Talks (Vietnam War), **3:** 868, 907
Parizeau, Jacques, **1:** 167
Park Chung Hee, **4: 1194-1196**
Parks, Rosa, **1:** 4
Parliament Act of 1911, British, **1:** 56, 255; **3:** 901
Parliamentary system of government, **5:** 1633
Parti Québécois, **1:** 166; **2:** 447; **3:** 920
Pasha, Jemal, **2:** 498
Pasok party, Greek, **4:** 1187
Passy, Frédéric, **2:** 359, 567
Patel, Vallabhbhai Jhaverbhai, **4: 1197-1198**
Patton, George S., **4: 1199-1201**

Paul VI, **4: 1202-1204**

Pearce Commission, **5:** 1414

Pearl Harbor, Japanese bombing of, **3:** 738; **4:** 1144; **5:** 1590

Pearson, Lester B., **4: 1205-1207**; **5:** 1499

Peng Dehuai, **4: 1208-1210**

P'eng Te-huai. *See* Peng Dehuai

People's Army of Vietnam (PAVN), **5:** 1540

People's Liberation Army (PLA), Chinese, **3:** 922; **4:** 1209; **5:** 1621

People's National Party (PNP) of Jamaica, **4:** 1018

People's Progressive Party (PPP), Guyanan, **3:** 766

People United to Save Humanity (PUSH), **3:** 762

Peres, Shimon, **4: 1211-1214**

Perestroika, **2:** 575; **5:** 1370

Pérez de Cuéllar, Javier, **2:** 531; **4: 1215-1217**

Permanent Court of International Justice, **3:** 886; **4:** 1330

Perón, Eva, **4: 1218-1220**, 1222

Perón, Juan, **4:** 1218, **1221-1224**

Peronism, **4:** 1222

Perot, H. Ross, **2:** 334; **4: 1225-1227**

Pershing, John J., **4: 1228-1230**; **5:** 1539

Persian Gulf War, **1:** 235; **2:** 493; **3:** 749, **4:** 1261; Britain and, **3:** 972; Morocco and, **2:** 634. *See also* Desert Storm

Pétain, Philippe, **3:** 676, 898; **4: 1231-1233**

Petrov affair, **4:** 1066

Petty-Fitzmaurice, Henry, **4: 1234-1235**

Philippine insurgent movements, **4:** 1031

Philippine Insurrection, **1:** 19; **4:** 1228

Philippines, martial law in, **4:** 1030

Ping-pong diplomacy, **3:** 867

Pinochet Ugarte, Augusto, **1:** 32; **4: 1236-1239**

Pius XI, **4: 1240-1242**

Pius XII, **4: 1243-1245**

PLA. *See* People's Liberation Army (PLA), Chinese

PLO. *See* Palestine Liberation Organization (PLO)

Pluralistic government, **5:** 1631

Podgorny, Nikolai, **5:** 1365

Poher, Alain, **4:** 1255

Poincaré, Raymond, **4: 1246-1249**

Poindexter, John, **4:** 1289

Point Four, Truman foreign-policy plank, **1:** 8

Pol Pot, **4: 1250-1252**

Pompidou, Georges, **4: 1253-1255**

Poole, Elijah, **3:** 979

Popular Front, French, **1:** 154

Popular Front for the Liberation of Palestine (PFLP), **3:** 746

Powell, Adam Clayton, Jr., **4: 1256-1258**

Powell, Colin, **4: 1259-1262**

Powers, Gary Francis, **3:** 847

Prague Spring, **2:** 435, 638

Prats, Carlos, **1:** 32

Pratt, Hodgson, **1:** 90

Pravda, **1:** 221; **4:** 1085

Presidential system of government, **5:** 1633

President's Summit for America's Future, **2:** 579

Princeton University, **5:** 1586

Profumo scandal, **3:** 961; **5:** 1583

Progressive Conservative Party, Canadian, in Alberta, **3:** 874

Progressive movement, **1:** 214; **3:** 883

Prohibition, **2:** 627; **5:** 1409-1411, 1587

Pure Food and Drug Act, **3:** 937

Pu-yi, **3:** 693; **4: 1263-1265**

Qaddafi, Muammar al-, **4: 1266-1268**

Quebec independence referendum of 1995, **1:** 167; 299

Quebec separatist movement, **1:** 166; **3:** 920; **5:** 1500. *See also* Bloc Québécois; Parti Québécois

Quezon, Manuel, **3:** 951; **4: 1269-1271**

Quiwonkpa, Thomas, **2:** 412

Quotations from Chairman Mao Zedong, **4:** 1026

Rabin, Yitzhak, **4:** 1213, **1272-1274**

Rabuka, Sitiveni, **2:** 429

Raeder, Erich, **2:** 417

Rafsanjani, Hashemi, **4: 1275-1278**

Railroad strike of 1910, French, **1:** 201

Rainbow Coalition, **3:** 763

Rakosi, Matyas, **4:** 1127

Ramos, Fidel, **1:** 43; **4: 1279-1280**

Rankin, Jeannette, **4: 1281-1282**

Rapallo, Treaty of, **3:** 928

Rathenau, Walther, **5:** 1442

Rawlings, Jerry John, **4: 1283-1286**

Reagan, Ronald, **1:** 234; **2:** 612; **4: 1287-1290**

Rebellion of 1914, South African, **1:** 164

Red Army, **5:** 1497

Red Guards, **3:** 767, 931

Red Record, A (Wells-Barnett), **5:** 1564

Re-establishment and Employment Act, **2:** 510

Reform Party, Canadian, **4:** 1023

Reform Party, U.S., **4:** 1226
Rehnquist, William H., **4: 1291-1293**
Reichswehr, **5:** 1387
Reid, Escott, **5:** 1441
Reid, George Houston, **4: 1294-1295**
Rejection Front, Algerian, **1:** 169
Religious Freedom Restoration Act, **4:** 1169
Renault, Louis, **4: 1296-1297**
Reno, Janet, **4: 1298-1300**
Reparations, German, for World War I, **2:** 371;
    4: 1193; **5:** 1443
Republic, **5:** 1632
Republic of Ireland Act, **2:** 395
Reynaud, Paul, **2:** 554
Rhee, Syngman, **3:** 851 **4:** 1194, **1301-1304**
Rhineland, **3:** 697
Rhodesian Front, **5:** 1413
Ribbentrop, Joachim von, **4:** 1086, **1305-1307**
Rickover, Hyman G., **4: 1308-1309**
Ridgway, Matthew B., **4: 1310-1312**
Roberts, F. S., **3:** 871
Robinson, Mary, **4: 1313-1314**
Rockefeller Foundation, **5:** 1360
Röhm, Ernst, **3:** 685
Röhm purge, **4:** 1191
Romanian constitution of 1965, **1:** 273
Romanian Winter Revolution, **1:** 274
Romanov Dynasty, **4:** 1142
Rommel, Erwin, **3:** 835; **4: 1315-1316**
Roosevelt, Eleanor, **3:** 721; **4: 1317-1320**
Roosevelt, Franklin D., **1:** 303; **3:** 951; **4:** 1091, 1317,
    1321-1324; **5:** 1437; Court-packing plan of, **3:** 731
Roosevelt, Theodore, **4: 1325-1328**; **5:** 1464
Root, Elihu, **4: 1329-1331**
Rope and Faggot: A Biography of Judge Lynch (White),
    5: 1566
Ross, Nellie Tayloe, **4: 1332-1333**
Rough Riders, **4:** 1327
Roxas, Manuel, **3:** 967
Royal absolutism, **5:** 1631
Ruhr region, French occupation of, **4:** 1193, 1249
Rundstedt, Gerd von, **4: 1334-1336**
Rusk, Dean, **5: 1359-1360**
Russia Leaves the War (Kennan), **3:** 817
Russian provisional government of 1917, **3:** 832
Russian Revolution, **1:** 220; **3:** 914; **5:** 1497. *See also*
    Bolshevik Revolution; Bolsheviks; December
    Revolution of 1905, Russian

Russo-Japanese War, **4:** 1141, 1230
Rwanda, genocide in, **2:** 611

SA. *See* Storm troopers (SA)
Saavedra Lamas, Carlos, **5: 1361-1362**
Sabry, Ali, **5:** 1365
Sacco and Vanzetti case, **2:** 523
Sadat, Anwar el-, **1:** 262; **5: 1363-1366**
Sahara, western, **2:** 633
Saint-Mihiel, **4:** 1035, 1072
Saipan, fall of, **5:** 1493
Sakharov, Andrei, **5: 1367-1370**
Salazar, António de Oliveira, **5: 1371-1374**
Salisbury, Lord, **1:** 95, 253; **2:** 364
SALT. *See* Strategic Arms Limitation Talks (SALT I);
    Strategic Arms Limitation Talks (SALT II)
Samouth, Tou, **4:** 1250
Sandinistas, **4:** 1177; **5:** 1375-1376, 1424
Sandino, Augusto César, **5:** 1375-1376, 1423
Sandline crisis, **2:** 429
Satō, Eisaku, **5: 1377-1379**
Satyagraha, **2:** 541-542
Saud, **2:** 494
Sauvé, Jeanne Mathilde, **5: 1380-1381**
Schacht, Hjalmar, **3:** 690
Schleicher, Kurt von, **4:** 1190
Schlieffen, Alfred von, **3:** 778
Schlieffen Plan, **3:** 942
Schmidt, Helmut, **1:** 186
Schröder, Gerhard, **5: 1382-1384**
Schuman, Robert, **1:** 16; **5:** 1426
Schuman Plan, **1:** 16
Schuschnigg Kurt von, **4:** 1306
Schwarzkopf, Norman, **4:** 1261
SCLC. *See* Southern Christian Leeadership
    Conference (SCLC)
Scopes "monkey" trial, **1:** 215
Scullin, James Henry, **5: 1385-1386**
Seale, Bobby, **3:** 857
SEATO. *See* Southeast Asia Treaty Organization
    (SEATO)
Second Turkish Army, **3:** 756
Second Vatican Council. *See* Vatican II
Seeckt, Hans von, **5: 1387-1388**
Seeme, Pixley, **3:** 948
Selassie. *See* Haile Selassie I
Senghor, Léopold, **5: 1389-1391**
Seven Pillars of Wisdom (Lawrence), **3:** 903

Shaba, **4:** 1080; **5:** 1510

Shah of Iran. *See* Mohammad Reza Pahlavi

Shamir, Yitzhak, **4:** 1213

Sharansky, Nathan, **4:** 1137

Share Our Wealth movement, **3:** 941

Sharpeville Massacre, **3:** 987

Sherif, Nawaz, **1:** 139

Sherman Anti-Trust Act, **3:** 814

Shevardnadze, Eduard, **5: 1392-1395**

Shining Path, **2:** 530

Shipley, Jenny, **4:** 1110

Shukairy, Ahmad al-, **1:** 45

Siad Barre, Muhammad, **1:** 79; **5: 1396-1399**

Sihanouk, Norodom, **5: 1400-1402**

Sikh Rebellion, **2:** 546

Silver Jubilee of George V, **2:** 560

Simpson, Wallis Warfield, **2:** 472, 561

Sin, Jaime, **1:** 42 **4:** 1031

Singh, V. P., **2:** 545

Singh, Zail, **2:** 545

Sinn Féin, **1:** 11, 151; **2:** 352, 394; **4:** 1171

Sino-Japanese War, **3:** 759; **5:** 1620

Sison, José Maria, **4:** 1031

Six-Day War, **2:** 377; **3:** 746; **4:** 1131, 1272

Sixteenth Amendment, **3:** 738

Sixth Plan, Georges Pompidou's, **4:** 1254

Six-year plan, Mexican, **1:** 257

Slim, William Joseph, **5: 1403-1405**

Smallwood, Joseph Roberts, **5: 1406-1407**, 1440

Smith, Alfred E., **5: 1408-1411**

Smith, Ian, **3:** 805; **4:** 1103; **5: 1412-1415**

Smith, John, **1:** 149

Smith, Margaret Chase, **5: 1416-1418**

Smuts, Jan Christian, **5: 1419-1421**

SNCC. *See* Student Nonviolent Coordinating Committee

Social Credit Party, Canadian, **1:** 131

Social Democratic Party (SDP), German, **1:** 184; **3:** 807

Social Democratic Party, Swedish, **1:** 189

Socialism, **5:** 1639; scientific, **5:** 1640; utopian, **5:** 1639

Socialist market economy, Chinese, **3:** 924

Socialist Party, French, **1:** 153; **4:** 1075

Socialist Unity Party (SED), East German, **3:** 712

Solidarity movement, **5:** 1547-1548

Solidarity Party, Polish, **3:** 783

Somalia, famine in, **1:** 81

Somme, Battle of the, **1:** 204

Somoza García, Anastasio, **4:** 1177; **5:** 1375, **1422-1425**

Song Jaioren, **5:** 1458

South Africa, formation of, **1:** 165

South African coalition government of 1933, **5:** 1420

South Africa's Truth and Reconciliation Commission (TRC), **1:** 239, **3:** 991, **5:** 1521

Southeast Asia Treaty Organization (SEATO), **2:** 444

Southern Christian Leadership Conference (SCLC), **1:** 4-5; **3:** 762, 856

South Korea, economic growth in, **4:** 1195

South Korea, 1961 coup in, **4:** 1194

South Pacific Summit of 1997, **2:** 429

Soweto Uprising, **2:** 384

Spaak, Paul-Henri, **5: 1426-1427**

Spain, democratic monarchy of, **3:** 793

Spanish-American War, **4:** 1228

Spanish Civil War, **2:** 518-519; Portugal and, **5:** 1372

Spencer, Diana. *See* Diana, Princess of Wales

Spirit of Independence, The (Rhee), **4:** 1303

Sri Lanka, Indian intervention in, **2:** 546

SS, **3:** 685

Stalin, Joseph, **1:** 221, 303; **3:** 982; **4:** 1085; **5: 1428-1431**; Tito and, **5:** 1489

Stalingrad, Battle of, **5:** 1624

Standard Oil, **3:** 814

Starr, Kenneth, **2:** 335

Stevenson, Adlai E., **5: 1432-1434**

Stimson, Henry L., **5: 1435-1438**

Stimson Doctrine, **5:** 1436

St. Laurent, Louis, **5: 1439-1441**

Stockholm Conference, **2:** 651

Storm troopers (SA), **2:** 581; **3:** 682, 685

Strategic Arms Limitation Talks (SALT I), **1:** 197; **2:** 597; **4:** 1148

Strategic Arms Limitation Talks (SALT II), **1:** 219, 263

Stresemann, Gustav, **1:** 202, 277; **5: 1442-1444**

Stroessner, Alfredo, **5: 1445-1447**

Student Nonviolent Coordinating Committee (SNCC), **3:** 856

Submarines, atomic, **4:** 1308

Submarine warfare, **1:** 133; **2:** 417; **3:** 688

Sudetenland, **1:** 120, 282; **4:** 1086

Suez Crisis, **2:** 445, 465, 476, 623; **4:** 1130

Suharto, **5: 1448-1451**, 1454

Sukarno, **5:** 1448, **1452-1455**

Sun Yat-sen, **1:** 286; **2:** 606; **5: 1456-1459**, 1601

Sun Yixian. *See* Sun Yat-sen

Suttner, Bertha von, **1**: 90
Sykes-Picot Agreement, **2**: 499
Syndicalism, **5**: 1631, 1643

Taba dispute, Israeli-Egyptian, **4**: 1100
Taft, Robert A., **5**: **1460-1462**
Taft, William Howard, **1**: 181; **5**: **1463-1466**
Taft-Hartley Labor Relations Act, **5**: 1461
Taiwan, Republic of China and, **1**: 288
Tammany Hall, **3**: 887
Tanganyikan African National Union (TANU),
    4: 1160
Tanks, developmnent of, **2**: 598-599
Tannenberg, Battle of, **3**: 688
Taschereau, Louis Alexandre, **2**: 446
Taylor, Charles, **2**: 413
Teapot Dome scandal, **2**: 346, 627
Tehran Association of Militant Clergy, **4**: 1277
Teng Hsiao-ping. *See* Deng Xiaoping
Tenth Indian Division, **5**: 1404
Teresa, Mother, **5**: **1467-1470**
Tet Offensive, **3**: 788; **5**: 1541
Thailand, independence of, **1**: 136
Thant, U, **5**: **1471-1473**
Thatcher, Margaret, **3**: 971; **5**: **1474-1477**
Theocracy, **5**: 1631
Theodore, Edward Granville, **5**: 1386
Thieu, Nguyen Van, **3**: 908
Third Army, U.S., **4**: 1200
Third International, **1**: 222
Thomas, Clarence, **5**: **1478-1480**
Tiananmen Square demonstrations and massacre,
    2: 391; **3**: 925
Tibet, communist Chinese invasion of, **2**: 367-368
Tilak, Bal Gangadhar, **5**: **1481-1483**
Timoshenko, Semyon K., **5**: 1623
Tirpitz, Alfred von, **5**: **1484-1486**
Tito, Josip Broz, **2**: 408; **5**: **1487-1490**
Tlatelolco, Treaty of, **2**: 548
Togliatti, Palmiro, **2**: 588
Tojo, Hideki, **5**: **1491-1494**
Tokes, Laszlo, **1**: 274
Tolbert, William, **2**: 411
Tongogara, Josiah, **4**: 1106
Tonton Macoutes, **2**: 450
Torrijos, Omar, **4**: 1155
Totalitarianism, **5**: 1630
Trade Disputes Act of 1906, British, **1**: 255

Trade Union Council, British, **1**: 92
Trades Union Congress (TUC), **1**: 245; **3**: 954
Trans-Canada Pipeline, **5**: 1440
Transvaal, **1**: 164; **5**: 1420
Travel rorts affair, Australian, **3**: 726
Trench warfare, **3**: 777
Trident Conference, **2**: 474
Trilateral Commission, **1**: 218
Tripartite Pact, **5**: 1492
Triple Alliance, **1**: 224; **2**: 469
Triple Entente, **1**: 224
Trotsky, Leon, **1**: 221, 284; **5**: **1495-1498**
Trudeau, Margaret, **5**: 1499
Trudeau, Pierre Elliott, **1**: 304; **2**: 589; **3**: 920;
    5: **1499-1502**, 1516
Trujillo, Rafael, **5**: **1503-1504**
Truman, Harry S, **2**: 445; **3**: 952; **5**: **1505-1508**
Truman Doctrine, **5**: 1507
Truth and Reconciliation Commission. *See* South
    Africa's Truth and Reconciliation Commission
    (TRC)
Tshombe, Moïse, **2**: 623; **3**: 946; **5**: **1509-1511**
Tubman, William V. S., **5**: **1512-1515**
Túpac Amaru Revolutionary Movement (MRTA),
    2: 531
Turkey, Greek invasion of, **5**: 1535
Turkish coup of 1960, **3**: 757
Turkish Revolution, **2**: 483
Turkish war of independence, **1**: 70
Turner, John Napier, **2**: 590; **5**: **1516-1517**
Tutsis, **2**: 608
Tutu, Desmond, **5**: **1518-1521**
Tweed, William Marcy, **4**: 1331
Twelfth Army Group, **1**: 179
Tydings-McDuffie Act, **4**: 1270
Tz'u-hsi, **5**: **1522-1523**

U-boats, **2**: 417
Uganda People's Congress (UPC), **4**: 1163
Ulbricht, Walter, **3**: 712; **5**: **1524-1526**
Umkonto we Sizwe, **3**: 986
U.N. General Assembly, **2**: 488
U.N. General Assembly Resolution 3379, **3**: 679
Uniform Crime Reports (UCR), **3**: 719
Union Minière du Haut-Katanga, **4**: 1079
Union Nationale Party, **2**: 447
Union Treaty, Soviet, **2**: 576
Unionist Party, British, **1**: 281

United Arab Republic (UAR), **3:** 745; **4:** 1130
United Federal Party, Southern Rhodesian, **5:** 1413
United Malay National Organization (UMNO), **1:** 1; **3:** 968
United Nations, **2:** 488; establishment of, **1:** 265; **2:** 596; Indonesian withdrawal from, **5:** 1454; management problems of, **1:** 176; Spain's entry into, **2:** 520
United Nations dues, United States and, **1:** 25, 40, 175
United Nations Educational, Scientific, and Cultural Organization (UNESCO), **1:** 266
United Nations Emergency Force (UNEF), **2:** 623
United Nations Palestinian Commission, **1:** 228
United Somali Congress (USC), **1:** 79
United States-Japan Security Treaty, **5:** 1378
Universal Declaration of Human Rights, **1:** 266; **4:** 1318
Universal Negro Improvement Association (UNIA), **2:** 551
U.N. Resolution 242, **2:** 458
U.N. Security Council, **2:** 488
U.S. Children's Bureau, **3:** 893
U.S. Department of Health, Education, and Welfare (HEW), **3:** 700
U.S. Joint Chiefs of Staff, **3:** 854; **4:** 1260
U.S. Mint, **4:** 1333
U-2 incident of 1960, **3:** 847

Vanier, Georges, **5: 1527-1528**
Vargas, Getúlio, **5: 1529-1531**
Vargas Llosa, Mario, **2:** 529
Vatican City, establishment of, **4:** 1120, 1241
Vatican neutrality in World War II, **4:** 1245
Vatican II, **3:** 780; **4:** 1202
Velasco Ibarra, José María, **5: 1532-1533**
Velvet revolution, **2:** 437, 639-640
Venizélos, Eleuthérios, **5: 1534-1536**
Verdun, Battle of, **4:** 1232
Versailles, Treaty of, **1:** 282, 309; **2:** 484; **4:** 1330; violation of, **2:** 463, 561; **3:** 697; war reparations and, **4:** 1193; Woodrow Wilson and, **5:** 1588. *See also* Paris Peace Conference
Vichy government, **3:** 677, 898; **4:** 1233; French colonies and, **2:** 460
Victor Emmanuel, **2:** 380
Victoria, **2:** 468
Vietminh, **3:** 703-704; **5:** 1540

Vietnam War, **2:** 535; **3:** 705, 788, 907; **4:** 1175; **5:** 1541; Australia and, **2:** 584; **3:** 709. *See also* Paris Peace Talks (Vietnam War)
Villa, Pancho, **4:** 1165; **5: 1537-1539**
VIP affair, **3:** 709
Vo Nguyen Giap, **3:** 704; **5: 1540-1543**
Voodoo, **2:** 450
Vorster, John, **4:** 1104; **5:** 1414, 1518
V-2 ballistic missile, **1:** 191
Vyshinsky, Andrei, **5:** 1429

Wafd Party, **5:** 1604
Waldheim, Kurt, **4:** 1216; **5: 1544-1546**, 1575
Wałęsa, Lech, **5: 1547-1550**
Walker, James J., **3:** 887
Wallace, George C., **5: 1551-1553**
Wang Ching-wei. *See* Wang Jingwei
Wang Jingwei, **5: 1554-1555**
War on Poverty, **3:** 786
Warren, Earl, **1:** 194; **4:** 1291; **5: 1556-1558**
Warsaw Pact, **4:** 1126
Washington Arms Limitation Conference, **3:** 732
Watergate scandal, **1:** 231; **2:** 507, 612; **3:** 789; **4:** 1148
Weimar Republic, **5:** 1443, 1485
Weizmann, Chaim, **5: 1559-1562**
Weizmann Institute of Science, **5:** 1561
Wells, Ida Bell. *See* Wells-Barnett, Ida B.
Wells-Barnett, Ida B., **5: 1563-1564**
West African Pilot, **1:** 83
White, Walter Francis, **5: 1565-1567**
White Australia policy, **3:** 733; **5:** 1568
White Guard, Finnish, **4:** 1022
White Revolution, Iranian, **4:** 1083
Whitlam, Gough, **2:** 524; **3:** 710; **4:** 1055; **5: 1568-1569**
Wiesel, Elie, **5: 1570-1572**
Wiesenthal, Simon, **5: 1573-1576**
Wilhelm II. *See* William II
William II, **1:** 224; **5: 1577-1580**
Wilson, Harold, **1:** 246; **5: 1581-1584**
Wilson, Woodrow, **1:** 182; **3:** 729, 937; **4:** 1330; **5: 1585-1588**
Wingate, Reginald, **5:** 1604
Women's Army Corps (WAC), **3:** 699
Women's Franchise Bill of 1918, **1:** 162
Worker priests, **4:** 1244
Workmen's Peace Association, **2:** 359
World Bank, **4:** 1045

World Court. *See* Permanent Court of International Justice

World War I, **1:** 27; assassination of Francis Ferdinand and, **1:** 133; **2:** 512; **5:** 1579; Australia and, **1:** 208; **3:** 733; Britain and, **1:** 56; **2:** 558; **3:** 871, 933; France and, **4:** 1231, 1247; Germany and, **1:** 133; **3:** 688, 942; Greece and, **5:** 1534; Italy and, **2:** 586; South Africa and, **5:** 1420; Turkey and, **2:** 481; United States and, **4:** 1229; **5:** 1587. *See also* Gallipoli campaign, World War I; Versailles, Treaty of

World War II, **2:** 473; **3:** 697; Australia and, **2:** 360; Britain and, **1:** 72, 204, 301; **2:** 562; **4:** 1088, 1097; Douglas MacArthur and, **3:** 951; French Equatorial Africa and, **2:** 462; Germany and, **2:** 417, 598; **3:** 835; **4:** 1315, 1335; Hungarian resistence during, **3:** 796; Ireland and, **2:** 395; Italy and, **2:** 380; **4:** 1120; Japan and, **3:** 693; **5:** 1493, 1589; Philippines and, **3:** 966; Portugal and, **5:** 1373; Soviet Union and, **5:** 1623; United States and, **1:** 178; **3:** 854; **4:** 1144, 1200. *See also* Burma campaign, World War II; Hitler, Adolf

World Zionist Organization, **5:** 1559

Wye River Agreement, **1:** 47; **4:** 1137

Xuanton. *See* Pu-yi

Yalta Conference, **2:** 596

Yamamoto, Isoroku, **5: 1589-1591**

Yamani, Ahmed Zaki, **5: 1592-1594**

Yeltsin, Boris, **2:** 576; **5: 1595-1598**

Yemeni Civil War, **2:** 496

Yilmaz, Mesut, **4:** 1181

Yom Kippur War, **2:** 376; **5:** 1364

Young Egypt Party, **5:** 1364

Young modernists, Egyptian, **5:** 1605

Young Plan, **5:** 1443

Young Turks movement, **1:** 68-69; **2:** 481; **3:** 755

Yüan Shih-kai. *See* Yuan Shikai

Yuan Shikai, **5:** 1458, 1554, **1599-1602**

Zaghlūl, Saʿd, **5: 1603-1605**

ZANU Liberation Army (ZANLA), **4:** 1106

Zapata, Emiliano, **3:** 728, 964; **4:** 1165; **5:** 1537, **1606-1608**

Zedillo, Ernesto, **5: 1609-1611**

Zhao Ziyang, **3:** 771; **5: 1612-1614**

Zhou Enlai, **2:** 445; **3:** 867, 923; **5: 1615-1618**

Zhu De, **4:** 1208; **5: 1619-1622**

Zhukov, Georgy Konstantinovich, **5: 1623-1625**

Zia-ul-Haq, Mohammad, **1:** 138, 144; **5: 1626-1628**

Zikist movement, **1:** 83

Zinoviev letter, **3:** 956

Zionist movement, **1:** 114, 122; **2:** 456; **4:** 1058; **5:** 1559-1560

Zulu Rebellion, **2:** 541

Zulus, **1:** 237